South African London

Manchester University Press

South African London

Writing the metropolis after 1948

ANDREA THORPE

Manchester University Press

Copyright © Andrea Thorpe 2021

The right of Andrea Thorpe to be identified as the author of this work has been asserted by them in accordance with the Copyright, Designs and Patents Act 1988.

Published by Manchester University Press
Oxford Road, Manchester M13 9PL
www.manchesteruniversitypress.co.uk

British Library Cataloguing-in-Publication Data
A catalogue record for this book is available from the British Library

ISBN   978 1 5261 4855 1   hardback
ISBN   978 1 5261 7459 8   paperback

First published 2021
Paperback published 2023

The publisher has no responsibility for the persistence or accuracy of URLs for any external or third-party internet websites referred to in this book, and does not guarantee that any content on such websites is, or will remain, accurate or appropriate.

Typeset
by New Best-set Typesetters Ltd

Contents

Acknowledgements		page vi
Note on terminology		viii
	Introduction: Through the 'eyes' of London	1
1	Peter Abrahams and Dan Jacobson: South African liberal humanists in postwar London	25
	Detour: 'I have always been a Londoner': Noni Jabavu, an unconventional South African in London	80
2	Swinging city: Todd Matshikiza's contrapuntal London writing	93
3	Waiting and watching in the city's pleasure streets: Arthur Nortje's poems set in London	140
	Detour: South African writers and London networks of black British activism	179
4	Securing the past: self-reflexive, retrospective narratives of London in J.M. Coetzee's *Youth* and Justin Cartwright's *In Every Face I Meet*	188
	Epilogue: Between the cracks of the city: transnational solidarities and fractures in Ishtiyaq Shukri's *The Silent Minaret*	235
	References	260
	Index	272

Acknowledgements

I am grateful for the support of my friends, family and colleagues in both South Africa and London.

I would especially like to thank Andrew van der Vlies and Nadia Valman for their invaluable help with this research. Sam Naidu has been an incredibly supportive mentor and collaborator over the past few years. Thank you to the brilliant members of the Intersecting Diasporas Research Group at Rhodes University for their warm collegiality. I owe so much to my friend and one-time MA supervisor Lucy Graham.

Thank you to my parents, Richard and Edith Buchanan, and my sister Rose, for all their love and support. Thank you to my wonderful in-laws Charlotte, Robert and Bob Thorpe in East London.

My late grandmother, Molly Malan, was a constant source of encouragement during my research, as was my wonderful grandfather, David Malan. I also remember my dear aunt, Vaughan Buchanan, who was so kind to me during the London-based phase of my research.

Thank you to all my dear friends who kept me in good spirits through different phases of this project, especially Tamaryn Napp, Megan Donald, Andrew Kuhn and Beth Wyrill. My sweet dog, Sparky, provided welcome laughs and companionship throughout.

My thanks go to the helpful staff at the Archives and Special Collections at the University of South Africa for their assistance with Arthur Nortje's papers and manuscripts. I would also like to thank the Archive of British Publishing and Printing at the University of Reading for providing access to the records of George Allen and Unwin, the London Metropolitan Archives for access to Hodder & Stoughton's publishing papers and the staff of Amazwi South African Museum of Literature for assistance with various research queries.

Many thanks to Makhosazana Xaba for her generosity in sharing conversations and materials concerning Noni Jabavu. And thank you to Lindelwa Dalamba for generously and enthusiastically thinking through Todd Matshikiza's legacies with me.

I am grateful for the financial support of the Oppenheimer Memorial Fund and the Andrew W. Mellon Foundation, at different stages of this research.

Many thanks to Rhodes University's Department of Literary Studies in English for hosting me during my Andrew W. Mellon Foundation funded postdoctoral fellowship, during which research on this book was completed.

Finally, thank you to my husband, Chris Thorpe, for his unwavering support: wherever we go, you are my light up ahead.

An earlier version of the study on Peter Abrahams was published in *English in Africa* in 2018, republished here in a different form with kind permission from the journal.

Sections drawing on research originally included in the following articles have been republished with kind permission from the respective journals published by Taylor & Francis:

- Andrea Thorpe (2018) The 'Pleasure Streets' of Exile: Queer Subjectivities and the Body in Arthur Nortje's London Poems, *Journal of Literary Studies*, 34:1, 1–20, DOI: 10.1080/02564718.2018.1447865 2.
- Sam Naidu & Andrea Thorpe (2018) 'I don't belong nowhere really': The Figure of the London Migrant in Dan Jacobson's 'A Long Way from London' and Jean Rhys's 'Let Them Call It Jazz', *English Academy Review*, 35:1, 26–37, DOI: 10.1080/10131752.2018.1461477 3.
- Andrea Thorpe (2018) 'I slipped into the pages of a book': intertextuality and literary solidarities in South African writing about London, *Safundi*, 19:3, 306–320, DOI: 10.1080/17533171.2018.1482882

Copyright © (1) 2018 JLS/TLW (2) 2018 The English Academy of Southern Africa (3) 2018 Informa UK Limited, trading as Taylor & Francis Group, reprinted by permission of Taylor & Francis Ltd, http://www.tandfonline.com on behalf of (1) JLS/TLW (2) The English Academy of Southern Africa.

Note on terminology

The term 'coloured', in most of the senses in which the word is used in the book, denotes South Africans of 'mixed-race' heritage – a complex and contested category of both apartheid race classification and self-designation. Coloured identity is discussed in detail in Chapter 3.

I have chosen to use the terms 'black', 'white' and 'coloured' in lower case, in order to avoid a replication of the capitalised 'Black', 'White', etc. of apartheid classificatory terminology. By using these terms without inverted commas, and without qualifiers such as 'so-called', I do not wish to reify constructed 'racial' categories, but rather to recognise the effect that these classifications had on South Africans' lived experience or modes of self-identification.

Introduction

Through the 'eyes' of London

> City, your lovely daughter
> became my admirer, so if I acquire
> you it is simply an act of affirmation.
> I will not be the voyeur, the quiet observer,
> a man called 'lucky' to be with such a chick,
> toting a lens at Nelson or saying
> 'nothing like English pubs'. No, I can tell
> A stodgy pint from an ale that sets the soul
> right, I can point to your history
> and add many memories from what is now
> a fascination bound to be lifelong. (Nortje, 'Trio', lines 1.1–11)[1]

These are the opening lines of 'Trio', a poem written by South African lyric poet Arthur Nortje, in London, in 1967. Nortje studied at Oxford University from 1965 to 1967 and frequently visited and wrote about London during this period. In this poem, the speaker's attitude towards the city is refreshingly far removed from any simple understanding of London as an imperial centre, or from predictable tropes of the colonial struggling to assimilate into the vast, foreign metropolis. Rather, the speaker 'acquires' the city, like an accent or a lover, and asserts that he will not be 'the voyeur, the quiet observer'; he is no gaping tourist, performing obeisance to the city's heritage by 'toting a lens at Nelson'. Instead, he navigates his way into the city's spaces through expert knowledge of its pubs, confidently adding his own 'memories' to London's 'history'. Nortje famously wrote many compelling poems about the 'isolation of exile' ('Waiting', 1967, line 1), yet here he writes about an infatuation with London, a lasting 'fascination' that we might assume could coexist with the alienation of the exile.

In the final line of the poem, Nortje's speaker calls London 'my eyes, my wavelength, lifeline' ('Trio', line 3.41). Instead of observing the city voyeuristically, the speaker looks *through* the city. London provides the South African exile with a lens or frame through which to see the world, including his home country. The speaker's close, even bodily identification with London means that he is on the city's 'wavelength', speaking its language, understanding its peculiarities and pleasures. If we extend this technological metaphor, derived from radio communication, we have the sense that something about London is speaking *to* the exile, offering him a way of being that both echoes and assuages his sense of isolation and displacement: a place within the frequency of modernity. For an exiled writer to describe the place of exile as a 'lifeline' seems almost redundant, as the condition of exile presupposes a need for escape from dangerous or unpropitious conditions into a more welcoming, or at least more tenable, space. However, by stacking 'lifeline' in a 'trio' with 'eyes' and 'wavelength', Nortje suggests that London provides more than just physical or practical refuge: it offers the exile a new, life-changing paradigm, and a new way of being that threads through his existence, like the 'lifeline' of palmistry.

What does it mean for an exiled South African writer, writing in the late 1960s, to position London as a metonym for modernity, in a poem that includes modernist tropes and images? 'Trio' is densely allusive, and the second, scenic section is punctuated by Eliotian injunctions ('Observe'; 'Remember these your footsteps') that echo the erratic, agitated tone of 'A Game of Chess' in *The Waste Land* (lines 2.4; 2.8). Nortje's modernist leanings are caught up in the late adoption of modernisms by postcolonial writers more generally, and thus this belated influence is not unique to South African writers. Peter Kalliney's study of late colonial and postcolonial modernist networks, *Commonwealth of Letters* (2013), significantly focuses on the years 1930–1970 because 'it was during this period that high modernist principles were institutionalized on a global scale' (2013: 10). Moreover, modernism, once thought of as the preserve of European and North American writers of the early twentieth century, has gradually been reframed not only as a continuous preoccupation with modernity rather than with a specific style or form, but also as encompassing texts that were previously categorised as 'postcolonial' and problematically as outside the scope of modernism and modernity. Simon Gikandi goes so far as to claim that 'without modernism, postcolonial literature as we know it would perhaps not exist' (2006: 421). South African writers like Nortje provide perspectives on belated postcolonial engagements with modernity that are significantly displaced from the 'margin' to the 'centre' of modernism (and Empire) itself.

As we see in Nortje's poem, a study of South African writing in London has the potential to produce interventions that are distinctive from analyses of contemporaneous writing set in South Africa. For example, Soweto poet Mongane Wally Serote's urban poems of the early 1970s similarly apostrophise urban spaces, but very different ones – including, in the case of 'Alexandra' (1972), the township. In 'City Johannesburg' (1972), a poem replete with images of alienating, urban modernity, Serote's speaker 'salutes' Johannesburg in an ironic gesture that speaks to the curtailment of his freedom in the city: 'My hand pulses to my back trousers pocket / Or into my inner jacket pocket / For my pass, my life' (lines 2–4). In Nortje's 'Trio', by contrast, the speaker moves freely through the city, partaking of its pleasures, although there is an underlying sense of existential claustrophobia, symbolised by the 'metal cages' of the Underground elevators (line 3.35). While representations of South African cities in the latter half of the twentieth century had perforce to address the fractured urban spatialities created by apartheid, portrayals of London in texts written by South Africans during this period engage both with the relative freedoms that London afforded in comparison to South Africa and with the alienation of exile in a city that was not uniformly welcoming.

South African writers in London look back at their country of origin through the 'eyes' of London so that space is layered within their texts. We see this briefly in Nortje's 'Trio', as he mentions a 'Rondebosch fracas' (lines 1.19), referencing a Cape Town suburb. Furthermore, London-based writing by South Africans often reaches beyond those dual localities to engage with other global spaces. This global vision is evident in 'Trio', which speaks of 'world-wide / affiliations' (1.12–13) within London, manifesting themselves in a litany of world news and American pop culture in the latter section of the poem. Temporalities are similarly interwoven in South African writing about London: just as the speaker in Nortje's poem can 'point' to London's 'history', so other South African writers layer 'memories' of both South Africa and London in contemporary narratives of London. Nortje's poem is just one of the more unexpected, interesting, creative responses by South Africans in London that challenge straightforward dichotomies of centre and margin, provide nuanced perspectives on exile and immersion, and decentre and complicate ideas of modernisms and modernity.

Englishness on the 'peripheries'; South Africanness in the 'centre'

Why is it London, and not Paris or New York or, for that matter, Manchester or Leeds, which affords such postcolonial critiques by South African writers? The answers to this ineluctable question, which this entire monograph elucidates, are both historical and conceptual. During apartheid, many South African writers found sanctuary of different kinds in London. London was both the centre of the international movement against apartheid and one of the headquarters abroad of the exiled African National Congress (ANC) from the 1960s onwards, following its banning in South Africa. The United Kingdom provided safe haven to South African anti-apartheid activists, intellectuals and writers whose work was considered seditious in their home country and, owing to its history as a former British colony, South Africans of all backgrounds shared linguistic and cultural connections with Britain. As Britain's media and publishing hub, London offered South African writers employment, provided opportunities to further their literary careers beyond the censorious limits of apartheid South Africa and was home to a network of artists and activists sympathetic to the plight of South Africa's fleeing intelligentsia. Yet London's appeal to South African writers goes beyond the South African exiles' and expatriates' notable presence in the city during the apartheid decades to encompass specific modes of critique and affinity.

Nelson Mandela, who has himself been regarded as representing 'the story of an African *quest for modernity*' (Boehmer 2008: 12, italics original), visited London briefly in 1962 during a six-month journey (otherwise entirely through Africa) to forge connections with other African nationalist groups and governments. The section in Mandela's famous autobiography, *Long Walk to Freedom* (1994), that describes his London visit goes some way towards answering another crucial question raised by the topic of my study: how is South African writing about London similar to or different from other 'postcolonial' or immigrant accounts of the city? Mandela writes, in the following dense passage:

> I confess to being something of an Anglophile. When I thought of Western democracy and freedom, I thought of the British parliamentary system. In so many ways, the very model of the gentleman for me was an Englishman. Despite Britain being the home of parliamentary democracy, it was that democracy that had helped to inflict a pernicious system of iniquity on my people. While I abhorred the notion of British imperialism, I never rejected the trappings of British style and manners.

I had several reasons for wanting to go to England, apart from my desire to see the country I had so long read and heard about. I was concerned about Oliver's[2] health and wanted to persuade him to receive treatment. I very much wanted to see Adelaide, his wife, and their children, as well as Yusuf Dadoo, who was now living there and representing the Congress movement. I also knew that in London I would be able to obtain literature on guerrilla warfare that I had been unable to acquire elsewhere.

In London, I resumed my old underground ways, not wanting word to leak back to South Africa that I was there. The tentacles of South African security forces reached all the way to London. But I was not a recluse; my ten days there were divided among ANC business, seeing old friends and occasional jaunts as a conventional tourist. With Mary Benson, a Pretoria-born friend who had written about our struggle, Oliver and I saw the sights of the city that had once commanded nearly two-thirds of the globe: Westminster Abbey, Big Ben, the Houses of Parliament. While I gloried in the beauty of these buildings, I was ambivalent about what they represented. When we saw the statue of General Smuts near Westminster Abbey, Oliver and I joked that perhaps some day there would be a statue of us in its stead. (Mandela 1994: 360–361)

The passage begins and ends with Mandela's reflections on the irony and ambivalence present in his attitude towards London. Mandela's 'confession' of his Anglophilia, his admiration of the British parliamentary system and his affinity for 'the trappings of British style and manners' are carefully qualified by an expression of his abhorrence of imperialism. Mandela's internal conflict between Anglophilia and anti-imperialism is summed up in his reaction to London's monuments: 'While I gloried in the beauty of these buildings, I was ambivalent about what they represented' (361). Other responses to London by subjects of its former colonies reproduce this disconnect between an aesthetic enjoyment of British architecture and manners and a condemnation of Britain's imperial history. South Africa's unique relationship with Britain may, however, explain Mandela's uneasy response to London, as well as his insistence on his ambivalent Anglophilia. South Africa has a long relationship with Britain dating back to the British takeover of the Cape in the late eighteenth century, which was followed by organised British settlement from 1820 onwards. In addition to the presence of an Anglophone white minority, British cultural values, literature and language were inculcated amongst black South Africans from the nineteenth century owing to the presence of mission schools, established by organisations such as the London Missionary Society, whose name itself gestures to the longstanding transnational nexus between London and South Africa. The relationship between Britain and South Africa is complex and deep-rooted, and this has resulted in South Africans developing significant and ambivalent relationships, characterised by both strangeness and familiarity, affinity and critique, towards the imperial hub, London.

In this passage from his autobiography, Mandela suggests the important role that literature has played in developing the expectations that South Africans have about London: one of his reasons for wanting to visit London is his 'desire to see the country I had so long read and heard about'. Mandela would have been schooled in the English literary canon at the Wesleyan mission school Clarkebury and at Healdtown College, where students were taught that 'the best ideas were English ideas, the best government was English government and the best men were English men' (Mandela 1994: 44). Mandela's emphasis on his reading as forming his preconceptions of London echoes the longstanding image of London as a 'literary' city. In a South African novel as recent as Ivan Vladislavić's *Double Negative* (2010), the protagonist describes his arrival at Heathrow (in the 1980s) as slipping 'into the pages of a book' (94). Mandela's prosaic remark and Vladislavić's bookish metaphor both suggest how South African perceptions of London are mediated through English literature. It is therefore no accident that South African writing about London is chiefly in English, apart from a few isolated examples of Afrikaans texts.[3] While literature in Afrikaans (the second most widely published language in South Africa) has a worldly trajectory, it has historically engaged with spaces other than London, particularly European cities – for instance, the so-called 'Sestigers' forged connections with Paris.[4] For South African writers, London comes to stand metonymically for English culture and literature even if, like Mandela, their attitude towards Englishness and Empire may be one of ambivalent critique. If London is in some ways a literary space, then the question to be asked is how the city's textual constructions inform South African writing about London, and how these intertexts are entangled with cultural influences from South Africa and with global forms of urban writing.

While Mandela expresses his ambivalent attitude towards London's historical buildings, born of his co-existing Anglophilia and anti-colonialism, he also lays bare the city's own paradoxes. London may have been the historical centre of the British Empire, 'a pernicious system of iniquity' (Mandela 1994: 360), but it is also one of the places where members of the ANC can meet and plan their opposition to another racist regime. London was a major centre for 'South African exile activists, organizations and activities' (Thörn 2006: 20). As a node in transnational activist networks, London provides Mandela with a different type of literature: in this case, rare material on guerrilla warfare which would aid the ANC in its armed struggle. John McLeod, in his seminal work *Postcolonial London* (2004), describes London as 'a much more complex and conflicted location than that implied by the totalizing and abstract concept of the undifferentiated colonial "centre"' (2004: 6). McLeod highlights London's significance 'in the evolution of postcolonial thought and action' (6), and in the rethinking of national identities.

In this section from *Long Walk to Freedom*, Mandela considers his position in relation to both South African and British national histories. As he looks at the statue of South African statesman and military leader Jan Smuts in Parliament Square, he imagines jokingly that he and ANC leader-in-exile Oliver Tambo might be commemorated there instead. At the time of Mandela's writing, his likeness had not yet been erected alongside that of Smuts; the statue was unveiled in 2007. The twenty-first-century commemoration of Mandela, and the lingering presence of Smuts in Parliament Square (Mandela is monumentalised alongside Smuts rather than 'in his stead'), not to mention the contemporary focus of decolonial activism on urban statuary and monuments, add another layer of irony to the passage in a present-day reading. Mandela's memory of foreseeing himself and Tambo as potentially notable South Africans and world statesmen suggests that being in and writing about London might offer a way to think about what it means to be South African and to imagine alternative dynamics of power and influence while reflecting on the global legacies of Englishness and Empire.

Critics such as Robert J.C. Young (2008), Simon Gikandi (1997) and Ian Baucom (1999) have argued that Englishness was forged on the peripheries of the Empire – that, as Gikandi puts it, Englishness was 'elsewhere' (x). I would like to push this interesting and counterintuitive argument in another direction, and to ask whether travel to London enabled South Africans not only to think about London and Englishness, but also to forge ideas about South Africanness. In order to answer this question, I explore South African representations of London from 1948 onwards. I have selected writers whose texts carry out important cultural work in formulating ideas of South African identity in relation to London, and focus on the writing of Peter Abrahams, Dan Jacobson, Todd Matshikiza, Arthur Nortje, J.M. Coetzee, Justin Cartwright and Ishtiyaq Shukri. The genres in which these writers express their observations about London include autobiography, literary fiction, poetry and journalism. The eclecticism of the texts which I will explore reflects the range of imaginative and narrative approaches that South African writers adopted towards the city of London. My aim is to provide an alternative and transnational history of both South African literature and London by exploring the interface between London and South African authors across a broad timespan. To return to Nortje's metaphor, if London provides the South African writer with new 'eyes' with which to see the world and himself, then what kind of literary responses spring from this alternative perspective?

Comparisons, contrasts and gender

Thinking about one space through the prism of another inevitably invites comparisons and contrasts. London may thus act as a foil, or a touchstone, for writers' ideas about South African politics and society, or about their own South Africanness. We see this counterpointing and comparison of spaces in the writing of Lauretta Ngcobo, a South African activist, teacher and writer who lived in London from 1963 until 1994. Her two published novels, *Cross of Gold* (1981) and *And They Didn't Die* (1990), are both set in South Africa. Like many writers, she found Britain much more conducive to a life of writing; she remarks in *Prodigal Daughters* (2012), a collection of South African women's writing in exile that she edited: 'One great gift that England brought out in me was giving me the opportunity to develop my skills as a writer. The lifestyle is calm and people leave you well alone to do what you want to do' (2012: 131). The inverse of Ngcobo's retrospective statement is that 1960s South Africa did not provide ample opportunities for writers, that the lifestyle was anything but 'calm' and that, as an activist who played an important role in the women's anti-pass march of 1956, she was never left 'well alone' by the apartheid authorities. In a 2012 interview, Ngcobo suggests another reason that London provided a greater opportunity for the writer to develop her 'skills', as she recalls how her lecturers at Fort Hare University discouraged female students from writing, and generally downplayed their intellectual contributions (eThekwini Living Legends 2012). In South Africa, therefore, black women writers were doubly oppressed, while Ngcobo remarks on the more progressive aspects of London society.

In addition to her novels written in London and her later edited collection, Ngcobo compiled an anthology of reflections by black British women's writers called *Let It Be Told* (1987). In her introduction to the volume, she compares London and South Africa less favourably, determining that while 'the British are past masters' in 'diplomacy' and while their parliamentary and legal systems might appear to be egalitarian, the 'individualized' discrimination experienced by black Britons means that British society is 'just as oppressive as some of the more blatant systems' such as that of apartheid South Africa (1987: 24–25). Ngcobo therefore does not present London as a purely progressive promised land in comparison to South Africa; she perceives and experiences racism in London too. Although the discrimination she and other black Britons face may not be as overt or violent as the state-mandated segregation of the apartheid regime, racism is present in more codified, similarly devastating forms that are particularly evident to hyper-race-conscious South Africans such as Ngcobo. Complicating Ngcobo's comparisons of South Africa and London is her assertion, in her own essay in the anthology, that her experience of racism in Britain seems 'mild by comparison' to the 'devastating' racist policies of South Africa (1987: 140). These nuanced statements about the relative effects of South African and British racism show Ngcobo wrestling with the incommensurability of London and South Africa, even as she attempts to adopt a comparative approach to critique racism in both spaces. Ngcobo's final assertion that her 'battles' are 'elsewhere' (1987: 140), a declaration of commitment to South Africa, accounts for her decision to set her works of fiction in South Africa rather than write about London in any sustained manner.

Since many South African authors, like Ngcobo, lived in London but set most of their writing in South Africa, it is worth asking *why* specific writers chose to include London as a setting, or indeed why some did *not* write about London to any great extent. A related question: why are all my case studies in this book focused on male writers? The absence of sustained or extensive writing about London by South African women says a great deal about South Africa's literary and social history. Ngcobo's commitment to writing about South Africa rather than London is certainly not unique to women. For instance, all of Peter Abrahams's early novels were set in South Africa. Ngcobo's comments about South Africa as a hostile environment for black women writers suggest one of the reasons why black women in particular have historically been sidelined in South African literature.

Black women's writing in South Africa was, as Barbara Boswell puts it, 'effectively sentenced to a metaphoric death which threatened to extinguish their attempts at creative expression', faced as they were by 'censorship, banning, imprisonment, harassment by the security police, exile and disenfranchisement' (2016: 1331). The first novel published by a black woman in South Africa was Miriam Tlali's *Muriel at Metropolitan*, as recently as 1975. Tlali had struggled to obtain a publisher for her Soweto-based novel, which was written in 1969. Previously, the only black women who had published full-length books were Bessie Head, writing from Botswana, her books published in New York and London, and Noni Jabavu, granddaughter of influential South African journalist and activist John Tengo Jabavu, who moved to London in 1932 at the age of thirteen to complete her education and lived there until returning to South Africa in the late 1960s. *Drawn in Colour*, published in London in 1960, was an account of Jabavu's 1955 trip back to South Africa and Uganda.

The absence of support for black women writers in South Africa does not, however, fully answer the question of why there are no extensive accounts by South African women set in this city that was home to many exiled South African intellectuals and artists. To do so we need to consider the relation between women writers and urban spaces more broadly, and therefore inversely suggest ways in which male South African writers approach London as a setting. Dorothy Driver has argued that the approach to city writing that emerged out of *Drum* magazine, an influential and popular publication that launched the careers of many black South African writers in the 1950s, was overwhelmingly masculine. Driver suggests that *Drum* both excluded and domesticated women. While the magazine provided an 'enabling community' for male writers, 'it was quite the reverse for women' (Driver 1996: 231). In an effort to construct a mode of urban modernity that subverted the National Party's onslaught on urban Africans, *Drum* 'became complicit in a wider effort to contain the "menace" and desirability of women within an ideology of domesticity', writes Rob Nixon. 'In the process, the public sphere was cast as inviolably masculine while the private sphere was feminized – notwithstanding the fact that most urban black women held jobs in the public domain' (Nixon 1994: 20). One might also consider Nortje's feminisation of London as a 'chick' whom he 'acquires' in the poem 'Trio', and how this masculine mode of sexual acquisitiveness is not open to the woman writer. City writing has historically been regarded as a male preserve, with figures such as the masculine *flâneur* looming large: he is the aimless wanderer in the city streets who stores up observations of the crowd to use in his art.[5]

In the works of Matshikiza, Nortje, Cartwright and Coetzee, in particular, we will see how South African writers re-appropriate, imitate, subvert or send up this European trope. Whatever their attitude to the figure of the *flâneur*, these writers are arguably participating in a male-dominated metropolitan literary tradition, drawing on a sense of urban modernity that was also given masculine overtones back in South Africa. Some writers, such as Lauren Elkin, challenge the characterisation of *flânerie* as a strictly masculine activity, based on its genealogy from Balzac through Poe, Baudelaire and Flaubert to Benjamin, arguing that '[t]o suggest that there couldn't be a female version of the *flâneur* is to limit the ways women have interacted with the city to the ways men have interacted with the city' (2016: 11). It is certainly true that South African women have written the city, even if they have not presented themselves as engaging in *flânerie*. After all, *Muriel at Metropolitan* is set in a furniture shop in Soweto, and many of Nadine Gordimer's novels present a finely drawn Johannesburg. Very few South African women writers, however, have engaged with the physical milieu and textual space of London, and this might be partly attributed to a broader absence of a well-developed tradition of urban women's writing in South Africa.

The relative scarcity of female voices in South African writing about London is testament to problematically masculine definitions of modernity in South African literature and culture more broadly. South African women writers may not write London in the same sustained way as their male counterparts, but Noni Jabavu's and Lauretta Ngcobo's writing, in particular, reveals vantage points from which I uncover diverse, potentially disruptive perspectives that work with and against the main textual studies in this book. Ngcobo elucidates the same sense of the relative freedoms that London affords for black South African writers as Matshikiza and Abrahams, yet in her writing this realisation is filtered through an awareness of the restrictions placed on her by her gender in both South Africa and London. At the same time, Ngcobo's intersectional activism in London in the 1980s deepens understanding of the networks and solidarities forged during that violent decade between black Britons and exiled South African writers. Jabavu's life and letters, alternatively, offer perspectives on London in the 1960s that are coloured not only by her gender but also by her provenance from South Africa's black elite, and her long immersion in upper-middle-class British society, affording her a uniquely ambivalent position from which to represent London. Because these women's writings diverge in many respects from the routes traced through the main studies in this book, I have chosen to present them as 'detours', drawn from the spatial lexicon woven through my analyses. Just as writers such as Matshikiza or Nortje critique modernist urban geographies and hegemonic conceptions of the modern subject through their subversive and playful texts, so the very presence of Ngcobo's and Jabavu's writing amongst male-dominated urban perspectives offers, like de Certeau's pedestrian trajectories (1984: 99), an unpredictable itinerary that introduces intriguing diversions into the cartography of the South African writer in London. These two feminine voices, along with the epilogue, which deals with Ishtiyaq Shukri's London-grounded transnational subjectivities, offer disruptive perspectives to the central studies. Their meandering and intersecting tracks complicate and deepen our understanding of South African London.

Writing London during and beyond apartheid

One of South Africa's most important women writers lived in London: I refer, of course, to Olive Schreiner, who lived in the city between 1881 and 1889, and again from 1913 to 1918. Travel to London helped Schreiner to further her literary career, as she arrived with the manuscript of *The Story of an African Farm*, which was published by a British publishing house, Chapman & Hall, in 1883. Anna Snaith has argued that writers like Schreiner connected London to British colonies not only through travel, but also 'by bringing colonial forms to the heart of empire' (2014: 23). For instance, Snaith discusses how Schreiner 'countered South Africa's "distance" from England through print culture', in the form of her journalism about the South African War (23). Snaith sets out her study of Schreiner and other colonial women writers writing between 1890 and 1945 (including Jean Rhys and Katherine Mansfield) in terms that inform my own approach to London writing:

> Their London writing, whether journalism, poetry, drama, fiction or memoir, deals in varying ways with the relationship between metropolis and colony. Constitutive of the city's modernity, their encounters with metropolitan writers and the cultural spaces of the city are an important, yet often overlooked, part of the history of modernist London and its literary networks. (Snaith 2014: 2)

I am similarly interested in studying the ways in which South African writers portray the relationship between South Africa and London, and I deal with a series of later historical moments that show the imbrication of late-colonial, proto-postcolonial and postcolonial temporalities. As mentioned in relation to Nortje's poetry, I also relate the writing of South Africans in London to broader histories of modernisms. Schreiner was associated with modernist networks during her time in London in the early twentieth century; however, drawing on Peter Kalliney's work, I am interested in studying South African literature that engages with later, globalised modernisms.

A great deal of research has already been generated on South African texts by writers who lived in London in earlier historical periods. Scholars have particularly focused on Schreiner and Solomon T. Plaatje, who visited London to protest the Native Land Act in 1914, staying on in the city until 1917, and visiting again in 1919.[6] The well-researched nature of this earlier period of South African writing in London is not, however, the only reason that I have chosen to concentrate on later texts. As well as being broadly postwar texts, the narratives I study in this book were all published after 1948, which was the beginning of formal apartheid in South Africa. Therefore, what these texts have in common is that they are a response to the apartheid context, displaced to a non-South African location that is a significant site of South African exile and emigration. London is read through apartheid, and vice versa. Apartheid affected individual South African writers in different ways, depending most importantly on their racial classification under South African law, but also on the moment in which they wrote. Even the post-apartheid texts discussed in this study look back to apartheid and its global and long-lasting resonances.

After the National Party came to power in 1948 and instituted a series of restrictive and racist laws, many South African writers relocated – either voluntarily or as political exiles – to London, finding in the city both a more tolerant society and a place where they could publish their work. The 1960s, in particular, saw an increase in the number of South African exiles in London, which explains the concentration of my case studies in that decade. My first chapter looks at texts from the 1950s (and briefly at Abrahams's 1940s publishing history); the second and third chapters are focused on work from the early and mid-to-late 1960s respectively; and the fourth chapter skips ahead to the 1990s and early 2000s, although J.M. Coetzee's *Youth* (2002) is also set in the early 1960s. The epilogue studies a novel set in the early twenty-first century. Notably, my study does not include any detailed discussion of South Africans writing about London in the 1970s and 1980s. During this time, the political situation in South Africa meant that even those writers living in London were more interested in writing about South Africa than about their host country; as Leonard Thompson puts it, when black resistance 'became more formidable than before' following the Soweto Uprising of 1976, South African writers 'conveyed the resistance message to vast audiences'

(1995: 228). I partly address this temporal gap in my detour into anecdotal but representative intersections between black British activists and South African writers in the 1980s and early 1990s.

Because my book is focused on dual locations, it is important to consider the simultaneous contexts of both spaces: this is a study of both postwar texts and apartheid-era and post-apartheid-era texts. Indeed, several of these writers engage with London as a postwar space. For instance, in Dan Jacobson's writing – his retrospective autobiography, published in 1985; his novel *The Beginners* (1966); a 1958 short story – he comments on the disappointment that bomb-scarred postwar London represents to a South African arrivant in the 1950s, brought up on imperial myths about the glory of the city. Equally significant is how these decades represent a postcolonial period, as colonies in Asia and Africa attained their independence from Britain in swift succession. London itself has been particularly fraught with questions of race from the 1950s onwards. After all, 1948 was an important date for race relations in Britain as well as in South Africa, since it was in this year that one of the first large groups of West Indian immigrants arrived on the *Windrush*. Although I focus on apartheid as the defining historical force informing the setting and themes of these texts written in exile, it is important to also consider synchronous events in Britain and elsewhere. My case studies will therefore layer the spaces of London and South Africa over one another, with a simultaneous recognition of the geographically specific and intertwined histories leading up to the specific moment invoked.

Past and present, here and elsewhere: London as palimpsest

Such spatial and temporal layering is more than just a methodological approach but is also thematised in South African writing *about* London. As we have seen in Ngcobo's writing, one way that writers bring these two spaces together is through comparisons and contrasts. In other writers' work, however, time and space are layered in even more complex ways. An example of one of these more multilayered, nuanced encounters between South Africans and London is found in Nadine Gordimer's *No Time Like the Present* (2012), a novel that considers how the post-apartheid moment is marked by the past. The novel's two protagonists, Jabu and Steve, a couple who were active in the struggle against apartheid, travel to London on holiday. There have been a number of post-apartheid novels which reverse this movement, which recount the return of 'exiled'

South Africans from London over the past decade, including Justin Cartwright's *White Lightning* (2002), Michiel Heyns's *Lost Ground* (2011), Ivan Vladislavić's *Double Negative* (2010) and Zukiswa Wanner's *London–Cape Town–Joburg* (2014). Like many of the earlier texts that I study here, these novels have spatially and temporally layered plots that include echoes of London, and the South African past, within their post-apartheid settings. What sets *No Time Like the Present* apart from these other contemporary texts that reference London, however, is that its activist protagonists were not exiled in London, but rather in Swaziland, and thus this visit to London is their first. In some ways the following passage therefore mirrors earlier South African texts that recount first impressions of London, while also offering reflections on the interconnected histories of London and South Africa:

> London not exotic, as arrival would be in China, say, even France, Germany. Descendants of those who lived as subjects of the overlord always know much about him, his habits. Both he and she had been 'brought up' with strong tea brewing in its pot; in Steve's case, also Andrew's bacon and egg breakfasts. London that her father had been taught was the heart of the mother country, the empire ('wider still, and wider, shall thy bounds be set' sung in school choir) of which his coal-mine village was part; London that was the 'home' elders in his father Reed's family referred to when going on a visit, although several generations hadn't been born or lived there. The famous parks legendary for soap-box speakers in tirades against this or that seemed to have fewer, and the shaven Hare Krishna, familiar from their place among black street hawkers on the pavements in Johannesburg, apparently had been succeeded by punks whose designer heads, ear- and nose-rings were reminiscent of ancient tribal distortion/decoration in her ancestry: a sign of one world, unbroken past and present, in contradiction (again) of the conflicts that were tearing life-fabric as a motorbike tore the street at Glengrove Place. (Gordimer 2012: 100–101)

Although this passage is set in the 1990s, the way in which Jabu and Steve's encounter with London is framed is similar in some ways to Mandela's attitude towards the city: both new arrivals to London approach the city from a position of prior knowledge. London is 'not exotic' because of the continuity it represents to those who come from former British colonies: 'Descendants of those who lived as subjects of the overlord always know much about him, his habits.' This enduring sense of continuity between South Africa and London, because of the anglicisation of South African culture, is evident even in such a contemporary text. In this passage, we also see how an attachment to Englishness is felt across race, as both Jabu and Steve approach London from the same perspective of familiarity.

Moreover, in this passage, Gordimer describes the complex, temporally criss-crossing intersections between London and South Africa. To some extent, London meets Jabu and Steve's expectations – it is not 'exotic' – but certain aspects of the city surprise them. The 'famous' Hyde Park Corner does not live up to its 'legendary' reputation, and their expectations of seeing Hare Krishna followers on London's streets, already a 'familiar' sight to these city-dwellers, are not met. Rather, they observe punks whose piercings are 'reminiscent of ancient tribal distortion/decoration in her ancestry'. Jabu perceives these continuities between South Africa and London as 'a sign of one world, unbroken past and present'. While both Jabu and Steve approach London as a historical centre of Empire and Englishness, the 'unbroken past and present' described here does not refer to London's English history, but rather to the shared and interconnected histories of South Africa and London, and even more broadly to shared global histories and cultural forms. In this passage, therefore, Gordimer underscores the multiple meanings of London, an English city that is layered with histories from other places.

John Clement Ball, in *Imagining London: Postcolonial Fiction and the Transnational Metropolis* (2004) focuses (like McLeod) on London's significance as a 'contact zone' in which transnational encounters occur.[7] 'As a palimpsest under which millennia of material history are layered, London is an English place; as the hub of a network of global relations, it has always been a transnational space', Ball argues (2004: 4). My examination of South African writers' relationship with London necessarily takes into account both its historical position in terms of Empire (and Commonwealth) and its constant remaking by its global citizens, including South Africans, into a more 'complex and conflicted location', and a site in which activism is encouraged and national identities are challenged, rethought and reformed. Moreover, my approach to London's literary history, focused through the lens of South African writing, does not see 'palimpsest' and 'transnational space' existing in a dialectic; rather, the 'millennia of material history' include noticeable injections of 'elsewhere' within their layers, so that the very notion of 'national' history is complicated. Into the understanding of palimpsest as layered history I interweave the notion of layered spaces. In the texts that I study, South Africa is written over, under and through London's history and present. Furthermore, South African writing about London invokes discourses, styles and references from spaces other than Britain and South Africa.

Sometimes, these global resonances are found within London itself, and in other cases, they derive from the diasporic and globalised nature of South African culture.

Like London's history, South African literature has been characterised as palimpsestic. Shane Graham, for instance, writes of the prevalence of hauntings and buried bodies within post-apartheid South African texts as a figure for repressed trauma and memory. He suggests that these 'tropes and devices' point to the 'present absence of a past that has been erased from the landscape, but which leaves marks of its erasure' so that 'what is called for in interpreting these works is a palimpsestic understanding of history as characterized by gaps, ruptures and phantom traces' (2009: 20). In South African literature, the layering and uncovering of history takes on specific resonances to do with the sublimation and memory of a particularly painful past. Both South African and British history are layered palimpsestically in London, so that texts set in the city recall traumatic moments in both national histories, and particular spaces within London provide points of reflection into both countries' pasts. Trafalgar Square is such a space replete with submerged and displaced histories: a monument to Britain's military history, the location of the South African embassy and site of many significant anti-apartheid rallies and marches. For Todd Matshikiza, Trafalgar Square raises the spectre of apartheid. In his autobiography, *Chocolates for My Wife* (1961), he recounts a visit to South Africa House, where he imagines that he is under surveillance by white South Africans, represented ghoulishly as 'numerous eyes, blue, green and fiery red, peering at me' (Matshikiza 1961a: 20). One of Nortje's poems, 'Cosmos in London' (1966), begins in Trafalgar Square and then travels to a scene of prisoners breaking rocks on Robben Island.

Nortje's comparison of the 'island' of England to Robben Island, where South African political prisoners were incarcerated, is a common trope in South African writing about London. 'Cosmos in London' includes the ambivalent lines 'It seems at times as if I am / this island's lover', which might refer to either Britain or Robben Island (lines 41–42). The island, Ashleigh Harris reminds us, was frequently employed as 'a rhetorical shorthand to describe the isolationism of the South African state during apartheid' (2018: 322), and Robben Island, furthermore, was envisioned as a 'site of fetishistic disavowal' (322) or a 'heterotopia' in the Foucauldian sense (323). South African writers in London engage with the already fraught trope of the island and reposition it alongside British geographies. This specific and instrumental twinning of South African and British spaces is employed emotively in Dennis Brutus's 1971 poem 'I walk in the English quicksilver dusk'. An activist and writer who famously campaigned for a sports boycott of South Africa, Brutus was imprisoned on Robben Island for sixteen months after breaking his banning order in 1963, and then remained under house arrest until leaving for London in 1966. He layers Robben Island and London in an untitled poem, published in 1971. While walking in the 'English quicksilver dusk' (line 1), he thinks of:

> the Island's desolate dusks
> and the swish of the Island's haunting rain
> and the desperate frenzy straining our prisoned breasts:
> and the men who are still there crouching now
> in the grey cells, on the grey floors, stubborn and bowed. (Lines 5–9)

Brutus brings these two locations together through a temporal marker, dusk, in order to express the pain and guilt of exile. At times in South African writing, London becomes metonymic of exile as a whole. Exile was a conflicted and ambivalent condition for South Africans abroad, who experienced alienation as foreigners displaced from their homeland but who also felt guilty about being able to escape the brutal realities of everyday life in South Africa. Some writers, especially, declined to designate themselves as 'exiles', since strictly speaking this term denoted political expulsion. For instance, Ivan Vladislavić dramatises the slippage of the term in *Double Negative* (2010), when a journalist asks the novel's protagonist, Neville Lister, how long he was in 'exile' in London, to which he quickly replies, with evident embarrassment: 'No, no, that is a political fate I never had to suffer' (144). Lister's distinction between his own fate and that of political activists is elided, however, when he declares an affinity for an ANC stalwart who has spent time on Robben Island: 'I had also spent ten years against my will on a small, inhospitable island' (169). Thus London and Robben Island are significant co-ordinates within the psychological cartography of the South African exile, navigation points from which to map their positions in relation to their home country and the struggle against apartheid.

Too late: disappointment and belatedness

That Neville Lister's assessment of England has transitioned from an exultant 'I slipped into the pages of a book' (Vladislavić 2010: 94) into this disillusioned view of the country as 'inhospitable' speaks to a larger sense of disappointment that many South African writers experience in London, partly *because* of the unrealistic – and often outdated – expectations of the city that they have derived from literature. In writing of the 1950s and 1960s in particular, as I earlier suggested, one can attribute this sense of disappointment in part to the depressed conditions of postwar London. John McLeod discusses Dan Jacobson's disappointing experience of setting out to find Virginia Woolf's home in Tavistock Square only to find a bomb site; this is 'a disequilibrating moment where the alliance of London, England, order and culture comes apart in the derelict and ruined spaces of postwar London' (2004: 60). For black South Africans, disillusionment about London sets in when they realise that the city is not as free from racism as they would have hoped. Other forms of disappointment endure in more recent South African texts set in London; for instance, in *No Time Like the Present*, Jabu and Steve realise they have come to London too late to see Hyde Park Corner in its heyday. In this sense, disappointment has a close relationship to the trope of belatedness, a term that has often been assigned to South Africa rather than London. South African narratives set in London not only layer time in the sense of recalling London's occluded past, or remembering South African history in London, but also reflect on the asynchronicity of both South Africa and London.

For writers like Lauretta Ngcobo and Peter Abrahams, South Africa is belated, old-fashioned and asynchronous, especially compared with London, because of the conservative and stagnant conditions of apartheid that hamper political and intellectual progress. South Africa, in this view, is not figured as prehistoric or non-modern in the racist sense that has often been applied to Africa as a whole, which sees it reflecting 'an "other" time whose logic and historical expression are incommensurable with the normative temporality of clock and calendar associated with Western modernity' (Ganguly 2004: 162), but rather as not participating in modernity because of the 'backward' conditions brought about by apartheid. In this schema, London frequently stands for South Africa's possible future – its relatively tolerant and multicultural society representing utopian possibilities. For some writers, belatedness is linked to a literary period in London, specifically the modernist, pre-war period. For example, David Lytton recalls how the well-known Afrikaans poet Ingrid Jonker visited London in 1964. Lytton took her to Soho and Fitzrovia, an area associated with modernist writers, including Woolf, T.S. Eliot and Dylan Thomas:

> We strolled up Charlotte Street to the abandoned centre of pre-war Bohemia, the Fitzroy, the Wheatsheaf, the Marquis of Grandsby.[8] There were no poets or painters now to point out. The territory where those flamboyant lions had roistered was now occupied by salesmen, PRO's and those unattached vagrants who neither make nor buy nor sell, but merely, it seems, know of a good thing, old boy. It was sad. No gay brigades challenging the form and content of contemporary life; only scavengers and squatters and a few sallow derelicts left on their bar-stools by the last outgoing tide.
> 'Anyway, this is where it all happened; the geography of all the memoirs.'
> 'I've come too late. I'm always too late.' (Lytton 1970: 208–209)

Lytton remarks on the disjunction between pre- and postwar London, but in this case it is not the ruined city that is disappointing, but the absence of the bohemian London poets of the pre-war era. Lytton follows the 'geography of all the memoirs' but, rather than being charmed at his tour-guiding, Jonker is dismayed at her belatedness. Throughout the day, she continues to bemoan her lateness: 'But I wish I could have seen Dylan Thomas. Why must I always be too late?' (211). Jonker's regret at never meeting Thomas and her pilgrimage to Fitzrovia pubs frequented by Thomas and Eliot suggest how South African writers were influenced by modernist literature way into the 1960s, as we also see in Arthur Nortje's rewriting of Eliotian and Baudelairean references and tropes. Her response to London exemplifies the complex multilayering of temporalities that occurs when South Africans encounter London, a layering that is further complicated by the interweaving of fictional narratives within their expectations and experiences of the city.

Unreal city, real city: making meanings from London

London thus plays a dual role in South African writing, as a 'real' city at a particular moment in history and as a textual, imaginative space, which stands for much more than itself and on to which writers project images not only of South Africa, but also of other places and other times, real and imagined. To think through this multivalent London, I wish to turn to a visual text: a documentary film, *Three Swings on a Pendulum*, made by the BBC in 1967, featuring South African writer Lewis Nkosi, one of the original *Drum* magazine journalists. Nkosi studied at Harvard University before moving to London, where he was the editor of the *New African* and worked for the BBC. The film sets out to determine whether 'swinging London' is an invention of the media or whether the city is indeed 'blooming'. Three immigrants, a Frenchman (Olivier Todd), an Australian (Robert Hughes) and a South African (Nkosi), spend a day looking for the 'real' London in the fashion boutiques of Carnaby Street, amongst the stalls of Portobello Road, in a 'Negro' jazz club and through interviews with ordinary Londoners and cultural luminaries such as playwright Arnold Wesker. The somewhat conservative Hughes and Todd frequently foreground the frivolity of London's 'swinging sixties' affectations and conclude that London, steeped in history like the 'muck of the Thames', will remain constant despite superficial social shifts. Nkosi, however, positions himself (or is positioned) as the advocate for the new, young London; he shares with the camp, 'swinging' zeitgeist a playful, even derisive attitude towards history. Interestingly, Nkosi's attitude towards London is aligned subtly with his South Africanness. The first scene in which we see Nkosi is at Hyde Park Corner, watching the spirited, humorous speech of a representative for the Coloured Workers' Association. Nkosi remarks, in a voice-over:

> As a black South African, living in exile, I find this a vastly comic, open-air cabaret show, yet beneath all that mock insult against the English, these blacks state the terms on which they would like to be accepted into English society. They know they have something unique to contribute. They want to be accepted, but they are not buying 'British at all costs'. (Gill 1967)

Nkosi begins his observations by clearly stating his position and perspective: as a 'black South African, living in exile', he observes Hyde Park Corner as a 'vastly comic, open-air cabaret show'. For Nkosi, the mocking speeches against British racism appear carnivalesque, disrupting the establishment in a way that would not be possible in South Africa. The slight distance afforded him by his position as a 'black South African living in exile' means that he witnesses the speeches as a show, as not quite real, almost as a display of British society put on for the foreigner. His South African background and his perspective as a black man in London, however, allow him to see 'beneath' the spectacle, as he determines the underlying motivations of black Britons: to be accepted and to be able to contribute to British society, though not 'at all costs'. From the film's opening moments, Nkosi sets out how his observations of London society are filtered through his South Africanness, and through his blackness.

Hailing from South Africa, a former British colony, means that Nkosi's attitude towards swinging London's camp nostalgia for the ephemera of Empire – Union Jack oven mitts, Boer War tea caddies, ironically worn military uniforms à la *Sgt. Pepper's Lonely Hearts Club Band* – is particularly ambivalent. In a Portobello Road shop filled with nostalgic bric-a-brac, he reads from a 1930s *Wonder Book of Empire*, in a tone dripping with irony: 'London is the mother city of an Empire whose children are scattered under every sky. ... It is the council chamber of the Commonwealth, which millions of many races look upon with love and reverence'. And upon entering a famous shop called 'I Was Lord Kitchener's Valet' Nkosi asks wryly: 'Has Lord Kitchener's domain shrunk to this little measure?'[9] His reference to Kitchener is significant, given the British general's involvement in the South African War, amongst other colonial conflicts. Nkosi seems amused at the diminution of the Empire to these nostalgic commodities, but his ironic attitude and incisive questions also undercut any sentimental longing for past glories; in an interview with a political cartoonist, he bluntly and smilingly asserts, 'You've lost the Empire now.'

While Nkosi is entertained by the curiosities of Carnaby Street and Portobello Road, he seems somewhat dissatisfied by London. Overlooking a smoggy, suburban London from the vantage point of a construction site lift, Nkosi remarks that London disappoints his expectations of an ideal city: 'My fantasy is to wake up to see London littered with the kind of café where you can meet anybody, famous or infamous.' Like other South Africans, Nkosi expresses his disappointment that London is not a truly modern city. In this case, his vision of a café society is closer to imaginings of Paris in the late nineteenth and early twentieth centuries, rather than to a London past, present or future. Thus, Nkosi dreams of another place and time superimposed over the contemporary city. He perceives some promising signs of vibrancy in London, as he reflects in the closing moments of the documentary that 'London now has the vitality, the colour and even the new extravagance I like' and that 'there is the expectation that something exciting is about to happen in the next pub or around the next street corner'. Even as he celebrates this new liveliness, however, he suggests that it is always deferred, always around the corner: this exhilarating futural London is tantalisingly out of reach. While the film is about a specific historical moment and place, Nkosi's reflections about London are shot through with different spaces and moments, real and imagined. Furthermore, the various roles that Nkosi takes on in this film – including sardonic, intellectual observer, colonial critic of the mother city and bohemian *flâneur* enjoying the city's pleasures – stage the diversity of positions and perspectives that exiled South Africans occupy within London.

South African London is the first substantial study to put South African writing specifically into conversation with studies of London. Over the past decade, critics have commented on post-apartheid South African literature's tendency to contest the nation as major context.[10] However, as is evident in a study of South African writing about London, South African literature has long been a corpus developed, written and published beyond its borders.[11] Not only do these London-based writers explore the connections between South Africa and Britain, but the global nature of the city feeds into the worldly reach of their writing. A study of South African writing in London develops our understanding of the historical development of South African culture and identity in response to the places of 'exile'. Recognising the longstanding intersections of national literatures and cultural histories seems particularly timely at this post-Brexit moment, since those who voted to leave the European Union were at least somewhat swayed by visions of a mythic British past unadulterated by foreign influence.[12] Furthermore, such a study also contributes to the contemporary debates and disruptive conversations within South Africa's public sphere about the interwoven nature of British colonialism and South Africa's histories and culture, following the paradigm-shifting intervention of the Rhodes Must Fall protests. With a sense of the sustained entanglements between Britain and South Africa then, and an understanding of the longstanding worldliness of South African letters, this study asks: what does it mean to be a South African writer in a city that is an English, British and global space?

Notes

1 All quotations to Nortje's poems are from Nortje (2000).
2 Oliver Tambo, the ANC leader who had moved to London with his family in 1960, and who joined Mandela on his travels across Africa.
3 For examples of Afrikaans novels with London settings, see André Brink's *Gerugte van Reën* (1978) and Karel Schoeman's *Die Hemeltuin* (1979).
4 'The Sestigers' were a group of Afrikaans-language writers led by André Brink and Breyten Breytenbach who aimed to revolutionise Afrikaans literature in the 1960s.
5 See, for instance, Janet Woolf (1985) and Elizabeth Wilson (1995).
6 See, for example, Boehmer (2002).
7 The concept of 'contact zones' was identified by Mary-Louise Pratt in *Imperial Eyes: Travel Writing and Transculturation* (1992: 8): 'the space of imperial encounters, the space in which peoples geographically and historically separated come into contact with each other and establish ongoing

relations, usually involving conditions of coercion, radical inequality and intractable conflict'.
8   The famous Fitzrovia pub's correct name is 'The Marquis of Granby'.
9   Dominic Sandbrook calls the shop 'a painfully trendy boutique on the Portobello Road, which overflowed with Union Jacks and imperial memorabilia' (2006: 450).
10 See, for instance, Samuelson (2010).
11 See van der Vlies (2007).
12 In contrast, London's first Muslim mayor, Sadiq Khan, expressed his opposition to closing the city off to the rest of the world, launching his #Londonisopen campaign, which includes assertions of tolerance and acceptance of 'difference', but is also firmly founded on a neoliberal agenda of encouraging investments; see Crerar (2016).

1

Peter Abrahams and Dan Jacobson: South African liberal humanists in postwar London

At first glance, Peter Abrahams and Dan Jacobson seem an unlikely pairing as subjects of a chapter. Peter Abrahams was a mission-educated, coloured South African, who moved to London in the 1940s, mixing there with key British Communists and African and West Indian Pan-Africanists before relocating to Jamaica in the late 1950s, where he died in January 2017 at the age of 97. Dan Jacobson was a white, university-educated South African writer of Eastern European Jewish heritage, who lived in London from the 1950s until his death in 2014. Despite differences in background and in the focus of their work, these South African-born authors are usefully juxtaposed: both lived in and wrote about postwar London, and in ways that provide a broad picture of the connections between London and South Africa in the late 1940s and 1950s.

This was a crucial period in the interconnected histories of both London and South Africa, Britain and Africa. These decades saw the end of the Second World War in 1945 and a rise in tensions in the early years of the Cold War. In 1948, an Afrikaner nationalist government came to power in South Africa,[1] ushering in their apartheid regime, while colonialism was on the wane in the rest of Africa as a number of African states won their struggles for independence. Britain, and particularly London, also experienced large-scale non-white immigration from the late 1940s onwards, starting with the arrival of West Indian immigrants on the *Windrush* in 1948. Many South Africans, including key intellectuals and activists, were exiled or moved voluntarily to London as the apartheid regime passed increasingly racist and freedom-constraining laws. In 1950 alone, four of the most devastating apartheid laws were passed: the

Immorality Amendment Act (prohibiting sexual relations between black and white South Africans), the Suppression of Communism Act (which was used to quell any non-parliamentary opposition to government, not only that deriving from the South African Communist Party), the Group Areas Act (enforcing residential separation of races and mandating the formation of semi-urban townships for black and coloured South Africans) and the Population Registration Act (by which all South Africans had to be racially classified). London was a key centre for South African exiles, both black and white, escaping this restrictive environment. An analysis of Jacobson's and Abrahams's London-based writing is relevant not simply for the sake of providing diverse perspectives on this significant historical moment, however. There are also similarities between their approaches to London: each writer invokes somewhat liberal-humanist ideas, forged by their English education in South Africa, in their engagement with 1950s London. However, their espousal of liberal humanism is both expressed and received in subtly different ways. In this chapter I provide a close reading and comparison of key texts about London by each author. But first I provide an overview of each writer's career and London-based writing.

Peter Abrahams was born Peter Henry Abrahams Deras in 1919 to an Ethiopian father and a coloured South African mother, in Vrededorp, a large Johannesburg slum. His tumultuous childhood included the early death of his father and his being sent to family in rural Elsburg, before returning to Johannesburg, where he lived with his aunt. Abrahams only started school at the age of eleven and had to leave aged fifteen, after which he worked odd jobs. While trying to find work at a market, he met a man who offered him work at the Bantu Men's Social Centre, which had been set up by white liberal South Africans for the benefit of young black men. Through his contacts at this centre, he was able to attend the Diocesan Training College in Grace Dieu, near Pietersburg, and then St Peter's Secondary School just outside of Johannesburg, where he was a classmate of South African writer Esk'ia Mphahlele. After leaving school he worked in Cape Town and then travelled to Durban. In 1939 he signed on to a ship as a stoker with the aim of eventually arriving in London, where he hoped to pursue his career as a writer. After two years at sea, Abrahams arrived in England in 1941. He lived in London – in Hampstead and then in Debden, Essex – until 1959.[2]

Shortly after moving to London, Abrahams, who had already been exposed to black radical thinking through his reading of American Harlem Renaissance writers, met key Pan-Africanist and anti-colonialist writer

George Padmore. Trinidadian-born Padmore studied in the United States, where he joined the Communist Party, which led to him being appointed head of black communist organisations in the USSR and in Germany. In the mid-1930s, he fell out with the Party when he took issue with the Comintern's reluctance to provide meaningful support for anti-colonialism and anti-racism. After being expelled from the Party, Padmore moved to London, where he became instrumental in Pan-African politics, focused around a group of activists that included Jomo Kenyatta and Kwame Nkrumah, who would go on to lead Kenya and Ghana, respectively, to independence.

Through Padmore, Abrahams also became deeply involved in Pan-Africanist, anti-colonial activities in London. He was briefly employed by the British Communist Party before, like Padmore, abandoning any formal attachment to communism. Abrahams, along with Padmore, West Indian activist Ras Makonnen and Kenyatta, was on the organising committee of a major Pan African Congress held in 1945 in Manchester, which drew together the various anti-colonial organisations in Britain (Ramdin 1987: 177). This movement, led by Padmore, was crucial in encouraging the independence movements of Ghana and Kenya,[3] and attempted to promote the unity of African peoples. Thus Abrahams and his associates planned the Empire's demise from its (increasingly de-centred) centre. Some of their activities were curtailed by the Second World War – they were prevented, for instance, from holding rallies in Trafalgar Square (James 2015: 51). Yet, as Tamara Sivanandan writes, the war also 'gave new impetus to this stirring nationalism in the colonies, helping to mature it, not least because of the wartime experience of soldiers drawn in to fight for the "mother country"' but also because the violence wrought by Europeans upon one another meant that 'Europe was ... subjected to a huge and disorienting change in perspective in the West/non-West relationship which it had not before experienced' (2004: 45). Abrahams thus participated in this maturing nationalist, anti-colonialist, Pan-African movement, not 'in the colonies' but in the capital of the 'mother country' itself.

By the late 1940s, however, Abrahams had broken ties with Padmore, and Kenyatta and Nkrumah had returned to Africa. In the 1950s, Abrahams's home in Essex became a kind of halfway house for new South African arrivals as he pursued his literary and journalistic career. In his autobiography, *The Coyaba Chronicles* (2000), he remembers 'endless streams of newly arrived South Africans, all sizes, shapes, genders, colours, coming to Debden for help to find their bearings in the 'world's greatest city' (Abrahams 2000: 173). During his years in London, Abrahams was extremely well connected, his network spanning the Atlantic and including African American writers Langston Hughes and Richard Wright, South African writers of the *Drum* generation and even extending to radical British figures such as Sylvia Pankhurst. Abrahams was, at times, a controversial figure. He was alternately seen as a communist, a voice of black South Africa, a dedicated Pan-Africanist and anti-colonialist, and a compromised 'native informant'. Apart from his writing, a biographical account of Abrahams's time in London alone reveals much about the interwoven histories of London and South Africa.

Abrahams broke ground for South African black writers in several ways. His *Song of the City* (1945), for instance, was the first novel by a black South African since Solomon T. Plaatje's *Mhudi* (1930). Abrahams is widely hailed as a major influence on subsequent writers and as a leading figure in the development of South African literature and African literature more broadly. While living in London in the 1940s, he wrote about South African society; for instance, *Mine Boy* (1946) narrates the experiences of a black mine worker who unites with white miners in Johannesburg to strike against the oppressive mine management, while *The Path of Thunder* (1948) is an interracial romance between a coloured teacher and an Afrikaner woman, set in a rural South African community. Abrahams wrote about London, however, in his journalistic account of his 1952 visit to South Africa, *Return to Goli* (1953),[4] and also depicted the city in his novel *A Wreath for Udomo*, which was published in 1956. It is on these key texts that I focus in this chapter. I will also reference Abrahams's political memoir, *The Coyaba Chronicles: Reflections on the Black Experience in the Twentieth Century*, which, although published more than forty years later in 2000, sheds light on aspects of Abrahams's 1950s texts. As well as providing historical and biographical details, it reveals how Abrahams developed his political views over time and how he positions himself in terms of a history of anti-colonialist thinkers.

Dan Jacobson was a much less controversial London-based writer. He was born in 1929 in Johannesburg to a Latvian father and Lithuanian mother, both of whom were Jewish and had fled the poverty and discrimination in their home countries to live in South Africa. Jacobson grew up in the diamond-mining town of Kimberley, where his father ran a butter factory. After his university studies in Johannesburg, he spent a year in London in 1950, before returning to South Africa. In 1957, he and his new wife, Margaret Pye, moved back to London. A prolific writer and professor at University College London, he lived in the city until his death in 2014. His early works, such as *A Trap* (1955) and *A Dance in the Sun* (1956), were set in South Africa, and were rural novels which focused on the relationship between black servants and their white masters. Later, Jacobson explored Biblical narratives in *The Rape of Tamar* (1970), and traced Jewish history in non-fiction works such as *Heshel's Kingdom* (1998), which is an account of his travels to his mother's homeland of Lithuania.

The two main texts in which Jacobson wrote about London were his short story about a white South African in London, 'A Long Way from London' (1958), and his novel, *The Evidence of Love* (1959), which focuses on an interracial relationship between a young coloured student and a white South African girl in London. *The Beginners* (1966) recounts the experiences of a Jewish family in postwar South Africa and is partly set in London. I will also deal with Jacobson's 1985 autobiography, *Time and Time Again*, while, as with Abrahams's *The Coyaba Chronicles*, recognising its status as a memoir, written many years after key events. While I will refer to all four texts, I will focus mainly on 'A Long Way from London', as this short story presents a compacted view of some of the most important issues faced by South Africans in London in the 1950s. I begin this chapter with an exploration of Abrahams's writing, and then focus on Jacobson's works in order to draw comparisons between the two writers. In this chapter, I explore how Abrahams and Jacobson share a commitment to writing and to culture that is underpinned by an attachment to liberal humanist principles, which is expressed in the way both writers represent London.

Peter Abrahams's early works: the politics of publishing black South African writing in 1940s London

In his autobiography, *Tell Freedom* (1954), Abrahams recalls a conversation he has shortly before leaving to work on a ship as a stoker. He tells an acquaintance that he 'want[s] to get to England' and when asked what he will 'do there', responds: 'I want to write books and tell them about life in this country' (Abrahams 1954: 299). This is certainly what Abrahams produced for much of the 1940s and early 1950s: writing about South Africa, mostly for an English readership. Fortunately for Abrahams, despite his being a very young immigrant writer in Britain, there was a great deal of interest in texts about South Africa at this time, particularly in those which were written by non-white South Africans. When Abrahams arrived in London, he brought with him most of the manuscript of *Dark Testament* (1942), a collection of short narratives, factual and fictional, set in South Africa. He submitted the manuscript to London firm George Allen and Unwin, known for publishing politically engaged, left-wing texts including the writing of Mohandas Gandhi and Bertrand Russell. Abrahams anticipated that his South African background would be of interest to the publisher. In the covering letter to his submission, he wrote:

> Depending on your reaction to my Mss. [manuscript] the following might interest you: I am a South African of Abyssinian and half-caste parentage and will be twenty-three years of age in March. The slim volumes of my poems were published in South Africa where largely due to the terrible lack of markets and encouragement of literary talent, there is an awful waste and loss of good material and creative people. [5](letter from Peter Abrahams to George Allen and Unwin, George Allen and Unwin papers, AUC 129/3)

After signposting his national and ethnic origins, Abrahams implies his motivation for moving to London: that he will find a place where his 'good material' and 'literary talent' will be nurtured, without consideration of his race. In *Tell Freedom*, he cites trade unionist Max Gordon, who encouraged him to leave South Africa for Britain: '[T]here's no room for you here. Who wants a writer?' (Abrahams 1954: 263). Abrahams was hopeful that London would prove a more propitious location for the development of his literary career.

The reception of his novels by publishers, reviewers and readers in London tended to place more emphasis on his position as a coloured South African writer than on the literary merits of his work. For instance, the reader's report for *Dark Testament*, written by the translator Bernard Miall, foregrounds the significance of Abrahams's race. Before even providing a summary of the text, Miall begins his report with:

> It would be interesting to know whether Mr Abrahams is a Jew, or a negro [sic], or a 'coloured' Jew.[6] It is really a matter of some importance. He speaks in some of these sketches of his 'negro body' and his blackness; but others describe the sufferings of the Jews, fellow outcasts with the negroes, but accepted if they have money. If he is a negro his book has a social significance which it could not claim if he were merely a Jew with a dash of African blood. (George Allen and Unwin papers, AURR/10/2/08)

Miall also suggests that, 'If it is the work of a negro it has a sort of curiosity value and a social significance independently of its literary merits and is a definite contribution to "coloured" literature'. He recommends the novel strictly 'as an example of negro writing'. Furthermore, he objects to some poems which Abrahams originally included in the text, claiming that they were 'neither African nor individual, but imitative and "modernistic"' (AURR/10/2/08). Miall insists on Abrahams's novel remaining authentically 'African', revealing his narrow understanding of what he classifies as 'African', which should not, he thinks, include references to modernism or even perhaps modernity. Despite the wartime conditions, which made bookselling difficult (the South African markets would have been difficult to reach during wartime, as Miall mentions in his report), Allen and Unwin published *Dark Testament* in 1942. This is testament to their belief that books written by a black South African would have 'a curiosity value' for English readers.

Abrahams was attuned to the problematic exoticism that was driving the marketing of his work in Britain. In December 1942, he wrote to his publisher, Stanley Unwin:

> In our telephonic conversation today I got the impression that you were trying to be patronising. The idea that the dust jacket, and my colour are selling the book is an unusually unpleasant picture to think up and I am at pains to understand it. … And even if you do think my colour is selling the book I should think it hardly polite to say it to the person concerned. (George Allen and Unwin papers, AUC 129/3)

The dust jacket copy and design for the 1942 edition of *Dark Testament* present Abrahams overtly as a black author. The stylised charcoal and watercolour sketch of a young man's face on the cover is tinted violet, but is shaded heavily to indicate blackness, and in spite of the autobiographical elements of the narratives (emphasised by the truth-telling 'Testament' of the title), the man's features bear little resemblance to those of mixed-race Peter Abrahams; his lips and nose are particularly exaggerated, in a manner harking back to typological ethnographic illustrations. The head of the young man looms above a lightly-sketched mine shaft and tower block, clearly representing Johannesburg, with a palm tree (not an indigenous South African tree) indicating a broadly exotic, African setting. Abrahams had no problem with being seen as a 'black' writer. According to South Africa's system of racial classification, Abrahams was coloured, but he self-identified as 'black' because of his part-Ethiopian heritage, and also because of his interest in Harlem Renaissance writers. However, he obviously wanted to be seen as a worthy writer in his own right, regardless of the 'curiosity value' that his background may have entailed; as Gareth Cornwell et al. suggest, alongside Abrahams's proud identification as a black writer, 'his work evinces throughout an impatience with racial categories and a keen awareness of the suffocating effect of generic identifications on the individual's sense of self' (2010: 16). The design of *Dark Testament*'s dust jacket, as well as Abrahams's reaction to Unwin's insistence on its importance, reveals the ways in which black writers had to submit to the patronising and compromised reception and presentation of their work in order to be published and sell books. For Abrahams, the indignity of these compromises was particularly pointed, considering the way in which his life had been circumscribed by considerations of race in South Africa. This exchange between Abrahams and his publisher, in which his literary worth was reduced to his skin colour, reveals how equally racist attitudes were present, albeit in more subtle forms, in London.[7]

Reviews of Abrahams's writing also foregrounded the ways in which his race played a role in his reception. For instance, he recalls in *The Coyaba Chronicles* how a reviewer in the *Manchester Guardian* wrote that: 'to see a dog dancing would be a noticeable event and people would not be too concerned about the quality of the dancing; the mere fact of the dog dancing would be remarkable. For a while I was known as the dancing dog amongst my friends' (2000: 42). More sensitive reviewers, however, foregrounded how his background made *Dark Testament* unique amongst literary accounts of South Africa. In the *Times Literary Supplement*, Jan Stephens begins his review with: 'Mr Peter Abrahams is a South African native. This fact dominates whatever he writes.' Stephens goes on to explain how Abrahams's viewpoint is an important counter-narrative to those of white writers who might emphasise a 'fine picture' of a 'solitary native walking delicately, in his ochre-coloured blanket' across an 'empty land', or who alternatively focus abstractly on the 'servant question' or the 'native problem' (Stephens 1943: 34). He concludes: 'It is high time Mr. Abrahams came along to remind us that ultimately it is not a matter of pictures or servants or political embarrassments but of a backward society that must eventually be educated and given generous opportunity' (34). Although Stephens's characterisation of African life without western intervention as 'backward' is indicative of a Eurocentric understanding of modernity, he foregrounds how Abrahams's work provides an invaluable, hitherto unseen perspective of black South African experience.

There were specific political reasons underlying British readers' interest in books about South Africa. South Africa became important in discourse around British imperialism after 1948 in particular; as Leslie James points out, 'Malan's victory most directly impacted ongoing debates about the governance of trusteeship and protectorate territories; provided a focal point for racial tensions in British colonial settler territory; and infused arguments about the economic and social conditions of coloured people under European domination with new potency' (2015: 92). Even before the start of formal apartheid in 1948, however, there was much interest in South African politics, which intensified towards the latter half of the decade. Discourse about South Africa was, as James suggests, caught up in a general sense of ambivalence towards Empire in postwar Britain. Ron Ramdin explains that 'British public sentiment towards Empire became increasingly ambivalent after 1945, as it confronted the impending loss of India, the uncertainty about Britain's presence in all parts of Asia, and the increasingly assertive independent mindset of the "white" dominions' (1987: 85).

Abrahams pinpointed exactly these issues in a 1952 *Observer* review of three books about South Africa: *The People and Policies of South Africa* by Leo Marquard, *The Dilemma of South Africa* by John Hatch and *Report on Southern Africa* by Basil Davidson. He notes the proliferation of books about South Africa and that 'few countries of comparable size and population have received such attention' but goes on to declare that this was 'as it should be, for the interests of Britain are intimately affected by what happens in the Union. The British Protectorates of Basutoland, Swaziland and Bechuanaland are either encircled by Union Territory or on the borders of the Union' and the British were therefore concerned about their protectorates being swallowed up by the Union under the South African National Party. He then suggests a more pertinent reason behind British interest in South Africa:

> But there is another and, in a sense, more challenging aspect of the Union's problem that is of importance to Britain. Britain is responsible for six territories in East and Central Africa that are faced with problems of race relations similar to those in the Union. In these territories, as in the Union, there is a small white minority and a large black majority ... It is easy enough for the British people to condemn what takes place in South Africa and ignore the same things in British territories. (Abrahams 1952a: 8)

Abrahams recognises how South Africa served both as a warning about race relations in British-ruled territories such as Kenya and Rhodesia, and as a catch-all for British anxieties about colonialism. By focusing on the racism of the National Party government in South Africa, the British public could ignore the oppression that still prevailed in British colonies. This had significant consequences for Abrahams as a member of an anti-colonial, Pan-Africanist group in London.

Though cognisant of the complicities and hypocrisies that informed liberal British interest in South Africa, Abrahams, as a writer trying to make a living in London, nevertheless benefited from this pointed interest in his home country. In *The Coyaba Chronicles* Abrahams reflects pragmatically on the necessity of appealing to a white readership, naming Langston Hughes as one of the few black writers who had 'broken free of the dependence on the white literary establishment for survival and progress as a writer'. He continues:

> We all, like it or not, write for white readers. They, after all, are the buyers of the books and the magazines. The publishers cater to their needs and interests. If we did not take account of those needs and interests, they would not publish what we wrote. In the process we became interpreters, conveyors of the black reality to the world of white folk in the forms most acceptable to them. If we did not write what was acceptable to them, we would not be published. (Abrahams 2000: 145)

The market for South African writing, and Abrahams's sense of his responsibility 'to write books and tell them about life in this country [South Africa]' (Abrahams 1954: 299) meant that all of his novels of the 1940s were set in his birthplace: *Dark Testament* (1942), *Song of the City* (1945), *Mine Boy* (1946) and *The Path of Thunder* (1948). Of his fiction in the 1950s, only *A Wreath for Udomo* (1956) is not set in South Africa. *Wild Conquest* (1950) is an account of the Afrikaner Great Trek, while his memoirs *Return to Goli* (1953) and *Tell Freedom* (1954) are largely set in South Africa. Abrahams's insistence on telling South African stories is foregrounded by the fact that even his 'war novel', *Song of the City*, which he intended to enter into a war literature competition run by publisher Hamish Hamilton,[8] was set in South Africa. This is quite a remarkable choice of setting considering Abrahams lived through the Blitz in London, albeit in Hampstead, away from most of the bombing in central and east London, though the bombs hit 'occasionally very close and – at least once – down our street and shattering our windows' (Abrahams 2000: 31). He had also worked on a merchant navy ship, at constant risk of being bombed, during the first two years of the war. Apart from his 2000 memoir, however, Abrahams never wrote about these events, and kept his literary gaze firmly focused on South Africa even when writing war-themed fiction.

The publishing history of *Song of the City* reveals a great deal about Abrahams's commitment to being published and sheds light on the networks in which he moved in London. Abrahams submitted two versions of *Song of the City* to George Allen and Unwin but was rejected both times (the reader was once again Bernard Miall). This was despite the support of prominent authors: a handwritten note by Stanley Unwin, located in Abrahams's file from George Allen and Unwin, records how: 'E.M. Forster has seen it [*Song of the City*] and likes it though suggests "growing pains"' (George Allen and Unwin papers, AUC 183/2, 85 & 86). Forster famously wrote the introduction to Mulk Raj Anand's 1935 novel, *Untouchable*, and it is significant that Abrahams's work was taken seriously enough that Forster, a well-known supporter of literature from the colonies, was asked to read it, perhaps due to the relative critical success of *Dark Testament*. His other 'Marxist' novel, *Mine Boy*, was similarly rejected by George Allen and Unwin, who wrote to Abrahams: 'We feel that you will probably be wiser to keep to realistic and psychologically truthful stories of coloured peoples' (7 October 1944; George Allen and Unwin papers, AUC 183/2, 85 & 86), intimating that they had expected something like the semi-autobiographical 'slice of native life' narratives that had made *Dark Testament* so successful. Both *Song of the City* and *Mine Boy* were subsequently published by Dorothy Crisp, a political commentator and publisher known for publishing radical works, often by colonial writers. The publishing history of Abrahams's early works is thus revelatory of the position of black writers in London in the 1940s. London presented a young, black writer like Abrahams with many opportunities, but his relationship with publishers and readers also entailed potentially limiting compromises and complicities.

Return to Goli: staging a trajectory towards liberal humanism

Abrahams's *Return to Goli* arose out of the rising interest in South African affairs and from Abrahams having become, after more than ten years in London, a respected commentator on African and South African issues. This book is an account of Abrahams's visit to South Africa – and briefly to Kenya – after a fourteen-year absence. The trip was sponsored by the BBC Third Programme, *The Observer* and the *New York Herald Tribune* in Paris, with the intention that Abrahams would test, and report on, the extent of the 'colour bar' in both South Africa and Kenya (Polsgrove 2009: 199).[9] It is chiefly a reflection on 1950s South Africa, and also frequently includes Abrahams's thoughts on the contrasts between South Africa and London. *Return to Goli* was commissioned with both colonial and metropolitan readers in mind. Abrahams explains his intentions for this book: 'I wanted to reach the hearts and minds of some of the 33,000,000 non-whites who live under the rule of the 3,000,000 whites in the vast areas of South, Central and East Africa. And I wanted to reach the hearts and minds of the whites too' (1953: 29). *Return to Goli* is primarily Abrahams's personal reflection on the living conditions of the different ethnic groups in South Africa, as defined by apartheid legislation, with sections entitled 'The Coloureds', 'The Indians' and so on. This trip also generated a series of regular documentary-style articles for *The Observer*. For instance, an article titled 'When a Black Man Comes to Town' (1952b) is a detailed description of the South African pass system. 'Degrees of Degradation' was billed as an 'African Documentary', and discussed the Group Areas Act (1952c: 5).[10] The volume of *The Observer*'s column space given over to Abrahams's articles is further evidence of London readers' interest in South Africa.

While *Return to Goli* is ostensibly about South Africa, its first section contains an account of Abrahams's years in London. He begins by contrasting South Africa and London, focusing on the relative liberty he experiences in London. Life in South Africa allowed Abrahams 'no self-respect, no dignity' (Abrahams 1953: 29) but in London, he 'had slowly built up the self-respect South Africa had not allowed [him] to have' (14). He did experience racism, however, particularly in his search for a job. Abrahams recognises, though, that the type of 'prejudice' he experienced in London was different from South African segregation:

> Of course I had found colour prejudice in England. But prejudice, painful as it is, is not quite the same as a bar. There were no barriers up saying I could not go here or there by law. The libraries and theatres were open to me, and so were the concert halls and museums and parks. There were people who did not want me, landladies who would not let a room to me, and there was the hardship of finding a job. But I could sit anywhere I chose in tram or train or bus, and the restaurants were open to me if I could afford their charges. (Abrahams 1953: 15)

Abrahams provides a slightly more nuanced view of race relations in London in *The Coyaba Chronicles*, writing about how there was little racism in the early 1940s because 'This was wartime Britain, and war, it seems, has this odd way of pulling people together' (2000: 26) and because there were few black residents in London in those years, most of whom were soldiers (31). However, with the 1950s came an influx of West Indian immigrants, and the beginnings of 'friction and tension between black and white in Britain' (118–119), which Abrahams wrote about in a series of articles for *Reynolds News*, the newspaper of the British co-operative movement. Although this racial 'friction and tension' would have been at its height in 1953, it made sense for Abrahams to emphasise instead the relative liberty of London in contrast to South Africa in order to reinforce his points, in the body of the text, about the dire situation in South Africa. In this section, he also sets out his intellectual and political development over the past decade, with London as both setting and catalyst. This trajectory is staged by Abrahams in order to reinforce his liberal humanist ideals, so that his picture of South Africa, contrasted with London, will be even more affecting.

Besides his Pan-Africanist friends, the other group with which he associated in London was the British Communist Party. In the early 1940s Abrahams worked at Central Books and then at the *Daily Worker*, first as a clerk, and then as a writer (Polsgrove 2009: 61), alongside leading Party members such as *Daily Worker* editor Bill Rust. He also met Party sympathisers such as suffragette Sylvia Pankhurst, who wrote to George Allen and Unwin about Abrahams in 1943 after meeting him; she asked if the publisher would consider employing Abrahams so that he could focus on his writing, which she admired.[11] In *Return to Goli*, Abrahams describes the attraction of communism for a young black man such as himself:

> But communism has a dynamic appeal all its own. It offers the idealistic young a fine faith to live and fight for: it promises that the poor and hungry and dispossessed shall soon inherit the earth: it offers a kind of social consciousness in a socially conscienceless world. And to me, and those like me who were not white, it offered freedom from the colour bar and imperialism and a future in which we would run our own affairs in our own lands. For the young, sensitive, idealistic, angry, frustrated and embittered non-European there can, on the face of it, be no greater prize than the communists offer. (Abrahams 1953: 16)

Abrahams, like many African activists, recognised the potential of communism as an aid to anti-colonialism. However, like many Pan-Africanists, he later renounced his attachment to the Communist Party in Britain, falling out with them after he failed to present *Dark Testament* for approval by the Party committee, and when they realised that he was not a card-carrying member (Polsgrove 2009: 61). Like other Pan-Africanists, he simultaneously continued to respect Marxist values, as is evident in the above passage. Even though, in the following paragraphs, Abrahams goes on to explain his relinquishment of communism, the hyperbolic nature of the prose here reveals that he is not entirely disillusioned with communism's revolutionary spirit. The listing of what communism 'promises', the polemical, chiasmic flourish of the phrase, 'offers a kind of social consciousness in a socially conscienceless world' and the stacked adjectives in 'the young, sensitive, idealistic, angry, frustrated and embittered non-European' (clearly a description of young Abrahams himself) underscore Abrahams's enthusiastic admiration of communist ideals.

Despite leaving the Communist Party in the 1940s, Padmore maintained friendships with leading communists, and it was he who secured Abrahams his job at the Communist-Party-run Central Books. As Abrahams recalls in *The Coyaba Chronicles*, Padmore 'was no longer a part of them, but he was not against them. He had no time for others who had fallen out with the Communist Party and then turned against it' (2000: 42). Leslie James points out how the black radical tradition in which Padmore and Abrahams were entrenched 'critically engaged with Western radical political ideas, pointing out the "incompleteness" of these ideas and the hypocritical and ambivalent ways in which they were applied to non-European peoples. For example, despite his break with organized communism Padmore, like many black Marxists, continued to engage with European radical political ideas' (James 2015: 9). To this end, Padmore published *Pan-Africanism and Communism* in 1956, which aimed to disentangle the history of black liberationist movements from the charge of being controlled by communist movements – a project particularly pertinent during the rise of the Cold War. This break from communism enabled the Pan-Africanist Federation, centred in London, to influence independence efforts more effectively. Ron Ramdin suggests that by 'liberating themselves from the weakening influence of doctrinaire Marxism which British communists … were trying to impose upon the African national liberation movements in order to exercise Stalinist control over them, the Pan African Federation was able to take an independent ideological position on the colonial question' (1987: 175).

Padmore's exit from formally organised communism was inspired by specific political events, such as the Third International's disbanding of the International Trade Union of Negro Workers in 1933 and the Soviet Union's trade in war material with Italy during the Italian-Ethiopian

War (Ramdin 1987: 144). Abrahams's refusal to toe the party line, however, derived from his position as a writer. As he explains in *Return to Goli*, he broke from the Party after being chastised for not being a Party member and for refusing to submit his novels for approval:

> I revolted. I would never submit my work for approval. And to hell! Keats was, and always will remain, more important to me than the Marxist 'classics'. I was beginning to feel as personally unfree as I had felt in South Africa. Marxism was inhibiting my desire to see the world and people in the round.
> ... But my association with the communists had not been wholly negative. As a result of it I had realised that people, individual people, would always be more important than causes for me. My business as a writer was with people, with human thoughts, conflicts, longings and strivings, not with causes. Painfully, I was slowly groping to a view of life that transcended my own personal problems as a member of one oppressed group of humanity. I felt that if I could see the whole scheme of things with the long eye of history I might be able to fit the problems of my own group into the general human scheme and, in doing so, become a writer. (Abrahams 1953: 16–17)

Abrahams invokes the language of individual freedom: 'I revolted' and an emphatic curse, 'And to hell!', before discursively qualifying these statements by explaining how this act of revolt fitted into his increasingly liberal humanist philosophy, in which 'people, individual people, would always be more important than causes'. This philosophy was derived from his position as a writer, as a reader and as a black, mission-educated South African, and was solidified and reinvigorated by his experiences and associations in London.

Many writers of this postwar period experienced similar breaks with communism in the name of freedom of thought and speech – what Carol Polsgrove calls 'the genre that explored [a] generation's great disillusion with communism', naming, amongst others, Lionel Trilling's *The Middle of the Journey* (1947), the collection of essays by ex-communists to which Richard Wright contributed entitled *The God That Failed* (1949) and, centrally, Ralph Ellison's 1952 novel, *Invisible Man*, which explores the nexus between Marxism and black identity through the fraught relationship between the protagonist and the Brotherhood (Polsgrove 2001: 69). Doris Lessing, the Rhodesian-born, London-based writer who was also involved with the British Communist Party, experienced a similar response to the political demand of 'commitment'. In her essay

'A Small Personal Voice', she expresses the conflict between speaking for 'individual people' and for 'causes', inspired by her experiences with communism: 'I think that a writer who has for many years been emotionally involved in the basic ethical conflict of communism – what is due to the collective and what to the individual conscience – is peculiarly equipped to write of the dangers inherent in being "committed"' (Lessing 1975: 12). Like Lessing, Abrahams counters a propagandist Marxist attitude towards literature with writing that is committed, not to causes, but to 'other human beings he influences' in a 'humanist' fashion (6). Just as Lessing gestures to humanism, Abrahams's defence of his move away from the Communist Party includes overt references to liberal humanist ideas and is thus an apt preface to his ideological manifesto in this first section of *Return to Goli*.

Liberal humanism, prevalent and contested in the 1940s and 1950s, has been viewed as a major shaping force in Abrahams's political thought and writing: Michael Wade, for instance, writes that Abrahams's 'central interest' is 'the problem of individual freedom in contemporary human affairs' (1972: 4). Michael Green argues similarly that liberal humanism is one of the discourses which 'dominated' Abrahams's writing (quoted in Distiller 2005: 126). Liberal humanism is a portmanteau of liberalism, a belief in the freedom of the individual to act, and humanism, which focuses on human agency and a concept of common humanity. Natasha Distiller usefully defines the term: 'Liberal humanism is liberal because of the notion of the autonomous subject it assumes and relies upon, and humanist because of the quality or attribute it posits of an essential, universal "humanness" shared by all subjects' (2005: 52). What liberal humanism denotes, and what it has been made to mean, are two different matters, and it has been critiqued as essentialist, Eurocentric and positing a male, white subject as representative of its concept of 'humanity'. In South Africa particularly, 'liberal' is a loaded term. Peter Blair traces how the liberal tradition in South Africa 'developed from a liberal paternalism imported into the Cape Colony as part of the cultural baggage of British administrators', who challenged the 'mistreatment of indigenous peoples' from the late eighteenth century onwards (2012: 476). Liberalism in South Africa was championed by the Liberal Party, founded in 1953, whose Vice-President was novelist Alan Paton. The party gradually became more radicalised, proposing a policy of universal suffrage; however, it was critiqued because of the impotence of its policies of non-violence in the face of atrocities such as the 1960 Sharpeville massacre (Blair 2012: 477). This view of the weakness of both liberal politics and literature is evident in a 1957 overview of South African literature by Anthony Sampson in the *Times Literary Supplement*, in which he writes that 'the trend and polemic of liberal literature is partly an echo of the faults and vagaries of liberal politics' since both evince 'the mixture of paternalism, guilt, sentimentality and evasiveness that has until recently characterized much liberal thinking' (1957: 500).

Furthermore, liberal humanism has historically been associated with English literature, as it was in this body of works that essential truths about humanity were thought to be found. These ideas were deeply entrenched in methods of literary criticism as well as methods of education. The latter was particularly important in South Africa, where English-style education was administered to black South Africans through the mission schools, such as Lovedale College and St Peter's. Several of these nuances and connotations of liberal humanism are referred to in the passage from *Return to Goli* quoted above. For instance, the canon of English literature is invoked: 'Keats' is more important to Abrahams than Marxist works. Furthermore, liberty is a key existential value: Abrahams does not wish to be 'personally unfree'. Lastly, Abrahams emphasises individuality and common humanity: he is more concerned with 'individual people' than with 'causes', and he hopes to 'fit the problems of [his] own group into the general human scheme and, in doing so, become a writer', thus circling back to the connection between liberal humanism and literature. British readers seemed to find this appeal to Romantic British literature out of place in Abrahams's writing. His George Allen and Unwin reader, for instance, commented that 'his gods are a curious trinity – Keats, Van Gogh and Lorca', while Jan Stephens, in his otherwise complimentary review, complained of Abrahams's 'alien influences' (1943: 34). Miall's and Stephens's comments evince western expectations that African literature, in order to be perceived as 'authentic', should be free from European influences. A thorough exploration of Abrahams's writing, however, shows that reading English literature was crucial to Abrahams's development as an intellectual and writer.

The passage in *Return to Goli* in which Abrahams sets out his 'revolt' and his realisation that 'people' are more important than 'causes' seems to present Abrahams's political ideas as following a straight line from Marxism to liberal humanism, influenced by his experience of personal freedom in London and catalysed by his encounters with the Communist Party. Some critics have certainly sketched out such a trajectory: Catherine Woeber, for example, writes that Abrahams's 'oeuvre shows how he turned in succession to Marxism …, liberal humanism … and

Pan-Africanism' (1997: 88). Wade argues that Abrahams's liberal humanism can be attributed to his 'personal experience of a very great contrast' between his very deprived, constrained existence in South Africa and the relative freedom he is afforded in London, which therefore explains Abrahams's 'feeling of identification and harmony with English society' and his 'conscious adoption of a fairly undiluted form of the ideology of English liberalism' (1972: 101). In my reading, however, Abrahams's turn from communism to liberal humanism is strategically staged in *Return to Goli*, and his liberal humanism was not 'undiluted' at all but was continually blended with strains of Marxism and anti-colonialism. Furthermore, Abrahams's liberal humanism did not spring directly out of his London experiences, but both originated from and was complicated by his background as a black, mission-educated South African.

Abrahams's statement in *Return to Goli* that 'Keats was, and always will remain more important to me' suggests that he had a long affinity with English literature and, by implication, with liberal humanism, dating back to his early life in South Africa. Distiller provides a useful discussion of the uses and permutations of liberal humanism in South Africa, which certainly helps us to understand Abrahams's ideas contextually.[12] While acknowledging that it may be true that 'the humanism which underlies the development of twentieth-century English studies is English, bourgeois, problematic: a smokescreen for gender and class oppression' that is 'linked to English nation building and to colonialism', she suggests that 'this analysis is produced from, and for, Anglo-American history', and that liberal humanism 'takes on different resonances in twentieth-century South Africa' (2005: 61). Liberal humanism, while certainly complicit in white privilege and Eurocentrism in South Africa, also informed the liberation movement, so that '[t]he liberal humanist subject in South Africa can also be the resisting, anti-apartheid cultural activist' (62). For example, Distiller discusses how Nelson Mandela's 1964 defence at the Rivonia trial was based on philosophies of liberalism and human rights. Joseph Slaughter, in *Human Rights, Inc.* (2007), similarly traces the simultaneous rise of human rights and the novel in the twentieth century, focusing on the Bildungsroman, which is significant given that both *Return to Goli*, and particularly *Tell Freedom*, are such tales of personal and intellectual development.

Distiller argues that the development of South African liberal humanism can be traced 'through the mission schools' humanist education policies, and Christianity, into the founding of the ANC, and thence into struggle politics' (2005: 77). She particularly focuses on Abrahams's autobiography, *Tell Freedom*, which 'explicitly engages with the advantages and complications of an education in English Literature' (101). According to Abrahams, before starting school, he worked in a smithy, where he met a young white woman who worked in the office and who read him the story of Othello from Lamb's *Tales from Shakespeare* (149). It was the possibility of being able to read books like this which encouraged him to go to school. Abrahams was then educated by missionaries at both Grace Dieu and St Peter's School, and was therefore exposed to Christian humanist, English and liberal ideas through his schooling. Catherine Woeber has foregrounded the immense influence of St Peter's School on South Africa's literary history; she writes that, before its closure in 1956, 'St. Peter's had been responsible for an entire generation of African intellectuals who recognised the contradiction between the Christian ethics of their education and the realities of colonial, and later apartheid society' (1995: 58). Other alumni of St Peter's included musician and writer Todd Matshikiza, novelist Arthur Maimane and ANC President Oliver Tambo. In *Tell Freedom*, Abrahams questions the contradiction between the Christian humanism they were taught at school and the realities of their treatment by 'Christian' white South Africans: 'God taught: "Love thy neighbour as thyself." ... The Church taught that we were all brothers in Christ, one with another ... And the whites, those who had spat on us and on others, were all Christians. The equation did not work out' (Abrahams 1954: 238). Abrahams also discovered Marxism while at St Peter's, and was already questioning the compatibility of Marxism and Christian humanism at this stage, asking: 'Had Marxism any room for the compassionate humanity that pervaded the life and teaching of Christ?' (251).

At St Peter's, and through his reading of English literature, Abrahams was steeped in liberal humanist ideals; and like other writers of his generation, he used these ideals to critique colonialism and apartheid. In *Tell Freedom*, Abrahams describes how his reading motivated his move to London. At the Bantu Men's Social Centre, he was exposed to American Harlem Renaissance writers such as Langston Hughes, Claude McKay, Stirling Brown, Jean Toomer and Georgia Douglas Johnson. This Centre was, Jonathan Hyslop writes, 'an important conduit for American influence on black intellectuals' (2008: 119). Founded in 1921 by an American missionary 'as a rather conscious attempt to moralize the leisure time of black men in Johannesburg' (Hyslop 2008: 119), the Centre offered reading material which influenced the political views of many of its users, including Abrahams. Abrahams recounts a dramatic scene in which a record by Paul Robeson – 'The voice of a black man!' – provides the soundtrack to his first reading of Du Bois, Weldon Johnson and Countee Cullen (Abrahams 1954: 192). Significantly, he appreciates Cullen because 'this man loved John Keats in a way I understood' (196). His reading of these authors over the next few months played a crucial role in his political development and his development as a writer: 'I became a nationalist, a colour nationalist through the writings of men and women who lived a world away from me. To them I owe a great debt for crystallizing my vague yearnings to write and for showing me the long dream was attainable' (197). Like the other men at the Centre, Abrahams was torn between Harlem and London, speaking of Harlem as the 'land of hope and opportunity' but equally referring to the absence of the 'colour bar' in England (199). For Abrahams, these two places were particularly represented by their literature.

Despite his interest in the 'New Negro' writers, it was Abrahams's reading of English poetry that confirmed his choice of England over America as an escape from South Africa:

> I tried to take stock of the two forces that pulled me, first this way, then that. And it seemed that America had more to offer me as a black man ... Yet England, holding out no offer, not even the comfort of being among my own kind, could counter that call because men now dead had once crossed its heaths and walked in lanes, quietly, unhurriedly, with such beauty that their songs had pierced the heart of a black boy, a world away, and in another time.
>
> I decided. I would go to England one day. Perhaps I would go to America afterwards. But I would go to England first. I would go there because the dead men who called were, for me, more alive than the most vitally living. In my heart I knew my going there would be in the nature of a pilgrimage. (Abrahams 1954: 200)

Abrahams expresses a feeling of common humanity with English poets, whose poems have 'pierced' his heart across time, and asserts a quasi-religious attachment to these literary heroes; to travel to England will be a 'pilgrimage'. Thus, Abrahams's reading of English literature – initially Lamb's *Tales from Shakespeare*, and later the Romantic poets – was crucial to his development as a writer, and informed his move into exile, as Distiller writes:

> Shakespeare inspired him to acquire education. Education gave Peter a love for English literature which provided him with access to the language. English allowed his political conscientisation via the works of African

American writers, which in turn liberated his sense of self as a black writer. All this means that he had to leave South Africa, and he chose exile in England because of his experience of English literature. (Distiller 2005: 147)

In the trajectory of Abrahams's intellectual development, diverse literary and political influences are interwoven. These different influences were to take on specific nuances in postwar London. It is also important to note that Abrahams's admiration of African American writing continued to inform his writing and thinking, as is evidenced by his longstanding epistolary relationship with Langston Hughes, who corresponded with a number of South African writers.[13] Abrahams later dedicated *A Wreath for Udomo* to Hughes. Even in *Tell Freedom*, after confidently stating his decision to make a 'pilgrimage' to England, Abrahams continues to imagine Harlem, rapturously: 'But Harlem! A Negro City! Imagine Countee Cullen walking down a street and meeting Langston Hughes! And then imagine Paul Robeson joining them! And Du Bois! And Stirling Brown ... Go on! Chuck in Pushkin too! And then let them talk! Imagine ...' (1954: 200).

It was to England that he went, though, and in *The Coyaba Chronicles* Abrahams suggests how his reading of English literature and his mission school education influenced his first encounters with London. His recalls his first visit to Hampstead Heath, one of the first places he went after his arrival in London:

It was all familiar from my readings. I felt oddly at home on Hampstead Heath. Being colonial and missionary-trained meant, in my case, knowing more about the 'mother country' than about the country in which I was born. The missionary schooling inevitably imbued me with the English vision of the way things are. My teachers at St Peter's in Rosettenville, outside Johannesburg and at Grace Dieu, outside the northern Transvaal Boer town of Pietersburg, had been graduates of Oxford and Cambridge, products of English religious orders. They transmitted their values to several generations of black South Africans. So I was freer on Hampstead Heath on my first day in London than I had been in any public park in the land of my birth. (Abrahams 2000: 27–28)

Abrahams's declaration that he feels 'freer' in Hampstead Heath than in a public park in South Africa contains a double meaning. Firstly, he is literally 'freer' because he is unconstrained by the racist laws and society that would have governed his movements in South Africa, particularly in public places such as parks. Secondly, the sentence in which he recalls his relative freedom significantly starts with 'So' and follows on from the previous statement; he feels 'freer' on Hampstead Heath precisely because his teachers 'transmitted their values to several generations of black South Africans'. These 'values' included liberal humanism, intertwined with an appreciation of English literature. Significantly, it is in one of the more pastoral spaces of London, Hampstead Heath, near where Keats lived, where Abrahams feels this 'freedom' and familiarity. This romanticised encounter on Hampstead Heath does not preclude him from understanding the more sober and complex realities of London, as he recalls in *The Coyaba Chronicles*, in which he writes:

> The London I entered was a great bustling metropolitan city at war, an imperial power fighting to hold on to that empire. And the teeming colonial subjects of that empire did not, on the whole, want England to lose that war, but they also did not want the empire to emerge unchanged from it. (Abrahams 2000: 27)

Thus his original idealisation of London, based mainly on pastoral Romantic poetry, is countered both by the urban realities of London and by his realisation of the inevitability of colonial resistance and the eventual dismantling of the British Empire. Although this was written years later, filtered through the lens of memory and a longer view of history, and should not perhaps be taken as evidence of Abrahams's immediate impressions of London, these two sides to Abrahams's encounter with London are present in his writing of the 1950s, specifically in *Return to Goli* and *A Wreath for Udomo*. He encounters postwar London both as figurative metonym and literal manifestation of the English values of liberal humanism he had been steeped in as a mission-educated black South African, and as the unstable centre of a crumbling empire.

In addition to the passage about his privileging of liberal humanism over communism after his fallout with the Communist Party, Abrahams reproduces a statement in *Return to Goli* he made in 1952 on the BBC Third Programme, which is informed by liberal humanist ideals that he claims have been developed in London but which, as we have seen, are a continuation of ideals already developed in South Africa. In this statement, Abrahams suggests that black African activists should harness the powers of love, rather than hatred, and should focus on common humanity rather than racial specificities and antagonisms. He suggests that:

> In the struggle to be free, many Negroes have arrived at a position where they would counter the white bigot's race-hatred with race-hatred against whites: many who have been humiliated because of their colour, joy openly

at the humiliation of a white person *because* he is white ... Large numbers of Negroes today counterpoise a black humanity against a white humanity. (Abrahams 1953: 20–21)

Abrahams illustrates and substantiates this viewpoint through incidents he experiences or witnesses in London. Thus London, which he had already acknowledged as mostly prejudice-free, serves as the testing ground for his ideas about race and black subjectivity. He presents four London-based 'depositions'.

Abrahams begins with reflections on his own attitudes towards race. Firstly, he recounts an incident in which, having just arrived in London, he travels on a bus, filled with the 'wonder of freedom' and a feeling of 'warm friendliness' towards others (1953: 21). He is startled, however, by the abrupt manner of a sour-faced bus conductor and becomes 'angry and bitter' at what he supposes is racism, thinking that 'South Africa was not so far away after all' (21), until the conductor treats a young white woman in the same unfriendly manner and Abrahams realises that his bad temper was not racially motivated. For his second deposition, Abrahams recalls how he felt obligated to inform a new landlady over the telephone that he was 'a Negro',[83] even though she had not asked for this information. He then moves on to discuss the behaviour and mindset of other black Londoners, telling of a West African friend who is 'using' the Communist Party and does not trust its white members. Lastly, he provides the example of a black friend who enjoys the cultural delights and freedom of London, and who has made friends with white Londoners and had affairs with white women, but tells Abrahams: 'I want to hurt them, to take revenge for everything that happened in South Africa. Something goes hard in me and I just want to hurt them as much as I can' (24). Out of these 'depositions', Abrahams offers the following conclusions:

> First, large numbers of Negroes tend to reach out for prejudice, even where it does not exist. Second, many Negroes tend to be double-faced and dishonest in their relations with non-Negroes. Their white friends, even their girl friends [sic], are dismissed, when not present, as 'like all whites'. Third, many Negroes are building up a colour bar of their own. They would counter South Africa's 'Reserved for Europeans Only' with their own 'Reserved for Negroes Only'. They would counter bigotry with bigotry, hate with hate, darkness with yet more darkness. (Abrahams 1953: 25)

As discussed, Abrahams had already developed these ideas in South Africa: of common humanity over bigotry and hate, even within the realm of race politics. The freer environment of London helped to reinforce these ideas, and Abrahams also selects and narrates these London-based incidents in order to foreground the possibility of a life outside of race. Abrahams concludes his 'declaration' with a description of the different levels of living, from the 'basic struggle' to that of the mind, and quotes Shelley's *Prometheus Unbound* to illustrate this superior level to which, he says, the black man must aspire; as Wade argues, Abrahams invokes Shelley to ensure that he has 'established the pedigree of his liberalism centrally in the English bourgeois romantic tradition' (1972: 99).[14]

Abrahams specifically states that these liberal humanist, non-racial ideas are facilitated by his living in London:

> But all of this had been worked out a long way from the seat of the problem. It was comparatively easy to work out a tolerant and humanist view of life in England. England had been kind to me. It had given me the chance to build a decent dignified life for myself. In it I had learnt to laugh and play, and found my love. It had given me access to forms of beauty. Its climate of mental freedom had allowed me to pursue my thoughts as far as they would go, and without fear. (Abrahams 1953: 27)

He therefore decides that these ideas have to be proven, that his 'faith had to be tested on the battlefield of race hatred' (28), which is why, he says, he travelled to South Africa in order to write *Return to Goli*. Whereas in *The Coyaba Chronicles* he acknowledges that he was sent by *The Observer* to test the 'colour bar', in *Return to Goli* he presents the journey to South Africa as a testing ground for his own ideology. Just as he chooses London-based incidents instrumentally to illustrate his vision of non-racial, common humanity, so Abrahams inserts *Return to Goli* as a milestone along his staged trajectory of intellectual and political development.[15]

In *Return to Goli*, Abrahams maps out London and South Africa as points along a spectrum of modernity and relative tolerance and prejudice. He draws on the common representation of South Africa as behind time, or out of time, in order to highlight the contrasts in freedom, progressiveness, even 'civilisation', between South Africa and London. Abrahams recounts a conversation he has with friends in South Africa about London:

> 'And you can just get on a tram or bus and sit anywhere, beside a White person, beside a White woman?'
> 'I am sure that somewhere in London now, in some full bus, some White woman has gone to sit beside some Black man.'

'And nobody takes any notice?'
'Why should they?'
'You mean it's natural.'
'Quite natural.' (Abrahams 1953: 150)

This conversation reveals the contrast in experiences of personal freedom between South Africa and London, which informs Abrahams's thinking about both his home country and issues of individual liberty and racism. His friend's incredulous question, with its incremental shift from 'beside a White person' to the even more unbelievable (for a South African) 'beside a White woman', reveals the gap in everyday experience between South Africa and London. Abrahams's measured and certain response, beginning confidently with 'I am sure', highlights the non-synchronous temporalities of London and South Africa: while 'somewhere in London now' a 'White woman' is taking her seat next to a 'Black man', this occurrence is unimaginable in 1950s South Africa. Abrahams's response, that this is 'quite natural', also foregrounds how he has come to see equality between races as almost unremarkable while in London. Upon his return to London, Abrahams once more highlights the differences between London and South Africa, using the same image of a black man and white woman associating with one another:

> I caught a brief glimpse of a young man and a woman walking together. They were both laughing happily. The man was Black and the girl was White ... How far away that other place was! Almost, it did not seem possible to believe that such a place existed in the modern world. (Abrahams 1953: 220)

Abrahams uses both spatial language – 'How far away that other place was!' – and a reference to temporality – it seems impossible that South Africa exists in the 'modern world' – to convey the contrasts between London and South Africa. Abrahams equates progress and modernity here with non-racism.

In the conclusion of *Return to Goli*, Abrahams re-emphasises how his attitudes towards race, liberty and humanity have been formed by his removal from South Africa to another, more progressive place, London, one that shares more of the positive attributes that Abrahams associates with modernity. He tells of his complex attachment to South Africa – although he is 'glad to leave the place' he is simultaneously 'sorry to go' because he is a 'child of Goli, forever involved in its problems' (Abrahams 1953: 203). Abrahams also feels vindicated for having left South Africa: 'Had I not gone frustration would have overwhelmed me and I would have gone bitter and sour. So many of those who had been children of my generation had grown into angry, bitter men' (202). In contrast to the somewhat prescriptive tone of his BBC radio statement, he acknowledges that he understands why '[s]ome of them [South Africans] had abused me for having lost my bitterness'. He particularly assigns their accusations to their lack of experience of the liberal environment of London: 'They had not lived as free men in a free world. They had not shared long hours in the capitals of the West with men and women who place freedom, friendship and tolerance amongst the rarest of human virtues' (202). Abrahams once more emphasises how liberalism is reinforced and enjoyed in 'the capitals of the West' (in his experience, Paris, and more significantly, London) in order to highlight the oppressive conditions in South Africa.

Responses to *Return to Goli* were mixed. Most notably Dorothy Pizer, George Padmore's wife, suggested in a letter to Richard Wright that Abrahams's trip to South Africa, sponsored as it was by western media institutions, and particularly his appearance on the BBC Third Programme, put him in a compromised position: 'Once a coloured fellow gets on the B.B.C. in any other programme than a colonial or commonwealth one, you can know for sure he's made his peace with the other side' (quoted in Polsgrove 2009: 118). Pizer suggested that, since Abrahams was allowed on the Third Programme and was sent to South Africa by a London newspaper, his views must have been less than radical. The BBC Third Programme, established in 1946, covered cultural and intellectual matters, and courted some controversy due to accusations of elitism, which explains Pizer's critique. Abrahams appeared on the Third Programme on several occasions, as part of a series of programmes about the 'colour bar' broadcast in 1952, mostly dealing with race relations in Africa, particularly Kenya and South Africa, but also occasionally discussing race issues in Britain (Newton 2011: 153).

By the time *Return to Goli* was published, the rift between Abrahams and Padmore (and Pizer) had been widening for several years, especially since Abrahams had divorced his politically active first wife, whom Padmore liked, and had lived in France for several years with his second wife. Abrahams added fuel to this fire when he addressed the Royal Institute of International Affairs in 1954, critiquing Nkrumah and the prospects of the Gold Coast by arguing that while black South Africans were defending 'Western European' values of liberalism and democracy, in the Gold Coast '[t]he ideas of Western Europe had not conquered' (quoted in Polsgrove 2009: 132). This was to prompt Padmore to criticise

Abrahams, also in a letter to Richard Wright, calling him a 'man who had sold his political soul for money and fame'. Padmore continued:

> Since Peter was taken up by his ofay [white] friends and dropped after they had made enough use of him to tell the spades back home how to behave as 'black Englishmen' – no bitterness – I have not seen the lad in years. He has deserted all his poor friends who helped him out when he was even poorer than they. May God help him to prosper and end up in Hollywood. I can even provide him with a title: 'From Johannesburg Slum to Paradise.' (Quoted in Polsgrove 2009: 133)

Padmore and Pizer's criticism of Abrahams reveals anxieties around collaboration, complicity and authenticity amongst black, western-educated African intellectuals in London in the 1950s. Leslie James writes of Padmore's 'ironic accusation' of Abrahams serving as an exemplar of a 'black Englishman':

> While Padmore enjoyed the opera and his journalism demonstrated a respect for British politics, he pitied those 'Africans and people of African descent ... who consider themselves more British than the Queen!' ... Put simply, for Padmore there was a distinction to be made: between personal respect for British political institutions and enjoyment of European culture, on the one hand, and Abrahams' involvement with organizations that Padmore believed did not reciprocate respect for African culture such as the BBC and the British Council, on the other. (James 2015: 149)

Furthermore, Padmore disapproved of Abrahams's focus on fiction writing over political journalism and activism: Abrahams recalls in *The Coyaba Chronicles* how Padmore was 'contemptuous' when he 'was too caught up in writing fiction to complete an assigned job' (2000: 39). Even though Padmore had abandoned communism himself, he objected to Abrahams leaving the Party in the early 1940s. Their debate over this issue, recalled by Abrahams in *The Coyaba Chronicles*, was focused on the incommensurability of being a writer and committed to a political party: 'For me, from the very outset, being a writer was incompatible with membership of any serious political party which demanded strict adherence to its principles and policies. They said this was "escapist", "idealist", "ivory tower" stuff' (2000: 60). Thus, while Abrahams believed in pursuing freedom as 'a writer's natural commitment' (60), hence his involvement in Pan-Africanism and anti-imperialism, he refused to be committed unquestioningly to a political dogma. Insisting on the need for solidarity, Padmore frequently objected to Abrahams taking on the role of 'the loving critic within the Pan-African family' (152). James points out that Abrahams was not alone in experiencing this treatment from Padmore; included under the contemptuous term 'café intellectuals' – those only committed to the anti-colonial struggle in words, rather than action or commitment – were Leopold Senghor, C.L.R. James and George Lamming (2015: 144).

As intimated above, Padmore's labelling of Abrahams as a 'black Englishman' was arguably disingenuous given that Padmore himself, as a West Indian who lived for decades in London, felt as if he were an 'outsider' when in Africa (James 2015: 144). Other Pan-African activists in London had similarly complex relationships with London and Africa; Abrahams, in an article originally published in the Jamaican *Holiday* magazine in 1959, described how Jomo Kenyatta, 'the most relaxed, sophisticated and "westernised"' amongst them 'enjoyed the personal friendship of some of the most distinguished people in English political and intellectual society'. While living in London, Kenyatta 'fought the British as imperialists but was affectionate towards them as friends' (Abrahams 1963: 138). Kenyatta was therefore, somewhat like Abrahams, 'westernised' in terms of his education and cultural interests, but nevertheless resolutely anti-colonial. That Abrahams was himself aware and self-critical of the pitfalls of becoming a westernised 'café intellectual' while supporting the Pan-Africanist, anti-colonial cause is evident in his novel *A Wreath for Udomo* (1956).

A Wreath for Udomo: London as 'The Dream'

A Wreath for Udomo is concerned with a group of African anti-colonialist intellectuals who live in London, some of whom return to their respective countries in order to lead their states to independence. It is widely believed to be a *roman à clef*, with characters loosely based on the real-life political figures with whom Abrahams associated. The protagonist, Michael Udomo, is partly a fictionalised version of Kwame Nkrumah, while the group's leader, Tom Lanwood, is a critical portrayal of George Padmore. The artist figure, Paul Mabi, is a stand-in for Abrahams himself (Polsgrove 2009: 135). The main fictional African countries of the novel, Panafrica and Pluralia, stand roughly for the Gold Coast (Ghana) and South Africa respectively, although their geographical positions are not equivalent, since Pluralia seems to be a short journey away from Panafrica; thus 'the major problems of Africa in the fifties are geographically juxtaposed for dramatic convenience' (Wade 1972: 133). After some planning and campaigning in London, and a romance with an Englishwoman called

Lois, Udomo returns to Panafrica, where he stages a revolution and becomes Prime Minister. He sells out his Pluralian activist friend, David Mhendi, to the white Pluralian government, in order to elicit the technical assistance of Pluralian engineers for a dam-building project. The Pluralians kill Mhendi and, in the novel's violent climax, Udomo is murdered by Party members who disapprove of his anti-tribalist stance. *A Wreath for Udomo* was published on the cusp of the Gold Coast's independence, which occurred in 1957, and was seen as a foreboding prophecy of the struggles to come, particularly between tribalism and 'western' democracy. Although the novel focuses on African independence struggles in general and particularly on the Panafrican Udomo, through the Pluralian characters, especially Mhendi, Abrahams also reflects on the South African political situation and its connections to both London and the rest of Africa.

A Wreath for Udomo is vague about its revolutionary politics, as Abrahams particularly avoided any overt references to socialism, despite the socialist elements of the revolution in the Gold Coast, his model for 'Pan Africa'. Carol Polsgrove asks:

> Simplifying the political picture is understandable in a novel, but why did Abrahams erase socialism from his imagined African future? He may have had Cold War sensitivities in mind, or he may have been trying to present a book that would appeal to a broad American and British audience with little knowledge of Africa – a book focused on the human feelings and relationships of an African generation caught between two worlds. (2009: 136)

If this is the case, one wonders whether Abrahams's overt repudiation of communism in *Return to Goli*, published only three years earlier, may not have been motivated by the same concerns. His publishers certainly seemed to appreciate Abrahams's effacement of socialism in *A Wreath for Udomo*. The novel's reception by its London and American publishers was markedly different from that of Abrahams's earlier South Africa-set works. While Allen and Unwin's reader valued the South African specificity of *Dark Testament* over its literary merit, the publishers of *A Wreath for Udomo* wanted to frame the novel as a 'literary rather than a political work' (Polsgrove 2009: 136). His American publisher, Harold Strauss of Knopf, complained to London-based Faber and Faber's Peter Du Sautoy about the 'tendency for book review editors to have novels reviewed by specialists in their subject rather than by literary critics'. He suggested to Du Sautoy that 'someone of very high literary reputation' should provide an advance review. Joyce Cary, author of the Nigerian-based *Mister Johnson* (1939), was approached and, to the publishers' dismay, designated Abrahams's novel '[a] good study of African nationalism, valuable in revealing both the conscious and unconscious motives at work in a movement which gathers momentum a great deal faster than Europe realizes' (quoted in Polsgrove 2009: 136). The publishers' attempt to present *A Wreath for Udomo* as a literary rather than revolutionary work suggests, firstly, the extent to which the Cold War affected literary output on both sides of the Atlantic and, secondly, the difference in approach to a Pan-African rather than a South African work, as a tale of Pan-African anti-colonialism was far more difficult to swallow, for the British reading public, than anti-racist South African literature.

London is represented in *A Wreath for Udomo* mostly as private domestic spaces in which meetings between the activists and others take place. In fact, the only public spaces of London ever mentioned in the novel are the pub in which Udomo meets Lois in the opening scene and the hall in which a colonial congress is held. No major landmarks, streets, parks or monuments of London are referenced. Abrahams focuses on the mingling of the African activists and their supporters in a series of rooms. Lois, Paul and Lanwood's apartments, all situated around Hampstead, are described in great detail. The activists live in their own world within these residential spaces. As Mabi later tells another activist, Adebhoy, 'London's an old city. It doesn't change for our coming or going' (1956: 225). This statement glosses over the impact the activists have on the city, simply through their presence and political activities, but it also reinforces the sense the reader has of the group as isolated from the rest of the city.

A passage recounting Udomo's first visit to Lanwood's flat, while seemingly simply descriptive, highlights how the activists' response to London's urbanscape illustrates their position within the city:

> Lanwood lived in a three-roomed flat in a mews off Hampstead Heath. The flat was, in common with all the others, above a garage. In the dim distant days of imperial glory, when Victoria was Queen-Empress of the most powerful throne on earth, these garages had been stables. The flats above them had been the quarters of those who looked after the horses and carriages of the great families. There were still watering troughs in the mews. But now little boys sailed paper boats on them in the brief months of summer. And there were still cobble-stones underfoot. (Abrahams 1956: 40–41)

In this description, Abrahams provides the reader with a sense of the history of the dwelling, during London's 'dim distant days of imperial glory', and also of the changes that had taken place over the past hundred years in the city. The class system has eroded: the stables of the gentry have been converted into flats for middle-class inhabitants, including African anti-colonial activists. The short sentence, 'And there were still cobble-stones underfoot', suggests, however, that remnants and reminders of Victorian London and its imperial values endure. The passage continues:

> Udomo stopped outside the mews and looked at the slip of paper. This must be it. Then he saw Adebhoy's car on the other side of the road. This was the place all right. He turned into the mews. His shoes clanked against the cobble-stones. He found walking on them awkward. Adebhoy had said it was the flat right at the end, in the left-hand corner of the mews. He pushed the bell that said 'Press'. He heard it ring faintly a long way away. He waited, turning his back on the door, watching a man polishing a shining black car outside the garage opposite. These people seemed to love working for its own sake. The thing was shining already. Suppose I'm just another damn nigger or darky to you – hey, Mister? (41)

That Udomo, who is at this point new to London, finds the cobblestones 'awkward' to walk on suggests his difficulty in adjusting to life in this foreign city with its imperial legacy. His anxiety at finding Lanwood's flat, evident in his self-reassuring 'This must be it' and 'This was the place all right', reflects his general difficulty positioning himself within London. This is compounded by his suspicions about the middle-class white man cleaning his car, whom he imagines may be racist. For Udomo, even London's suburban streets contain reminders of Britain's history and the ever-present possibility of racism.

London appears in the first section of the novel, entitled 'The Dream', while Part Two, set in Africa, is called 'The Reality'. The group of activists in London, the 'brains trust behind the anti-colonial organisations' (Abrahams 1956: 23) are, as Kolawole Ogungbesan describes them, 'rootless people living a bohemian kind of life' whose existence is 'summed up by the word "dream", and it is a dream which is very much divorced from the African reality' (1979: 101). London is a place where writing, thinking and meeting take place, whereas it is Africa where the revolutionary 'action' will occur. In London, the activists' ideas of Pan-Africanism and anti-colonialism are developed and support is drummed up for African independence, in the form of publications and representations at congresses. Udomo, the protagonist and man of action in the novel, argues that his 'dreams of liberation' are not 'dreams' at all: 'Or, if it is, it is more real to me than what you call reality' (Abrahams 1956: 96). Udomo's attempts to realise these dreams have tragic and violent results, partially because he cannot reconcile his western ideals of modernity and industrialisation with the so-called 'tribal' or 'traditional' sensibilities of his people.

Thus, Abrahams represents the intellectual arguments of the anti-colonial group, developed in London, as detached from the political and social realities of Africa. Lanwood in particular is seen as out of touch, reflecting (and perhaps caricaturing) Padmore's comment to Richard Wright, 'I will fight for a free Africa and Asia, not live there' (quoted in Polsgrove 2009: 134). When Lanwood's leadership becomes heavy-handed, Pluralian freedom fighter David Mhendi tells him: 'It's easy enough for you to sit in London and be godlike'. When challenged about this statement, Mhendi addresses the rest of the group:

> He's good at sneering at other people. Well, has he tried to lead a movement? Not in London where he's safe, but in Africa? Movements are led by more than godlike speeches and pontifical books from the safety of London. Go out to Africa! Fight there! And then come and lecture me about self-discipline. (Abrahams 1956: 42–43)

In this passage and elsewhere, Mhendi (who is also, significantly, the only major South African/Pluralian character) presents Abrahams's concerns about his and his associates' ambiguous position as Africans in London. *A Wreath for Udomo* is focalised through various characters, with some sections of free indirect discourse. Furthermore, the narrative is very dialogue-heavy, meaning that we hear the characters' opinions with minimal narrative comment. Catherine Woeber has suggested that 'Abrahams has always expressed forcefully-held opinions through his characters' (Woeber 1997: 102). In *A Wreath for Udomo*, the diversity of viewpoints held by the characters provides questions and provocations rather than 'forcefully-held opinions'. The different positions of the characters vis-à-vis London and Africa suggest Abrahams's own questions about his place in relation to these two spaces.

It is also through Mhendi that Abrahams critiques the idea of collaboration between 'liberal' British politicians and colonial leaders, and Africans. At a congress on African affairs in London, Mhendi berates a paternalistic British politician, saying: 'I'm tired of all your talk about multi-racial commonwealths and freedom and protecting our so-called backward brethren from us. I'm tired of the whole lot of it because I've heard it so often' (Abrahams 1956: 70). He goes on to suggest that the 'pioneers' of their 'movement' (liberal British politicians) 'would not have had the nerve to talk about a multi-racial commonwealth of free and equal partners knowing all the facts of the Pluralian situation today' (71). Through the character of Mhendi, who represents a South African freedom fighter, Abrahams critiques the detachment from Africa that London entails on two fronts, amongst black African intellectuals and white liberals who are involved in African affairs.

While Tom Lanwood has been seen as a scathing portrayal of Padmore, the character is also inspired by Abrahams's own complex relationship with Africa and London. When Lanwood travels to Panafrica after Udomo has become Prime Minister there, he feels out of place and eventually books a passage back to London, thinking to himself:

> Truth is I'm homesick for London. Hadn't realised how used I'd grown to London till now. Silly to have thought I could wipe out thirty years of my life as though they didn't matter. What was that little song I'd always jeered at?
>
> *Maybe it's because I'm a Londoner*
> *That I think of her wherever I go ...*
>
> Now, at last, when you're too old to support it, you're facing reality, aren't you, Tom? (Abrahams 1956: 258)

For Lanwood, the 'reality' of Africa forces him to acknowledge his own 'reality' – that London is truly his home and he is more a Londoner than he is an African. He takes London with him to Africa, and thinks of 'her' wherever he goes, because of a long familiarity with the city and because he has become attached to 'English' values of liberalism and modernity. Similarly, in *Return to Goli*, Abrahams expresses, upon his departure for South Africa: 'Really, *it* [London] was home, not the place I was bound for' (1953: 13).

The title of the novel's first section, 'The Dream', takes on a specific meaning in relation to the potentially autobiographical writer figure of Paul Mabi, an artist figure with liberal sensibilities, who may be another cipher for Abrahams himself. Wade describes him aptly: 'Mabi, besides being Europeanized to his fingertips, represents a specially sensitive version of the liberal outlook; his artistic occupation is unmistakably symbolic' (1972: 135). Although Mabi visits Panafrica, he eventually returns to London and chooses his own friendships and personal ideals over 'the cause', horrified and discouraged by Udomo's betrayal of firstly his British girlfriend and then more crucially his Pluralian friend, Mhendi. Mabi is unsure, however, whether his choice of liberalism and loyalty over political action and expediency, à la Udomo, is wise or effective, as he explains in a letter to Lois, Udomo's one-time British girlfriend:

> But you and I, were we right with our private moralities? Can a man betray love and friendship, the gods we worship, and still be good? I think you'll still say no. Then how explain Udomo? I know the wrong he did you and Mhendi. But I also know the good he did Africa. (Abrahams 1956: 309)

On one hand, Udomo is the hero of this novel; as the title implies, the text is a 'wreath' in the sense of an elegiac tribute to Udomo, and his violent and expedient road to independence is celebrated as a victory for anti-imperialism. However, Udomo is presented as morally bankrupt and egotistical, betraying friends and lovers in his rise to power and ultimately being brought down by trusting his tribalist allies over his westernised friends. Despite his doubts, Mabi chooses the 'dream' of London over the 'reality' of Africa, and suggests to Lois that he hopes they can continue to 'dream as we dreamed before Udomo came and brought reality into our lives'. London is therefore presented as a refuge from the 'realities' of Africa, but Abrahams recognises the problematic nature of using exile in London as an escape from Africa's problems. Carol Polsgrove helpfully points out that 'Mabi's *mea culpa* suggests that the book may in part be an effort to work out Abrahams's own conflicts and confusions about the freedom struggle and his role in it' (2009: 135). Mabi also voices Abrahams's liminal, somewhat rootless position between Africa and London, despite his belonging to a group of activists. Mabi tells Lois:

> You've known us and the thing that binds us together for many years now. Of our own free will, if there is such a thing, we've elected to live to for a cause. We would liberate a continent. That is what we live for. Someone once told me we are the lost generation: we don't belong to the past of our own people and we have not found a place in your world. (Abrahams 1956: 39)

Given the autobiographical attributes of this character, Mabi's speech is perhaps an indication that Abrahams may not have felt as 'at home' in London as he had elsewhere declared. Thus the character of Mabi contains both the struggles which Abrahams experienced and expressed in writing: his questions around the validity of his liberal humanist ideals, and his occupation of a space between London and South Africa.

In 1957, Abrahams was commissioned by the Colonial Office to write a history of Jamaica, published as *Jamaica: An Island Mosaic*. In Jamaica, Abrahams found what he felt was a plural, free society, where he and his family could live with dignity (Polsgrove 2009: 135). The family moved to Jamaica in 1959, and Abrahams lived there until his death. His early idealisation of London and English liberal humanism had a great deal to do with his searching for a place where he could belong, given his rejection of the 'sickness' and 'hatred' of South African society, but it was in Jamaica that he eventually found a home. His time in, and writing about, London paved publishing inroads for black South African writers who followed. Todd Matshikiza, in a 1960 letter to Langston Hughes, suggested that Abrahams had not thoroughly explored the racism experienced by black Londoners: 'London for the Black man isn't even a fool's paradise. One day someone ought to take out those dirty old carpets and give them a good solid, shaking and airing. It is a great pity that Peter Abrahams left without doing it sufficiently' (in Graham and Walters 2010: 114). It is possible Abrahams did not 'sufficiently' shake out London's carpets because he was focused on the problems of apartheid and colonialism, but also perhaps because London represented, however ambiguously, the liberal touchstone to which he compared the unfree realities of South Africa. For another South African author active in the early 1950s, London was similarly the site where liberal humanism was tested and explored.

Dan Jacobson: different worlds and literary homelands

Dan Jacobson, a South African writer who also lived in London in the 1950s, explored the limits and uses of liberal humanism in postwar, postcolonial London in his short story 'A Long Way from London' (1958). While Jacobson shares some commonalities with Peter Abrahams in terms of his experiences in London and his relation to English liberal humanism, the two authors also differ in important ways owing to their specific South African backgrounds, and his work offers a productive contrast with Abrahams's writing. While Abrahams frequently invokes liberal humanism to present his anti-colonial, anti-racist views to his British readers, Jacobson both critiques and defends liberal humanism by comparing this philosophy with irresponsibility and neo-Toryism.

Growing up in South Africa, Jacobson, like Abrahams, imbibed English culture and education, particularly a love for English literature. Jacobson's hometown, Kimberley, had a long history as part of the British Colony in South Africa, and an association with imperialists such as Cecil John Rhodes. Jacobson's ideas about England and Englishness were formed by both the books that he read and his English-style education. He recalls in his 1985 autobiography, *Time and Time Again*, how:

> My parents from one world,[16] this constrained yet half-abandoned world around me, I read in book after book of yet another: of England, Britain, to whose empire Kimberley and the country as a whole was still supposed to belong, and because of whose empire I was being brought up to speak English and to go to a school which modelled itself as much as it dared on some vague notion of an English public school. As so many others have done, in so many varying climes, I found it wasn't the reality of the countries from which the books and movies came that I was compelled to doubt, but the reality of the country I lived in: this undescribed and uncertified place where not a single thing, from the sand underfoot to the occasional savage thunderstorm overhead, was as other places were. (Jacobson 1985: 8)

In this passage, Jacobson describes how the England he read about in books became more real to him than the land surrounding him. Here we see an echo of Abrahams's declaration that the English poets were, to him, 'more alive than the most vitally living' (1954: 200).

Like Abrahams, Jacobson's education entailed a valorisation of canonical English literature and 'culture', and a tradition of liberal humanism interwoven through these texts and cultural values. Jacobson acknowledges, in *Time and Time Again*, that he is a disciple of English literary critic F.R. Leavis. He describes meeting Leavis at Cambridge and prefaces the anecdote by calling him 'one of the writers whom I had appointed to be a mentor' (1985: 126). Significantly, it is the humanist, universalist aspects of Leavis's criticism that appeal to Jacobson, which he relates to his exile status:

> What could have suited me better? There I was, having chosen to sunder myself from South Africa and to settle in England; and here was Dr Leavis, in prose which again and again seemed to reach to the heart of certain literary works, implicitly proposing an ideal community which could be experienced (if anywhere) only inside my own head, but which nevertheless felt more like the real thing than any other I could imagine myself joining. It was as if the 'Republic of Letters', to use a phrase Leavis would probably have abominated, had been opened up or transformed into a homeland: a place in which I could be naturalised without seeking a licence from any authority other than that of my own tastes or talents, inclinations or ambitions. (Jacobson 1985: 127)

Thus Leavis's ideas about literature allowed Jacobson to occupy a space outside of South Africa or London – a 'homeland' – for which he needed no documentation or nationality, which would especially appeal to an exile. One can appreciate how this philosophy would have been attractive to Abrahams as well, who was unable to go back to the land of his birth, but who was (even more than Jacobson) a foreigner in London, for all his Anglophilia. Both Abrahams and Jacobson attempt to transcend nationality through reading and writing, by dwelling in the 'Republic of Letters'. In 'A Long Way from London' Jacobson explores the extent to which the imaginary 'homeland' of letters and high culture might detach writers from the realities of apartheid South Africa, where 'homeland' was to take on very different connotations within racist apartheid geography.

Despite their ideological similarities, Jacobson's background and his education differ from Abrahams's in several ways. Firstly, as he was white, education was not difficult to attain or unique amongst his contemporaries, since all white South African children were provided with adequate education. As we learn in Abrahams's memoir, *Tell Freedom*, higher formal education for black South Africans was rarer, and when obtained (in the 1940s, generally through a mission school) meant that the student entered into a black, middle-class elite, which provided a certain kind of privilege, but also potentially entailed compromises and complexities of class and race. Secondly, while Abrahams's liberal humanism, at least in its formation, was based upon Christian principles, Jacobson's is strictly secular. Thirdly, one of the most marked differences between Abrahams and Jacobson is that while Abrahams was critiqued for his espousal of liberal humanism by contemporaries and critics, Jacobson's liberalism was largely received as something unremarkable amongst his generation of white writers. Lastly, Jacobson's background as a Jewish South African with immigrant Eastern European heritage plays into his adoption of English liberal humanism; as he notes, his parents are from another 'world', and this background informs his empathy for other types of 'outsiders' within South African society. Thus, while Abrahams and Jacobson both invoke a liberal humanism informed by a colonial South African education in order to speak to the concerns of apartheid South Africa, their invocation of such an ideology has different roots, and has been differently received. Their espousal of this ideology had particularly complex resonances when they both travelled to liberal humanism's place of origin, London, in the tumultuous period of the demise of British colonialism in the 1940s and 1950s.

The themes and image of London explored in Jacobson's short story 'A Long Way from London' reveal aspects of his position as a white, liberal, English-speaking South African writer in London in the 1950s, which are also reflected in his London-based novel, *The Evidence of Love* (1959). This novel provides an interesting counterpart to Abrahams's works, as it reflects on the experiences of a 'Cape Coloured', Kenneth Makeer, who moves to London to study law. Kenneth, like Abrahams, is a Pan-Africanist and a member of the Free Africa Society. Another parallel between *The Evidence of Love* and Abrahams's writing is the theme of interracial love – the novel's main concern is the romantic relationship between Kenneth and a white South African woman. Abrahams depicted interracial romance in *The Path of Thunder* (1948) and in the relationship between Lois and Udomo in *A Wreath for Udomo*. Interracial romance is also significantly a trope employed in the service of a liberal humanist vision of race relations, in which love both triumphs over the racial divide and is thwarted by a discriminatory society.

I will focus mainly, however, on 'A Long Way from London', as it presents a compelling exploration of the guilt and shame that attended liberal South Africans in London. This short story, first published in 1955 in the *New Yorker*, is the title narrative of *A Long Way from London* (1958), a collection mainly comprised of pieces set in South Africa, aside from the title story. Although this short story was not first published when Jacobson was living permanently in London, he nevertheless recalls in his autobiography, *Time and Time Again*, how he had already begun to 'commit' to living in London at the end of his first year there in 1950 (1985: 116). Furthermore, the issues and incidents contained in this story would have been derived from his experiences in London in 1950. The choice of this title for the collection reflects its content, which is mostly comprised of South African narratives, where the society that is depicted is 'a long way from London'. For instance 'The Box' is a seemingly autobiographical story about his friendship with a young black servant during childhood, while 'The Riot' tells of an episode of unrest amongst black factory workers in his home town and 'The Zulu and the Zeide' recounts a relationship between an elderly Jewish immigrant to South Africa and his devoted black servant. The collection was republished by Little, Brown with the title *The Zulu and the Zeide* in 1959, perhaps because, as with Abrahams's *Dark Testament,* the publishers were aware of the market for South African fiction and wished to distinguish the work's setting more overtly.

The phrase 'A Long Way from London' takes on a specific meaning in relation to the title story, which is set in London, but which includes South African and African characters and sets up a complex relationship between South Africa and London, which are a 'long way' from each other in more than just geography. Its central character is a South African-turned-Londoner, Arthur Panter, who must rethink his self-imposed distance from South African concerns after an encounter with his South African mother and a Tanganyikan student. Through this story, Jacobson questions the positions which white South African immigrants to London, particularly white South African writers, occupy in relation to their home country and its political and social conditions. Significantly Arthur is a writer and member of the London literati, a published poet who works at 'a fairly arty publishing house' (1958: 153). and therefore an examination of his attitude towards South Africa and England takes on larger implications, becoming an exploration of the responsibility of the South African writer.

'Not civilized enough': continuity and disappointment in London

Jacobson's short story begins with an arresting description of Arthur Panter's attitude towards London. We learn he is not 'impressed' by London:

> Any fool of a South African can come to England and be impressed. Be so impressed that he even begins to feel there is something a little shameful about the fact that in the country he comes from most of the buildings are new, and summer is in December and winter is in July – not as it is in England, not as it is in all the books he has ever read.
>
> Just as any fool of a South African can come to England and refuse to be impressed. He can complain that the buildings are old and dirty, and that Johannesburg has taller buildings and is more modern in any number of respects, especially with regard to such things as the supply of hot water and the number of motor cars to be seen on the streets. (Jacobson 1958: 151)

These thoughts about the differences between South Africa and London, and the dual perspectives from which these two spaces could be viewed, are filtered, with a degree of authorial irony, through the consciousness of Arthur Panter. There is clearly an element of satire in Arthur's reported assumption that all a (white) South African in the 1950s would find 'shameful' about their country would be its different climate and newer buildings, rather than the truly shameful racial discrimination present in South African society. Arthur is impressed by neither space, regarding those with an overly developed reverence for England's monuments as 'tourists' and those who prefer the more modern buildings of South Africa as 'Philistines' (151). In this passage, the two spaces are significantly figured by their 'buildings'. While this may be literary metonymy, Panter also shrugs off the racial issues in South Africa by focusing on impersonal architecture.

We soon learn that, although he views South Africa as 'colonial, tawdry, second-rate' (151), unlike some émigrés he surprisingly does not view London as 'more civilized': there is no clear dichotomy between the two spaces, despite the contrast implied by the story's title. Rather, 'Arthur Panter refused to be impressed by London, by England, by anything in the country, because it *wasn't civilized enough*' (151–152, italics original). Although he hails from a tiny, rural village in the Eastern Province of South Africa, he objects to London, which he finds 'ugly, dirty and dreary', with Westminster Abbey crawling with tourists, the City having been bombed, Mayfair having been 'sold to perfumery firms and public relations consultants':

> Nothing that there was suited him. It had all been spoilt. While other South Africans in England tried to assimilate what was in front of them to what they already knew, Arthur Panter had priced it all, and knew that it wasn't worth the effort. True, there was nothing else: he could never go back: he would die in the desert airs of the Eastern Province; but all the same, England wasn't civilized enough. (152)

The gap between what Arthur and the other South Africans 'already know' about London and what is 'in front of them' is what motivates him to dismiss the city as 'not civilized enough'. As was suggested in the earlier passage, these mental images of London are formed through 'all the books he has ever read' (151). English colonial education and the privileging of English literature have led South Africans to develop a romanticised vision of England, particularly London, which is at odds with the real London they encounter.

Reading English literature has also inspired in Arthur elitist notions about 'civilisation', associated with colonial discourse. English culture, according to imperial ideology, is supposed to occupy the highest rung on the ladder of civilisation, whereas that of the colonies is, in Arthur's words, 'second-rate'. There are also self-evidently racial implications to this hierarchy of culture. Since this idea of England – and particularly its hub, London – as the pinnacle of 'civilisation' is a myth developed for the colonised, rather than a material reality, Arthur obviously finds this utopic ideal 'spoilt', particularly by commercialism, which he sees as ruining his cultured, pastoral, static vision of England with the trappings of modernity. Jacobson purposely uses commercial language, however, to convey the irony of Arthur's position: he has 'priced it all' and has found it not 'worth the effort'; even though he is objecting to the capitalist tawdriness of public relations firms and tourism, he is a consumer too, of propagandistic English imperial ideology. Abrahams's *Return to Goli* contrasts London's more liberal, progressive society with racist South Africa, which is positioned as existing outside the 'modern world'. In Arthur Panter's temporal schema, however, London, despite being preferable to provincial South Africa, is not 'civilized' because it is too modern. Throughout the short story, Jacobson reflects on the ironies of Panter's understanding of 'civilisation', which is informed by Panter's background as a white, English-speaking South African.

Jacobson's own removal to London provokes reflection on the strangeness and particularity of his South African 'Englishness', both in 'A Long Way from London' through the eyes of Arthur Panter and some twenty years later in his autobiography. In *Postcolonial London*, John McLeod analyses Jacobson's first impressions of London as recalled in *Time and Time Again*, and reads this passage as participating in a dialectic of continuity and disappointment experienced by many postcolonial arrivants in London, particularly in the postwar period. For Jacobson, being in London 'afforded him the opportunity to encounter the substance of English life which he had only previously encountered imaginatively through his reading of literature' and he feels that 'London, England, civilization, continuity, culture, order – each seemed seamlessly allied with each other' (McLeod 2004: 59). At the same time, as McLeod points out, Jacobson is disappointed, most significantly by his attempt to see Virginia Woolf's house in Tavistock Square, which was a bomb site. This 'is a disequilibriating moment, where the alliance of London, England, order and culture comes apart in the derelict and ruined spaces of postwar London' (McLeod 2004: 60). This moment is certainly reminiscent of Arthur Panter's declaration that 'It had all been spoilt' and how he and other South Africans struggled to 'assimilate what was in front of them to what they already knew' (Jacobson 1985: 152).

Jacobson's simultaneous experience of having his expectations both met and thwarted by postwar London makes its way into several of his other texts, demonstrating its significance in shaping his relationship to London and Englishness. In *The Evidence of Love*, the narrator reflects on the common experience of South Africans who come to England; this passage reprises formulations of familiarity, strangeness and disappointment:

> What it means for a South African to come to England can perhaps best be compared with what it means for a provincial in England to come to London, or a provincial in the United States to come to New York. But the comparison is untrustworthy, no more than a dim metaphor. How can one explain what England is to the South Africans who come to the country as visitors, tourists, immigrants, students? To them England is truth, and it is dream; England is reality, and it is pure vision. England is like a mirror in which they see their deepest selves reflected, the selves they have sought for and never found, and have known only by the sense of incompleteness that haunted all their previous day; yet England is chillingly, vastly, uncomfortably strange, with a strangeness made only the more poignant by the sense of dream-familiarity that accompanies it. England is their own past; yet they have never seen it before: England is all they have hoped for; yet it is a disappointment that endures and endures, long after they have left her or settled in her. (Jacobson 1959: 121)

Jacobson's mapping of province and metropole puts London at the centre – England is the imperial centre to which (English-speaking) South Africans return, and London is the metropole to the English provinces. He expands this spatial description to a series of contradictions: England is 'dream' and 'vision', but also 'reality'; it is a 'mirror' in which they see their true selves but remains unknowable; it is what they have hoped for but is (as Arthur Panter finds) a 'disappointment', because it is 'uncomfortably strange' and does not meet their long-held expectations. In Jacobson's later novel *The Beginners* (1966), partly set in late 1940s London, the city appears to the protagonist, Pamela, and her mother as shabby and ruined, which they specifically attribute to postwar conditions: '[O]f all the cities they had visited the pall of the war still seemed to hang most heavily over London. It was dark, shabby, grimy, defaced, soiled; its people seemed wearier than those on the continent, their clothes and houses dirtier' (Jacobson 1966: 294). As in 'A Long Way from London', the city is 'spoilt', although not by commercialism but by the effects of war.

The sense of 'incompleteness' and mystery (a perception of the 'unknowable') that Jacobson attributes, in *The Evidence of Love*, to South

Africans encountering London for the first time, is a phenomenon that he apparently processed throughout his writing life. He describes the impressions he felt on arrival in London in an article published twenty years later in the *Times Literary Supplement*. Jacobson recalls how, upon his arrival in London, he was 'convinced at once that I was in the presence of some complicated and tantalizing riddle whose terms I could not begin to define, and whose answer it was impossible for me to guess at' (Jacobson 1971: 884). He reiterates the same 'classic experience' recounted in 'A Long Way from London' of 'having things at last made clear to him' through witnessing places and things he has 'hitherto only read of in books or seen in paintings and films' and repeats the Biblical idiom of 'seeing face to face instead of darkly; of knowing more perfectly that which had been known only in part'. In this later piece of writing, however, he uncovers another reason, besides the friction between idealistic, possibly outdated depictions of England presented to colonial readers and the shabby postwar realities of the city. In an epiphanic passage that suggests a working-out of this previously mysterious disappointment, Jacobson explains that:

> [T]o see face to face is to see, also, what one had never really wanted to admit fully to oneself: namely, that those books, films, comics, pictures, and even commonplace words which one had grown up with, were not one's own, as one had imagined them to be (after some surreptitious adjustment) – they were 'theirs'. They belonged to the world with which they were congruent; they belonged to these people, who lived in this place; they were more private, even perhaps more limited in their meanings, than one had ever suspected. (884)

This 'paradoxical sense of exclusion and withdrawal', Jacobson suggests, leads eventually to a critique of colonialism and British exceptionalism, which he implies underlaid the disappointment-on-arrival he felt and represented through his fictional characters: 'I still think I was right, twenty years ago, to decide that English culture was a more private affair, a more local show altogether, than the spreading abroad of its language and empire had allowed me to imagine' (884).

Read through Jacobson's later explanation, Arthur Panter's disgust at the realities of 1950s London can be perceived as a critique of the effects of empire upon the colonial subject, particularly on white, English-speaking subjects who imagine a sense of assimilation into English culture and society, which is not upheld by the more 'private' and 'limited' meanings of Englishness that exclude him. Jacobson's critical re-examination of the trope of colonial disappointment in the metropole thus illuminates texts dealing with similar 'disequilibriating moments' (McLeod 2004: 60) on the part of South African arrivants: moments that may suggest a sense of exclusion, entailing a critique of colonialism and cultural imperialism in addition to a provincial belatedness.

In contrast, in Abrahams's remembrance of his first encounter with London on Hampstead Heath, he does not recount any disappointment, but only continuity: the place is 'familiar' from his 'readings' and he feels 'oddly at home' (Abrahams 2000: 27–28). As mentioned, Abrahams does not comment in any of his writing on the effects of war either, except in *The Coyaba Chronicles*, briefly explaining how wartime affected race relations in London. His failure to experience the disappointment felt by Jacobson and many other colonials when encountering familiar-but-strange London can be attributed to Abrahams's focus on his relative freedom in London: as a coloured South African he is more interested in being 'freer' in London than in the land of his birth than he is in any potential discontinuity between 'real' London and that of his imaginings and readings. While Abrahams's familiarity with London because of his reading is comparable to Jacobson's, London ultimately represents to him not a realised or unrealised past but a possible future. In *A Wreath for Udomo*, London is designated 'The Dream', but it is not dreamlike because it is a partial and thus surreal manifestation of their imaginings. Rather, it is the place where they can dream of a better future for Africa. In 'A Long Way from London', Jacobson reflects on this disjunction between what London means to white South Africans and black migrants. In doing so, he draws on his own experiences of familiarity, strangeness and disappointment when encountering London, and therefore turns his critique back on himself.

White hands: neo-Toryism and assimilation in London

Jacobson's central focus in his short story, and the question triggered by its climactic incident, is whether social and political responsibility should be assumed, or shrugged off, by white South Africans who live in London. Arthur's focus on London's and South Africa's buildings and other impersonal landscapes – he refers to 'the desert airs' (Jacobson 1958: 152) of the Eastern Province, rather than its people – has foreshadowed his real preoccupation: his abandonment of any type of position regarding racial discrimination and segregation, which he may have had to take on in apartheid South Africa. Believing that, unlike the rest of London, he is 'civilized right up to the minute, or even a little beyond it' (153), he positions himself beyond politics or race issues:

> For instance, one of the reasons why Arthur had been so glad to leave South Africa was because in South Africa one had to be a 'liberal', lest one find oneself among the supporters of the South African government, and supporters of the South African government were even more unspeakable than South African 'liberals'. But in Britain one could be as irresponsibly neo-tory as one liked. (153)

Jacobson's third-person focalised narrative allows him to ironically present Arthur's antipathy towards South African liberals. Arthur, in his quest to abandon his South Africanness, eschews the sentimental paternalism of South African liberals and embraces neo-Toryism instead. Neo-Toryism (although it has come to have different meanings at different times in history, and in different countries) refers here to a blend of liberalism and conservatism, including anti-communism, which developed in the 1950s. In the sense that Jacobson uses this term to describe Arthur, it conveys a shrinking from revolutionary action and a libertarian approach to society; Arthur, in other words, supports the status quo in London and avoids any radical political action. He is embarrassed by his 'poor old mum', who sends him money to deposit into accounts of anti-apartheid organisations in London and who encourages him to attend anti-apartheid events (154). Although Jacobson ostensibly sets up Arthur, the fastidious 'neo-Tory', as an anti-hero in contrast to his liberal, well-meaning mother, the story will ultimately question the efficacy of both ideologies.

Ignoring his mother's spurs to political activism, Arthur retreats into 'civilised' pursuits, such as writing avant-garde poetry, and attempts to blend into London society. Although his attachment to Englishness is complicated by the fact that his idealistic visions are 'spoilt' by the realities of London, he has nevertheless taken pains to assimilate into the city's masses, a response to that sense of 'exclusion' that Jacobson perceived upon his own arrival in London. Arthur has 'lost any trace of a South African accent' (153) and we learn that 'he dressed like an Englishman, and carried an umbrella to work every morning. Certainly no one could have accused him of being, in appearance, a son of the wide-open spaces' (153–154). Even his face has 'acquired that secretive, tentative English look' and his hands are 'after three years, quite white' (153). Jacobson's focus here on Arthur's complexion as denoting Englishness prefigures the issues of race and racism which dominate the latter half of the story. Arthur can assimilate into English society because he is white, even whiter after three years away from the South African sun, making him a credible imitation Englishman. When he learns that his mother is determined to visit him in London, he is most concerned about her markers of South Africanness, that her accent would be 'like a South African's' and that her 'sun-faded complexion' would make her 'look different' (155).

Upon her arrival at the train station, his mother draws attention to herself not through her own appearance, but rather because she is accompanied by a black Tanganyikan student, Mr Manwera. Recounted through Arthur's consciousness, the first description of the man focuses on his physical blackness: Arthur finds himself 'at surprisingly close quarters to a round and shining face, shining like coal' (158). Arthur's impressions of Manwera are provided in almost psychoanalytical terms, as an image from a dream, which he immediately interprets:

> Arthur thought him beyond belief, the possible product of a fragment of his own mind that he was not yet neo-tory or irresponsible enough to acknowledge without a feeling of discomfort. In England one did not need to be a 'liberal', but, Arthur felt, one could still blush with embarrassment for the man. (159)

This short passage offers a range of insights into Arthur's state of mind as a white South African Londoner. As there were certainly black immigrants in London in the 1950s, the fact that this dark-skinned man is 'beyond belief' says more about Arthur's wilful ignorance of black Londoners than anything unusual about his presence in a London train station. It is also 'beyond belief' to him that this black man is in his immediate vicinity, being introduced to him by his mother. Manwera's presence evokes the 'fragment' of Arthur's mind which is concerned with racism and the situation in apartheid South Africa. He disingenuously suggests that his 'embarrassment' on Manwera's behalf resembles liberal empathy, but since it is sparked by his disgust at the Tanganyikan's cheap-looking yellow hat, 'a hat that should never have been made' (159), Arthur is projecting his own elitist, and essentially racist, embarrassment at being seen with the man rather than any kind of empathy. Here, Jacobson provides a subtle criticism of the potentially patronising characteristics of liberalism.

Although Manwera is not only a 'fragment of his own mind', as a character in this story he certainly serves to represent a part of Arthur's thinking: his presence disturbs Arthur's neo-Toryism. More broadly, Jacobson is interested in exploring the 'fragments' of Panter's mind, to question the ideological attachments of white South Africans who move to London and gravitate towards English culture rather than acknowledging their implication in the inequalities of apartheid South Africa. Certainly, as we have seen, Jacobson was just as enamoured of certain aspects of Englishness as Arthur, but critiques those who would use their 'escape' from South Africa to London as a means of escaping moral responsibility. In doing so, he validates his own liberal humanism, although he also foregrounds the weaknesses of liberalism through the character of Arthur's mother.

Mrs Panter, who teaches at a mission school for young black girls, is concerned with Mr Manwera's fate, and immediately promises Manwera that Arthur is 'the one who'll help you with everything' (158). She explains to Arthur that, although Manwera is not South African, it is the apartheid government that has forced him to relocate to London: 'He was studying in South Africa, but then the Government said that no more foreign-born Africans could study in the Union, so he's had to come here' (160). In contrast to Arthur's attitude of embarrassment – he tries to get rid of the man soon after meeting him – Mrs Panter befriended Manwera on the boat, pitying him because of the racist attitudes of the other South Africans during the journey. She declares to Arthur: 'It was dreadful. I *hate* South Africans. Though I shouldn't say that because I'm one myself. But it was unforgivable' (160, italics original). Like Arthur, she has a complex attachment to South Africa, but for different reasons: she both identifies as South African and hates white South Africans because of their racism. Arthur, on the other hand, overly identifies himself as a Londoner, though he is disgusted by many aspects of London, to avoid acknowledging either his own racism or his responsibility to act in response to racism in South Africa.

Through Manwera's eyes: London as a vast toy-town

Arthur discovers – to his shock – that his mother has offered to share their taxi with Manwera, and so they travel back to Arthur's flat. It is on this journey that the story moves, for the first time, from Arthur's consciousness into that of Manwera. This allows Jacobson to imagine the anxieties and fears of a young black immigrant to London, eliciting sympathy from the reader towards Manwera, in contrast to Arthur's 'embarrassment' on his behalf:

> Mr Manwera had been quite dazed by his arrival. He had sat quietly throughout their taxi-ride with his hands in his lap: his idea of a big city had been formed by the glimpses he had had of Durban and Cape Town, and the smallness and closeness of so many of the buildings in London had surprised him. But so too had the length of the drive in the taxi. In him there was an apprehension of danger in being drawn into the shining, tiny toy-town that he had seen about him – the toy-town that, like something in a dream, he had also seen to be huge, to be bloated, to be something beyond the farthest reach of his sight, the widest pacing of his feet, the farthest stretch of his imagination. In these spaces one could be lost, in this confinement one could be trampled upon: there was no way out. (Jacobson 1958: 161–162)

London is figured in surreal terms, 'like something in a dream', as both small and cramped, and large and overwhelming. It is a 'shining toy-town' with 'small' and 'close' buildings, but it is also 'huge', 'bloated' and beyond comprehension or imagination. Manwera perceives both London's cramped, crowded streets and its vast, overwhelming size as menacing. He is afraid of being 'lost' and 'trampled upon' in this alien city. While for Arthur London does not quite live up to the city he knows from literature, for Manwera, whose idea of a city has been formed by the metropolises of South Africa, London is beyond his imagination and frame of reference, and is thus frightening. Manwera, as a black Tanganyikan, alone in London, also has more reason to feel isolated and afraid than Arthur does.

This passage is echoed by Jacobson's own initial impressions of London, as recollected some thirty years later, in his autobiography, *Time and Time Again*. Of his first walk around central London, he recalls:

> Already, on that walk, I was struck by what was for me one of London's most surprising features: its spaciousness, the size of its streets, squares and public places. (The size of the city itself was another matter, and quite distinct from what I am speaking of here: in a way, the area the city as a whole covered did not come as such a surprise to me, partly because I could not, and still cannot, grasp it: it is beyond reckoning, beyond the widest span of one's imagination.) I suppose I had heard so much about the 'tight little island', about England being 'cramped', 'crowded', and 'pinched' – and had also heard so much about the 'wide open spaces' of South Africa, about the 'vastness' of the veld – that somehow in my mind

there was an expectation that everything in England would really be small, reduced in scale, somehow toylike. (Jacobson 1985: 76)

Similar terms are used in both passages: London's vastness is beyond 'the farthest stretch of his imagination' in the former passage and 'beyond the widest span of one's imagination' in the latter. In both passages there is a recognition of London's simultaneously cramped nature and vast scale. However, while Jacobson had 'an expectation that everything in England would really be small, reduced in scale, somehow toylike', an expectation somewhat challenged by the scale of the city, for Manwera, it is the 'toy-town' characteristics of London that surprise him. There is a significant difference in tone and mood between the two passages. In Jacobson's autobiography, the spatial aspects of London are calmly remarked on, as a matter of interest, but when he filters these impressions through Manwera's consciousness, there is a proliferation of terms referring to confinement and threat: he has 'an apprehension of danger' and is concerned that there will be 'no way out'. The differences between Manwera's understanding of London's sublime spatiality and those of Jacobson himself highlight the black African's relative isolation in London, in comparison to that of an English-speaking white South African. In the short story, this passage also sets the stage for the scene which succeeds it, highlighting the callousness of Arthur's reactions towards the isolated young man.

'I thought that people would be more kind in London': disrupting neo-Toryism

The climactic encounter between Arthur and Manwera serves to disrupt the central character's smug irresponsibility and elitism and poses important questions about the position of white South Africans in London. Upon their arrival at Arthur's flat, Arthur learns that Manwera was supposed to stay with a friend, but that this friend has left a letter for him in Southampton, stating that he is away and will meet Manwera at the East Africa Office in eleven days' time. His friend did not leave any address, meaning that Manwera is homeless and friendless for a fortnight. Arthur is immediately irritated by this situation rather than sympathetic: "'I've never heard of a man actually writing a letter ..." He did not finish the sentence; he waved his white hand above the cup. "What are you going to do?"' (Jacobson 1958: 166). As in the story's opening scenes, Arthur's complexion – his 'white hand' – is referenced at this crucial moment, since his lack of empathy for Manwera is caught up in the privilege he is afforded as a white South African. Although Manwera has not asked to stay, Arthur brusquely tells his mother, not even addressing Manwera himself, 'He certainly can't stay here' (167). Manwera objects to his presumption and makes to leave, saying, 'I thought that ... people would be more kind in London than they are' (167). Manwera's expectations of London have been undermined once more. His statement that he thought that 'people would be more kind in London than they are' is partly a veiled comparison between South Africa and London. Since he experienced discrimination in South Africa, which eventually culminated with him being thrown out of the country, he perhaps had higher expectations of Londoners, but instead he finds yet another racist white South African. Manwera's reaction also undermines Arthur's supposed 'civilisation': his elitist attitudes have in fact made him uncivil and uncivilised, unwilling to help a friend of his mother's who is stranded in a big city.

Mrs Panter, embarrassed by her son, begs Manwera to stay, but he pointedly tells her: 'Your son is very rude'. Mrs Panter, however, has a different interpretation of Arthur's behaviour, telling Manwera that he is being treated 'as an equal' because 'things' are 'different' in London. She suggests, 'Perhaps that's something neither of us understand, coming from where we do' (168). Mrs Panter therefore argues that Arthur, as an assimilated Londoner, is treating Manwera in a colour-blind manner, and that if he were to give him special treatment and help him find a place to stay, this would be patronising and paternalistic. Mrs Panter's explanation evinces a liberal humanist attitude, positing a universal humanity, which does not see race. Given all that we have learnt about Panter and his attitude towards Manwera and South Africa, however, interpreting his behaviour as egalitarian is a red herring. Manwera clearly does not believe this explanation. He tells Mrs Panter politely, 'You will perhaps telephone me', but when she asks for his telephone number, he shouts with noticeable 'aggression' that he hasn't 'even got one' (169). Manwera therefore puts Mrs Panter's theory about Arthur's actions into question. Manwera is 'equal' in terms of deserving respect and kindness, neither of which were afforded to him, but his situation is also not equivalent to that of a white South African like Arthur upon moving to London. Manwera is completely alone and does not even have a telephone number at which he can be contacted. Arthur's neo-Toryism, resulting in his irresponsibility in the face of inequality and suffering, has failed him in this situation, just as it is an ineffective and selfish attitude towards apartheid South Africa.

In the short story's conclusion, Jacobson critiques the inefficacy of liberalism alongside his representation of the callousness of neo-Toryism. Mrs Panter begins questioning her explanations on Arthur's behalf. Arthur, appealing to English ideas of gentility, suggests that Manwera left so suddenly because he felt 'it was the gentlemanly thing to do, after he'd insulted me like that', to which Mrs Panter responds: 'I suppose that would be the best reason for his going. It would be even worse if he went for any other reason … Wouldn't it Arthur?' (170). The 'other reason' is Arthur's racism, which he is at pains not to acknowledge, wishing to see himself as beyond race issues now that he has left South Africa. Arthur's mother says nothing about this incident during the two weeks she stays with him, but the event clearly continues to bother him, and he wishes that he could have challenged his mother on the subject, something which she avoids:

> [S]he had said that they would say no more about it, and she was as good as her word. Too good, from Arthur's point of view – chillingly good. Had it been only Mr Manwera who had lied on that morning about the reasons for Arthur's behaviour? It is a torment to Arthur to think that his mother may well have known what she was doing, and that she may well be, in the mission station in the sad, sandy Eastern Province, even more ashamed of him than he in London had been of her. (171)

Thus Arthur's embarrassment about his mother and his home country – a kind of colonial cringe – is inverted and he suspects that his mother may have lied about her assessment of the incident, and be ashamed of him and his unkind behaviour towards Manwera. His attitude of elitism and irresponsibility has been disturbed by his mother's reaction to his cold treatment of a friendless black man in London.

Through the figure of Panter's mother, who becomes a muted voice of conscience in the story's conclusion, Jacobson valorises liberal humanism over neo-Toryism. However, through Mrs Panter's inaction (she could, presumably, have found Manwera through the East Africa Office), her readiness to explain away Arthur's racism as colour-blind liberalism and her silence, Jacobson also points to some of the weaknesses of liberalism. Despite the reader's natural sympathy for Mrs Panter's well-meaning benevolence towards Manwera, Arthur's neo-Toryism and his mother's liberalism ultimately have the same effect. In Colin MacInnes's 1957 novel *City of Spades*, one of the characters, a Colonial Department Welfare Officer, allies irresponsibility and liberalism, explaining: 'A liberal ... in relation to the colour question, is a person who feels an irresponsible sympathy for what he calls oppressed peoples on whom, along with the staunchest Tory, he's quite willing to go on being a parasite' (MacInnes 1957: 11). While Jacobson would perhaps not go as far as MacInnes's character in equating liberalism and irresponsibility, his focus on Mrs Panter's silence and inaction may indicate that Jacobson is aware of the limitations of his own humanist but politically quietist position in relation to South Africa. Jacobson's 1956 novel, *A Dance in the Sun*, similarly questions the efficacy of liberalism; as Peter Blair suggests, it depicts white English-speaking South Africans 'struggling to translate liberal inclination into practical action' (2012: 483).

Specifically, given Arthur's occupation, 'A Long Way from London' may offer a critique of white South African writers who chose to relocate to London and immerse themselves in the city's bohemian circles, abandoning any attachment to South Africa or Africa or responsibility towards its problems, or only playing liberal, sentimental lip-service to South African concerns. Manwera, an African who has been cast adrift by the South African government's actions, thus comes to symbolise the reality of South Africa, which Arthur pointedly chooses to reject. Although Jacobson himself had a complex affinity with English culture – unlike Arthur, who certainly would never have addressed South African social realities in his poetry – he continued to write and think about South Africa after settling in London. In addition to Jacobson's earlier South African-set novels, *The Trap* (1955), *A Dance in the Sun* (1956) and *The Price of Diamonds* (1957), the other short stories of *A Long Way from London* are set in South Africa, as is one of his most successful novels, *The Beginners* (1966). Many of his narratives focus particularly on the unequal relationship between black and white South Africans. Although he was to move on to other themes in some of his later work, he nevertheless did not shrug off his South African origins and continued, in his writing, to think about South Africa in addition to other aspects of his identity, such as his Jewish heritage. 'A Long Way from London' represents an important moment in Jacobson's thinking around his South African identity and his settlement in London in the 1950s and in this story he examines the validity of liberal humanism, and the responsibility of white South African writers towards their country of origin.

Conclusion

The writing of Peter Abrahams and Dan Jacobson about London in the 1950s weighs the political responsibility of the writer alongside a sense of artistic liberty – a balancing act that is not unique to this decade, either in South African or in global literary history. Since both writers emerged from a tradition of liberal humanism that had strong ties to Englishness and English literature, the locus of 1950s London both offered a sense of continuity with their literary attachments and political ideologies and challenged and disrupted these somewhat belated ideas. In Jacobson's case, this disruption is evident in his disappointment at the ruined nature of postwar London, and through his questioning of the ethics of detachment from South African affairs, both intellectually and spatially. For Abrahams, the challenge to his liberal humanism was manifested in the reactions of his anti-colonial associates, while he simultaneously questioned his dual affiliations to English literature and artistic freedom and to representing black experience and contributing to decolonisation and Pan-Africanism. Through their writing, Abrahams and Jacobson raised questions about the role of South African writers, who were increasingly, necessarily, in exile after 1948.

For several decades, shades of liberal humanism and the influence of English literature continued to inform both South African writers' approach to London and their critiques of the racism they encountered in both South Africa and Britain. As we shall see, Todd Matshikiza, who was from the same generation as Abrahams, was similarly mission-educated and steeped in English literature. He lived in London at a slightly later moment, however, when racism in both South Africa and Britain was even more visible, and he attempted to shake out London's 'dirty old carpets' in a more vigorous fashion than Abrahams (Graham and Walters 2010: 114). J.M. Coetzee's *Youth* (2002) looks back to this period through the eyes of a protagonist who, not unlike Arthur Panter, attempts to shed his South Africanness by becoming English. As in Jacobson's self-reflexive short story, Coetzee uses his London setting to ask questions about the responsibility of the South African writer, and the role of the writer in relation to political engagement and commitment more generally. In a 1970 poem, Arthur Nortje famously declared, 'some of us must storm the castles / some define the happening' ('Native's Letter', lines 35–36), yet his poems set in London reflect his guilt and ambivalence at not being directly involved in the struggle against apartheid.

As we see in Abrahams's and Jacobson's writing, London, as a place of exile and an English place, represented a significant locus amidst these important debates about identity, artistic independence and the role of the South African writer during apartheid.

Notes

1. The 1948 general election was won by the Reunited National Party, which was formed in 1940 when D. F. Malan's Purified National Party (a group that had broken away when the National Party was absorbed into Smuts's United Party in 1935) was reunited with J. B. M. Hertzog's National Party faction, which left the United Party over their decision to enter the Second World War on the side of the British. The Reunited National Party became known as simply the National Party in 1951.
2. Abrahams's residence in London was interrupted by two years in France.
3. Padmore would later work as one of Nkrumah's advisors in Ghana.
4. 'Goli' (or eGoli) is the alternative Zulu name for Johannesburg.
5. All archival material related to George Allen and Unwin's correspondence with Peter Abrahams and the publication of his work is derived from the Archive of British Publishing and Printing at the University of Reading.
6. Perhaps Miall postulated that Abrahams was Jewish because of his Jewish-sounding surname, and because a number of the characters in *Dark Testament* are Jewish.
7. Unwin apologised for giving the impression that he was 'trying to be patronising', assuring Abrahams: 'Nothing was further from my thoughts' (letter from Stanley Unwin to Peter Abrahams, 11 December 1942, George Allen and Unwin papers, AUC 129/3).
8. George Allen and Unwin to Peter Abrahams, 11 December 1962, George Allen and Unwin papers, AUC 129/3.
9. See also Abrahams (2000: 121).
10. This story was linked, in this edition of *The Observer*, to a front page report about the launch of the Mass Defiance Campaign, entitled 'First Steps in Mass Defiance of Malan'; the report was followed by a teaser bearing the headline and page number of Abrahams's article, evincing Abrahams's position as an expert commentator on key South African events.
11. Pankhurst's request is noted in a letter from George Allen and Unwin to Peter Abrahams, 26 January 1943; George Allen and Unwin papers, AUC 156/2.
12. Distiller's book, *South Africa, Shakespeare and Post-Colonial Culture* (2005), is particularly focused on the uses of Shakespeare in South Africa, which is certainly relevant to Abrahams. As will be discussed, one of the texts which most influenced him was Charles Lamb's *Tales from Shakespeare*. Furthermore, Distiller's comments are relevant to the broader development

of liberal humanism and the uses of literature in general. See also Schalkwyk (2013), which focuses on the reception and invocation of Shakespeare by Robben Island prisoners in service of anti-apartheid ideals.
13 This correspondence is collected in Graham and Walters (2010).
14 Abrahams uses the same quotation from Shelley as an epigraph for his novel *The Path of Thunder* (1948).
15 Another example of his staging of his intellectual development is the Lamb's *Tales from Shakespeare* incident in *Tell Freedom*. Woeber asserts that he could not speak English at this point, and that he rather 'structured his childhood memories around his education' in order to 'draw a clear trajectory of the growth of the poet's mind' (quoted in Distiller 2005: 134).
16 Here, Jacobson references his parents' Eastern European, Jewish backgrounds.

Detour

'I have always been a Londoner': Noni Jabavu, an unconventional South African in London

A week after delivering his controversial statement that became the introductory chapter of *Return to Goli* on The Third Programme on 7 February 1952, Peter Abrahams participated in a follow-up discussion. For this programme he was joined by Sierra Leonean writer Davidson Nicol and South African-born writer Helen Nontando Jabavu, known professionally and socially simply as Noni Jabavu.[1] According to the *Radio Times*, another programme in March 1952, 'The Conflict of Cultures', featured Jabavu and Nicol once more alongside Abrahams, discussing 'racial misunderstanding and prejudice' and giving 'their own experience, as Africans, of the effect of these tensions on individuals'.[2] Abrahams's joint showing with Jabavu on at least two BBC programmes offers a glimpse into Noni Jabavu's prominence as a commentator and public figure in London in the 1950s and 1960s. *Drawn in Colour: African Contrasts* (1960), an account of her travels in South Africa and Uganda, mirrors Abrahams's *Return to Goli* in its subject matter, gesturing towards a minor 'return to South Africa' genre. Jabavu's biographer, Makhosazana Xaba, a pioneer scholar of this under-researched writer, wrote an obituary of Jabavu following her death in 2008, and contacted Abrahams for a comment, but his response was terse: 'yes he knew Noni while he lived in Britain' but 'no they were not friends' and 'she was a "Black Briton"'; he preferred not to comment on her books though he had read them (Xaba 2009: 218). Abrahams's dismissive labelling of Jabavu as a 'Black Briton' suggests the complexities of assimilation and identity faced by long-term South African exiles in London, which he also experienced, particularly around the time that *Return to Goli* was published. Abrahams's comment to Xaba also lays bare the difference between himself and Jabavu, despite their shared South Africanness. Unlike Abrahams's teleological trajectory, as set out in *Telling Freedom* (1954), from the slums of Vrededorp to the dream realised of becoming a writer in London, Jabavu's background was even more deeply interwoven with the development of South African liberalism than that of Abrahams.

Noni Jabavu was the granddaughter of influential South African journalist and intellectual John Tengo Jabavu, editor of South Africa's first isiXhosa newspaper, and she was the daughter of the equally well-known newspaper editor and owner, and founder of the All African Convention, Davidson Don Tengo Jabavu. Her mother was Thandiswa Florence Makiwane, sister to Cecilia Makiwane, the first registered professional black nurse in South Africa. D.D.T. Jabavu completed his schooling and had been educated at the University of London, before returning to become one of the founding members of staff of the University of Fort Hare. Noni was likewise sent to England to be educated at the age of thirteen in 1932, attending the Mount School in York and living with social reformer and botanist Margaret Clark Gillett and banker Arthur Bevington Gillett.

The Gilletts were family friends of the Jabavus and were also close friends of General J.C. Smuts, as Jabavu explains in a column for the *Daily Dispatch*, a newspaper based in East London, South Africa, during a brief stint as a writer for that publication in 1977.[3] She describes being introduced to her soon-to-be guardians at Smuts's Cape Town home where the three families enjoyed a pleasant afternoon. She later recalls 'sprightly Oom Jannie' joining the Gillett family on a holiday to the English countryside, which coincided with Jabavu's fourteenth birthday. Smuts gifted her a 'copy of a speech he had delivered at St. Andrews University' wherein 'he developed a theory that freedom was not for the uncivilised black people of South Africa' (Jabavu 1977: 6). Jabavu remembers thinking that: 'Old politicians are capable of unpredictable actions!' (6). This lightly sardonic criticism of the limits of Smuts's liberalism is, however, put into conversation with Afrikaner Nationalist Prime Minister B.J. Vorster's declaration that 'liberals are more hateful, worse than communists, despoilers of the Afrikaner identity'. Jabavu concludes the article by asking: 'What would the Reverent Christian gentleman make of this small slice of non-racial South African behaviour abroad?' (6). Jabavu forges a contrast between Smuts's 'non-racial' behaviour towards Noni and her family co-existing with his underlying beliefs in racial hierarchies, and the draconian policies of separation espoused by Vorster in the 1970s, leaving it up to the reader to consider her rhetorical question. Such lived experiences of the contradictions of South African liberalism affords her a keen critical perspective towards its 'hidden racial transcripts' (Mkhize 2018: 430), alongside an appreciation of the cultural capital such alliances with Cape liberalism granted her family and herself.

After completing her schooling, Jabavu started studying at London's Royal Academy of Music but lost interest in her studies just before war broke out, and during the war she was recruited to work at a munitions factory as an oxyacetylene welder. The starkly different perspective from which Jabavu witnessed some of the overlapping circles she and Abrahams moved in during the war is evident in an anecdote recounted in a letter written to long-time friends Denis and Jean Keenan-Smith in 1995, in which she remembers her 'long-forgotten phase as a SHOP STEWARD' (letter from Noni Jabavu to Denis and Jean Keenan-Smith, 22 August 1995, Amazwi South African Museum of Literature). She recalls the sexism she experienced as one of the first seven women who was called up into the aircraft production line. After training to work on Halifax bombers, the women were sent to De Havilland's aeroplane factory in north London; she describes them as 'Seven shrimps in an ocean of male chauvinist workers whose jaws dropped at [the] sight of us'. A ladies' restroom had not been organised for the newcomers, so they were forced to leave the factory and use a public bathroom. Remembering her reaction to this indignity, Jabavu explains how her privileged upbringing allowed her to become the 'voice' for the young women, 'as the other six girls were too awed by the beastly, officious Floor Manager. To me he seemed only a type of "jumped up" chauffer [sic] or footman, none of whom had awed me during my adolescence in my guardians' home'. Her forthrightness not only resolved the practical problems faced by the women but led to their union membership. In her commentary on this outcome, Jabavu differentiates herself from the other, working-class women:

'We'd never heard of such things, or rather / hadn't, my fellow females came from families that knew about them but had never been required to speak up for themselves. Thus I was appointed "Shop Steward", & floundered happily in a field entirely new to me!' She goes on to explain that: 'what interested me most, at the time, was my exposure for the first time to the working classes. It was like being among foreigners, a new "tribe"!'. Several South Africans in London, including Arthur Nortje, Todd Matshikiza and J.M. Coetzee, express this 'fascination' with the British working classes, steeped as they are in a version of colonial Englishness that elides working-class British culture.

For Jabavu, however, brought up in England since she was a teenager and immersed in the upper-middle-class echelons of British society, her reaction arguably owes more to amused voyeurism than to a self-reflexive anthropological perspective on British society. She associates her memory of meeting notorious Stalinist and Communist Party stalwart Harry Pollitt (through her shop steward role) with her guardian Arthur Gillett's disapproval of the 'young commies in the bosom of the family' who were 'ever wanting to go sell the *Daily Worker* up at the Morris motor works' which he financed; he forbade them to use the family motor car for such a 'ridiculous jaunt' (letter, 22 August 1995, Amazwi South African Museum of Literature). While Jabavu does not state her opinion on her guardian's stance, the tone in which this anecdote is recounted, albeit some fifty years later and five years after the fall of the Berlin Wall, evinces a very different relationship to radical politics than that of Peter Abrahams's conflicted rethinking of his relationship to the Party. For Abrahams, the Communist Party in London offered him his first job in the city and helped him to forge anti-colonial and literary networks, while, for Jabavu, her brief brush with union stewardship was fodder for an interesting story and an opportunity to delve into an unfamiliar world.

After marrying her first husband in 1941, a member of the Royal Airforce who was later killed in combat, Jabavu gave birth to her daughter Tembi.[4] During her pregnancy, she was among the evacuees from London to the Lake District, 'away from the Blitz', as she recalls in a letter (22 August 1995, Amazwi South African Museum of Literature). After the war, she remained in London, working as a journalist and a presenter and producer for the BBC, and it was during this period that she interacted with Abrahams on the Third Programme. Her marriage to film director Michael Cadbury Crosfield in 1951 set in motion what she was to call 'the peripatetic print of [her] feet' (Jabavu 1962c: 323), since Cadbury Crosfield first founded the Uganda Colonial Film Unit, which meant the couple lived in Uganda from 1955 to 1960, and later worked as a films adviser to the Jamaican government, necessitating a sojourn in Kingston from 1962 to 1967. Like Abrahams and his wife, their 'mixed' marriage contravened apartheid laws and thus prevented frequent visits to Jabavu's home country. Later in life, even after the marriage failed, Jabavu was to live in Kenya and Zimbabwe, with sporadic visits to South Africa, eventually returning in 2002 to East London, South Africa, where she died in 2008. London was, however, a formative place for Jabavu, where her two books were published and where she developed her networks and experience as a journalist.

One such significant experience for Jabavu was her short-lived editorship of the *New Strand* magazine, from 1961 to 1962. As Makhosazana Xaba remarks, this was her first editing position and she was the 'first black as well as the first woman to be editor of this prestigious magazine' (Xaba 2019). The original version of *The Strand* was issued from 1891 until 1950 and included contributions from literary luminaries such as Agatha Christie, Arthur Conan Doyle and Rudyard Kipling. Appointing Jabavu as the first editor of the revived magazine was thus testament to her considerable renown as a London literary figure following the publication of her first memoir. Her appointment was notable enough to elicit a full feature from US magazine *Ebony*, which had been founded in 1945 and which targeted African American readers. In the feature, Jabavu is described as a 'little, brown-skin woman, whose glamour and sophistication leave no clues to a childhood spent in a Bantu community in South Africa' ('New Strand Editor' 1962: 81). Her supposedly provincial upbringing is emphasised in order to draw the reader through contrast and surprise, since the phrase 'Bantu community' suggests rural or even 'tribal' antecedents, though later the writer acknowledges that Jabavu 'continues a family tradition of journalistic pioneering started by her grandfather, John Tengo Jabavu – the first Bantu to establish a newspaper in South Africa' (84). The photographs accompanying the *Ebony* story are mostly of Jabavu in London, walking in Hyde Park, waiting for a double-decker bus, with a guardsman at Whitehall, suggesting the anomalous nature of a South African in London by presenting her against such ubiquitous landmarks. The sequence of day-in-the-life style photographs also emphasises Jabavu's 'glamour and sophistication', for instance by depicting her leaving her office in a business-like skirt-suit, 'smartly dressed', as the caption puts it, with possibly patronising overtones. Despite this slightly sensationalist initial hook, the article attributes her appointment to her 'many literary accomplishments' and to her 'sparkling wit and literary common sense', quoting *New Strand* co-owner Ernest Kay's assessment: 'Miss Jabavu has led such a varied life that she will bring a completely fresh outlook to the magazine. She certainly couldn't be conventional if she tried' (81).[5]

One of the photographs accompanying the article presents her with her 'personal secretary', with the caption reading: 'Mrs Kathleen Anscombe ... takes dictation from her boss. Besides her native Xhosa language and English, editor speaks French and Swahili' (81). As with the 'smartly dressed' descriptor, her gender, as well as her South African background, is what makes these unremarkable work scenes remarkable – note the reference to 'her boss' as if this power dynamic is remarkable. The feature foregrounds her gender throughout, describing her in the lede as 'Noni Jabavu, author, globetrotter, housewife, mother' (81), including details about her parental and marital status that would probably not be mentioned in a similar profile of a male editor. The article also concludes with Jabavu's comment, 'I am a married woman first and a career woman second' (85). *Ebony*, extending their editorial mission to celebrate 'the positive everyday achievements' of black men and women 'from Harlem to Hollywood' beyond the United States' borders (Staples 2019), celebrates Jabavu as a groundbreaker, making it in the metropolis despite her supposedly provincial South African background.

The gendered limits that she pushes against through her new executive position, while certainly also present in the article, are, however, subtly re-asserted through mentions of her motherhood, marital status and attractiveness. Jabavu would have faced the same racism as her male South African counterparts in 1960s London, even if her proximity to upper-middle-class Britons lent her a certain degree of privilege. In addition, as we see through her treatment in the *Ebony* article, she had to negotiate sexist expectations, as she established herself as a writer and editor in London. The remark about being a 'married woman first' is in her own words, so one might also ask how, alongside her 'unconventionality', part of that negotiation involved a certain degree of conformity to such gendered societal norms, just as she asserted her power in the sexist munitions factory workplace by appealing to her previous experiences with a 'jumped up' chauffeur or footman (letter from Noni Jabavu to Denis and Jean Keenan-Smith, 19 July 1985, Amazwi South African Museum of Literature).

Without ascribing to Jabavu a specific mode of resistance to class, race or gender oppression, it is also worth thinking through Pumla Gqola's suggestion that ambiguity can be part of a strategy against oppression; she suggests, drawing on Yvette Abrahams's work, that ambiguity may be 'deliberately partaking in the post-colonial processes of resistance through subversion and mimicry' (2001: 18). Certainly, a complex shifting of allegiances between her affinity for left-wing politics, her own ambitions as a writer and journalist, and her immersion in both South African liberalism and British bourgeois life is represented through a similar process of performativity and self-reflection to that seen in the writing of Arthur Nortje and Todd Matshikiza.

In her monthly editor's columns for the *New Strand*, Jabavu provides insights into her life in London and the tensions between her London working life and her connections elsewhere, including South Africa and Jamaica, where her husband was still living. In the author's note to *Drawn in Colour* (1960), Jabavu writes, 'I belong to two worlds with two loyalties; South Africa where I was born and England where I was educated'. Such a dual loyalty, but even beyond this, a truly multilocational perspective, is evident in her *New Strand* columns.

Despite her pioneering role as the first black and female editor of the magazine, Jabavu only touches on racism obliquely in her columns. In her first column, Jabavu immediately addresses the daunting nature of taking on the editorship of such a historic title, opening with the question frequently aimed at herself, 'How does it feel to become Editor of a new "quality" magazine intended to fill the gap created by the death of that most celebrated journal of yesterday and similar name?' (1961: 68). She continues: 'When the projected publication of *The New Strand* was announced last

September, along with the news of my appointment as Editor (which dismayed one "Keep Fleet Street White" campaigner), that question was asked by absolutely everyone I met' (68). Jabavu parenthetically acknowledges the potential racism underlying the surprise expressed at her appointment but underplays such a reaction by painting the racist campaigner as a lone voice. In a later column she similarly mentions racism in London only as an aside. While holidaying on the French Riviera, she writes:

> Marvellous Menton – for even momentarily taking my mind off London's 'hot' money houha, 'dear' money doldrums, 'crisis' Bank rate, Sir Cyril 'Speculating' Osborne ('if 50,000 West Indians a year come to live in Britain, what of vice, health? But of course this is not colour prejudice'!), bingo, slump in steel, The Rhine Army – 'Exercise Spearpoint'... (Jabavu 1962a: 101)

In a list of London's contemporary concerns, including financial crises and planned anti-nuclear military operations, Jabavu references Member of Parliament Cyril Osborne, whose call for a ban on large-scale immigration to Britain from the 'new commonwealth' was a precursor to Enoch Powell's anti-immigration proposals. While Jabavu swiftly dismisses suggestions that such proposed limits on commonwealth migration do not constitute 'colour prejudice', this racist parliamentary proposal is only mentioned in passing alongside other troublesome aspects of life in London. At no point in her editor's columns, furthermore, does Jabavu ever overtly mention apartheid, despite the Sharpeville massacre having occurred less than a year before she assumed her editorship. An advertisement by the anti-apartheid International Defence and Aid Fund (IDAF), printed on the facing page of Jabavu's February 1962 editorial, asks, 'Have you forgotten Sharpeville?' Of course, Jabavu had not forgotten: she continued to be devoted to and concerned about conditions in her home country, as evinced in *Drawn in Colour* (1960) and in her other journalism, including her later work for the *Daily Dispatch*. But in her *New Strand* columns, she does not overtly mention the struggle against apartheid, focusing rather on musings about writing, literature and, overall, on travelling and occupying different spaces.

In an intriguing passage from her February 1962 column, Jabavu recalls an epiphany she experienced concerning the influence of her South African upbringing, and particularly her isiXhosa linguistic background, on her writing. She remembers waking up suddenly in her Westminster flat to a vivid realisation:

> My subconscious, burrowing away beneath the prolonged unhappiness, had hit on the deep laid reason why I was in trouble with my writing. It was because all along, I had been trying without being aware, to make English sound and read like my own language. I had been writing long sentences, trying to force them into the shape that they would take in that language, with its alliterated concordial agreement of syllabic inflexion in suffixes and prefixes. This is a major characteristic of the South African tongue that I learnt in infancy. (Jabavu 1962b: 198)

Jabavu calls this 'discovery' of the 'hidden patterns woven in to [her] make-up by the accident of birth' one of the 'major experiences' of her life, 'on a par with falling in love'. She recalls: 'It was so disturbing that I left my bed, got dressed, went for a solitary walk in nearby St. James's Park to calm my agitation by contemplating the sleeping pelicans' (Jabavu 1962b: 198). Her description of the walk in St James's Park as offering an antidote to her disturbing realisation of the influence of isiXhosa linguistic patterning suggests how London somehow facilitates this realisation and is the place where it can be worked out.

The 'shock' of recognising that her South Africanness, despite her many years in Britain, has followed her to London, is no less momentous than John's realisation that he is 'unable to live without a country' and his turn towards South African historical narratives in J.M. Coetzee's *Youth* (2002). Jabavu, however, does not regard her tendency towards isiXhosa syntax as something she can incorporate into her English writing, but as an impediment; she describes herself as 'plagued by the temptations of my foreign alliterative background' (Jabavu 1962b: 201). The only sense in which she perceives her background as a gift is that it offers her a degree of empathy with the writers submitting work to the *New Strand*: 'Nevertheless, my sufferings have helped open my eyes to some of *their* deep-laid and unconscious temptations, inclinations, affinities' (201). In a notably geographical metaphor, Jabavu describes herself working alongside the writers: 'I gain new vistas across the torturous territory of the written word as I try to put myself in their shoes when dissecting with them the possible inner patterns or conflicts that dictate the way in which they write' (201). Jabavu's South Africanness redirects her meandering yet pioneering route through London's literary world, so that, even as she eschews South Africa's sentence-level influence, she gains new perspectives through her transnational background.

In common with many South African writers in London, Jabavu writes about the loneliness she feels in the city. Her experiences of isolation are, however, not associated with the alienation of the exile. When she describes, in a March 1962 *New Strand* editorial, how 'travelling and roving brings its *miseries*' involving 'mornings of loneliness and distress because of enforced separation from one's family and other nearest and dearest' (Jabavu 1962c: 327), one can surmise that she is referring to her distance from her husband based in Jamaica, yet the use of 'family' also suggests her distance from her South African loved ones. The city itself, despite her occupation of a privileged position within it, seems to increase her loneliness so that, 'Waking alone in the flat which David Hicks has designed as my beautiful London pied-à-terre means desolation' (327). Jabavu imagines a rural idyll apart from noisy London, 'a permanent home in soothing scenes' (329). Although she was first schooled in York, she declares, 'In England, I have always been a Londoner' (329), reinforcing the centrality of the city to her adult life, but she asserts that, contra Dr Johnson, she is now 'tired of London' (329). Her idealisation of country life as a respite from London and from travel is interspersed with her assertion that 'My home in South Africa was in the country' (329), suggesting a yearning after rural life quite contradictory to the depiction of Jabavu as the urban sophisticate in the *Ebony* article.

In the following month's column, Jabavu continued to describe her disillusionment with London in terms that are not dissimilar from other South African writers' expressions of disappointment with the city. Writing from Jamaica (the column is titled 'From a Mobile Desk' rather than 'From the Editor's Desk'), Jabavu considers her relatively recent and disappointing first impressions of Bloomsbury: 'For one who is a writer and admires "the Bloomsbury Set" of fifty years ago, I had a shamefully cursory acquaintance with that renowned region of books until last year. Then I was astonished to discover that it is debilitating beyond endurance!' (Jabavu 1962d: 453). Like Arthur Panter who bemoaned that 'it had all been spoilt' (Jacobson 1958: 152), or David Lytton's recounting of Ingrid Jonker's disgust at Fitzrovia, 'now occupied by salesmen, PRO's and ... unattached vagrants' (Lytton 1970: 208–209), Jabavu expresses her disenchantment with the tawdry commercialism of the former enclave of the modernist literary elite, from the plethora of 'offices' to the 'bill-posted private enterprise car park' and the 'gim-crack shacks in Tottenham Court Road labelled "Magic", "Fish Bar", "Souvenirs"!' (Jabavu 1962d: 453) Despite her long-time familiarity with the city, Jabavu holds on to idealised visions of London unspoilt by the realities of mid-twentieth-century urban life. Her expression of disappointment may not be, like Dan Jacobson's, a coming-to-terms with her own South Africanness, but along with her descriptions of alienation, this sense of disillusionment is interwoven with an émigré's yearning for a place where she can be at peace, fulfilled and at home.

In the same column, Jabavu compares Bloomsbury – 'that book-lined jungle of filthy streets' – to the 'mangrove swamps' of the West Indian island she is writing from. Out of this comparison, she draws an ambiguous assessment of West Indian writing and its relation to place:

> More distracting from work they may be; but how infinitely more conducive to art! I see now why the West Indies has produced its magnificent short story writers – like Samuel Selvon. I am staggered that many of these authors emigrate to live and write in London, of all places! But I supposed this is because in order to 'recollect in tranquillity' it is sometimes necessary for writers to travel *away* from the surroundings that nurtured their art ... and distracted them from their work. (Jabavu 1962d: 453)

According to Jabavu's circular reasoning in this passage, London is not conducive to art, because it is 'filthy' and ugly, yet London is nevertheless where great works are written because its lack of beauty prevents distraction, affording writers distance from their country of origin they frequently write about. The uneven flow of global economic and cultural capital is occluded by Jabavu's surprise that 'many of these authors emigrate to live and write in London, of all places!' Such a geographic conundrum could equally apply to Jabavu's own writing life at this point. London is the place where she misses her home and her loved ones in South Africa and Jamaica but is also the city that affords her an editorial platform and an audience and is where her two books were published. As for many South African writers, and transnational writers more broadly, London comes to stand as both a literary city that affords useful or even life-saving distance from the homeland and a place of 'misery' and disappointment, an unhomely, lonely metropolis.

Even though she was born in the same year as both Todd Matshikiza and Peter Abrahams and lived in London at a similar time, Jabavu stands apart from her contemporaries, and not only because of her gender, which meant she faced narrow sexist expectations in her professional life. Through her journalism and letters, we witness Jabavu as a different type of writer from her South African counterparts who first arrived in Britain much later and as adults, self-exiled in response to the South African situation. Jabavu, despite her iconoclasm, her lack of 'conventionality' as Ernest Kay put it, is immersed in an upper-middle-class English society. Yet, she still perceives her own writing and the world around her through her South African background, which is as inescapable as the circuitous rhythms of her mother tongue shaping the sentences she writes for high-brow London magazines. Jabavu moved through London's media and publishing institutions with arguably even more ease than her male compatriots, and so her life in London tells a different South African story abroad, equally marked by homesickness and travel but also by less anxiety about her place in the munitions factory, editor's office or chic Bloomsbury apartment. The complexity of Jabavu's life and writing, which does not fit into more well-worn tropes of masculine apartheid-era exile, has perhaps influenced the lack of scholarship on this pioneering South African woman, which will hopefully change in light of recent responses to the centenary of her birth.[6] As Noni Jabavu is reinstated in South Africa's national literary archive, we should not lose sight of the multiple places which shaped her life and work, and which she in turn shaped, including London, the fulcrum of her writing career.

Notes

1 See BBC Genome Project, Radio Times 1923–2009, programme listing, 'The Last Freedom', Third Programme, 7 February 1952. http://genome.ch.bbc.co.uk/47772bb2251d41008516f6a4a6ea09f9.

2 See BBC Genome Project, Radio Times 1923–2009, programme listing, 'The Conflict of Cultures', Third Programme, 6 March 1952. http://genome.ch.bbc.co.uk/33006f9a5b3a4d7786277837ba71d01d.
3 At the time of Jabavu's tenure as columnist, the editor of the *Daily Dispatch* was Donald Woods, a well-known journalist, anti-apartheid activist and friend of Steve Biko, who went on to expose the truth behind Biko's death in police custody through his writing.
4 According to *Ebony* magazine, he was a 'Royal Airforce Man killed in combat' ('New Strand Editor' 1962: 82).
5 The article explains: 'Although married to film director Michael Cadbury-Crosfield, scion of wealthy English Quaker family, she still uses her maiden name, Jabavu, and the title "Miss" as pen name and in her professional life' ('New Strand Editor' 1962: 82).
6 See Xaba (2019).

2

Swinging city: Todd Matshikiza's contrapuntal London writing

South African jazz musician, composer and journalist Todd Matshikiza, renowned for his work on the musical *King Kong*, lived in exile in London between 1960 and 1964. Inspired by 'images of travel and freedom' (Matshikiza 1961a: 127) and desiring a better life for their two young children, Matshikiza and his wife, Esmé, departed for London in August 1960, before the rest of the *King Kong* cast brought the show to London in February 1961. In April 1959, almost a year before his departure for London, Matshikiza wrote about travel to London in a column he contributed to *Drum* magazine:

> I hear the Coons have arrived in London. I hear the Coons will do London. I hope London doesn't do the Coons. I hear London's mighty big. Can swallow Joh'burg many times. Showbiz can be tough in London. There are big names there, an' big places. Ted Heath an' the Albert Hall. Johnny Dankworth an' the Hippodrome.[1] They say London is 'big'.
>
> Ten years ago my friend, Alfred Fish, who gives everything a go from ping-pong to hypnotherapy, got a passport, in which he described himself as a musician. He was jes' waiting for London to tell him his job at Ciros night spot is in the bag. That was ten years ago. I met him the other day. He's still around. Says he hears London is a big town. Says he hears people don't throw pennies around there.
>
> But if the Coons can crack London open, there's lots more goods we can fly out there. (Matshikiza 2000: 14)[2]

An analysis of this passage – the first substantial reference to London in Matshikiza's writing – reveals his characteristic style and his perspective on both South Africa and London. Matshikiza's use of the term 'Coons' in this passage is self-consciously ironic. Literally, he refers here to the Cape Town Minstrels, also known as the 'Kaapse Klopse', troupes of musicians who perform in the Cape Town Minstrel Carnival (previously known as the 'Cape Town Coon Carnival'). Their style of dress, make-up and music is partly inspired by the 'blackface' tradition of American minstrels, an influence which takes on complex resonances considering that the Carnival's performers are members of Cape Town's coloured community. The Minstrels' 'superimposition of this North American theatrical character onto the Capetonian carnival landscape has raised difficult, politically charged questions around the issues of wilful racist caricaturing', Nadia Davids explains, listing the following in particular: 'problematic public enactments of creolized and indigenous identities; processes of trans-Atlantic cultural exchange, appropriation, and ownership; and patterns of interface between performance and cultural memory' (2013: 88). The term 'Coon' itself has a self-evidently racist etymology. Matshikiza is all too aware of the complex racist connotations of the epithet: he mentions, in a January 1960 *Drum* column, how a music shop clerk called him and his friends 'coons': 'And he wasn' talking 'bout the Cape Town Coon Carnival' (2000: 41). Despite the ambivalent origin of the Carnival's symbols and original name, Davids insists that the Cape Town Carnival is 'an instance wherein blackface is invoked as a powerfully transformative mask, not a racist caricature' (2013: 89). She reads the annual celebration as a rewriting and reimagining of its historical sources: 'through the Carnival's processes of appropriation and replication, it imprints the original (the image, the song, the popular figure) with new resonances and textures and in doing so creates something that though still in dialogue with its source, has become an entity both different and self-sustaining' (92). Davids furthermore draws on Denis-Constant Martin's suggestion that 'the appropriation of blackface within the Carnival' emerges from 'excitement and hope' that informs the creation of an 'alternative, non-white modernity' (quoted in Davids 2013: 92).

The Carnival's complex history – both its potentially problematic elements and its celebratory validation of the presence of Cape Town's coloured community within the city's streets – provides an illuminating lens through which to read this passage and Matshikiza's writing more broadly. Firstly, in addition to its literal reference to the Cape performers, the derogatory, racist connotations of 'Coon' are intentionally jarring here: the repetition of the epithet in the chiasmic sentences 'I hear the Coons will do London' and 'I hope London doesn't do the Coons' is an almost incantatory reminder of the racism experienced by black entertainers.

The appropriation of racist tropes such as blackface or the word 'Coon' by Carnival performers does not efface the histories of these elements, and this would be even more notable at a moment in which a term like 'Coon' was still used as a common racial slur, as Matshikiza references in his later column. It is therefore no coincidence that Matshikiza chooses to focus on the minstrels' tour to London, when riffing on the global aspirations of black jazz musicians such as himself and his friend. Matshikiza was attuned to the exoticism which shadowed performances by black musicians for white audiences such as the London tour of the 'Coons'. As I shall explore in this chapter, his anxieties about playing up a certain image of blackness for white audiences in South Africa and London grew out of his experiences of working on *King Kong*.

Not only is the work of the Cape Town minstrels a touchpoint for concerns and hopes about finding a British audience, but the ambivalent Carnival performance is a useful analogy for Matshikiza's approach to his self-writing. In his journalism and his autobiography, *Chocolates for My Wife* (1961), Matshikiza, like the Carnival performers, appropriates and reimagines personas and texts. In so doing, he forges a hopeful, resistant mode of identification that also inscribes what Martin calls an 'alternative non-white modernity' (quoted in Davids 2013: 92). This reinscription of symbols, signs and tropes takes on specific resonances in his writing set in London, in that he uses these elements to map both the differences and the continuities between South Africa and London.

One of the significant global imaginaries evoked in Matshikiza's writing is African American culture and identity. Just as the 'Coons' of the Cape Town Carnival adopted African American signs, so Matshikiza engages with American jazz culture through his writing style, as is evident in the above passage. He draws on 'jazzy' slang – 'London's mighty big'; 'Showbiz' – and employs an African American argot, evident in abbreviations ('an" for 'and'), and the phonetic rendering of accent ('jes" for 'just'). Furthermore, Matshikiza adopts a self-consciously naive persona in this passage, performing a wide-eyed perspective on 'mighty big' London, which can 'swallow' Johannesburg 'many times'. Matshikiza takes on the role of the inexperienced colonial, amazed by tales of the imperial metropolis, but in an ironic fashion. His syntax is also noteworthy: short, repetitive sentences create a song-like rhythm, contributing to his intentionally naive tone. These stylistic and tonal elements of Matshikiza's writing intersect with his observations about London. His adoption of a credulous tone, for instance, is well suited to his exploration of the golden hopes and harsh realities the city presents, especially for a musician like himself or his friend, Alfred. London represents an opportunity for success in 'showbiz' but is intimidating because it is so 'big'. Yet his tongue-in-cheek naivety also contains a playful critique of patronising attitudes towards black South Africans who are positioned as provincials supposedly in awe of the 'big', bustling metropole. Like the minstrels' performance, Matshikiza's staging of awestruck reverence for London's 'big names' and 'big places' presents a caricature played for laughs that also includes a subtle critique. Matshikiza ends this section on a hopeful note, clearly wishing he (and his musical endeavours) might be amongst the 'goods' flown to the city. Even this seemingly light-hearted conclusion to the anecdote hides a barb: it takes a troupe of minstrels who, regardless of the nuanced history of their performance style, would likely be read as caricatures in Britain, to 'crack' open London. By calling black South African musicians 'goods', Matshikiza underscores the commodification of black South African music. Matshikiza also conveys here the quiet desperation of black South African musicians who long to escape stultifying apartheid South Africa by travelling to London. Despite the humour, his friend, Alfred Fish, is a pathetic figure, longing for London but stuck in Johannesburg. A year after this column was written, Matshikiza became one of those 'goods' flown out to 'crack' London.

Born in 1921 in Queenstown in the Eastern Cape province, Todd Matshikiza, like Peter Abrahams and a number of other black intellectuals of his generation, received his secondary education at St Peter's School in Rosettenville. He went on to obtain a diploma in music from Adams College in Natal, and a teacher's diploma from the Lovedale Institute in Alice in the Eastern Cape, where he taught English and Mathematics for a number of years. In addition to his renown as a jazz musician and composer, Matshikiza is well known in South Africa as a composer of choral music; his famous work 'Hamba Kahle' was composed during his time at Lovedale. In 1947, he left for a teaching post in the Eastern Transvaal, but soon moved to Johannesburg, where he took up various jobs, including music teaching and working at Vanguard Booksellers, to support his career as a musician. He met his future wife, Esmé, soon after his arrival in Johannesburg, and they were married in 1950. When *Drum* magazine was launched in 1952, journalist Henry Nxumalo roped in his musician friend as one of its original writers, even though Matshikiza had 'never written prose before' (Nicol 1991: 82). While writing regularly for *Drum*, including his much-loved column, 'With the Lid Off', Matshikiza continued to focus on his musical career, notably composing 'Uxolo', a large-scale choral composition for Johannesburg's seventieth anniversary celebrations in 1956, and playing with popular jazz groups the Manhattan Brothers and the Harlem Swingsters. He is most famous for composing the music and some of the lyrics of the hit musical *King Kong*, which was staged in South Africa in 1959 and was taken to London's West End in 1961. Alongside Matshikiza, many of *King Kong*'s other cast members and musicians, including singer Miriam Makeba and trumpeter Hugh Masekela, stayed in London after *King Kong* ended its run.

Matshikiza's reflections on the first two years of his stay in the city are presented in two forms: in the monthly columns he wrote for *Drum* magazine, called 'Todd in London', and in his 1961 memoir, *Chocolates for My Wife*. Both these texts are written in what *Drum* editor Anthony Sampson and other journalists called 'Matshikeze' – a 'breathless, explosive style which enchanted the readers' (Sampson 2000: 10). Matshikiza's accounts of early 1960s London present a meaningful engagement with the interplay between London, South Africa and a wider global black imaginary. He sets up a counterpoint between London and South Africa that allows him to read the histories and colonial legacies of both places, while expressing transnational solidarities with a global black diaspora. Liz Gunner argues that writing about *Drum* figures 'has not on the whole examined how they fitted into larger black diasporic patterns after their departure from South Africa' (2005: 54). A study of Matshikiza's London writing offers not only new perspectives on an important South African intellectual, but also a fresh look at how the approaches to modernity and transnational black subjectivities forged in Sophiatown inform writing about the former imperial metropolis.

'Authenticity' and exoticism: *King Kong* and 'race' in London

The period during which Todd Matshikiza wrote about London (1960–1961) was crucial in terms of race relations in both South Africa and London. British Prime Minister Harold Macmillan delivered his 'Winds of Change' speech to the South African Parliament in February 1960, in which he outlined Britain's official policy concerning African independence and Britain's opposition to South Africa's policy of apartheid in particular. The Sharpeville massacre occurred in March 1960, in which sixty-nine black pass-law protesters were brutally gunned down, and in May 1961 South Africa declared itself a republic, severing its ties with the Commonwealth. In London, the Notting Hill riots of 1958 had also brought questions of racism and black immigration to the fore. These events, although not overtly mentioned in Matshikiza's writing, inform his engagement with racism in London and South Africa. When *King Kong* travelled to London, the reception of this production was caught up in attitudes towards race amongst Londoners in the early 1960s, as was the response to Matshikiza's writing. Liz Gunner comments on the ambivalence of this moment in London's history, in which London was 'moving between a kind of late-imperial cosmopolitanism and a reactive British "nativism" in this period of flux and realignment, when the newly independent status of previous African colonies perhaps played its part in bringing about a shift in ideas on the transference of culture' (2005: 53). Gunner argues that writers of the *Drum* generation hailing from 'Sophiatown and Johannesburg, that most African and cosmopolitan of places' were well-positioned to act as 'cultural broker[s] and interpreters[s] across contending modernities at such a time' (53). It was at this moment of fluid and often paradoxical attitudes towards race and Africa that *King Kong* came to London.

In the wake of the Fugard Theatre's 2017 revival of *King Kong*, which was received by music critics and historians with some ambivalence,[3] it is worth reconsidering the legacy and travels of this South African musical, which has attained 'iconic' status[4] but which has a troubled, even problematic history. While I will provide a brief discussion of the musical's history and reception in London, I am mainly interested in how *King Kong* influenced and informed Matshikiza's writing. Firstly, Matshikiza writes about his experiences of developing the musical for its South African run and about his involvement in the London production. Secondly, as I have already intimated, his awareness of the exoticisation that black performance artists' work often entails feeds into his writing, even at the level of form and tone. Thirdly, the musical's ambivalent success and popularity in South Africa and in London provide a glimpse into how South Africa figured in the British imaginary, and how perceptions of apartheid South Africa intersected with British engagements with racism and anti-racism. *King Kong* sustained British awareness about South Africa and served as a staging-ground for debates about how apartheid should be resisted. Paul Gilroy, for instance, in a 2018 interview, frames a discussion of his longstanding interest in South Africa by recalling: 'I had been taken to *King Kong*, the musical, as a child by my parents' (Gilroy 2018).

King Kong was based loosely on the life of South African heavyweight boxer Ezekiel Dhlamini, who won the heavyweight title for black South Africans in 1953 before becoming embroiled in gangsterism. He was eventually convicted of murdering his girlfriend and committed suicide in prison. Dhlamini's nickname was 'King Kong', an undoubtedly racialised reference to the mythical giant gorilla, and he was a symbol of black masculine power and resistance. His descent into crime in the townships, however, witnessed to the massive social problems experienced by black South Africans, which severely hindered their chances of success and happiness. As Matshikiza recounts in *Chocolates for My Wife*, he covered the trial of the boxer for *Drum* magazine in 1957 and, owing to his interest in the topic and his reputation as a composer and musician, he was asked by producer Harry Bloom to write the music and some lyrics for the production. Well-known South African jazz trombonist Jonas Gwangwa, who was a member of the *King Kong* orchestra, notes that even the plot of *King Kong* was somewhat compromised: 'The problems that arose were ... you cannot really tell the truth, you know? It was alleged that [Ezekiel Dhlamini] committed suicide, but we believed that he was killed in prison and thrown into a dam that was being built ... That was just the whole apartheid South Africa ... that couldn't allow people to tell the real story' (quoted in Ansell 2004: 103).

The other, somewhat ambiguous 'story' of *King Kong* was the production's public image of convivial interracial collaboration. South African *Drum* editor Tom Hopkinson wrote in *The Observer* that *King Kong* 'has smashed a tiny hole in *apartheid*' and is a 'triumph of black and white co-operation' (1961: 21, italics original), but the musical's reception in South Africa and especially in London was not unproblematic. Matshikiza's son, John, suggests that '[i]f *King Kong* was able to make it to the West End of London in 1961, it had as much to do with the exoticism of an all-black cast jiving their hearts out in the middle of London as with any artistic merit' (2000: 100). Michael Titlestad points out that reviews of the London production of *King Kong*, while sympathetic, often included a patronising slant to their praise. A reviewer for the *London Times Weekly Review*, for instance, described *King Kong* as 'a piece of naïve but vital indigenous art' (quoted in Titlestad 2004: 98). Lindelwa Dalamba situates the reception of *King Kong* in London in the context of debates around 'authentic jazz' in 1960s England, so that 'British reviews of *King Kong*'s music are framed by the modernist trope of hot rhythm as black music's "vital essence"', with *King Kong* appearing as a representation of the apparently African 'source' of jazz music (2013: 99). Furthermore, Dalamba cites a *Daily Mail* review that 'segued' from discussing the merits of *King Kong* to a treatise on the 'immigration problem' within England, which suggests that some reviewers felt the need to situate the escapist all-African musical within a broader context of English race relations (Dalamba 2013: 99).

On the other hand, some liberal London audiences accused *King Kong* of not accurately reflecting the inequalities of South African society and wished that the production had taken a more overt anti-apartheid stance. David B. Coplan writes that 'international attitudes towards Africa had left South Africa behind' as in 1960 'African nationalism, independence and cultural resurgence were already dominant movements' so that 'a liberating "anything goes" shocker in South Africa was in England simply an advertisement for the social status quo' (2007: 216). For instance, English theatre critic Robert Muller wrote that *King Kong* was '[p]olitically ... about as dynamic as a bag of laundry ... One swallow of black and white collaboration doesn't make a summer of South Africa's bleak shame' (quoted in Coplan 2007: 216). Coplan suggests, however, that these critics were '[s]taggeringly blind to the situation in South Africa', since they misunderstood how the staging or development of an overtly political production would have been thwarted by the apartheid authorities. As it was, *King Kong* encountered much resistance in South Africa simply because of its 'racially-mixed' cast and crew. In contrast to the reviews Titlestad and Dalamba mention, which viewed *King Kong* as authentic 'indigenous art', Coplan suggests that the production was 'also damned, ironically, by white play-goers who expected an "African" (traditional) display, and so were disturbed by its modern, hybrid nature and considered it "inauthentic"' (2007: 216). British critics' assessments of *King Kong* as authentically African or as not sufficiently African show how the imperial concept of the exoticised African other who is outside of modernity continued to shape English attitudes towards South Africans (and black immigrants of other nationalities) in the 1960s, even amongst so-called 'liberals'.

Matshikiza expressed his misgivings about the London reception of *King Kong* in an opinion piece published in the *New Statesman* in February 1961. Matshikiza begins by referencing a *Telegraph* review of *King Kong*: 'Someone suggests ... that the British public should see and support as far as possible the all-native South African Jazz Opera, *King Kong*, for it would be sad for the poor Natives if they were to travel the whole distance to flop in London after the opening night, to return to the misery of the land of their birth' (1961b: 315). He rejects this patronising attitude, asserting that '*King Kong* must stand or fall by his own strength or weakness, in London or anywhere else in the world' (Matshikiza 1961b: 315). His piece in the *New Statesman* is accompanied by an article by Martin Jarrett-Kerr, a British clergyman and literary critic who was involved with the Union of Southern African Artists – the sponsors of the show – in which he discusses the 'minor' and 'reluctant' compromises that this organisation had to make to promote multiracial music within the apartheid context (Jarrett-Kerr 1961: 316). Matshikiza, on the other hand, clearly sets out in his article the many compromises that were made, specifically musically, in the production of *King Kong*, and his feeling that his contribution was sidelined and consciously westernised for London audiences by the play's white producers, a subtly different criticism from that of the London reviewers who called it 'inauthentic'. He argues that his original score, which included more of the South African marabi and mbaqanga styles that he favoured,[5] 'slipped out of [his] hands' (Matshikiza 1961b: 315).

Matshikiza's misgivings about the integrity of his compositions and his contributions to the show being respected are conveyed in *Chocolates for My Wife*, too. As the show was being rehearsed and developed for the West End stage, he describes feeling on the brink of a nervous collapse because he had been listening to his music and watching it go 'from black to white and now purple' (Matshikiza 1961a: 125). He also recounts his dreams of having his brain matter sucked out with straws by 'pale-skinned, blue-veined people' – a clear metaphor for the white producers' exploitation of his ideas – and recalls asking the producers to stop writing his name 'in the register from the bottom' while their names appeared at the top (123). According to Matshikiza, *King Kong* was already compromised by the unequal politics of its development before it hit the London stage and became subject to the alternately condescending or hostile reception by London audiences. Furthermore, the interest around *King Kong*'s arrival, evident in its extensive media coverage (as seen in the inclusion of these two lengthy articles in the *New Statesman*), suggests that race issues and the relationship between England and her former colony, South Africa, were of great interest to English readers.

Besides its importance as a subject in his writing and a backdrop to the autobiographical experiences he describes, Matshikiza's work on *King Kong* was crucial to the development of his only full-length literary work, *Chocolates for My Wife*. The archival records of his publisher, Hodder & Stoughton, reveal that the publisher's interest in Matshikiza was causally linked to his renown as the composer of *King Kong*. Hodder & Stoughton's editorial director, Robin Denniston, was friendly with anti-apartheid clergyman and significant Sophiatown figure Trevor Huddleston and with former *Drum* editor Anthony Sampson, whose 1956 book *Drum: A Venture into the New Africa* he had published while working at Collins.[6] Denniston's interest in securing Matshikiza's manuscript is notable, likely deriving from his relationship with British liberal figures who supported Matshikiza and from the popularity of *King Kong*, which garnered attention in London even before it was staged. Matshikiza writes in *Chocolates for My Wife* of the flurry of media reports which surrounded his arrival in Britain, when the 'newspapers quickly heard that there was a black rather well-known South African recently arrived in London' (1961a: 39).

Denniston wrote to Matshikiza in October 1960, 'very anxious' about how the book was 'coming along' and urging him to write as 'quickly as possible' while his 'impressions of London' were still 'fresh, and before the *King Kong* Hiroshima' (19 October 1960, Hodder & Stoughton/ Todd Matshikiza file, London Metropolitan Archives).[7] A memo written by Denniston in January 1961 underscores the public and publishing interest in Matshikiza ahead of *King Kong*'s opening night. He also draws attention to Matshikiza's own reasons for wanting to publish as soon as possible. It reads in part:

> [Matshikiza] is now very poor and determined to write his book. I have seen 10,000 words of this, and it is quite as good as I had hoped. He is going to write another few thousand words, and then ask us to give him an advance. I mention this because several publishers, including in fact Jonathan Cape, have offered him £150 without any obligation to see anything. He is, in fact, going to be, for a long or a short time, a very sought-after person, and if we want him we shall have to pay for him. Personally there is no-one I want more. (27 January 1961, LMA)

While reading both *Chocolates for My Wife* and the 'Todd in London' *Drum* columns, which Matshikiza continued to send back to South Africa, it is important to consider Matshikiza's position as a 'very poor' South African in exile, who was at the same time a 'sought-after person' and both at the centre and margins of one of South Africa's most famous exports to London.

'Word jazz with an American accent': *Drum*, Matshikeze and Englishness

The 'jazz opera' *King Kong*, in its subject matter if not always its musical style, referenced a Johannesburg-based, Sophiatown-focused culture that drew on American, and specifically African American influences, as we have already seen in the excerpt from one of Matshikiza's *Drum* columns. As one of the original *Drum* journalists, Matshikiza helped to usher in the 'New African' values that the magazine personified in its reincarnation under new editor Anthony Sampson, in contrast to its paternalistic, tribalist origins as *African Drum*. Lewis Nkosi described the *Drum* staff as 'the new African[s] cut adrift from the tribal reserve – urbanised, eager, fast-talking and brash' ([1965] 1983: 8).

One of the models for this mode of urban blackness was the literature of the Harlem Renaissance. As we have seen, Peter Abrahams captures the attraction of this 'affirming precedent' in *Tell Freedom* (1954) when he reflects rapturously on Harlem, 'A Negro City!' (1954: 200) and explains how reading the Harlem Renaissance crystallised his proud political identification as a 'colour nationalist' (238). Abrahams and many of the other *Drum* writers, such as Esk'ia Mphahlele, discovered Harlem literature years before the Sophiatown 'renaissance' of the 1950s.[8] Stéphane Robolin traces the routes of the 'New Negro cosmopolitanism of early twentieth-century which contributed greatly to the rise of urban-centred New Africanism that surged through black South African cityscapes, as iconized in the bustling culture of Sophiatown' (2015: 23). Just as early twentieth-century modernist influences were assimilated and rewritten by many South African writers, so the influence of early twentieth-century African American writers such as Booker T. Washington and W.E.B. DuBois was drawn upon in later decades by 'South Africa's black urban literati and cosmopolites of the 1950s' (2015: 23). Rob Nixon explains the enduring significance of Harlem's influence in 1950s South Africa, when successive laws such as the Group Areas Act (1950), the Bantu Authorities Act (1951) and the Natives Resettlement Act (1954) were passed in order to drive black South Africans out of urban areas, such as Sophiatown, into rural 'homelands'. Nixon suggests that 'in Harlem literature', some South African writers 'recognized a world that was black and urban, spoke of the trauma and promise of displacement, and defeated all "tribal" categories' (1994: 16). This 'idea of belonging to the city' was under pressure because of apartheid legislation, Nixon writes, so that 'their affiliation with a bold city strain of African American writing became, to adopt an apartheid term, a tonic form of "unlawful association"' (16). The fact that this 'unlawful association' was related to urban belonging becomes significant to representations of London by black South African writers.

Robolin makes the important point that, while the histories of 'violently maintained racial segregation' in the US and South Africa have inspired comparative approaches because 'their patterns of race-based oppression and resistance are at times strikingly resonant', thus enlivening the identification and solidarity across borders which Nixon writes about, the national histories of the US and South Africa have also been 'intertwined' in more tangible ways (2015: 5). Furthermore, when discussing the literary solidarities between the two spaces, Robolin's warning against racially based essentialism and over-simplification of the affiliations between African Americans and black South Africans is worth bearing in mind; he reminds us that the transnational engagements between black American writers and their South African counterparts were the 'product of deliberate exchanges and efforts to forge connections across oceans, without the ineluctable consequence of received lineage or a putatively inevitable shared racial bond' (17). While it is not in the ambit of this study to trace the circulation of texts and ideas that forged such transatlantic connections, I concur that implying a mystifying sense of 'kinship' is an unhelpful way of characterising this relationship, and so my reference to Matshikiza's appeal to a 'global black imaginary' in this chapter should not be taken as a shorthand for such an essentialising approach.

When it comes to more contemporary African American literary influences, J.U. Jacobs has suggested that African American writers such as Ralph Ellison influenced the development of the distinctive *Drum* style (1989: 10), as did the work of poet Langston Hughes, who corresponded regularly with many of the *Drum* writers, including Matshikiza; epistolary relationships constituted one of these forms of 'deliberate exchanges' which Robolin discusses. Recall, for instance, the exchange of letters between Richard Wright and Peter Abrahams. As Jacobs and Nixon both argue, however, Sophiatown's cultural connections with Harlem went beyond literary modes, as strains of jazz and blues were interwoven into 'Sophia's literary idiom' (Nixon 1994: 16), just as these musical styles influenced Ellison's writing, for instance. Beyond these literary influences, Matshikiza's style and that of *Drum* magazine more broadly owe a great deal to jazz and its culture, scene and language, originating in America, and engaging with global black subjectivities. As with literary affiliations, the rising popularity of jazz amongst urban black South Africans in the 1950s has been attributed to the parallel experiences of African Americans and black South Africans, as Coplan has suggested. Both experienced migration in the early twentieth century from rural to urban areas, leading to 'overcrowding, poverty, segregation, personal harassment, economic exploitation', which resulted in 'the emergence of performance styles that served comparable expressive needs' (Coplan 2007: 178). Again, this comparative approach and parallel assumption of certain 'performance styles' should not be read as an esoteric bond based on 'racial' likeness; jazz is implicated in routes of unequal capital and cultural imperialism, and complex webs of circulation, even as it transcended national boundaries and served potentially empowering purposes.[9]

Matshikiza's style thus reflects these networks between jazz, black America and South Africa: he writes what Coplan calls 'word jazz with an American accent' (2007: 208). Michael Titlestad explores the origins and impact of Matshikiza's 'word-jazz' in detail in *Making the Changes: Jazz in South African Literature and Reportage* (2004), arguing that, through its evocation of American jazz-scene slang, 'Matshikeze' subverts its restrictive South African context: '"Matshikeze", in its black Atlantic relational reach, shrugs off these controls by unravelling, in diasporic jazz dialect, the hypostasised subject positions that were the cornerstone of apartheid ideology' (51). The links between the writing of Matshikiza and the other *Drum* writers, through jazz, to a black global identity became a source of political resistance, so that 'writers on the *Drum* staff sought to articulate not just the local concerns of their readers, but their place in a global imaginary' (51).

Referencing Paul Gilroy's influential work *The Black Atlantic* (1995), Titlestad emphasises the disruptive and dislocating effects of Matshikiza's writing style, arguing that '"Matshikese", through this act of relational interpolation, inaugurated an influential language of counter-identification that various black South African writers would emulate' (2004: 51). Matshikiza's jazz-infused style and vocabulary enable him to take part in both 'relational interpolation' – allowing him to transcend, even deterritorialise (to use Deleuze's concept broadly) the space in which he lived by referencing another space – and counter-identification, asserting jazz and African American civil rights culture in the midst of the restrictive apartheid regime. Not only does he directly reference jazz music and include African American slang and inflections, but the form of Matshikiza's writing is also improvisational, mimicking the creative spontaneity of jazz; Titlestad suggests that '[r]apid changes in register, code-switching, repetition and a flexible approach to structure' (2004: 53) allow him to 'play' in the 'machine of apartheid symbolic power' (51).

How *Drum* writers like Matshikiza positioned themselves within a global imaginary influenced their representations of London. Liz Gunner considers how Lewis Nkosi, another exiled *Drum* writer, approached London, arguing that his background in the 'global ecumene'[10] of Sophiatown meant that he 'arrived in London ... already a very cosmopolitan young man', one who 'must have felt in many ways at home in the London of imperial twilight, the early 1960s' (2005: 51). Similarly, *Drum*'s jazz-inflected, Harlem-inspired approach to urban life provided Matshikiza with a model of city writing that he employed in a bold, self-assertive manner in his London-based texts. To his writing in both *Chocolates for My Wife* and his 'Todd in London' *Drum* columns Matshikiza also brings other, more South African influences. Lindelwa Dalamba goes so far as to suggest that his writing 'has little to do with jazz beyond content', and that his anecdotal 'morality tales' are in the oral traditions of isiXhosa '*amabali* (stories) or *iintsomi* (myths)' (2018: 316). Thus, Dalamba argues, the 'pulp culture' to which *Drum* responded and perpetuated, was something 'Matshikiza negotiated rather than embraced through "Matshikeze"' (319). If 'jazz' can stand for a broader global black imaginary and flow of transatlantic influences and subjectivities (as Titlestad and Jacobs see it), then I argue for a synthesisation of these theoretical uses of 'jazz' with Dalamba's important insistence on Matshikiza's interweaving of South African cultural traditions with his negotiation of other perspectives and personas. Dalamba's focus on 'negotiation' is especially salient to my study of Matshikiza's London writing, since, as we have seen in the rich passage initially discussed, his oscillation between different registers, languages and personas stages this process of negotiation, these dizzying shifts signalling the very counter-identification and resistance that Titlestad foregrounds. Such multiple identifications through writing took on especially multi-faceted resonances in his London work.

Furthermore, the Harlem Renaissance and American jazz culture were not the only transnational influences on Matshikiza's writing. Rob Nixon points out that, '[a]s a foreign influence on Sophiatown culture, America did not pass unrivalled: one feels throughout the literature of the place and era the strong tug of the writers' almost uniformly English, mission school education' (1994: 12). Despite beginning his writing career about a decade later, Matshikiza's background bears many similarities to that of Abrahams. They both attended St Peter's School and thus shared with other *Drum* writers like Mphahlele an English-language, mission-school education. Matshikiza's upbringing was arguably even more anglicised than Abrahams's. His birthplace, Queenstown, had been founded in 1853 as a military outpost designed to protect British subjects from attack during the Frontier Wars against the AmaXhosa. Matshikiza's family had strong links to England and English culture: as he recounts in *Chocolates for My Wife* his father 'had been a civil servant, musician, language interpreter in the law courts, a great civicist and English scholar' (1961a: 29), the extent of his imperial background evident in Matshikiza's recollection of him sitting 'in conference with the big, white men planning how Africa would receive and entertain His Royal Highness, the Prince of Wales in 1929, on his Royal Visit there' (49).

Besides his training at St Peter's, Matshikiza attended Lovedale College, which was one of several influential schools set up by English missionaries for the education of black South Africans. As Leon de Kock explores in *Civilising Barbarians* (1996), while English education allowed black South Africans a degree of power within the colonial system, it was also 'centrally implicated in consolidating, in representational forms, the modes of othering which Africans had to negotiate in order to achieve the social and cultural empowerment of education' (1996: 45). That Matshikiza was an English teacher, that his home language was English and that his family achieved middle-class status through the 'socio-cultural capital' (188) of English education is all evidence of the work that English missionaries and imperialists carried out in the south-eastern corner of South Africa. As de Kock writes, English was 'both a means of transmission and a state of ideality – the place where "civilisation" was cultivated' (45). Todd Matshikiza was a product of this 'civilising mission', but he was also attuned to the compromises it entailed. Because of his English education, Matshikiza was well-versed in the classics of English literature, as is evident in his London memoirs.

When arriving in Baker Street underground station, he is reminded of hearing Arthur Conan Doyle's Sherlock Holmes tales as a child:

> I went down the escalator in the fairyland of Baker Street where I had read Sherlock Holmes watsoning away at the baskervilles.
> My elder brother Temba had read me to bed on that hound way back in South Africa. There was not a footprint I would have not outwatsoned brother Temba upon that night. There was not a book in a brown cover and written in the English language and covered in Harley streets that I could not that evening have uncovered for my brother Temba. (Matshikiza 1961a: 49–50)

Reading English literature has informed Matshikiza's understanding of London, so that these narratives constitute the background to his walks around London, and Baker Street becomes a 'fairyland' overlaid with stories. Walking is a metaphor for reading in this passage: Baker Street is where he has 'read' Sherlock Holmes, rather than a place which merely invokes memories of Conan Doyle's detective stories. Matshikiza is like a detective, 'outwatson[ing]' the literary layers of the city and 'uncover[ing]' its bookish history, the textual 'footprints' traceable in London's streets.

He also uses language playfully here, turning the Conan Doyle character Dr Watson into a verb, thus reimagining and destabilising iconic English texts even as he acknowledges his immersion in English literary culture. It is significant that it is a memory of reading, or rather being read *to* by his brother, which connects South Africa to London and past to present in this passage. Despite their very English origins, the Sherlock Holmes stories map an imagined route from London back to South Africa, and to Matshikiza's childhood, underlined by his further assertion: 'So when this Englishman said to me this is Baker Street Station my brother Temba came to me and said, "Elementary, dear Watson"' (Matshikiza 1961a: 50). This intertextual moment foregrounds both the centrality of English literature to the worldview of middle-class black South Africans such as Matshikiza and how canonical English texts are reimagined for purposes beyond their original narratives, just as Abrahams draws on Keats to support anti-colonial and anti-racist positions.

Matshikiza's musical education was intertwined with English influences too, and Matshikiza recalls how he and his fellow teachers prescribed English songs like 'Down Vauxhall Way' and taught 'perfect' English diction (Matshikiza 1961a: 27). He also remembers a well-known 'black South African concert impresario' who 'added prestige to our aspirations for English' as he was the 'only black man to have ever worn the bowler hat in South Africa' and had 'been to London to study elocution' (28). By subtly mocking these aspirations to Englishness on the part of black South Africans, Matshikiza subverts the idea of Englishness as the height of 'civilisation'. London may be a 'fairyland', reminding Matshikiza of his childhood reading, but he is nevertheless subtly critical of the anglicisation of black South Africans.

Despite both invoking their English education and childhood reading within the setting of London, Matshikiza's playfully rendered invocation of Arthur Conan Doyle's popular detective stories is far removed from Abrahams's reverence for Keats on Hampstead Heath. Besides deriving from a difference in temperament – Mphahlele describes Matshikiza as 'bristling with life', with a 'kind of deep-seated irony' (quoted in Nicol 1991: 86) – Matshikiza's more irreverent approach to London's cultural history can be attributed to the sardonic, hard-boiled persona he had developed as a *Drum* journalist and jazz musician. Abrahams, despite contributing to *Drum* magazine, did not live in Sophiatown during the 1950s. Although many of its journalists were middle class and educated in the liberal English tradition, the American culture so influential to *Drum* magazine had a 'more scattered, cross-class appeal' (Nixon 1994:

12). Moreover, the broad readership of *Drum* led its writers to abandon standard English frequently, peppering their journalism with *tsotsitaal* – Afrikaans-based 'gangster speak' combined with 'English and vernacular languages' and strains of American film diction, invoked by writers like Can Themba and Matshikiza 'as a mark of their classlessness' (Nixon 1994: 33). The popular American and demotic local influences upon black South African writing in the 1950s meant that Matshikiza did not approach London in a reverent manner as the source of high literature and culture, despite his anglicised education. Moreover, the fluid class boundaries of Sophiatown and *Drum* made Matshikiza even more sensitive to the peculiar class dynamics he encountered in London, alongside the British racism he observed.

Style and audience in Matshikiza's *Drum* columns and autobiography

That Matshikiza hails from a South African background shot through with both English and African American cultural threads contributes to the complex spatial webs he creates and enters into when writing about London. For instance, in a passage in *Chocolates for My Wife* describing a bus trip through central London, Matshikiza reveals both the complex relationship between England and South Africa, and his 'jazzy' style:

> 'Let's go and see Piccadilly Circus.' And we sat on the top deck so's to view freedom from above. Past Prince Albert's Memorial in Hyde Park and John-Anthony said, 'Is that how the house looked so big Daddy and full of picture things an' all that big. Was he a giant prince, Daddy?'
> And boys and girls were painting pictures of London. They sat there feeling free. Prince Albert didn't step down an' say what you doing on my monument, you monster. Or Queen Victoria come out an' say what you doing sunbathing naked in my park jus' because the sun is shining once a year in England. The queen was wearing long pearls an' cullinan diamonds right round. Also ostrich feathers and an ivory fan and things like that which relaxed the English bathing in the long, long years that built their houses right up against each other when we came and space was short. (Matshikiza 1961a: 32)

Matshikiza again employs an African American accent evident in frequent abbreviations. The passage is also very rhythmic, with the repetition of 'Daddy' at the beginning of the passage, and later the repeated phrase 'an' say what you doing', creating a sing-song effect. Minimal punctuation and the strings of short words, for instance in 'long, long years that built their houses right up against each other when we came and space was short', also lend the passage a noticeably rhythmic lilt. While celebrating the freedoms the city affords its inhabitants, Matshikiza provides subtle commentary on colonialism and historical links between London and South Africa. For instance, Queen Victoria is wearing 'Cullinan' diamonds, sourced from the Transvaal in South Africa, as well as ostrich feathers and a fan made of ivory – a recognition of the historical relationship between London and South Africa, which was largely based on the exploitation of these types of valuable minerals and animal products.

Titlestad has argued that 'Matshikeze' constitutes a form of 'historiography', asserting 'genealogies' from elsewhere and thereby disrupting 'apartheid's linear historicity'; using an appropriately musical metaphor, Titlestad suggests that Matshikiza's writing style '*swings* within and between layered archives of history' (Titlestad 2004: 55, italics original). In his writing about London, Matshikiza not only invokes the histories of a global black imaginary through his form and references, but also reflects on the intertwined histories of South Africa and London. His 'historiographic' writing counters a sense of London's history as linear and purely English, just as his references to other spaces and countercultures in his South African writing disrupt apartheid's racist teleology.

In the above passage, Matshikiza destabilises London's imperial legacies by adopting a comic tone, particularly in his subversive ventriloquising of Queen Victoria. Both *Chocolates for My Wife* and his *Drum* columns are replete with humour. His regular 'With the Lid Off' columns for *Drum* were renamed 'Todd in London' when he moved into exile, and these columns are mock-epistolary in style, set up as letters from abroad and structured as a series of short, snappy sections which each end with a punchline. Matshikiza addresses the *Drum* readers directly, with an assumption that they will understand his references. For instance, he writes, 'Hey girls, Dixie Kwankwa is here', referring to a South African singer who has moved to London (Matshikiza 2000: 88). He even ends one of the 'letters' in a familiar epistolary fashion: 'Auntie Charlotte you were right about the dogs here, and the cold weather. Please send me some lovely South African sunshine ... and moonshine' (2000: 81). While it also has its share of humour, and is similarly episodic, *Chocolates for My Wife* is slightly more discursive and lyrical than the *Drum* columns.

Given that Matshikiza may have anticipated that *Chocolates for My Wife* would be banned by the South African censors, which it was (in its initial hardback form),[11] one might posit that he had aimed the book at a British or more generally international readership, knowing that it could not be read by many South Africans. It is interesting that Hodder & Stoughton's readers' and editors' reports only obliquely foresee the possibility of censorship. Robin Denniston's report on the marketability of *Chocolates for My Wife* lists five different markets for Matshikiza's autobiography ('Market', 20 June 1961, LMA). Firstly, Denniston mentions his 'influential circle' of acquaintances in both 'Africa and England'; secondly he refers to the 'many thousands' of 'people who enjoyed King Kong'. Thirdly, he deals with the South African market where 'Todd was one of the best known blacks in the Union by virtue firstly of his music, then of his politics, thirdly as a journalist on *Drum* and fourthly as a great character', but he does acknowledge the possibility that the book might be banned: 'If we can get it into the country, and this is a big if, I can think of several book shops who should order in hundreds'. Significantly, the fourth market Denniston highlights is the 'African market' in Britain since, 'There are a number of African organizations and a growing interest in African affairs in the provinces as well as London'. He posits *Chocolates for My Wife* as an alternative to 'worthy but dull indictments of apartheid' and hopes that it 'may lead some of the more old-fashioned liberals to think again'. He markets the autobiography as playing into and challenging metropolitan ideas about apartheid and Africa in general. Denniston's final suggested readership for *Chocolates for My Wife* is 'the general marked for third programme satirical books'. The reference to the cerebral BBC 'Third Programme' radio station to describe satirical literature is interesting considering the criticism faced by Peter Abrahams a decade earlier over his affiliation with this British institution.[12] Despite its potential to make 'old-fashioned liberals ... think again', Denniston foresees that the book will be legible within certain British intellectual, liberal traditions and networks. When *Chocolates for My Wife* was published, the blurb on the dust jacket highlighted Matshikiza's connections to Trevor Huddleston and to Alan Paton and also included reviews of *King Kong*, so that Matshikiza was strategically positioned in relation to people and works with which British readers would be familiar.

This does not mean, however, that the text is particularly transparent to non-South Africans. There are frequently sentences in isiZulu or isiXhosa, for example, left untranslated, which suggests that, despite the possibility of censorship, Matshikiza was at least partly interested in addressing his fellow black South Africans, as he did in his *Drum* journalism, rather than speaking to a white, British audience. Fortunately, the editorial staff of Hodder & Stoughton seemed particularly keen to maintain the integrity of his voice and style. One reader, Elsie Heron, recommended that the editors 'let all stand, words, detailed descriptions, unbridled feelings, the lot, for to change or cut them ... would be largely pointless, and weakening in its effect'. She emphasised that 'the style' should not 'be tampered with at all; it is Matshikiza and unlike anyone else' (Heron Reader's Report, 19 June 1961, LMA). In response to a slightly critical report from Harper Brothers, with whom Denniston attempted to negotiate a US deal for the book, Denniston replied, 'I myself worked with him with the greatest care over the book, but felt that it was wrong not to let him write in the way in which he wanted to, and indeed he is very reluctant to accept editorial advice except on small matters' (Denniston to Melvin Arnold, 7 November 1961, LMA). Unlike the arrangers and producers whom Matshikiza saw as altering his compositions from 'from black to white and now purple' (Matshikiza 1961a: 125), Robin Denniston was sensitive to Matshikiza's standing and talent as a writer, intellectual and public figure and allowed him a great deal of creative liberty.

In order to ensure that Matshikiza's position within the networks of the South African literati was clear to British readers, Denniston asked well-known novelist Alan Paton, with whom Matshikiza had worked on the musical *Mkhumbane* (1960), to contribute a comment for the marketing of the book. He wrote to Denniston: 'No-one writes quite like Todd Matshikiza. He has his own wry humour, and in spite of humiliation, which he describes faithfully, he keeps a strangely level head' (Paton to Denniston, 18 October 1961, LMA). Matshikiza's adoption of 'wry humour' throughout much of his writing can be attributed to his background as a writer in 1950s South Africa. Firstly, humour and irony were a coping mechanism for many oppressed black South Africans. Lewis Nkosi writes that '[f]or a black man to live in South Africa in the second half of the twentieth century and at the same time preserve his sanity, he requires an enormous sense of humour and a surrealistic kind of brutal wit' ([1965] 1983: 254) and suggests that black South Africans identified with Langston Hughes's description of African Americans who 'laugh to keep from crying' (28).

While Matshikiza does not shirk from pointing out the racism present in both South Africa and London, he does so in a tone of ironic detachment in order to avoid melodrama, side-step trauma and present the facts unsentimentally. Secondly, adopting an ironic tone often helped to convey the 'surrealistic' absurdity of the South African situation, with its nonsensical, though brutal, laws; as Nkosi explains: 'At best an account of what a black man goes through in his daily life sounds like an exaggerated Kafka novel' ([1965] 1983: 25). These daily conditions are made to seem even more ridiculous, in Matshikiza's writing, through their contrast with London's relative freedoms. It is worth noting that Nkosi references a modernist, European author, showing how the *Drum* writers were influenced by modernism, particularly in their engagement with absurdism. While Matshikiza is less explicit about his literary influences, there is certainly a modernist tinge to his non-linear, stream-of-consciousness narrative in *Chocolates for My Wife*, as is evident in the passage quoted above, which provides the same perspective on London as Elizabeth's journey in Virginia Woolf's *Mrs Dalloway* (1925), in which central London is similarly viewed from the top deck of an omnibus. Furthermore, some of his African American influences, including Langston Hughes, have been designated as Afro-modernists. Thus Matshikiza drew on both canonical modernism and global engagements with modernity in his depictions of South African and London city life.

Several other writers of the *Drum* generation, including Lewis Nkosi and Arthur Maimane, lived in London during the 1960s. During his time in London, Nkosi worked at the BBC, and wrote essays, literary criticism and radio plays, some of which are set in London, later publishing the novel *Mating Birds* in 1983.[13] Maimane also worked at the BBC; his novel, *The Victims*, set in South Africa, was published in 1976. However, Matshikiza was the only *Drum* writer who took on the setting of 1960s London in any sustained manner in a full-length published text. Studied together with his *Drum* columns, *Chocolates for My Wife* provides a unique window into this moment in which South African writers, activists and other artists were increasingly living in exile in London. Through Matshikiza's writing, Sophiatown comes to London, and the intersections between the two places give rise to commentary on both South African and British society.

Peering eyes and familiar faces: South Africa in London

Aside from the way in which Matshikiza's style references another space, and thus partakes in 'relational interpolation', he also sets different spaces in counterpoint in a more concrete sense, since he thinks about contemporary South Africa within London. Michael Titlestad aptly describes how, in *Chocolates for My Wife*,

> [Matshikiza] deploys an almost rapturous counterpoint in setting the lived realities of apartheid South Africa alongside the author's initial

experience of life in the United Kingdom. The narrative zigzags between the two contexts as new experiences evoke memories of growing up and becoming a composer, performer and writer in an intractably racist country. (Titlestad 2004: 154)

Matshikiza's 'contrapuntal', 'zigzagging' method feeds into the deterritorialising, interpolative aspects of his writing, as he engages with London as a space while thinking of, and through, South Africa. I would argue for a productive synthesis of Titlestad's two concepts – a contrapuntal approach and a historiographic method – through a particular application of Edward Said's idea of contrapuntal reading. Said argues that we should read cultural texts 'contrapuntally' rather than 'univocally', with a 'simultaneous awareness both of the metropolitan history that is narrated and of those other histories against which (and together with which) the dominating discourse acts' (1994: 60).[14] The significance of the 'counterpoint' in Said's use of the appositely musical metaphor is that neither melodic strain dominates the other and both are indispensable to the complete composition; accordingly, 'metropolitan' histories cannot be understood without considering how they are intertwined with narratives from the 'margins' – and vice versa. Rather than using Said's mode of literary analysis to read Matshikiza, I want to suggest that Matshikiza *reads* and writes London in this contrapuntal and historiographic manner. Matshikiza both sets up a counterpoint by comparing the 'lived realities of apartheid South Africa' alongside his experiences of London, and invokes the counterpointed, interdependent histories of South Africa and London while introducing strains of 'other histories', such as those of a global black imaginary. His straightforward comparisons between places, and his historiography of South Africa and London, work together to disrupt the 'dominating discourses' of both imperialism and apartheid. Matshikiza's multifaceted, historiographic contrapuntalism is exemplary of the multilayered temporal and spatial approach of many South African writers' depictions of London, and mirrors my own methodology of foregrounding 'marginal' narratives about the 'metropolitan' space.

In Matshikiza's 'rapturous counterpoint', London is often set up as a place of refuge and freedom, suggesting either overtly or implicitly that South Africa represents the inverse. For instance, in the opening passage of *Chocolates for My Wife*, Matshikiza describes Britain, and specifically London, in sublime terms:

> Arrival. The English Channel dressed up in the most beautiful blue and white, the most gorgeous of satins as my family and I flew across towards

London airport. I kissed her, the English Channel. I kissed her each time the jet plane dipped a wing, a nose, a dive to give us a glimpse of great London where we were heading. (1961a: 7)

The relief that Matshikiza expresses in this moment can be explained by the series of humiliating and traumatic experiences he has undergone in South Africa, recounted in a retrospective section towards the end of *Chocolates for My Wife*. These events culminate in his being harassed on the street by policemen, who mock him for bringing home a box of chocolates for his wife. In London, when he experiences either the city's relative freedoms or instances of racism, he reads these moments through his South African memories.

One of the ways in which the lingering trauma of apartheid is represented in Matshikiza's autobiographical writing is through his encounters with white South Africans in London; indeed, it seems that Matshikiza cannot escape them. In a *Drum* column, Matshikiza describes taking his children to feed the pigeons at Trafalgar Square and comments on the 'infectious' politeness amongst the crowd, which is quickly contrasted with the extreme racism of white South Africans who revile any contact with black people:

You find yourself automatically helping the ladies up or down the steps or buying pigeon food for them and they say, 'Thank you very much. Have some of mine nex' time.' So I was happy as usual that Sunday when a young white woman dropped a handkerchief and I rushed to pick it up for her. She grabbed it out of my hands an' said, '*Oo, Here, God!*' The man with her exclaimed, '*Magtig, Jesus!*'[15]

I wonder where they came from. (Matshikiza 2000: 72–73)

As in many South African narratives set in London, Trafalgar Square is an important symbolic site in Matshikiza's writing, and he foregrounds its role as a monument to British military success, as well as its centrality for South Africans due to its proximity to the embassy at South Africa House. In *Chocolates for My Wife*, Matshikiza describes a visit to South Africa House. Although he has been told he can get his 'South African papers' at the embassy, he claims that this is merely an excuse to go inside; motivated by a 'naughty streak' (1961a: 18), he says to himself:

Eenie meenie mina mo
Catch a nigger by his toe
Go inside and then you'll see
Is Africa for you or me. (19)

Matshikiza thus aims to confront the absurdity of apartheid South Africa's laws and regulations by entering the type of official space from which he would be barred in South Africa, but in London, where his rights of movement and association are not curtailed. Although South Africa House is in the centre of London, his experience within its walls causes Matshikiza to relive the trauma of the surveillance and humiliation he underwent in South Africa. He enters the reading-room to which he is directed, significantly lined with books of South African statutes, and when he looks up, he sees 'numerous eyes, blue, green and fiery red, peering at me', a vivid image of menacing, panoptical surveillance. Even more disturbingly, he finds himself 'in the silent, mute company of the "South African Native Bronze Heads"', a series of sculptures by state-patronised sculptor Anton van Wouw. Overwhelmed by these racially stereotyped images of '*Native Awaiting Sentence*' and '*Sleeping Kaffir*' (19), Matshikiza bolts out the room and, paralysed by shock, ends up standing for hours in the freezing rain.

South Africa House, particularly from the 1960s until the early 1990s, was the target of anti-apartheid activism in London, as it represented the official presence of the South African government. Afrikaner nationalist ideology was visibly presented in the High Commission's artworks, which have since been re-curated. The High Commission's artworks included murals that represented stereotyped and racialised images of black South Africans; as Annie Coombes writes, 'virtually all the murals cannot escape the charge today of either covertly or overtly representing a vision of the past that has since proved to be the foundation upon which apartheid's discriminatory logic was cemented' (2003: 290). The same applies to Van Wouw's well-known bronzes called 'African studies', small sculptures of black South Africans in various poses and activities, of which Matshikiza names two examples: *Native Awaiting Sentence* and *Sleeping Kaffir*. Other titles of these works include *The Laughing Basutu* and *The Dagga Smoker*. Certainly one can understand Matshikiza's revulsion towards such stereotyped depictions of black South Africans. This incident in South Africa House illustrates what London allows Matshikiza to escape from: surveillance, by the police and white South Africans in general, and (at least partly) from antiquated racial stereotypes such as those represented by the Van Wouw statues. In London, Matshikiza is free from the control of the South African government and police force; but is he able fully to escape South Africa or his South Africanness?

The fact that he remains outside, so focused on his traumatic experience that he does not notice the rain, would suggest that total escape from the psychological effects of apartheid is not possible. Titlestad argues that jazz and its association with a wider global black imaginary constituted one of the avenues through which 'individuals and communities ... faced up to the apartheid panopticon and devised ways of eluding its gaze (albeit fleetingly)', thwarting its 'technologies of surveillance' (2004: xiii). This incident at South Africa House suggests the 'fleeting' nature of this strategy of evasion and self-assertion in the face of the insidious presence of the apartheid machine's functionaries, reminiscent of Mandela's assertion that 'the tentacles of South African security forces reached all the way to London' (1994: 360). Furthermore, this moment in Matshikiza's autobiography is a reminder of the lingering effects of the trauma inflicted by apartheid, which endures even outside of its borders.

As he leaves South Africa House, Matshikiza comments on British symbols of imperialism and jingoism within the square, as he studies the plaque below Nelson's Column, depicting 'soldiers weathering a stormy sea'. He soon notices on one of the panels a 'Negro soldier with a face full of pride' and imagines that his 'rifle seemed to point in the direction of the gold-plated Springbok on South Africa House'. He then quotes Nelson's famous statement written under the plaque, 'England expects every man to do his duty' (Matshikiza 1961a: 20). Matshikiza turns his traumatic experience within South Africa House into a desire for black resistance, as he re-appropriates a slogan of British patriotism and turns it into an injunction to take up arms against apartheid, by linking it to the black soldier's belligerent pose. While Matshikiza's suggestion of violent action against the apartheid government may be taken as angry wishful thinking in a particular moment, rather than as an overt political statement promoting an armed struggle, it is worth noting that *Chocolates for My Wife* was published in the same year in which the armed wing of the ANC, Umkhonto we Sizwe, was formed. By imagining the black soldier taking aim at South Africa House, he therefore echoes debates about the effectiveness of non-violent resistance within South Africa at the time.

Not only does he literally encounter white South African racism within London, but Matshikiza's traumatic memories of South Africa are frequently layered over London spaces. For instance, in a London pub, Matshikiza is 'suddenly carried away to the Coloured Bar in Queenstown, South Africa' (Matshikiza 1961a: 37). He recalls the racist and humiliating treatment of black patrons by the Queenstown barman, Smith, who would force them to drink excessively till they blacked out and would then stuff sawdust in their mouths while they were sleeping. After recounting this horrific story, Matshikiza snaps back to his London present: 'But I was thinking nearly aloud in this pub in Kensington, so Smith wasn' true. The pub in Queenstown wasn' here. What's more, Smith wasn' there' (38). Matshikiza has escaped the humiliations of apartheid South Africa, meaning that sadistic 'Smith wasn' there', but South Africa is simultaneously made present because of his memories of moments of brutalisation.

At times, these memories intersect with experiences of discrimination within London itself, so that the dialectic between the two spaces becomes more ambivalent. A clerk at an eye hospital where Matshikiza goes to receive treatment fires a series of incisive questions at him, including an accusatory, 'Have you come to live on the dole?' (Matshikiza 1961a: 12). Matshikiza becomes increasingly angry:

> His goose had been boiling higher and higher in me since I met his face. He looked a dirty, pinkish-yellowy brown like South African Coloureds playing White. His eyes were a muddy brown graced with darts of green to help him pass. His mind was a cross between a successful playwrite [sic] and a dismal flop.
>
> And when my mind told me this, his goose was cooked. I blew up. 'Don't you go asking me silly questions. I've come for help. Not for yelp. And if I'm not getting it you can keep it.'
>
> Now what did I say. Stranger in the land misusing the hospitality. The man's face had reminded me of a face I had seen somewhere. (12)

Not only does the man's face remind Matshikiza of a 'South African Coloured' who attempts to pass as 'white', an embodiment of the effects of South Africa's arbitrary race classification laws, but he bears a similarity to a specific face he has 'seen somewhere', not in South Africa, but in London. Matshikiza explains that the clerk's face takes him '[b]ack to Kensington to a pub with Lionel Ngakane. It was the barman's face' (2). Overhearing their conversation in Afrikaans, the barman talks to Matshikiza and the South African actor Lionel Ngakane (famous for his role in the 1951 film version of *Cry, the Beloved Country*). The barman claims that he is Rhodesian, but Matshikiza later hears him talking to other patrons and discovers that is he is South African and was in the police force but has hidden his identity from Ngakane and Matshikiza because he '[c]ould have had something to do with these two maybe in Johannesburg' (13). The overbearing British clerk accusing Matshikiza of leeching off the state is thus compared to a South African policeman who has enforced brutal laws against black South Africans and who might still be spying on black, politically-active exiles in London. Matshikiza thus compares the controlling and discriminatory nature of Britain's bureaucratic state apparatuses to the more overt forms of oppression in South Africa.

Matshikiza's complex, criss-crossing counterpoint between South Africa and London enables his critique of comparable racisms and methods of domination and surveillance in both locations. Like other South Africans writing London, Matshikiza reads memories and traces of South Africa in amongst his experiences of London. His playful, satirical style of writing allows him to play with perceptions and reality, present and past, as metaphor morphs into metonymy. For instance, a simple comparison, 'The man's face had reminded me of a face I had seen somewhere', changes into a statement of fact, 'It was the barman's face', in the next paragraph (12). Matshikiza combines the paranoia that apartheid South Africa invokes with a playful destabilisation of fixed identities, as he undercovers the lies and obfuscation of the apartheid regime. The man at the NHS looks like the coloured South African playwright 'playing White' (12), who reminds him of the barman disguised as a Rhodesian who might be 'Sergeant Diedericks who told the court he doesn't fear Natives or God' but who admits he is 'afraid' of being found out by black South Africans in London (13). It is no wonder then that the suspected policeman is later seen reading Leslie Charteris's *The Saint* on the Underground (13), presumably tailing Matshikiza while reading popular fiction about a shadowy master spy and criminal who famously adopted many aliases.

'He calls us "Sir"': anonymity and naming

Against the control and surveillance he has been subjected to in South Africa, Matshikiza insists on anonymity and autonomy within London. For instance, he describes in a September 1960 column how he is approached on the Underground by an Afrikaner working for the government's Publicity Bureau in London – the tourism or information department of South Africa House. The young man has overheard Matshikiza talking to a South African friend about 'Kipe Town' and asks him 'if youse both come from home'. Matshikiza coldly replies: 'Jong, this is London. You mind your own business' (Matshikiza 2000: 72). Matshikiza's form of address, 'Jong' (literally Afrikaans for 'youngster') is deeply coded; it is both a colloquial form of address (similar to 'mate') but also denotes a young black male servant. In London, Matshikiza can turn this potentially infantilising form of address against these white government officials and can be assimilated into the mass of other Londoners.

In a monologue presented for the BBC's Home Service's *Tuesday Talk* radio show on 6 February 1962, Matshikiza speaks of how the pass book he was forced to carry in South Africa, ostensibly an identity document, paradoxically 'testified to [his] lack of identity'. In London, however, he is able to declare, 'But I have an identity now. And I have the right to be anonymous' (British Library Sound Archives). It is significant that one of the observations he makes in his first *Drum* column on Londoners is that 'none of them are not minding their own business' (2000: 67). In the opening chapter of *Chocolates for My Wife*, he similarly remarks, with mock resentment, that 'The English people look at you, but they do not see you. And here I was with my family, boasting our black faces in the white land, and welling up with resentment that nobody was taking any notice of us' (1961a: 11). He revels in this right to 'be anonymous', even as he asserts his 'identity' in London. In other immigrant writing on London, such as George Lamming's and Sam Selvon's novels, the disinterested nature of Londoners is seen as a symptom of an alienating, lonely city, but Matshikiza celebrates anonymity as a welcome relief from the interference of the apartheid government and its supporters and spies.

As part of his contrapuntal method of comparing London and South Africa, Matshikiza contrasts how he is designated in each space. In his first London-based column, published in August 1960, he marvels at the immensity and diversity of London, and comments on how he is situated within this multicultural city. The column begins, characteristically, with an incredulous, Americanised exclamation:

> Shucks! Where does one begin to tell the story of a city so big? ... There are hundreds of black people here, but the Englishman calls us all Coloured. No, I am wrong, he calls us 'Sir'. He uses the word 'Coloured' politely because he does not make any difference between Xhosa, American Negroes, Basutho, Jamaican or Zulu. (Matshikiza 2000: 67)

Matshikiza's commentary on the Englishman's designation of black Londoners is subtle. While the Englishman politely calls him 'Sir', a courtesy not afforded him by most white people in South Africa, there is still something unsettling about being lumped into the undifferentiated category of 'Coloured' upon his arrival in London along with dark-skinned people from all over the globe. The broader British definition of 'Coloured', describing non-white people in general, while still potentially derogatory, makes apartheid's racial and ethnic differentiations seem absurd in their specificity, particularly as 'Coloured' denoted an arbitrarily defined group of 'mixed-race' people in South Africa.

Despite being labelled as 'Coloured', Matshikiza finds that he is at least properly named in London. In *Chocolates for My Wife*, he explains his astonishment on being correctly addressed upon his arrival at the airport:

> The Air Hostess at London Airport called our names. There were letters of welcome awaiting us at the Airport.
>
> 'Mr and Mrs Matshikiza!' It was thoroughly astonishing, she was pronouncing the terribly awkward, long, difficult name correctly, with the accent properly on the second syllable. Well, it was my own fault that even my best white friends in South Africa could not pronounce my name. They had never practiced the 'Native' name because over there I was Todd 92867. To them I was Todd. To the Administration I was 92867. Perhaps that was why Dr. Ralph Bachelor, a white South African, had written to me in London and named me Mechichesa. ... But if this English lassie at the airport was pronouncing my name the right way at first shot either the Special Branch had caught up with us and practised her, or England was going to be great fun. (1961a: 9)

In South Africa, Matshikiza's name is westernised ('Todd' rather than his isiXhosa first name, Tozama), botched ('Mechichesa') or effaced by a dehumanising number, but in London it is carefully and correctly pronounced. Matshikiza takes the correct pronunciation of his name at the airport as an omen that England will 'be great fun', yet he suggests the darker side of naming by jokingly wondering if the 'Special Branch' (apartheid South Africa's spies) are after him. Being named can be gratifying, but it can conversely signify surveillance and control. We see, once more, the underlying paranoia about being watched which has 'caught up' with Matshikiza and has followed him to London.

Matshikiza is also known as a 'South African' for the first time in London, something he has never been called within his home country. In that first 'Todd in London' column, he remarks how, on the flight to London: 'I looked at my passport which described us not as Coloureds, not as Natives, not as Bantu, but as South African citizens, approaching the great city of Rome' (2000: 68). In his 1962 BBC talk, Matshikiza explains how, on his flight's stop-over in Rome, he is approached by a white South African who wants to know whether he is the 'South African gentleman' named in a newspaper article entitled 'Native Composer and Wife Fly to London':

> I was shocked at this double distinction – a gentleman and a South African. Of course my passport described me as South African, but it was the only document that had ever done so. You see, in South Africa, only Coloureds, those of mixed ancestry, and Whites are called South Africans. But if you are neither White nor Coloured, you are not a South African at all. And unless you are an Asiatic, you are a Bantu – a Native. And everywhere you go, you have to carry a pass, which is a book of 96 pages. So I thought, now I am out of South Africa, I am considered a South African. (British Library Sound Archives)

Thus leaving South Africa, in the strange and estranging logic of apartheid, is precisely what allows Matshikiza to think of himself as 'South African', although this is a complex act of self-designation, as Matshikiza acknowledges. This encounter during his flight foreshadows Matshikiza's interrogation of race, identity and nationality while he is dislocated from his home country in London. While he identified with a global black imaginary, being allowed to call himself South African was of particular importance to Matshikiza, more so perhaps than for someone like Abrahams, who identified more broadly as 'African' and who was particularly invested in this Pan-African affiliation during his involvement in anti-colonial activities in London. Esmé Matshikiza has commented that

> [Todd] had so much inborn faith in himself and who he was and where he came from that he was extremely self-confident about being a South African. I don't like to use the words a 'black South African', because for him that was totally irrelevant. There was no question about it, he was a South African and had a right to be there, he was part of the soil, it was his ancestral home. (Quoted in Nicol 1991: 83)

Matshikiza's attainment of a national identity, by means of his passport and the designation he is given by others as he travels to London, confirms the belief he already has in his rights as a South African, despite the efforts of the apartheid regime to rob black South Africans of that identity. In his autobiographical writing, Matshikiza asserts that identity without pandering to or even overtly addressing British readers.

Rallies, meetings and mutual suspicions: anti-apartheid politics in London

Although Matshikiza may never have been a card-carrying member of any political party,[16] he was engaged in anti-apartheid activities while in London, evidenced by his involvement in a fundraising concert put on by the Anti-Apartheid Movement (AAM) in St Pancras Town Hall in 1963.[17] Esmé Matshikiza has asserted that Matshikiza was 'by emotion and sentiment a supporter of the ANC but he was not uncritical of the party or of individuals'. She comments that '[h]e was an observer of the situation more than anything else but at the same time identified with it' (quoted in Nicol 1991: 83). Nelson Mandela and exiled ANC leader Oliver Tambo visited the Matshikizas during Mandela's 1962 visit to London, arriving at their north London flat late at night. The last time they had met had been at the opening night of *King Kong* in South Africa. According to Esmé Matshikiza, Mandela described how he was certain he would be arrested upon his return to South Africa, whereupon she asked him why he would then choose to go back. Mandela replied, 'I'm the leader of the people and the leader of the people must be with his people' (Smith 2010: 260). Esmé Matshikiza's question foregrounds how London served as a potential place of refuge, where South African activists could escape arrest and imprisonment.

London provided not only a space in which anti-apartheid activists could meet together without sanction, but also where they could garner support for their cause from the British public and politicians. In a 'Todd in London' column from October 1960, Matshikiza refers to a rally in Trafalgar Square, 'where Alfred Hutchinson was addressing a meeting recently with Tennyson Makiwane, Dr Yusuf Dadoo and other South Africans' (2000: 79). This may refer to the rally which kicked off the 'boycott month' of March 1960, where speakers also included ANC Youth League member and Treason Trial defendant Tennyson Makiwane, alongside anti-apartheid cleric Father Trevor Huddleston, British Labour leader Hugh Gaitskell and Liberal MP Jeremy Thorpe. The proposed boycott of South African goods was widely supported by British people and was fuelled by the Sharpeville shootings in March 1960. The Boycott Movement changed its name to the Anti-Apartheid Movement (AAM) that year; this London-based organisation started with South African exiles and a few British supporters and grew to become one of the 'most important organizations in the transnational [anti-apartheid] solidarity network' (Thörn 2006: 20). Matshikiza reports, however, that at this early AAM meeting '[a] few Englishmen tried to break up the meeting shouting "Keep Britain white"', similarly to Noni Jabavu's lone campaigner who wanted to 'Keep Fleet Street White' (Jabavu 1961: 68). These racist words are soon mitigated by the fact that the 'Englishmen' are quickly arrested for 'disturbing the peace' (Matshikiza 2000: 79). In contrast to South Africa, where the activists would have been detained on a charge of disturbance, here it is their brash detractors who are censured by the police. While acknowledging the presence of racism in London, Matshikiza also expresses his appreciation of the relative freedoms afforded by English society and policing.

Alongside his sympathy with the ANC and its leaders, Matshikiza is critical of those who would exploit the cause of black South Africans for selfish purposes. For example, in *Chocolates for My Wife*, he describes a rally led by one 'Fikile Sono', a South African 'refugee' who is billed as 'hot stuff' (1961a: 59).[18] The hyperbolic tone in which Matshikiza glosses the advertisement for the rally conveys his misgiving about Sono's showboating activism:

> The pamphlet read hot, blue, black.
> *'Africa needs you, brother, more than ever. Roll up! Roll up!*
> *Will you not heed the call? Come one, come all.*
> *Meeting extravaganza. Gala extraordinary.*
> *Biggest and fullest attendance of the most important even in the history of mankind.*
> ...
> *Your best opportunity to meet the man most wanted by the South African Special Branch, dead or alive.*' (1961a: 59, italics original)

Although his rally is well attended and his statements in support of a 'free Africa' are met with cheers, Sono turns out to be a charlatan, more interested in British women, smart clothes and glamorous parties than in the struggle against apartheid. Suspicions abound that he is a spy for the apartheid government, and he eventually reveals to Matshikiza that he is 'not spying on Congress for the South African Government. But I am spying for the American Government for the South African Government' (65). Matshikiza's convoluted clauses – 'for the American Government for the South African Government' – evoke the web of suspicion and surveillance that surrounded anti-apartheid politics, which involved global actors, including the United States' Central Intelligence Agency (CIA). It is well established that the CIA worked to undermine the ANC by funding anti-communist alternatives, and some claim that the CIA provided the tip-off that led to Mandela's arrest in 1962 in Rivonia (Schmidt 2013: 113). Whether or not Sono is a double agent of some kind, or whether he is indeed just a common-or-garden apartheid government spy after all, the inclusion of this fictional (or at least fictionalised) spy figure[19] in Matshikiza's autobiography points to the climate of mutual suspicion and Cold War era paranoia that characterised South African political activities in the 1960s, even in the 'freer' atmosphere of London.

Although it was easier for activists and intellectuals, both white and black, to meet freely in London, the sense of community and equality amongst South Africans was often uneven. In his radio talk 'Apartheid Apart', presented for the BBC Home Service, Matshikiza discusses at length the complexities involved when white and black South Africans meet together to socialise and organise political activities in London. Characteristically observant, he comments on how South African jazz forms a significant background to these gatherings: 'At a typical South African night, everyone boasts of his collections of South African jazz records. This music is not thought much of by white South Africans at home, but in London, South African jazz is the thing we go for, Whites even more than Blacks' (British Library Sound Archives). Matshikiza recognises how South Africans, particularly white activists, often over-perform their South Africanness when in London, in this case by listening to South African jazz.

During the rest of the monologue, Matshikiza studies the possible cracks in the apparently unified multiracial gatherings of anti-apartheid supporters in London. Although it seems that 'all are united in the cause of freedom for South Africa', Matshikiza finds himself 'wondering how far everyone truly identified with all these expressions of unity and freedom'. He lists overheard snippets of conversation that reveal the suspicion each South African has about the other: 'That chap here was playing White in Cape Town'; 'That chap says he's a student, but man, he's dumb. We think he's Special Branch'; 'Man, I hate the way these South African Whites crawl around us in London. They didn't when they lived in Parktown'.[20] Matshikiza thus reveals how the South African community in London is always provisional and anxiety-provoking because of the country's historical racial schisms. He concludes, however, on a hopeful note, remarking on how exile facilitates transparency within the anti-apartheid movement:

> What interests me is how the natural tensions and inevitable mutual suspicions are working themselves out in London. What do we find in this great, free city? We Africans find ourselves in a new position in our movement. We can assert our rights firmly and freely. And because we find ourselves in a society where everyone has equal political rights, we gain new confidence. We meet experienced British politicians and learn from them. We attend meetings and international conferences. We meet foreign statesmen and leaders of independent African nations. We become more articulate. Again, White South Africans are joining us openly. And in London, differences can be worked on out in the open. (British Library Sound Archives)

In this broadcast monologue, Matshikiza articulates how London serves as a place of meeting, a site not only of organised political gatherings, such as those at Trafalgar Square, but also of more informal meetings between white and black South Africans, and between South Africans and Britons. In these meetings, he hopes that 'natural tensions' can be 'worked on out in the open'.

'I found myself wandering ...': getting lost in London

The 'openness' that Matshikiza experiences in London is manifested in the freedom with which he traverses the city. The incident in which Matshikiza ignores the white South African from the Publicity Bureau takes place, significantly, on the Underground, and the passage in which he and his family travel by bus past the Albert Memorial likewise sets a commentary on freedom within a journey via public transport. Licence to travel across London on unsegregated public transport is meaningful for Matshikiza, considering how the movement of black South Africans in urban areas was restricted by the pass system. As part of the 1950 Group Areas Act, South African pass laws – which already governed the movements of black men – became even stricter. All black South Africans had to carry a pass book with them at all times when outside their designated townships or homelands, and could only move in such areas with the permission of a white employer. In *Chocolates for My Wife*, for instance, Matshikiza recalls being stopped after a *King Kong* rehearsal by policemen, who ask for his pass: fortunately he has a letter from the musical's director. Resistance to the pass laws culminated in the Sharpeville protests and massacre in March 1960 – a few months before Matshikiza left South Africa for London. Thus, the mobility of black South Africans is especially fraught in this early 1960s moment.

As well as referring to public transport, Matshikiza frequently recounts his walks around London, which reminds one of de Certeau's suggestion that a city's meaning is made and countered through its pedestrians; 'their intertwined paths give their shape to spaces' (1984: 99). In the midst of the mappable, 'planned' or 'readable' city, de Certeau posits an everyday, 'migrational' use of space by its inhabitants, whose unpredictable, rambling routes counter the over-determining power implied by panoptical perspectives of the metropolis, which consider the city as a predictable grid of well-planned streets (93). De Certeau's description of disruptive modes of walking in the city can be used as a metaphor for other kinds of acts and subjectivities that subvert forms of discursive power. For instance, Titlestad invokes de Certeau's 'walks' to elucidate how jazz, and 'jazz writing' like Matshikeze, has been employed as a language of counter-identification in South Africa. Like pedestrians, who occupy and move between spaces in unforeseen ways and 'gradually destabilize the panoptical "order of things"' (Titlestad 2004: 8), so Matshikiza's 'improvisational' writing oscillates ('swings') between spaces and temporalities, undercutting dominant discourses and histories in both London and South Africa.

Chocolates for My Wife, particularly, is filled with accounts of Matshikiza's wanderings around London, which lend the text its meandering, stream-of-consciousness feel. For a black South African banned, in his own country, from freely entering the city unless he had permission from an employer, a seemingly nonchalant statement such as 'So I found myself wandering through London Streets down Trafalgar Square' (Matshikiza 1961a: 18) becomes a radical statement of freedom, as he moves purposelessly through the city's centre. Matshikiza frequently gets lost in the city, as recounted in this passage from a 'Todd in London' column in December 1960:

> I had an appointment for twelve o' clock. I left at ten to give myself time to look around this fabulous, great city of the world where every nation under the sun is to be found. I took my passport and my reference book as well, in case. Off I zoomed in a fast underground train without asking everyone if it was the right train to Leicester Square where most of the theatres are. Ask nobody. Boy from Joh'burg knows everything. (Matshikiza 2000: 82)

He soon realises the folly of his big-city bravado, as he takes the wrong train and misses out on a job because he is late for his appointment. Although he becomes temporarily lost, there is little sense of the disorientation experienced by a figure like Jacobson's Manwera, who has only had 'glimpses' of 'Durban and Cape Town' (1958: 161–162). Matshikiza's confident sense of being a 'Boy from Joh'burg [sic]' means that he boldly sets out to explore 'this fabulous, great city of the world'. He praises London's worldliness, its diversity and expansiveness. As in so much of Matshikiza's London writing, however, the shadow of apartheid South Africa hovers over his freedom, as he quips about taking 'his passport' and 'reference book' (pass) with him on the Underground. Similarly, in an anecdote recounted in *Chocolates for My Wife*, Matshikiza sets off for a walk in Kensington, and his wife has to tell him, 'You can leave those papers bulging in your pocket behind now, you know', to which he jokingly replies, 'Shucks, you're right. I'll go into the street an' see who the hell is going to ask me for my pass' (1961a: 33). Although in the passage above, Matshikiza tries to find his own way through London, he soon learns the London habit of asking policemen for directions: he describes them humorously as helpful automatons: 'There was something very lonesome in the crowded police helmets that made me want desperately to put a sixpence in the slot each time they volunteered promptly, "Firs' set o' traffic lights, secon' turnin' on the right, pas' the roundabout and firs' left, right."' (40). The underlying irony, of course, is that in South Africa, the police would be trying to prevent his movement around the city, or at least would be asking *him* the questions.

The same sense of anxiety and relief around uncensored mobility through the city is conveyed in jazz trumpeter and fellow King-Konger Hugh Masekela's 2004 autobiography, when he recalls his experiences in London during the same time period. In lieu of a reference book, he would carry his passport with him, and a glimpse of a British policeman would send him reaching for his back pocket 'the same way a gunslinger reaches for his pistol in a western film' (Masekela and Cheers 2004: 114). Like Matshikiza, Masekela had to remind himself that 'in England the police were there to protect and not harass me, something that took me a very long time to get used to. Being able to walk around freely, enter any establishment, not worry about curfew, socialize with anybody – all this was new to me' (114). Matshikiza and Masekela's parallel experiences of habitually travelling with identificatory papers in their back pockets and reacting to British policemen with a novel sense of relief shows how, as Masekela puts it, the 'apartheid laws had become etched into [his] subconscious' (114) but also how being in London puts the trauma entailed by apartheid's surveillant society into stark and even absurd relief.

In Matshikiza's writing, getting lost is therefore presented as empowering or as a normal part of city life that does not provoke anxiety. In one incident recounted in his autobiography, however, he employs the metaphor of losing one's way to express the alienating effects of exile. The anecdote begins, like many of Matshikiza's sections, with a description of his wanderings around London: 'I lost my way home but wandered instead in the direction of the crowded Kensington High Street along with the holiday-makers whose curiosity was walking them toward Harrods' (Matshikiza 1961a: 47). He continues:

> I found myself standing at a corner listening to a street violinist. He was about sixty years old, hunchbacked but very intimately, positively present in the street that morning.
> That was the different Saturday morning. Back home was also warm, sunny, busy and energetic. This London street violinist was more than all

of that. He was also personal. He was fiddling away at Liszt's Hungarian Rhapsodies. He was old but inspired. He was white and I was black. He stood there hunched over his music and as possessively over his violin as a loaf of grimy brown bread in a Johannesburg mayoral dustbin. Then his greasy cap lying on the ground, then his few pennies in the cap, then my dirty black hand and body dropping a coin in the white beggar's cap, then his tear-stained face and glassy eyes that hadn't slept since last night. ...

When he stopped he said his name was Lombardo. 'The las' time I played for colonial gen'lman like you was crying also, thinking far away.' Then he chuckled quietly out of a cavity toothless with age.

He said, 'For colonial gen'lman I wish good morning like that, always.' That's how I found my way back home. (1961a: 47)

Matshikiza draws comparisons between 'home' and London on a summery Saturday morning: both are 'warm, sunny, busy and energetic'. However, the street violinist exceeds even these positive attributes and Matshikiza experiences a real moment of communion with him when listening to his music, even as he brings a South African's hyper-awareness of race to their interaction: 'He was white and I was black'. Through the violinist's words, we learn that Matshikiza has been moved to tears, 'thinking far away', but the man's warmth and 'inspired' performance has also brought him 'home'. The spirit with which he plays, a reminder of beauty and gentleness in the midst of deprivation, has brought Matshikiza's thoughts back to South Africa.

While this is a sublime moment of connection between Londoners, we are also reminded of Matshikiza's sense of alienation in the city. Although he may enjoy his wanderings in London, he feels his distance from 'home', and must feel his way back, temporarily, through encounters like this. It is significant that he finds his way home through music. Despite the emphasis placed on Matshikiza's jazz affiliations, we must remember that he was equally steeped in the traditions of western classical music through his formal musical training, and so the violinist's performance of Liszt's *Hungarian Rhapsodies* charts a course back to Matshikiza's own musical background in South Africa, even as its Eastern European provenance invokes other spaces within London. Just as the announcement of Baker Street Station invokes childhood memories of his brother reading him Sherlock Holmes stories, so the street violinist's rendition of Lizst maps a course 'back home'. European works of music and literature are thus overlaid with personal resonances for Matshikiza.

Music also forms the background to many of Matshikiza's other wanderings and encounters in London, especially in the West End. For instance, in *Chocolates for My Wife*, he recounts a night out at the glamorous Pigalle nightclub, which is filled with 'sparkling champagne, royal introductions, Parisienne waitresses, Spanish wine-stewards and two hours of exhilarating entertainment by the American Negro singer and actor, Sammy Davis, Junior' (1961a: 73). In a particularly rich, impressionistic passage in an October 1960 'Todd in London' column, Matshikiza describes a flâneuristic trajectory through cosmopolitan Soho:

> The other day we went to a restaurant in Soho where there are hundreds of palate-tickling Continental eating places. We passed through narrow, winding streets filled with entertainment houses with pictures of French women dancing naked. Others stood fully dressed in a passage with red lights. Chinese girls were smoking in their narrow skirts, slit through the sides from the knee to the thigh, dreaming at you through their slit eyes. Men dressed in top hats an' tail coats, and women in mink and pearls were climbing out of their Cadillacs to see and hear Count Basie at the Trocadero. Round the corner was the Ritz Hotel where one of Nkrumah's ministers was punched in the nose. We passed the Cameo News Theatre where world news is flashed every hour, and we saw 'South African Emergency Lifted'. We ended up at the 'Man in the Moon' restaurant to eat *Fegato Di Vitello Al Burro*, which is calf's liver in butter. Of course we went to watch down at the 'Bunch of Grapes' where Can Themba must come and write the Memoirs of the House of Truth. (Matshikiza 2000: 77–78)

Here we see what Esmé Matshikiza, in an interview, calls '[t]he wonder of Soho and its night-life where London never sleeps. The theatre, cinema, opera, all unsegregated' (quoted in Bernstein 1994: 326). In Matshikiza's description, the excitement, glamour and diversity of the Soho setting is evident in the 'Continental eating places', racy images of 'French women dancing naked', 'Chinese girls' in slit skirts and wealthy patrons going to watch famous pianist Count Basie. These observations, though, are interrupted by a reminder of African politics (the Ritz is where 'one of Nkrumah's ministers was punched in the nose').

What Matshikiza is enjoying here is not so much a specifically English scene, but rather an international, diverse, cosmopolitan version of the city. That the lifting of the South African emergency is mentioned in passing certainly does not mean that Matshikiza views this event as unimportant. In fact, by interrupting this catalogue of Soho's delights with a reminder of South African conditions, Matshikiza demonstrates once more how it is impossible to escape the resonances of South Africa, even within glamorous Soho. He also imagines that *Drum* writer Can

Themba would enjoy writing the memoirs of the 'House of Truth' in a Soho pub: this is what Themba called his Sophiatown home, where black intellectuals, artists and musicians would meet. Matshikiza thus draws a direct link between the pleasures of Soho and the libertine, intellectually lively atmosphere of Sophiatown.

Furthermore, Soho is implicated in ambivalent racial politics, as a careful reading of this passage will reveal. There have been a number of studies of 'cosmopolitan' Soho and all which that adjective, and the area itself, have come to signify, and certainly this passage exemplifies some of the cultural imaginings of Soho as a place where cosmopolitanism existed, as Judith R. Walkowitz puts it, 'in tension with conventional norms and attachments to the nation' (2012: 6). More symbolically, the locus of Soho might be said to represent a utopian vision of a hybridised, multi-ethnic meeting-place. Simultaneously, many of the elements mentioned in the Soho streets suggest a recurring theme of the commodification of the other – whether foreign women, as seen in the Chinese and French women in Matshikiza's description, or black entertainers, as is evident in the popularity of Count Basie and Sammy Davis Junior. Walkowitz explains that Soho has always been a place where 'ethnic entrepreneurs', be they restaurateurs or musicians, have 'adapted their commerce to suit British tastes and travel fantasies' (2012: 7). Matshikiza's description of Soho thus reveals a side of London in which the racism that sparked the Notting Hill riots co-exists with a purportedly inclusive 'cosmopolitanism' which nevertheless entails a potentially exploitative exoticism – something to which Matshikiza, as a jazz musician and because of his experiences with the musical *King Kong*, would have been highly attuned.

Matshikiza's wanderings through London are an expression of de Certeau's errant pedestrians' shortcutting of surveillant power, and his meandering routes take him into spaces in which he provides a contrapuntal reading of the city that destabilises dominant narratives of both London and South Africa. Furthermore, his accounts of these walks are written in an improvisational, jazz-inflected language and form that is itself playful, disruptive, and invokes other global spaces and imaginaries.

'They got locations for us': seeking a home in London

If the freedom London affords the black South African exile in the 1960s is symbolised by his nonchalant wanderings around the city, its limiting aspects are presented most trenchantly in Matshikiza's struggle to find a home for himself and his family. He observes in a December

1960 column how, 'If you are a black man you have to try three times harder than the white man who is also hunting for a place to live. Huge 'planes from all over the world zoom into London every five minutes and shiploads of West Indians every week' (Matshikiza 2000: 84). He realises that this is due to the informal segregation of London's different areas. In the following *Drum* column, published in January 1961, Matshikiza recounts a visit to Nigerian friends in Notting Hill Gate, which the Matshikizas are told 'is the place where most black people live because the fat landlords won't let you live in Garden Hampstead if you're black' (2000: 87). Even more frustratingly, when they finally happen upon an advertisement for a flat stating 'Coloureds Preferred', it turns out to be a cruel ruse by 'a Fascist organisation painting swastikas and sending Coloured people walking all over London on useless errands'. Matshikiza's sadness at this event is conveyed in *Chocolates for My Wife* through the reported words of his young daughter, who says: 'I wish I were a tree. Then there is nothing to worry about' (Matshikiza 1961a: 69).

In *Chocolates for My Wife*, Matshikiza describes desperately scanning the local newspapers for accommodation listings:

> We had now techniqued the whole process of screening through the advertisements for accommodation. We drew a circle in ink on the likely possibilities. We pencilled thinly around the remote possibilities. At the end of each triple newspaper session our reading material resembled our newspapers back home, after we had pencilled around such constant references as 'kaffir', 'coolie', 'hotnot', 'bastard' or 'bitch'.
>
> I've always wanted to make an engraving of those pencil marks. There was a time they resembled a Dalian *surréalité*. (1961a: 48)

In this case his method of 'relational interpolation' – of thinking about South Africa within London – leads him to remark on the similarities, rather than the contrasts, between the two places, as the London newspaper resembles publications 'back home' due to the advertisers' racist terms. As in Nkosi's reference to Kafka in order to describe South African conditions, Matshikiza conveys the absurdity of the advertisers' racial distinctions by comparing the pencil-marked newspaper to a modernist, surreal artwork. *Drum* writer and fellow London exile Bloke Modisane similarly invoked Salvador Dali, in his autobiography, when comparing the 'wasteland' of bulldozed Sophiatown to one of the artist's canvases ([1963] 1990: 33). London is frequently characterised as a palimpsest upon which successive layers of history are scrawled, but Matshikiza's image of an engraving is equally suggestive. His pencil and pen marks demarcate the spaces in which black immigrants are able to live, pinpoint the lexicon through which racism is inscribed in London and make the paper resemble the scored-out page of a publication that has been through the censor's hands, once more bringing London and apartheid South Africa together in a moment of relational interpolation.

As is evident in Matshikiza's appeal to his Nigerian friends for help and his remark about the 'shiploads of West Indians' arriving in London, Matshikiza is aware of the shared experiences of black Londoners and expresses feelings of brotherhood with other black immigrants, which is particularly evident in the following passage in *Chocolates for My Wife*:

> Let me take a try and exploit this burning thing within me that's dying to throw fraternal blessings, greetings, good wishes, at each black man passing by.
>
> 'Hello, brother man, in your broad-brimmed Stetson. My brother Noble wore that hat when I was a kid an' Louis Armstrong played "Gut Bucket Blues", way back in '29.'
>
> 'Hi, brother. You won' smile, but them there blue lyrics in your face, "I got it bad, and that ain't good", maybe we've got something in common. I'm off to see an Englishman about a South African.'
>
> ... Black woman in London streets off shopping. I'm looking in her direction asking to be recognised. She and her black man don' even smile. Get you'se up in the mornin' early. Time to go hunting for rooms. But I didn't know that.
>
> But I didn' know that the black man walking down the Strand wasn' looking for my common curry. I thought how nice it would be if all the black men in the all the Black world and all the white men in all the White World... (1961a: 41)

Matshikiza's sense of identity with the black men and women he encounters on his walks is based on his participation in a global black imaginary, associated with the genres of blues and jazz: one man's hat reminds him both of his brother and of Louis Armstrong's 'Gut Bucket Blues', while in another's face he sees 'them there blue lyrics' from the Duke Ellington standard 'I Got It Bad (And That Ain't Good)'. He knows that he and the other black Londoners have shared experiences of discrimination and hardship in London, when searching for accommodation, for instance. Despite his 'burning' wish for kinship with the other black Londoners, he finds their interest is not reciprocal, concerned as they are with their own quotidian difficulties, and his half-expressed desire for community – 'if all the black men in all the Black world'

– remains unfulfilled. In this passage, Matshikiza recognises that 'fraternal' feelings between himself and other black Londoners are sometimes fraught: that despite their common experiences in the city, and despite his feelings of affiliation with a global black imaginary routed through jazz, solidarity frequently falls short. Matshikiza therefore experiences London as meeting-place where he works out his position within the cartography of global black experience, but at times these attempts at solidarity mark his difference as a South African, disrupting a sense of broad transnational blackness.

As we see in this passage, one of the experiences which he shares with his fellow black Londoners is his difficult search for jobs and his experience of racism in this search. We recall his light-hearted optimism about the potential success of South African musicians like himself who move to London, in his April 1959 *Drum* column: 'But if the Coons can crack London open, there's lots more goods we can fly out there' (2000: 14). In another column, written in July 1960, he notes how 'there is such a great demand for black South African musicians here that I'm sure our guys would walk into jobs blindfolded, straight from the 'plane'. He provides the disclaimer: '*But you must work hard*, chaps. The money is good, but you must be damn good, too' (2000: 75, italics original). Despite Matshikiza's early optimism, Esmé Matshikiza explains that job-hunting in London was as difficult as house-hunting:

> Todd had one disappointment after another. He had a job lined up at the BBC. But he took an ANC concert party to perform at the independence celebrations in Algeria; and when he came back they asked him why he had gone to Algeria; and told him the job was off. A bitter blow, from which he never recovered. He did part-time work for them, and the odd freelancing journalistic work. Our many English friends were helpful and supportive; but there was nothing for someone like Todd in a cultural environment where the school or university to which you went determined the type of job you were, or were not, able to do. This was Britain in the 1960s – warm and welcoming and available at one level, totally insular at another. Todd could not adjust to this culture, nor could he be reconciled to exile. His soul started to die then. (Quoted in Bernstein 1994: 326)

As Esmé Matshikiza intimates here, the Algeria incident lays bare the limits of British liberalism. It is noteworthy that he missed out on a BBC job because he performed in Algeria at the ANC celebrations of the former French colony's newly minted independence in 1962, as this incident raises questions about British attitudes towards anti-colonial revolutionary movements. The official British government approach to

Algeria, although not outwardly supportive of the National Liberation Front (FLN), was not exactly sympathetic to France's position either. Historian Martin Thomas argues that 'the British government regarded Algérie française as an anachronism which France could not maintain indefinitely'. Furthermore, 'Harold Macmillan's Conservative administration also rejected the French claim to be fighting the Cold War in Algeria against leftist pan-Arabism' (Thomas 2002: 172). This latter point is worth bearing in mind in this case, or else one might surmise that the BBC's wariness concerning Matshikiza's support for the new Algerian government might be motivated by anti-communism.

More likely, the BBC's questions for Matshikiza may have been caught up in the ambivalent relationship between British institutions and the ANC in the early 1960s, which was of course not unconnected to Cold War politics. Håkan Thörn has pointed out that the ANC's forming of a military wing, Umkhonto we Sizwe, in 1961 meant 'the end of the carefully built international image of the organization as the "the moderate alternative"' to the Pan African Congress (2006: 54). Nelson Mandela, who headed up Umkhonto we Sizwe, visited Algeria during his 1962 trip across Africa that culminated in London (and the Matshikizas' doorstep) to spend time in an FLN guerrilla training camp (Thörn 2006: 54). The ANC's increasing support of an armed struggle alienated some liberal supporters in the West, and the organisation only managed to gradually regain support from a broader swathe of anti-apartheid activists in the 1970s (Thörn 2006: 55). The suspicion with which the BBC viewed ANC-aligned Todd Matshikiza was thus implicated in these early days of growing distance between liberal British institutions and an organisation that was moving away from its non-violent origins. Although Matshikiza did not express his support for an armed struggle against apartheid overtly, as I have discussed, his description of the soldier depicted below Nelson's Column pointing his rifle 'in the direction of the gold-plated Springbok on South Africa House' (Matshikiza 1961a: 20) suggests that he saw the need for a more robust form of resistance against the apartheid government, as does his involvement in celebrations of Algerian independence won through guerrilla tactics. Moreover, this moment of rejection shows that despite Matshikiza's early absorption and legibility within British liberal institutions, and publishing, media and theatre circles, colonial attitudes and British chauvinism would always limit the degree to which black South Africans could assimilate into cultural spheres in London. Matshikiza was expected to perform a certain role as an exciting new writer and composer, but once his politics became unpalatable or his associations questionable, he was rejected by institutions that had previously embraced him.

If British institutions felt ambivalent about Matshikiza, the feeling was mutual. As we have seen, Matshikiza's experience of London as 'warm and welcoming and available at one level, totally insular at another' explains why he could call London 'a great, free city' in his BBC monologue, after complaining to Langston Hughes in an October 1960 letter that 'London for the Black man isn't even a fool's paradise' (in Graham and Walters 2010: 114). Matshikiza sent a copy of *Chocolates to my Wife* to Langston Hughes in November 1961 with the following note, which sums up his disillusionment with London: 'We meant to write each day, then we are put off from writing by having to cope with the English and their land. And if I have paid them any compliments in this book, it was in error' (in Graham and Walters 2010: 132).

Chocolates for My Wife concludes with a particularly acerbic commentary on 'race' and space in London:

> In London my favourite pub is the Bull and Bush where I go to meet my friend Fred. He's going to find us a nice London home. When I first met him I asked him where the African people live in London, like in Joh'burg they got locations for us. Fred said earnestly, 'Well, looking at it this way, I know the zones go something like you'll find the English in British West Hampstead, the Jews in Goldschtein's Green, and the Indians in Belsize Pakistan. The other races are scattered all over the place. (Matshikiza 1961a: 127–128)

This passage begins with a direct – although ironically couched – counterpoint between Johannesburg's 'locations' (urban areas where black South Africans were forced to live) and London's 'zones'. Matshikiza reads London's spaces through South Africa's absurd, racist terminology, recognising that there is informal ghettoisation along ethnic lines in London, captured in wordplay that conveys the global nature of London and the dislocated spatiality of the city. The typically English 'park' of 'Belsize Park' is turned, linguistically and culturally, into *Park*-istan. In a particularly dislocating formulation, West Hampstead is called 'British West Hampstead' because of its concentration of working-class British residents; as Matshikiza explains in a January 1961 *Drum* column, 'West Hampstead is the home of the working class who calls this part the proud British West' (2000: 88). West Hampstead's white 'working class' who call themselves 'British' claim this category for themselves, suggesting inversely that Londoners of other races are not 'British'; this formulation is therefore a reminder of the racism and insularity present in London. Amid these ethnically or class-defined spaces, 'other races', including, presumably, black South Africans, are 'scattered all over the place'. Even though Matshikiza has experienced racism in this somewhat segregated city, in this conclusion he recognises that black Londoners have a degree of freedom; in contrast to South Africa's system of 'locations', they are not assigned by law to specific areas. But there is certainly an air of ironic pathos in Matshikiza's hope that Fred will find them a 'nice London home'. London is *not* Matshikiza's 'home' – he has been forced to live in exile in a sometimes exhilarating, sometimes hostile city. Although he is not assigned a 'location', which is as freeing as anonymity, he is also out of place; he literally cannot find a place to live, and he experiences alienation. Like the trope of getting lost and being far from home, the act of being 'scattered about' in London implies disintegration as well as freedom.

Although Matshikiza declared in a letter to Hughes, as early as November 1960, that he and Esmé had 'already decided to quit this cold and damp people-less place' (in Graham and Walters 2010: 118), they only left London in 1964, moving to Zambia, where he worked as a broadcaster. Matshikiza wrote his last 'Todd in London' column in 1961 and published *Chocolates for My Wife* later that year. According to John Matshikiza, by 1961 'the romance with the British way of life was beginning to pall, and he was desperately missing South Africa' (2000: 90). Matshikiza continued to experience profound homesickness when in Zambia, and after the death of two of his brothers in South Africa, he declined further and died of a sudden illness in 1968.

Both Matshikiza's *Drum* columns and his autobiography provide a nuanced commentary on his first years as an exile in London. In his London writing, Matshikiza foregrounds the intertwined histories of South Africa, London and other spaces. Through his employment of 'Matshikeze', he engages with a global black imaginary, further extending the worldly reach of his writing and providing a playful mode of counter-identification that takes on new resonances in London. His descriptions of London are set in counterpoint with his memories of South Africa, resulting in moments of 'relational interpolation' during which each space interacts with and comments on the other. The intricate webs of spatiality and temporality in Matshikiza's work provide a paradigmatic example of the often subversive, contrapuntal historiographies carried out by many South African writers in London.

Notes

1. Johnny Dankworth and Ted Heath were both well-known British jazz musicians and band leaders.
2. Matshikiza's 'With the Lid Off' and 'Todd in London' columns are collected in *With the Lid Off: South African Insights from Home and Abroad 1959 – 2000* (2000), which also includes articles by his son, John Matshikiza.
3. See Christopher Ballantine, 'Revisiting Todd Matshikiza's King Kong' and Mareli Stolp, 'Review: King Kong, Legend of a Boxer, dir. Jonathan Munby', both in *South African Music Studies*, 38 (2018).
4. For instance, the 2017 Fugard Theatre revival of *King Kong* was marketed as 'The iconic South African hit musical'.
5. South African jazz sub-genres which combined western jazz with traditional African musical elements and instrumentation.
6. In the preface to *Drum: A Venture into the New Africa*, Sampson thanks 'Robin Denniston of Collins' (1956: 12). Denniston also went on to publish Anthony's Sampson's later books, such as the popular *Anatomy of Britain* (1962) under Hodder & Stoughton.
7. All archival material related to Hodder & Stoughton's correspondence with Todd Matshikiza and the publication of his work is derived from the Hodder & Stoughton papers in the London Metropolitan Archives (hereafter LMA).
8. Despite not living in South Africa during the 1950s, Abrahams contributed to *Drum* and associated with many of the magazine's writers. He also judged the short story competition which Can Themba won, launching Themba's career as a journalist.
9. For a careful study of these routes of cross-cultural influence in the origins of South African jazz, see Ballantine (2012).
10. Gunner quotes this phrase ('global ecumene') from Hannerz (1994: 184).
11. See McDonald (2009: 105). Matshikiza was also 'listed' under the amended Suppression of Communism Act in April 1966, meaning that his work could not be distributed within South Africa.
12. Indeed, Matshikiza appeared on the Third Programme several times, an 'illustrated talk' on South African jazz in 1956 – recorded in South Africa – and a programme of 'African Protest Music' he introduced and curated in 1962 (see *Radio Times* archive, http://genome.ch.bbc.co.uk).
13. See Gunner (2005).
14. I have been influenced in my use of Said by Alexander Greer Hartwiger's article, 'The Postcolonial Flâneur' (2016), in which Hartwiger similarly applies Said's contrapuntal method to a 'reading' of the city.
15. In Afrikaans, literally: 'Oh, Lord, God!'; 'Mighty, Jesus!'; idiomatically: 'Good God!'.
16. As reported by his son, John Matshikiza, in *With the Lid Off* (2000: 223).

17 'We Sing of Freedom' programme, Anti-apartheid Movement Archives, 1963, MSS AAM 1463, www.aamarchives.org/file-view/category/18–1960s.html?s_f_id=4025.
18 Sono is referred to as 'Fakile Sono' and then 'Fikile Sono' on the same page and a number of times subsequently – the first mention of his name appears to be a typographical error.
19 As far as I could tell, there is no known activist or political figure of this name, though of course this may be an alias for a real-life individual.
20 Parktown is a suburb of Johannesburg which was demarcated for white South Africans only during apartheid.

3

Waiting and watching in the city's pleasure streets: Arthur Nortje's poems set in London

One of Arthur Nortje's most famous poems, 'Waiting' (1967), begins with these memorable lines:

> The isolation of exile is a gutted
> warehouse at the back of pleasure streets:
> the waterfront of limbo stretches panoramically –
> night the beautifier lets the lights
> dance across the wharf.
> I peer through the skull's black windows
> wondering what can credibly save me. (Lines 1–7)

'The isolation of exile' is compared to an empty warehouse in London's docklands, a symbol both of commerce and the ruin and waste inherent in modernity: the warehouse is 'gutted', suggesting visceral violence and abandonment. It no longer serves its purpose, as it is emptied of commodities for trade. Nortje suggests that the loneliness felt by the exile entails an emptying-out of the self and one's identity, which leads to a lack of purpose and meaning. The docklands imagery here, however, intimates that this isolation is not only a consequence of physical displacement from one's home country ('exile') but is also associated with a larger sense of existential alienation emanating from life in urban modernity. London, and specifically the Thames and its banks, as in T.S. Eliot's *The Waste Land* (1922), is made to symbolise the qualities of twentieth-century modernity. The empty warehouse is not only 'gutted', but is hidden behind 'pleasure streets', a phrase which conjures up images of bodily desire and satisfaction in drinking houses and brothels. The glamour of these 'pleasure streets' is an obfuscating façade for the bleak reality of 'exile'. Yet, the poem moves between the desolate and the beautiful, suggesting that the 'pleasure' experienced in these streets may be just as deeply felt as the 'isolation': in the following lines, 'the waterfront of limbo stretches panoramically – / night the beautifier lets the lights / dance across the wharf'. The speaker is in 'limbo', 'waiting' for certainty and for a sense of belonging, in between and out of place in 'exile', but this state is represented lyrically as a beautiful, 'panoramic' view, by a set of lights reflected in the water. At night, even the gutted warehouse blends into this attractive waterfront panorama and becomes part of the speaker's enjoyment of London after dark. His focus oscillates between enjoyment and isolation. In the next line, the speaker 'peers' out of 'black windows', yet despite the continuation of the architectural imagery, these are not the windows of the empty warehouse. We have now entered the speaker's body, his 'skull', and rather than experiencing bodily pleasure in the city, he is 'wondering what can credibly save [him]'. His eyes are significantly 'black', suggesting that his engagement with London, and with his own body, is filtered through an inescapable awareness of his race. Thus, in these few lines, Nortje moves between London as setting and London as symbol, and between pleasure and loss: between the gutted warehouse and the pleasure street. This is both a productive and a conflicted space.

In Arthur Nortje's poetry, London is the stage upon which he performs various personae, which enable him to reconfigure and renegotiate his own position as a 'coloured', 'exiled' South African writer. London, through its literary associations as an embodiment of modernity, allows Nortje to create a nexus between physical displacement from South Africa, his ambivalence about his mixed-race origins, and the psychological and social alienation intrinsic to late twentieth-century life. In Nortje's London-based poetry, he depicts his attempts to work out his identity and his positionality and national or cultural belonging via his engagement with the city through his body. Ralph Pordzik suggests that Nortje's poetry 'stands halfway between the first generation of modernist-inspired South African poets, such as Dennis Brutus, and the Soweto poetry of the 1970s with its programmatic claim to a literature of radical change, of candidness and of representational accuracy' (1998: 35). My reading evinces how Nortje's poetic engagement with London informed both the starting point of this development – his engagement with modernism and modernity – and provided a subject and setting that enabled his trajectory towards a confessional poetic voice.

The meanings of 'exile' in Nortje's London poems

Arthur Nortje was born in 1942 in Oudtshoorn, in the Southern Cape, to Cecilia Nortje, a coloured South African woman, and a white Jewish student. He grew up in Port Elizabeth, mostly in the coloured township of Gelvandale, living with his aunt and with family friends, all of whom encouraged his reading. At Paterson High School in Port Elizabeth he was taught English by the poet and activist Dennis Brutus. Nortje completed a Bachelor of Arts at the University College of the Western Cape, the assigned university for coloured students under apartheid, where he majored in English and psychology. During this time he published a number of poems. After working for a short period as a teacher in Port Elizabeth, Nortje left South Africa in 1965 to take up a scholarship at Jesus College, Oxford, arranged by the National Union of South African Students (NUSAS). At Oxford University, Nortje read for his degree in English literature, receiving tuition on such writers as Chaucer, Shakespeare, Milton, Fielding, Wordsworth, Keats, Austen and Dickens, amongst others. When originally thinking about leaving South Africa, Nortje had considered moving to Canada, as he had friends there, including Joan Cornelius, a love interest from South Africa, to whom many of his poems are addressed. In July 1967, after the completion of his Oxford degree, Nortje left for Canada to take up a teaching post at Hope Secondary School in British Columbia and then briefly at a school in Toronto. In July 1970, he returned to Oxford University as a BPhil student, and a number of London poems derive from that year. In December 1970, however, he died in Oxford, having taken an overdose of barbiturates.[1]

In the sizeable body of criticism on the poetry of Arthur Nortje, now recognised amongst the finest of South Africa's postwar lyric poets, the chief paradigm through which the work has been viewed has been that of exile. 'Exile' is certainly a word and subject which recurs frequently in Nortje's poems; 'Exiles Silenced', for instance, is a 1962 poem about the 'mute fury' of exiled activists (line 16). An early poem written in Oxford is entitled 'Spring Picture in Exile', suggesting that he has entered this exilic state in which he must 'slog among the ruins and the crushed roots': he feels disconnected from his origins (his 'roots') (line 16). 'In Exile' (1966) describes a wind-swept street scene in either London or Oxford which reminds Nortje of South Africa; without these reminders of home, though, 'the soul decays in exile' (line 16). Exile is also of course a central term in 'Waiting', as discussed above. No wonder, then, that critics have noted the prevalence of the 'isolation of exile' in Nortje's poems, foregrounding his liminal state 'on the fringes of this new society', as Jacques Alvarez-Pereyre puts it (1984: 162), or 'on the margin of modern society', as Dirk Klopper writes (Nortje 2000: xxix).

Critics have also emphasised the loss and trauma that exile entails, which is evident in Nortje's poetry. Wole Soyinka groups Nortje with other exiled postcolonial writers and describes his poetry as 'permeated with the visceral protest of a sensibility that tries hard, but cannot reconcile itself with a condition of forced exile'; Nortje had to come 'to terms with the contradictions of this liberating vista, England, which spelt freedom and self-realisation but which, nevertheless, inserted a real territory of loss' (2002). One cannot deny that Nortje's poetry depicts this 'real territory of loss', but his reaction to 'exile' and the use of the term and concept in his poetry is more complex and ambivalent than with some other 'exiled' postcolonial writers, for a number of reasons. In complicating Nortje's exile, I draw on the work of Sarah Nuttall, who argues in favour of a reading of Nortje's poems that emphasises his immersion in Britain, and particularly in London, as well as his alienation. Nuttall suggests that 'in addition to the powerful framework of exile … Nortje's work has much to tell us about the still latent histories of diaspora in the African context' and that his London poems 'reveal a familiarity with and even an embeddedness in the city which still has to be adequately discussed by critics' (2004: 42). In this chapter, I respond to this critical lacuna. London is the locus in which Nortje's 'exile' is experienced and also somewhat ameliorated and complicated by his familiarity with the city and his experience of pleasure within its streets. This is encapsulated in 'Return to the City of the Heart', a poem written during a brief visit to London in March 1970, in which Nortje suggests that London provided comfort during the 'isolation of exile': 'Despite the irony, she, city, / suckled my exile' (lines 52–53). While Nortje characterises himself as an 'exile', the city 'suckles' him, providing motherly nourishment and comfort; there is 'irony' here, as he acknowledges, because the place of exile provides comfort for the exile. It is this 'ironic' relationship that I wish to explore. Moreover, Nortje employs irony and a variety of performative personae to represent and work out this relationship.

Even before arriving in Britain, Nortje's response to the term 'exile' was complex. Following the 1960 Sharpeville massacre, increasingly tyrannical laws were enforced upon black South Africans. For instance, the Unlawful Organisations Act of April 1960 outlawed anti-apartheid parties such as the African National Congress (ANC) and the Pan

Africanist Congress (PAC). In July 1962, the General Law Amendment (or Sabotage) Act was passed, 'thereby silencing 102 anti-apartheid activists, including the novelist Alex La Guma and the poets Dennis Brutus and Cosmo Pieterse, and forcing the closure of most of the leading oppositional periodicals of the time' (McDonald 2009: 33). Peter McDonald explains the effect of this systematic 'silencing':

> Following the terms of the Suppression of Communism Act, this new 'gagging clause' banned various writers and journalists as persons, removing their rights of association, among other things, but it also made it illegal for them to be quoted in public. In the years ahead, the government would use this kind of legislation to silence most of the established black writers of the 1950s and 1960s and the leaders of the Black Consciousness movement in the 1970s. (McDonald 2009: 33)

Nortje thus arrived in the United Kingdom at the same time that many other South African activists and writers were fleeing their home country, often for London, because they were banned by the apartheid authorities, found the racism in South Africa untenable or feared for their life or liberty. In a letter to his friend James Davidson, who lived in Canada, Nortje sums up the political and intellectual mood of this period:

> News from this side of the world is sadly lacking. Nobody seems to be big enough to hit the headlines any more. All in jail, languishing; or retired from active this and that (the term 'Politics' is either taboo or obsolete, one does not know which); or exiled by choice like you and Rosemary and Gerald Jeftha; or planning to move out, like –?! Latest departures is that of Frank Landman and his wife. Theirs are exit visas – more of us are becoming persona non grata. Do you wonder now why those who want to be safe and popular refuse to THINK? It is dangerous – all you can think is that we are in rats' alley where the dead men lost their bones. (Arthur Nortje to James Davidson, 15 March 1964, Manuscript Collection: Arthur Nortje, UNISA Archives, Accession no: 61, File no 4.6)

Nortje highlights how 'politics' and even 'thinking' more generally became 'dangerous' after Sharpeville, resulting either in self-censorship, imprisonment or exile on the part of intellectuals and activists. He references a line from T.S. Eliot's *The Waste Land* (1922) – 'I think we are in rats' alley / Where the dead men lost their bones' (lines 115–116) – to describe the bleakness of the situation in South Africa, just as he later references Eliot in his London-based poems to convey the 'isolation of exile'. 'Exile' in the South African context held specific historical and political connotations, associated with the anti-apartheid struggle and particularly with the members of the ANC.

As Nortje was not an active anti-apartheid activist and had not been banned or had his poetry censored, he had a tenuous claim to the strictly politicised term 'exile', which he acknowledges in 'Autopsy' (1966), a poem about Dennis Brutus, which begins:

> My teachers are dead men. I was too young
> to grasp their anxieties, too nominal an exile
> to mount such intensities of song (Lines 1–3)

Unlike the 'broken guerrillas, gaunt and cautious / exit visas in their rifled pockets' ('Autopsy', lines 21–22), Nortje was not forced out of the country for political reasons. Rather, he felt compelled to leave South Africa to further both his academic and literary career, and to escape the indignities imposed upon him by the apartheid regime. This produced in him a sense of ambivalence and even guilt around the term 'exile'. Nortje expresses his desire to leave South Africa in a 1964 poem, 'Finally Friday'. Responding to the oppressive torpor of 1960s South Africa, in which 'the end of black resistance' has been announced on national radio, he imagines the 'voice of the world' saying to his 'Coloured education' (lines 10–11):

> Go now, brown man, go and find me
> In Rome the eternal metropolis
> Paris under the Eiffel tower
> London by the Thames, New York,
> Toronto, further West, a continental
> trek, the soul's great odyssey, returning
> to Cape Town under the mountain tomorrow
> where the world will be a wedding. (Lines 12–19)

In this poem, displacement from one's home country is figured not so much as a loss, but rather as an opportunity to discover the 'voice of the world' on a journey through modern, cosmopolitan metropolises that include London. In an earlier draft of the poem, the line 'London by the Thames, New York' was originally 'In London, by Shakespeare's dear old river', later replaced with 'In London, by Spenser's dear old river', foregrounding Nortje's vision of London as a literary city (Manuscript Collection: Arthur Nortje, UNISA Archives, Accession no 61, File no 2.5, 2.1.2.). Nortje expresses the idealistic hope that his exile to any of these cities will be a temporary, soul-transforming 'odyssey' west, following the movement of the sun, which will end in a joyful return to a utopian Cape Town.

While 'odyssey' has classical connotations, suggesting an epic journey, 'trek' is significantly a South Africanism that is specifically associated with the 'Great Trek' of the Boers from the Cape Colony into the interior in the mid-nineteenth century. Graham Pechey writes of the word 'trek':

> If from the start this exodus of Afrikaners from British rule was hedged about by the obvious Old Testament parallels, this monosyllable that represented that exodus was nevertheless firmly anchored in an everyday world of things: *trek* delivers the mundane and the mythological in the same breath. (Pechey 2004: 14)

The word developed beyond its South African connotations and made its way into global English in the twentieth century, through its use in Wilfred Owen's 'Strange Meeting' (1918): 'They will be swift with the swiftness of the tigress. / None will break ranks though nations trek from progress' (lines 28–29). Pechey explains that, for Owen, '[t]he act of dropping *trek* into that place is a poetic move of huge importance: never before had it carried such accumulated weight of implication, and never again could it be innocuously deployed' (2004: 15). Pechey explores how South African poet Roy Campbell, whom Nortje would almost certainly have read, paraphrased Owen's line in 'The Sling' (1933): 'Where none break ranks though down the whole race treks' (line 56). Rather than representing migration into an empty interior then, 'trek' comes to signal, in Owen's and Campbell's poems, the decline of civilisation. Nortje's use of 'trek' here undermines the optimistic tone of these lines through its association with Owen's and Campbell's pessimistic view of modern civilisation. Nortje reminds the reader of the word's mythical Afrikaner origins and re-appropriates the term ironically, to describe the journey of a young coloured South African not into the interior of South Africa, but beyond the country's shores. In this way, he echoes Ingrid Jonker's employment of the word in her 1960 poem 'The Child Who Was Shot Dead by Soldiers at Nyanga', written in response to the Sharpeville massacre, in which she imagines how 'the child grown to a man treks all over Africa / the child grown to a giant travels through the whole world / without a pass' (lines 23–25). In both Jonker's poem and Nortje's, 'trek', despite its South African etymology, is used to describe travel beyond South Africa.

The last line of Nortje's 'Finally Friday' is similarly layered with meaning: not only is the statement 'the world is a wedding' a Talmudic saying indicating a sense of celebration, an injunction to seize the moment, it is also the title of a short story by American writer Delmore Schwartz, published in 1949. In the conclusion of this story about a group of bohemian intellectuals in 1940s New York, one of the characters proposes that 'The world is a wedding' and explains it thus:

> I don't mean to say that this life is just a party, any kind of party. It is a wedding, the most important kind of party, full of joy, fear, hope and ignorance. And at this party there are enough places and parts for everyone, and if no one can play every part, yet everyone can come to the party, everyone can come to the wedding feast. (Schwartz 1949: 79)[2]

It is plausible that Nortje may have read this story, but even if he had not, Schwartz's explanation of this phrase foregrounds its association with a messianic vision of inclusivity, where 'everyone can come to the party', something that would have appealed to Nortje as a coloured South African excluded from many sectors of South African society. The importance of this phrase for Nortje is also highlighted by an anecdote recounted by South African writer Richard Rive in his autobiography, *Writing Black* (1981), in which Rive recalls how he was introduced to Nortje through Cosmo Pieterse. Nortje read some of his poems aloud to Rive, and Rive questioned 'a line which went something like "All the world will be a wedding"'; Rive reports that Nortje then 'argued interminably about its appropriateness and suitability' (Rive 1981: 29). The importance of this hopeful vision was associated with Nortje's literary aspirations. In his 'Oxford Journal', which he kept from 1965 to 1967, he writes about having his poems published: 'it's ... very exciting to find an outlet. It makes you feel that the world is a wedding' (Oxford Journal: 29, Manuscript Collection: Arthur Nortje, UNISA). Exile for Nortje thus represented not only a necessary time abroad before a non-racist South African regime could be ushered in, but also a realm in which he could achieve his personal aspirations of finding an 'outlet' for both publication and creative freedom, as well as a sense of inclusion in a literary milieu.

Nortje was aware of his status as a 'nominal' exile when leaving South Africa and thus his use of the term in his poetry is loaded and provisional. Nortje's anxieties around the South African connotations of 'exile' were inflected by the perennial tension between the role of the poet and the role of the activist. Nortje's affiliation with organised black resistance against apartheid in South Africa was ambivalent; although he joined Jacari (Joint Action Committee Against Racial Intolerance) while in the United Kingdom and expressed solidarity for the struggle in several poems, he claimed 'I'm not strictly an organization man' (Oxford Journal: 139, Manuscript Collection: Arthur Nortje, UNISA), and, in 'Native's Letter' (1970), explains his position as a poet: 'some of us must storm the castles / some define the happening' (lines 35–36). Nortje both sympathised with and distinguished himself from political exiles and political activists, seeing the 'commitment' of the writer as 'defining' events in South Africa and abroad, exposing the truth and myth underlying the 'happenings' and, most importantly, defining and negotiating his own position as a coloured South African in relation to both home and 'exile'. This axiom may appear as a statement of liberal neutrality but can also be read as conveying a wistful, regretful tone, as if he knows that the glory belongs to those who 'storm the castles'. It is worth bearing in mind that, as David Bunn notes, coloured South Africans had an 'uncertain status in opposition movements' until the late 1960s (1996: 40). It is also possible that his hesitation around active participation in the anti-apartheid struggle had much to do with his complex relationship to blackness. Dirk Klopper suggests that Nortje was uneasy, for instance, about being awarded a NUSAS scholarship intended for a member of the black community, towards which he felt a contradictory sympathy and estrangement (2004a: 13).

Nortje uses the setting of London as a trigger for references to the political situation in 1960s South Africa. In the same way that Matshikiza engages in relational interpolation in his texts, spatiality in Nortje's poems is fragmented, enacting the displacement of exile, and these references to South Africa also give rise to an exploration of his position in relation to the anti-apartheid struggle. In 'Cosmos in London' (1966), the poem's title denotes a sense of other spaces contained within London. The first two stanzas are set in Trafalgar Square and in a jazz club in Kentish Town which echoes with 'sonorities of elsewhere' (line 16). Then we move to a memory of Nortje's 'friend in drama' performing as Macbeth back in South Africa (line 9). The 'friend in drama' referenced in the poem is actor, playwright and poet Cosmo Pieterse: Nortje describes how he 'once did Macbeth / loping across like a beast in Bloemfontein' (line 17), a performance which he also describes in a letter to a friend. In the letter, the location of the performance is different, but some of the wording is the same, as Nortje remembers 'the brilliant Shakespearian actor' Pieterse's 'superb headlong loping as a brutish Macbeth some time ago in Port Elizabeth' (Arthur Nortje to James Davidson, 15 March 1964, Manuscript Collection: Arthur Nortje, UNISA Archives, Accession no: 61 File no 4.6). Pieterse worked for the BBC World Service in London and edited anthologies of plays and poems for the Heinemann African Writers Series, including *Seven South African Poets* (1971), in which Nortje's work was published posthumously. The poem, in its title and its scope, thus references both specific South African figures and moments, and broader themes and spaces.

My identification of Pieterse as the 'friend in drama', moreover, illuminates Nortje's play on words in the title, as 'Cosmos in London' is turned into 'Cosmo's in London', an announcement of the exile's presence that resonates with the poem's themes. The poem ends with the Robben Island scene and with the speaker's desire to bring South African activists (some of them imprisoned) to London. The content of 'Cosmos in London' thus exemplifies the contrapuntal method of much South African writing about London, and the approach of this book too. It also brings home the longing, guilt and trauma experienced in exile. Yet the title evokes even more: what does it mean that the cosmos, the 'world', is found in London? Since South Africa is the only other country mentioned, does this speak to South Africa's internal cosmopolitanism, or imply that South Africa is the speaker's whole 'world' beyond London? Furthermore, few South Africans can read the word 'cosmos' and not think of the small pink and white flowers that carpet the Highveld every spring. Yet cosmos flowers are not indigenous to South Africa: a South American plant, they were originally germinated from bags of horse feed brought in from Mexico by the British during the South African War (1899–1902). The word 'cosmos', including its worldly connotations, speaks through the imported flower back to the interconnected colonial histories of Britain and South Africa, and towards thinking and writing about these entangled identities and narratives within London during the latter half of the twentieth century.

The poem begins with that London location that is important to many South Africans writing London: Trafalgar Square, where 'Pigeons perch on our shoulders as we pose / against the backdrop of a placid embassy, / South Africa House, a monument of granite' (lines 5–7). As in Matshikiza's writing, South Africa is present in London in the form of its deceptively 'placid', but also coldly 'granite' embassy. However, the poem does not travel at this point back to South Africa, but to a jazz show at 'the Tally Ho saloon at Kentish Town' (line 10). As the band plays, it is a sonic memory, and a collective one, shared by Nortje and his 'friend in drama', that triggers thoughts of South Africa: 'our minds echo sonorities of elsewhere' (line 16). Although the connection between the jazz band and thoughts about South Africa is not overtly explained, Nortje implies the networks between South Africa, jazz and resistance. The sound-memories that are evoked in this moment are the cheering of the crowd at Pieterse's performance of *Macbeth* and the chanting of the slogan, 'Oh come back Africa!', a reference to the ANC's rallying refrain, *mayibuye iAfrika!*, also variously translated as 'Bring back Africa' or 'Let Africa return' (lines 17–23). As Annie Gagiano suggests, Nortje uses the saying not only to express his sympathy with South African activists, but also 'to express his own yearning' (2004: 130). He similarly evokes this call for a South African renaissance, and for South Africans to return to their homeland, in 'Waiting' (1967):

> Come back, come back mayibuye
> cried the breakers of stone and cried the crowds
> cried Mr Kumalo before the withering fire
> mayibuye Afrika. (Lines 18–21)

While Nortje did not participate in any organised manner in the struggle and rather focused on 'defining the happening', in 'Cosmos in London' and 'Waiting', he, like Pieterse, uses the ANC slogan to register his solidarity with anti-apartheid activists.

The next stanza moves to the struggle's symbolic centre, Robben Island, with the rhythmic lines: 'There was a man who broke stone / next to a man who whistled Bach' (lines 25–26). The distance between London and Robben Island is figured by the juxtaposition of the improvisational jazz music in the Tally Ho saloon with the stone-breaking work song, set in counterpoint with the prison guard's whistling of Bach. The contrast between the two spaces is further explored when the poet declares:

> Tobias should be in London. I could name
> Brutus, Mandela, Lutuli[3] – but that memory
> disturbs the order of the song, and whose
> tongue can stir in such a distant city? (Lines 33–36)

After calling the exiles back to South Africa ('come back, Africa!') and imagining Robben Island while in London, Nortje now yearns for the South African activists to travel to London, a place which provides freedom and shelter. The names refer to Dennis Brutus, ANC leader Nelson Mandela, ANC President Albert Luthuli and the activist, scientist and NUSAS chair Philip Tobias. However, this recitation of names in connection with London 'disturbs the order of the song'. Imagining these activists in London causes the song to fail, because 'whose / tongue can stir in such a distant city?' In 'All Hungers Pass Away' (1970), Nortje similarly calls Britain 'a land where rhythm fails' (line 8). 'Cosmos in London' continues:

> The world informs her seasons, and she,
> Solid with a kind of grey security,
> Selects and shapes her own strong tendencies
> We are here, nameless, staring at ourselves. (Lines 37–40)

London is found, as Michael Chapman comments, to 'be pernicious: stifling to the dangerous hopes and dreams of a young South African political idealist', because of its 'security' (1979: 67–68). In the absence of the named political activists, the exiled South Africans are 'nameless', staring at themselves in futile narcissism.

Even though exiles such as Nortje enjoyed the 'security' of Britain, exile could be stultifying and guilt-inducing; as he writes in 'From the Way I Live Now' (1970), 'Unjustly do / I live the way I do now, / accepting smiles and favours for my buried ones' (lines 22–23). While Nortje's protest 'song' falls silent in London, the suffering endured by the prisoners on Robben Island provides inspiration for the exile: 'It seems at times as if I am / this island's lover, and can sing her soul' (lines 41–42). In the poem's final lines, he demonstrates the powerful symbolism of Robben Island by employing the image of the sea crashing against the island, to represent the unrelenting torment of exile: 'The rat-toothed sea eats rock, and who escapes / a lover's quarrel will never rest his roots' (lines 47–48). While London is the locus of exile, Robben Island symbolises both the source of displacement – the apartheid state – and the organised struggle from which exiles are removed. 'Cosmos in London' serves as a poignant reminder that while Nortje is immersed in the pleasures of London, such as sitting in Trafalgar Square in the sunshine or listening to jazz music in a club, he simultaneously experiences the loss and trauma of being wrenched from his homeland, and ambivalence about the potency of writing about South Africa from stultifying Britain.

'Exile' was thus a fraught designation for Nortje, containing a sense of the tenuousness of his claim to exilic status, his guilt at escaping the brutal realities of South Africa while others suffered, as well as the real difficulties of adjusting to a new country. Furthermore, in Nortje's poems, 'exile' takes on a further, metaphorical meaning, aligned with the existential exile of the modern subject. Always open to the irony, slipperiness and multivalency of every term, Nortje frequently grafts broader concerns of the alienation associated with capitalist modernity, represented by metropolises such as London, on to the narrower sense of geographic 'exile'. Many critics have complicated Nortje's exile by forging connections between Nortje's physical displacement from South Africa and his sense of alienation as a coloured South African in apartheid South Africa. Adam Schwartzman suggests, for instance, that even before his 'literal exile', Nortje, 'through his engagement with the experience of 1960s South Africa ravaged by bannings, arrests and forced removals ... had made the language of displacement, estrangement and isolation his own' (1999: 4–5).

Nortje traces the origins of his displacement within South Africa in a 1970 poem written in London, 'Questions and Answers', which includes a section entitled 'Exile from the first':

> Exile was implanted
> in the first pangs of paradise. This land became
> a refuge for adventurers.
> And who remembers history
> need not trouble my
> head with tales. I underwent fire
> baptism, reared in rags, schooled
> in the violence of the mud. (Lines 1–7)

Nortje references the Garden of Eden to convey the corruption of the 'paradise' of South Africa by imperial 'adventurers', which necessarily entails 'exile'. In the third stanza, Nortje also refers to his disavowing white father as a symbol of this corruption:

> white trash
> coursing through my blood
> for all the unalienable seasons,
> and I have an incurable
> malaise that makes me walk restlessly
> through the sewers of these distant cities. (Lines 28–32)

His father's bloodline is 'trash' and Nortje's lineage results in 'malaise' – both disease and a sense of being 'ill-at-ease'. Nortje's lack of belonging, Jacques Berthoud argues, cannot be understood outside its author's history as coloured; 'by virtue of its location in his personal biography, his neurosis has public resonances' (1984: 7). Drawing on the work of Homi K. Bhabha, Dirk Klopper similarly suggests that 'Nortje's location as subject is the postcolonial site of marginality and hybridity', due to his mixed racial descent, his disavowal by his white father and his childhood on the margins of South African societies, in the townships of Port Elizabeth. Like Schwartzman, Klopper claims that '[i]t would be erroneous to attribute Nortje's alienation to his having lost a sense of community on leaving South Africa' because 'even in South Africa, he felt himself to be incomplete and indeterminate' (2004b: 877). Thus, according to these critics, Nortje's background as a coloured South African results in an internal sense of displacement, and South Africa's diseased state, inextricable from Nortje's personal 'malaise', leads him to physical exile in 'these distant cities'.

Drawing on the writing of South African novelist and academic Zoë Wicomb, I seek to challenge the usefulness of situating Nortje as 'incomplete', indeterminate' and 'marginal'. While the deprivation and dispossession Nortje was subject to as a coloured person under apartheid would have led to a sense of a loss and anxiety, one should not fall into the trap of assuming a cause and effect relationship between his coloured identity and his sense of alienation, particularly when adopting Bhabha's ideas about hybridity. In her essay 'Shame and Identity: The Case of the Coloured in South Africa', Wicomb has critiqued the application of Bhabha's theories to narratives of South African coloured life as overly essentialist and implying a pre-existing racial 'purity'.[4] She furthermore suggests that aligning coloured existence with the concepts of liminality, marginality and hybridity plays into 'the tragic mode where lived experience is displaced by an aesthetics of theory. How, one is tempted to ask, do people who live in communities inhabit, spookily and preciously, a rim of inbetween reality? Symbolically, of course, and therefore ... in silence' (Wicomb 1998: 101). Although Nortje's lived experience as a coloured South African is important in the ways in which it plays into his sense of exile, applying concepts of hybridity and marginality to Nortje's work may narrow our understanding of his life and poetry. I wish to extend Wicomb's scepticism around theorisations of hybridity and marginality in relation to 'colouredness' into my analysis of his poems set in London, and to combine this openness to ways of being beyond liminality with Nuttall's suggestion that a critical lacuna exists around Nortje's 'familiarity' with and 'embeddedness' in, rather than only his isolation from, the city.

I read Nortje's London-based poetry as presenting a bodily engagement with the city, simultaneous with an exploration of the various forms of alienation (geographic, psychic, social) he experiences in London. Furthermore, my reading of Nortje's experiences of pleasure in London is underpinned by an understanding that sexuality and the body are charged sites for coloured South Africans. Wicomb suggests that shame is a central concept through which one can understand 'the textural construction, ethnographic self-fashioning, and political behaviour of coloureds in South Africa' (1998: 92). Because the origins of coloured South Africans are associated, as in texts such as Sarah Gertrude Millin's eugenicist novel *God's Step-Children* (1924), with miscegenation and coloured women's alleged promiscuity, Wicomb suggests that shame has been a defining characteristic of coloured self-image. In a footnote in her essay, Wicomb presents Nortje as an example of the complex relationship between coloured South Africans and the ANC, referring to David Bunn's comment on Nortje's 'problematic relationship with the ANC' which is 'suggestive in relation to the explicit, self-loathing references to miscegenation and colouredness in Nortje's poems' (1998: 104n). Wicomb also quotes excerpts from Nortje's poems 'Immigrant' and 'Waiting' as epigraphs to her interconnected collection of short stories, *You Can't Get Lost in Cape Town* (1987), and the title of 'Ash on My Sleeve', a story about exile and return, is derived from the last line of 'Waiting'.

What Wicomb calls 'self-loathing references to miscegenation and colouredness' can be seen in 'Exile from the first' (1970), although it is not blackness that is shameful here, but the 'white trash coursing through [his] blood' (line 28). The title of 'Dogsbody Halfbreed' (1970) is even more overtly self-loathing. Not only does shame play into Nortje's relationship to blackness and black activism, and thus also his ambiguous situation as an 'exile' in London, it also feeds into his representation of sexuality and pleasure in his poems as a means of being in and engaging with the city. In Nortje's writing set in London we see a dialectic between self-loathing and pleasure, as well as between engagement and isolation, which he depicts performatively through his poetry.

London as a literary city: intertextuality and identity

In his London-based poems, Nortje tries out not only different versions of himself, but different literary personae through his engagement with various literary influences, which are both inspired by and mediate his engagement with the city. Nortje drew on the work of late Romantic and modernist urban poets, especially T.S. Eliot and Charles Baudelaire. Nortje's close friend Raymond Leitch has suggested that 'Eliot was the most important influence', recounting how he and Nortje would read poetry together: 'his favourite poems that I can recall ... were two Eliot poems, 'Gerontion' and *The Waste Land*. We read through *The Waste Land* several times' (Raymond Leitch: Letter to Hedy Davis (Cassette Tape), 14 October 1979, Manuscript Collection: Arthur Nortje, UNISA Archives). While Nortje's frequent references to Baudelaire and Eliot may suggest a provincial belatedness, by the end of his life Nortje began to reach towards 'a literature of radical change, of candidness and of representational accuracy', as Ralph Pordzik writes (1998: 35). David

Bunn similarly suggests that '[h]ad Nortje survived, his later work suggests he would have found new strength in the identity politics of the Black Consciousness movement' (1996: 42). While perhaps not achieving the radical forthrightness of poets such as Oswald Mtshali, Mongane Serote or Mafika Gwala, Nortje's poetry includes a more committed critique of racism and capitalism than might be expected from his use of traditional forms and some of his more conservative or canonic literary influences, and this is particularly evident in his later London poems. Furthermore, he interwove the influence of late nineteenth- and early twentieth-century urban poets with the confessional lyric mode associated with American and British poets of the 1950s and 1960s, and utilised this personal, radical voice to interrogate his subjectivity as a coloured poet in exile.

Confessionalism was a 'reaction to the perceived stuffiness and excessive formalism of the academic poetry of the 1940s and 50s' and was loosely defined by 'an inscription of the intensively personal' (Cockin and Morrison 2010: 169). Al Alvarez famously anthologised this new school of poetry, in which he included Sylvia Plath, in *The New Poetry* (1962), and wrote of these confessional poems: 'In the seriousness of what I have called new depth poetry, the openness to experience, the psychological insight and integrity of D.H. Lawrence would, ideally, combine with the technical skill and formal intelligence of T.S. Eliot' (32). Nortje was an admirer of Plath, as is evident in his poem 'For Sylvia Plath' (1966), in which he empathises with Plath's complex relationship with her father. He references both Alvarez and Plath in an entry in one of his notebooks, which reads: 'Stop Press! Saw in Observer a beautiful photo of Sylvia Plath and Epitaph For A Poet: 4 poems said by Alvarez to have been written in pre-death feverish haste' (Notepad B, Manuscript Collection: Arthur Nortje, UNISA Archives). In a journal entry, Nortje also notes that he admires confessional American poet Robert Lowell, although he wonders if Lowell 'goes too far' (Oxford Journal: 88, Manuscript Collection: Arthur Nortje, UNISA) and he mentions reading Christopher Middleton and Wallace Stevens. In Britain he was exposed to these contemporary poets through the *New Statesman* and Stephen Spender's leftist journal *Encounter*.[5] These poets were reworking the lyric form into something more personal, even psychoanalytical, and Nortje's poems are similarly invested in self-analysis. Nortje's use of the confessional mode means that speaker and poet often appear identical in his poems. While most of Nortje's poems seem to be introspective, he frequently takes on personae and different voices in his poems in order to carry out this self-scrutiny. Furthermore, these personae are often related to specific literary modes, as we shall see particularly in his reference to the trope of the late Romantic, Baudelairean *flâneur*.

In his poems, Nortje displays an awareness of the loaded nature of his influences, and rewrites and builds upon his sources. He is specifically interested in positioning himself as an urban poet and a poet of modernity, which is why it makes sense that his London poems would be the most allusive. By locating himself as an urban poet, Nortje not only represents himself as immersed within the milieu of the city, as a respite from the 'isolation of exile'; he writes against a negative, fixed construction of coloured identity. Nortje's intertextuality can be read as a process of experimentation with different identities and modes of expression, to understand and reconfigure his identity as a coloured South African writer. He is thus critical of the literary forms in which he has been schooled and immersed. In a poem written in Cape Town, 'At Mowbray Waiting' (1963), Nortje represents the tension between English literary traditions and South African realities, through an ironic depiction of the act of reading gentle pastoral poetry within the brutalised South African cityscape. A glimpse of an incongruous 'big red bus among the orange others' at a Cape Town bus stop elicits hopes of travelling to London, and he rouses his 'sad little self from thoughts / of Keats under autumn on his sweet little island' (lines 1; 7–8). In this poem, London, England, English literature and the literary life operate as metonyms of one another, just as they do for Peter Abrahams. In the last line, while waiting to travel to 'Athlone desert' on Cape Town's arid and impoverished Flats, he declares: 'I have not been to London to announce my freedom' (line 16). The 'freedom' he hopes to 'announce' is in part associated with creative freedom, as embodied by the Romantic poet, but the red bus also represents the cosmopolitan glamour of the metropolis. This image of the red London bus, as a symbol of freedom and idealism, recurs in 'London Impressions' (1966):

> And big red buses, I thought I would never catch
> sight of the gentle monsters
> when I was young and shackled for my sharpness
> in the Union of South Africa. (Lines 2.21–24)

Romanticism has informed white Anglophone representations of the South African landscape from Thomas Pringle onward, as J.M. Coetzee has traced in *White Writing: On the Culture of Letters in South Africa* (1988). Nortje, however, suggests in this poem that 'thoughts / of Keats under autumn on his sweet little island' (line 8) are incompatible with the 'groaning mountain', hellish 'subways' and most importantly with his 'sad little self', juxtaposed through its rhythmic and syntactic similarity with 'sweet little island'. David Bunn uses passages from Nortje's journal to illustrate how he came to reject the 'Romantic hermeneutics of the lyric' in favour of his 'body' as the 'only place of imaginative refuge' (1996: 42). In this early poem, we see the beginning of Nortje's critique of Romanticism. Sarah Nuttall builds on Bunn's ideas about Nortje's bodily topography and suggests that his engagement with London is depicted in his poetry as occurring *through* his body. Nortje's interrogation of Romantic landscape paradigms within South Africa caused him to distrust ideas of idealised communion between place and self and led to a focus on the body as a site of meaning.

While Nortje may have realised that the Romantic approach to landscape writing was unsuited to the setting of South Africa, he found that the late Romantic and modernist urban lyricists, particularly T.S. Eliot and Charles Baudelaire, provided productive literary models. Andrew van der Vlies has suggested that, in Zoë Wicomb's writing, references to T.S. Eliot 'might ... be regarded, as markers of intertextuality, as having a broader function: either specifically, for all that Eliot *himself* connotes; or generically, as references to a canon (or *the* canon) in general' and, moreover, that this is how Eliot's work 'seems to function in so much South African writing and cultural discourse' (2011: 427–428). When noting the frequent allusions to Eliot in Nortje's work, it is possible to see this reliance as a mildly reactionary impulse, a method of assuring his reader of his familiarity with the tropes of the modernist lyric, in order to be taken seriously as an urban poet and a literary figure.[6] Nortje, not unlike Wicomb herself, uses references to Eliot self-consciously, even playfully at times, although this may be simultaneous with his desire (despite his avowed iconoclasm) to situate himself within the canon. Nortje's use of modernist images and concepts is furthermore caught up in the late adoption of modernisms by 'postcolonial' writers. Peter Kalliney's study of late colonial and postcolonial modernist networks, *Commonwealth of Letters* (2013), significantly focuses on the years 1930–1970 because 'it was during this period that high modernist principles were institutionalized on a global scale' (10). Kalliney cites T.S. Eliot's *The Waste Land* as a particularly influential text for colonial and postcolonial writers.

Nortje drew from *The Waste Land* a depiction of sullied, corrupted London, which he employed to represent both his position within the

city and also his broader sense of psychological malaise. We see this in
the opening section of 'Chelsea Visit' (1965), which begins thus:

> Dim among mists a starfish floats, the sun
> Of London autumn, leaves with everything.
> The wind has found its trembling orphan's nooks,
> though some, soft with the weight of rain, are trodden
> pulpy in the concrete of embankment.
> I scan a lacing shower pearl the water. (Lines 1.1–6)

Echoes of the opening of Eliot's 'The Fire Sermon' are evident: 'The river's tent is broken: the last fingers of leaf / Clutch and sink into the wet bank. The wind / Crosses the brown land unheard' (lines 173–175). In 'Chelsea Visit', not only does this image of 'pulpy' leaves suggest the 'broken', corrupt nature of the city; it specifically evokes Nortje's state of exile. Amanda Bloomfield suggests that '[a]n image that emerges repeatedly throughout his work is his exiled self, represented through the windswept leaf', which, like the exile, 'is disconnected from its home', 'has no roots' and is 'tossed about with no direction or purpose' (2004: 33). For instance, in the bleak 'Wayward Ego' (1970), thought to be Nortje's last poem, the speaker describes how 'Nights on the street find us windswept' (line 17). The leaf (the newly arrived exile, 'orphaned' from his mother country) can either find a 'nook' or 'be trodden / pulpy' under the weight of loneliness and alienation (Bloomfield 2004: 34). 'Chelsea Visit' also includes several images of dirt and contamination which remind one of the polluted Thames in *The Waste Land*: Nortje describes dirty swans which 'drift sullied on the ebbing river' and gulls which 'squawk among their smutty majesties' (lines 2.4–5).

Nortje's sense of disillusionment is then transferred to a description of a female acquaintance, whose living situation is reminiscent of the 'typist home at tea-time' in *The Waste Land*:

> That girl in her Chelsea rooms,
> (or should it be because I found her
> living with a man and grown more slender)
> that scruffy slut in a grotty flat! (Lines 2.9–12)

The real-life inspiration for this image of a 'girl in her Chelsea rooms' can be found in Nortje's Oxford Journal, in which he recounts a visit to a South African acquaintance in her 'Chelsea flat', and although he is 'expecting to carouse and unashamedly hog her flesh', he finds her 'living with a S.A. chap' in her 'grotty basement' (Oxford Journal: 46, Manuscript Collection: Arthur Nortje, UNISA). The vehemence of his insults towards the woman is therefore linked with sexual disappointment, as he admits: 'or should it be because I found her / living with a man' (lines 9–10). Nortje's reaction to female concupiscence is suggestive of a fraught response to shame and sexuality. The adjectives 'scruffy' and 'grotty' chime with the 'smutty' swans, suggesting that the sordid scene he finds in the girl's Chelsea flat is continuous with the alienation and disappointment he finds in London as a whole.

In the poem's concluding section, though, Nortje transfers this sense of corruption to South Africa, represented by 'stinking tombs' and the 'opulent squalor of too much sunshine' (lines 3.3–4). Here Nortje perhaps draws on the work of South African writer Alex La Guma, whose 1962 naturalist novella *A Walk in the Night* employs descriptions of disease, decay and detritus to convey the effects of apartheid upon a Cape Town coloured community: in *A Walk in the Night* the city is described as 'plague-ridden', filled with rubbish and 'general decay' (1962: 19). In 'Chelsea Visit', the Thames's 'thickets' remain 'fetid' too (line 3.5), however, which suggests that despite its 'intimate, desirable beauty' (line 3.8) London may not represent an escape from suffering or isolation for Nortje: there is continuity between corrupt London and squalid South Africa.

In 'Chelsea Visit', Nortje also draws on an earlier urban writer and influence on modernists such as Eliot: Charles Baudelaire. There is plenty of evidence, in his journal, for Nortje's reading of Baudelaire. For instance, in a discussion of Dadaism, he writes: 'The line of revolt runs from de Sade through Nietzsche and Baudelaire, where it crystallises as ennui and breeds "Sympathetic Horror"' (Oxford Journal: 71, Manuscript Collection: Arthur Nortje, UNISA). The latter is the title of one of Baudelaire's poems ('L'Horreur Sympathique'), and both 'revolt' and 'ennui' are sentiments which are evident in Nortje's London poetry. In 'Chelsea Visit', Baudelaire's influence can be perceived in the 'fetid thickets' (line 3.5) of the Thames, which echo the 'foetid marshes' in South African poet Roy Campbell's 1952 translation of Baudelaire's 'Elevation'. Although 'foetid marshes' is an admittedly loose translation of the '*miasmes morbides*' which the speaker entreats his soul to flee, it is highly likely that Nortje may have encountered Baudelaire's *Les Fleurs du Mal* in Campbell's translation. Furthermore, the image of the swans in Nortje's poem may correspond with Baudelaire's 'The Swan', in which the bird is compared to 'other exiles that we knew / Grandly absurd, with gestures of the mad' (lines 6–7) and which includes a description of a black African woman: 'the starved and phthisic negress / Tramping the mud, who seeks, with haggard eye, / The palms of Africa' (lines 13–15). The reference to 'The Swan' is significant given that, as Matt Houlbrook writes, its speaker 'is one of the most well-known figures in the literature of urban modernity', and the poem is amongst Baudelaire's key works which 'have articulated a vision of the city that has become the dominant model for how we understand modernity' (2005: 16). The concluding lines of 'Chelsea Visit' similarly present a muddied (South) African woman, aware of her distance from her homeland: 'I seek no answers, cradling your muddied face / so far together have we come from home' (lines 3.11–12).

In 'Chelsea Visit', Nortje invokes both Baudelaire and Eliot, because their visions of a corrupt, alienated city allow him to articulate his feelings both towards his exile and towards South Africa. His choice of London as setting for so many of his poems may be inspired by the writing of these urban poets, as the metropolis is a more powerful symbol of alienation than the less cosmopolitan Oxford. While Nortje's invocation of Eliot specifically speaks to the literary imagining of London, his gestures towards Baudelaire suggest that London, in Nortje's poetry, represents more than the British capital, but is frequently figured as the universal, cosmopolitan metropolis of modernity that was hinted at in the list of cities in 'Finally Friday'. In a line of thought that runs through Karl Marx, George Simmel, Theodor W. Adorno, Walter Benjamin and Jean-Paul Sartre, among others, industrialised, capitalist modernity, centred on the metropolis, is seen to entail alienation. Not only does this result in the alienation of the worker from the means of production (as Marx suggests), but also, through the commodification of relationships and the deepening of class divisions, it causes the alienation of people from each other and from themselves. Nortje thus uses the alienating metropolis of London as a symbol of his exilic state (both geographic and psychological) and, furthermore, he critiques these other forms of contemporary social alienation, which are particularly evident in 1960s London.

'The pace and tone of other voices': *flânerie* and language

Baudelaire's reputation as an urban poet is entangled with the trope of the *flâneur*, the dissolute, bohemian stroller who enjoys the pleasures of the city but is also detached from the 'crowd', as is evident in poems such as 'To a Passer-by' (1857). Baudelaire derived the figure of the 'passer-by' or *flâneur* from Edgar Allan Poe's short story 'The Man of the Crowd' (1845). The simultaneously detached and immersed nature of the *flâneur* within the city may have chimed with Nortje's own psychological and social condition as an exile. Keith Tester argues that '*flânerie* can, after Baudelaire, be understood as the activity of the sovereign spectator going about the city in order to find the things that will occupy his gaze and thus complete his otherwise incomplete identity; satisfy his otherwise dissatisfied existence; replace the sense of bereavement with a sense of life' (1994: 7). Walter Benjamin, the most influential commentator on Baudelaire, describes how Baudelaire's gaze, the gaze of the 'allegorist' and of the '*flâneu*r', as it falls on the city, 'is the gaze of the alienated man' (2006: 40). Furthermore, Benjamin suggests that the *flâneur* 'stands on the threshold – of the metropole and of the middle class. Neither has him in its power yet. In neither is he at home' (40).

Nortje similarly occupied a liminal, unhomed space within Britain: like Benjamin's *flâneur*, he found himself occupying an uncertain class position. One of the most important sites of class positionality in Nortje's work is language. Nortje's contradictory class affiliations as an exile in Britain are discussed by David Bunn in relation to Baudelaire's *flâneur* and to language:

> For the South African exile, Britain (or should I say London) is a heady introduction to international culture beyond the carceral apartheid state. However, British exile soon brings with it the realization that in order to be truly at home, one has to break through the race/ class association by learning the language of the ruling elite. Some of the most poignant moments in Nortje's journal are his short vocabulary lists, containing words like *frisson*, *manqué* and *donnée*, terms one uses to spice up one's conversations in sophisticated company. 'Britain', he remarks proudly in 1966, has done two things: 'made me start to become selective, betokening an upswing in taste; made me start to become self-confident. I truly begin to feel equal to the place, can swing its slang' [Oxford Journal: 67, Manuscript Collection: Arthur Nortje, UNISA]. Sadly, such vocabulary lists contain the basic elements for a negative redefinition of the beleaguered self, along the lines of Baudelaire's urban flâneur. (Bunn 1996: 38)

While Nortje certainly encountered British class politics, which would have differed markedly (but not entirely) from the race/class complexities of South Africa, in my view he dealt with these dynamics more critically than Bunn suggests. Firstly, the lists of words that Bunn mentions are not 'designed to spice up one's conversations in sophisticated company' but are meant for use in Nortje's poetry. At least one of the words on the list, 'manqué', finds its way into a poem: in 'From the Way I Live Now' (1970), Nortje considers that some Londoners may consider him a 'radical manqué' (line 21). Rather than illustrating a 'sad' desire to emulate the British elite, the borrowed word is used to highlight Nortje's disgust and guilt at living '[u]njustly' in 'centrally-heated freedom' in Britain, while black activists die in South Africa for their ideals (lines 22, 4). Secondly, these vocabulary lists, whether of words 'pinned down from the French' or other poetic and demotic words, demonstrate Nortje's playfulness with language, his desire to 'trust to that inner voice testing and hearing new sounds and phrases as they come through the brain's wind tunnel' (Oxford Journal: 67, Manuscript Collection: Arthur Nortje, UNISA).

Moreover, scattered throughout his journals and poems are experiments with different British registers, which allow Nortje both to comment on British class structures as an outsider and to insert himself, even temporarily, into the fabric of London through his mimicry of British speech. The journal passage quoted by Bunn above, in which Nortje asserts that he can 'swing [Britain's] slang', is not related to the list of French words, but rather to his use of British colloquialisms. Some of these British idioms are evident in 'Chelsea Visit', firstly in the description of 'leaves with everything' (line 1.2). This may be an oblique reference to the popular 1960s saying 'chips with everything', referring to the typical 'greasy spoon' diner menu.[7] *Chips with Everything* was also a 1962 play by Arnold Wesker that dealt with class conflict through its dual narratives of an upper-class soldier and a working-class socialist in London's East End; Nortje was familiar with Wesker's work, referring in his journal to the playwright's 1958 play, *Roots*, another 'kitchen-sink drama' depicting the struggles of a working-class woman (Oxford Journal: 87, Manuscript Collection: Arthur Nortje, UNISA). Wesker's fame in 1960s London is also witnessed by his inclusion as an interviewee in the aforementioned film featuring Lewis Nkosi, *Three Swings on a Pendulum* (1967). Although Nortje's tone could also be read as disparaging, by evoking chip-shop slang and Wesker's class-conscious play, Nortje suggests an affinity – or at least a fascination – with the British working class.

The poem 'London Impressions' (1966) is particularly full of conversational English. For instance, the statue of Nelson in Trafalgar Square is covered in a 'patina of pigeon shit' (line 5). This poem includes an assertion of Nortje's increased familiarity with Britain, particularly London, which is partly based on the acquisition of British modes of speech: 'I do not want to cross the road again, / having learnt the value of other faces, / acquired the pace and tone of other voices' (lines 19–20). Nortje frequently employs the concept of acquisition to explain his relationship to London: for instance, in the title of 'Fragment in Acquired England'

(1966) and in 'Autopsy' (1966), in which he writes of 'the towns I've acquired' (line 21). The connotations of the verb 'to acquire' are of both ownership and knowledge, and are often specifically linguistic: one acquires a language or an accent. In 'Trio' (1967), he elucidates what the acquisition of London's accent may entail, by comparing his relationship to the city with a love affair with a woman: 'I will not be the voyeur, the quiet observer / a man called "lucky" to be with such a chick' (lines 1.4–5). As I discussed in the introduction, in this poem, Nortje claims his distance from the figure of the camera-toting tourist and differentiates himself from the *flâneur*, who is often characterised as a 'voyeur'. His familiarity with the city is proven by what he says, or rather does not say: 'nothing like English pubs'. The irony and humour in this poem, evident in cheerful colloquialisms such as 'stodgy pint' and 'such a chick', convey Nortje's sense of pleasure in the city. He is familiar with the language of the city and is thus not a voyeuristic *flâneur*, but rather an active participant in the life of the city. In this way, Nortje's relationship with London is figured through the metaphor of language acquisition, and he uses various registers to indicate his complex class affiliations.

Nortje's playful, performative approach to his own identity as a coloured South African in London is foregrounded in an episode recounted by Raymond Leitch. Upon Nortje's return to Britain in 1970, Leitch feared that his friend had become a 'supercilious Oxford man' but was relieved when they were reunited: 'His speech was still unmistakably "Baienaar". Instead of comporting himself with Oxfordian propriety, he pranced through the West End like a Cape Town coon, singing "slaamse moppies" and clutching two gallon cans of pipkin' (quoted in Bunn 1996: 38). Despite his time in Oxford, Nortje's speech, at least in his South African friend's company, remains tinged by his upbringing in Port Elizabeth ('Baienaar' is an Afrikaans term for a native of that city) and he performs his coloured South African identity within the London streets, singing satirical songs, ghoema 'moppies', in the 'slaamse' dialect, dancing like a 'Cape Town coon'. Both 'slaamse' and 'coon' have potentially pejorative connotations: 'slaamse' denotes Muslim coloured South Africans, but also describes the Cape coloured Afrikaans vernacular, designated less problematically as 'Kaaps'. As mentioned in my discussion of Matshikiza's use of the word, 'Cape Town coon', while certainly containing the racist connotations of the epithet, also has a more specific connotation in the Cape coloured community, referring to a minstrel in the annual Cape Town Carnival. In this carnivalesque moment, Nortje resists his absorption into Oxford's polite academic society and South Africa's white English literary establishment, while also performing a caricatured racial identity – the 'Cape Town coon' – as a subversive, even bitter, act of re-appropriation. This performance of identity is achieved through language, through both his 'Baienaar' accent and his use of 'slaamse' slang.

The 'moppies' Nortje is singing are themselves a paradigm of his approach to his poetry: according to musicologist Denis-Constant Martin, 'ghoemaliedjies' (traditional Cape Malay songs), from which 'moppies' derive, 'were used to make fun of people, especially if they were or pretended to be in positions of authority and prestige, and to make fun of particular situations, even if they were rather distressing'. Martin explains that Afrikaans 'moppies' have 'preserved this legacy' and are 'comic songs' defined by musical 'bricolage' (2014: 113). In his poetry, Nortje both adopts this satirical, irreverently subversive attitude towards Britain's elite, and also shares with the writers of 'moppies' the technique of 'bricolage', drawing on different registers, languages and sources in his poems.

'I have drunk up nights': pleasure and shame

In the anecdote recounted by Leitch, Nortje's performance of colouredness is associated with drunkenness: he is clutching 'two gallon cans of pipkin' (ale), but his consumption of alcohol also reflects his experience, and portrayal, of London as a series of 'pleasure streets' ('Waiting', 1967: line 2). In the poem 'Trio', discussed above, the pleasures of London are likewise associated with drinking and with sex: London is a 'chick', 'acquired' by the speaker, and his familiarity with the city is associated with his knowledge of its alcoholic offerings. Through his identification with decadent, bohemian poetry such as that by Baudelaire, Nortje depicts an engagement with the city that is caught up in a dialectic of ambivalent pleasure and self-loathing. In his poetry, Nortje frequently aligns himself with the figure of the 'libertine', a specifically Baudelairean word and concept, one who is outside of moral and social (especially sexual) norms.[8] This liberal attitude towards sex and middle-class propriety, both heterosexual promiscuity and queer sexuality, is intertwined in complex ways with his colouredness. Brenna Munro, building on Wicomb's writing about shame, suggests that 'coloured identity' is 'categorically sexualised; to be coloured is, in the apartheid imaginary, to be the product of taboo miscegenation between black and white – just as homosexuality in South Africa has often been interpreted as a product, in the broadest sense of the word, of the colonial encounter' (2012: 92). Furthermore, drawing on Grant Farred's work, Munro suggests that '"impurity" produces shame but at the same time, perhaps, its own kind of freedom, and even a hospitality towards sexual transgressions' (113). Nortje's identification with hedonistic poetry can be seen either as an expression of this 'freedom' or, in a more subversive manner, as an open expression of 'shameful' sexual practices so as to rob them, and by inference his colouredness, of their associations with shame. We see this performative response to the construction of coloured identity in the 'slaamse moppies' episode recounted above, too. Nortje's poems thus both acknowledge shame and self-loathing, while simultaneously protesting his disregard of bourgeois standards of morality, significantly worked out against the backdrop of London, a permissive, modern city. Nortje's poems set in London, particularly his later works, are, I would argue, an exploration of queer sexualities.

The other poet whom Nortje names as representative of the figure of the libertine is Arthur Rimbaud, the French symbolist poet who famously lived in London from 1872 to 1873, while involved in an intense and eventually violent affair with fellow writer Paul Verlaine. After their affair ended when Verlaine shot and injured him, Rimbaud again lived in London for a few months with the poet Germain Nouveau in 1874, having given up poetry after his famous prose poem, 'A Season in Hell', was completed in 1873. In his journal, Nortje refers to Rimbaud as the inspiration of an unpublished poem: 'I refer to Rimbaud, whose brilliant and sensation-ridden career as a poet ended abruptly when he gave up at 19, retired to a queer's sordid existence in "acquired London" and later died of the carnal disease in Ethiopia' (Oxford Journal: 52, Manuscript Collection: Arthur Nortje, UNISA). Rimbaud in fact died of bone cancer rather than venereal disease, while working for a trading company in Abyssinia (present-day Ethiopia). Once again, Nortje employs the concept of 'acquisition' to indicate both familiarity and foreignness. Nortje also specifically foregrounds Rimbaud's life in London rather than his bohemian life in Paris, for instance, thus aligning himself with Rimbaud as a libertine and exile in London. What is notable here is of course his use of 'queer', which would have been a pejorative term as well as a commonplace synonym for 'homosexual' at the time. Despite his characterisation of homosexual relationships as inherently 'sordid', I want to suggest that Nortje's poetry, particularly his late London poems, can themselves be read as queer.

In calling Nortje's poems 'queer', I am not attempting to 'out' Nortje as a closeted homosexual poet. I am less interested in assigning Nortje a definitive sexual identity than in how he queered his poems, through references not only to homosexuality but also to non-normative sexuality and social behaviour, and in how this queerness played into his engagement with London in his poetry. In my approach, I draw on Brenna Munro's discussion of Richard Rive's sexuality and writing, in which she uses José Quiroga's suggestion that '"standard" epistemologies of "coming out" do not always make sense of texts from outside the Anglo-American cultural arena' (2012: 117). Furthermore, I employ the broad, inclusive definition of 'queer', which David M. Halperin explains as '*whatever* is at odds with the normal, the legitimate, the dominant'; a 'positionality' that is 'available to anyone who is or who feels marginalized because of his or her sexual practices' (1997: 62, italics original). As a coloured South African, Nortje is 'marginalized because of his ... sexual practices'; as mentioned, he is already 'sexualised' in South African society, through his origins as the 'product of taboo miscegenation' (Munro 2012: 113). Nortje seizes and owns his marginalisation and sexualisation through his representation of non-normative sexual experiences in the city, but his poems set in London move between a sense of self-loathing and pleasure: despite his celebration of his own 'queerness' in all senses of the word, the residue of shame is never fully erased.

In reading Nortje's poems as 'queer', I agree with Diana Adesola Mafe who has observed that '[i]f nothing else, Nortje's sexuality was ambiguous – another part of his identity and self-expression that was obscure and contradictory' (2008: 446). Where I diverge from Mafe is that she situates Nortje as 'emblematic of the feminization of the tragic mulatto in American literature and the more explicit linking of coloured masculinity with homosexuality in twentieth-century South African discourses' (431), while I am interested in how the 'queerness' of his poetry intersects both with the Romantic and modernist intertexts he invokes, and with urban subjectivities that are particularly relevant to his poems set in London. Nortje's 'coloured' identity is inextricable from these engagements with queer sexuality, but in many of his poems queerness is also negotiated through his evocation of certain tropes of city living. The metropolitan setting of London therefore enabled his engagements with queer subjectivities.

One of the most interesting engagements with queerness in the city in Nortje's oeuvre occurs in 'Identity' (1967), a poem which includes an ambiguous encounter with a man in the public toilet at Paddington Station. It begins with a sexualised reflection on the speaker's identity:

Infinities of images clash in my mirrors.
The fashionable urges that turn out to be

> sterile, complacent as the moon in June.
> Miscellaneous notions violate me. (Lines 1–4)

The speaker's 'infinities' of identities, which clash in his 'mirrors', are associated immediately with sexual desire – 'fashionable urges' – which both turn out to be 'sterile' and 'violate him'. Sterility here may suggest homosexuality or unconsummated, frustrated sexual desire, even masturbation. In the second stanza we move to the encounter in the public toilet:

> Familiar gesture in the gents
> at Paddington Station: the wristy aesthete
> in pinstripe trousers, pale lizard, beckoned:
> porcelain tiles reflected me vaguely declining. (Lines 5–8)

Here we are in the realm of the cruiser, a figure whom Mark W. Turner reads as an alternative to the figure of the *flâneur*. He suggests that cruising 'emerges as a counter-discourse in the literature of modernity and as an alternative street practice in the modern city, a way of both imagining and inhabiting the spaces of the city that challenge other ways we have come to understand urban movement, in particular through the overdetermining figure of the *flâneur*' (Turner 2003: 7). Turner focuses on the public urinal as a 'precarious' and 'liminal social space in which a unique interplay between public and private sustained complex opportunities for privacy and sexual encounter' (49). That the man's gesture is 'familiar' to the speaker suggests the 'established modes of symbolic exchange' of the public urinal, which Turner writes about, in which men 'insinuated a word, gesture or movement into public space, demonstrating their desires to those in the know' (50). While the speaker declines the man's sexual invitation, his familiarity with the code of the urinal and the qualification, 'vaguely', suggest that he may not be entirely antipathetic towards the man's intentions. It is worth noting, however, that the description of the man as a 'wristy aesthete' and 'pale lizard' is somewhat stereotyped, an image of an effeminate and sly, bloodless gay man which suggests, once more, that Nortje was not immune from the casual homophobia of the 1960s. Any sense of condemnation is, however, countered by the ambivalent, self-reflective tone of the rest of the poem.

For instance, in the following stanza of 'Identity', the speaker suggests that he cannot judge the 'wristy aesthete', as he is similarly transgressive:

> Can I speak of probity, who now
> work for the garbage man, stuffing the bin
> full of tissue paper, sugar packets, anything
> on which a poem was ever written? (Lines 9–12)

There is a suggestion of masturbation here, associated with writing poetry, which is represented as wasteful and self-indulgent. Writing poetry is, for Nortje, a queer act, radical and subversive, but perhaps morally suspect and resulting in self-loathing. In the next two stanzas, we return to the streets of the city and are presented with further ambivalent encounters with men. Firstly, we have a different type of exchange, a commercial one, as 'a man with twenty watches on his forearm / flicks his sleeve down to the shake of my head' (lines 15–16). The similarity between this encounter and that in the public toilet – the gestural invitation, the act of refusal – suggests a depiction of sexual relationships as transactional, even predatory or acquisitive. The next stanza includes a familiar trope of cruising: the knowing glance in the crowd:

> Soft as a pig's heart muscle in a queue
> down the Edgware Road, or in Leicester Square,
> a revealing smile was prelude to a
> supple suggestion i e room to shave. (lines 17–20)

Nortje's naming of London streets implies that cruising is facilitated by London itself; the city enables sexual freedom. The conversational tone of the explanation of the 'supple suggestion' behind a 'revealing smile', with the abbreviation 'i e' and the equally enigmatic 'room to shave', implies the speaker's immersion in the codified, secret language of queer culture in 1960s London. In the next stanza, though, he subverts this interpretation:

> Do not interpret this only, the odd
> encounters, the sought liaisons. See me
> tickled at the bourgeois games on Saturdays (Lines 21–23)

The reader is urged not to read too closely into the 'odd encounters' described in the poem, as the speaker reasserts his bourgeois respectability. We are thus teased in this poem with '[m]iscellaneous notions' about the speaker's (and by implication, Nortje's) sexual identity. The speaker defends himself against having his identity fixed: he is both queer and bourgeois, immoral and disgusted by perversity, he has 'sought liaisons' but declines them. Nortje's insistence on multiple, co-existing identities, although they are figured as sexual identities in this poem, also undermines the overdetermination of racial identity under apartheid South Africa; as Diana Mafe suggests, Nortje's poetry, through its 'queer' references 'reminds us of the "different" ways in which mixedness disturbs neat categories of identity' (2008: 450).

The dialectic between self-loathing and pleasure in Nortje's poems, associated with sexuality and colouredness and figured in his flâneuristic activities in London, is best explored through a close reading of a series of five poems written in September 1970: 'Supremely Individual', 'I Have Drunk Up Nights', 'What Is Mundane', 'Love of Perversity' and 'Natural Sinner'. These poems are all Shakespearian sonnets, and the formal structures of the poems contrast with their contents, which foreground the chaotic, even self-destructive nature of city life. 'Supremely Individual', for instance, continues the complex self-construction of 'Identity' and presents the speaker as 'Supremely individual, flamboyant, proud / insane and thirsty for a stable life' (lines 1–2). His complex identity is significantly worked out 'in cosmopolitan dives of some metropolis' (l.5). The city of London and its seedy pleasure houses ('dives') are where he comes to realise that 'The smelly and the raw / crowds that disgust me are also those I adore' (lines 13–14). Like the figure of the *flâneur*, the speaker is both part of the crowd and detached from it, and experiences simultaneous admiration and disgust for the 'smelly and the raw' both in himself and in others. The second poem in this sonnet series, 'I Have Drunk Up Nights', begins in a confessional mode that is continued in 'What Is Mundane' and 'Natural Sinner':

> I have drunk up nights and spent the days
> in wild pursuits, life of the libertine:
> do not repent, confess, seek remedies.
> The bourgeois sinners are banned from where I've been. (Lines 1–4)

These confessions are presented in the past perfect ('I have drunk ...'), which reminds one of the prevalence of this tense in Eliot's 'The Love Song of J. Alfred Prufrock' (1925): for example, 'I have measured out my life with coffee spoons' and 'I have seen the moment of my greatness flicker' (lines 51, 84). Both poems present a retrospective overview of the speaker's life. However, while Prufrock regrets his timidity and fastidiousness, Nortje confesses his seizure of life's pleasures: he has 'drunk up nights' while Prufrock has refused Marvell's injunction to '[squeeze] the universe into a ball' (line 92). One could thus read this series of poems as writing back to 'Prufrock', as a defiantly different kind of retrospective that affirms pleasure, but also includes an underlying sense of regret and self-loathing, as does Eliot's poem.

The reference in 'I Have Drunk Up Nights' to banning 'bourgeois sinners' reminds one of the censorship laws in South Africa; while many of his contemporaries are 'banned' from expressing themselves in their home country, in London Nortje can assert his freedom by carrying out his own banning order against the British elite. Sarah Nuttall explains the ambiguity present in these poems: while Nortje 'asserts that he has been to "places" where others haven't been, that are "unknown" to others', he also 'reveals that he hasn't been able to escape the notion of the forbidden'. What emerges, then, is 'a further suggestive contradiction in Nortje's readings of the flesh – on the one hand it is the site of discovery and exploration, and a way of thinking and writing the self, new kinds of selves, into being: on the other hand is the need, near death, to confess to his "transgressions"' (Nuttall 2004: 96). Once more, self-loathing and shame are held in tension with an affirmation of the life of the libertine within the city. 'I Have Drunk Up Nights' concludes with an invective against the bourgeois life:

> I speak
> to you for whom spittoons are made, who
> buy furbelows and leopard skins, antiques.
> Will you not read it, this my poetry,
> calling it uncouth: it makes you sick?
> You serve your tea in china that's authentic. (Lines 9–14)

Not only does the speaker differentiate himself from the 'bourgeois sinners', he specifically lashes out at the fastidious British literary elite who may find his poetry 'uncouth'. He expresses disgust at the ostentatious consumerism of these bourgeois critics: their purchase of unnecessary 'furbelows' (ornaments), 'antiques' and leopard skins from Africa; unlike his raw poetry, the most 'authentic' thing about this group is their 'china'. Nortje expresses his ambivalent sympathy with the 'raw and the smelly crowds' while critiquing the consumerism of the British middle class and high capitalist society as a whole.

'What Is Mundane' continues the theme of the previous poem, revelling in London's sexual and other bodily pleasures. This poem's confessions are contained in the second quartet, after the speaker has expressed his aim of transforming the 'mundane' into the 'sublime' (line 1):

> I have tasted potatoes, edibles, all that flesh
> can offer: lain in luxury with rich women,
> and homosexuals, bums, rag-pickers so obsessed
> me I could watch them all for hours in fascination. (Lines 5–8)

Nortje's use of punctuation in these lines is ambivalent. One could gloss the second and third line as: '[I have] lain in luxury with rich women, and [have also lain with] homosexuals, [while] bums [and] rag-pickers so obsessed / me'. On the other hand, the comma after 'rich women' may signal the start of a new clause, whose verb is 'obsessed'. In other words, the lines could be read as: '[I have] lain in luxury with rich women, and [furthermore] homosexuals, bums [and] rag-pickers so obsessed / me'. As in 'Identity', this ambivalence prevents the reader from being able to fix the speaker's sexuality. The 'fascination' that the 'homosexuals', 'bums' and 'rag-pickers' hold for the speaker is reminiscent of a voyeuristic *flânerie* that implies a certain detachment from these figures, and a relationship of scopic power. Though the speaker can sympathise with those excluded from the bourgeois city, he can also pass as a respectable man in (but not necessarily *of*) the crowd. The image of the 'rag-picker', however, is particularly meaningful, as it alludes to Baudelaire's poem 'The Rag-Picker's Wine', and to Baudelaire's prose exposition of this figure as one who, by collecting and sorting the city's rubbish, 'collates the annals of intemperance, the capharnaum of waste' (Benjamin 2006: 108). Walter Benjamin interpreted the rag-picker as 'an extended metaphor for the poetic method' since 'Ragpicker and poet: both are concerned with refuse, and both go about their solitary business while other citizens are sleeping' (108). Through the association of the rag-picker with the figure of the bohemian poet, collecting and sorting source material from the city's streets, Nortje expresses his affinity with this figure, rather than merely a voyeuristic fascination. In the following poem, 'Love of Perversity', the speaker expresses his unease about his class position as he 'loaf[s] among the well-to-do / and not among the louts and down-and-outers, tramps' (lines 7–8).

In the last of the five September 1970 sonnets, 'Natural Sinner', Nortje presents his (or his poetic persona's) dissolute life in London as directly related to his colouredness; its first stanza reads thus:

> I have preyed on my emotions like a mantis
> have lain with Soho prostitutes and gambled
> a month's rent in machines that gobble sixpences,
> and have sufficiently recovered from the shambles (lines 1–4)

The speaker's destructive introspection is represented by the pun of the 'preying' (praying) mantis, which is immediately associated with London through the 'Soho prostitutes', who are specifically located in London's most bohemian and cosmopolitan district. In the second stanza the metaphorical site is no longer the city but the body, which is represented as the source of his verse, and is grotesquely figured as a worm-ridden piece of meat from which the verse has been 'forced' (line 8), albeit not 'bellestrically / but in a measured music of a sort' (lines 5–6). Ironically, it is self-corruption, related to the dissolution experienced through the partaking of the city's pleasures, which results in the 'measured music' of the sonnet. This is akin to the Romantic conceit of worldly experience providing the poet with inspiration. The last stanza of this poem relates the speaker's pleasurable and self-destructive experience of the city and his ironically productive bodily and mental corruption to his origins as a coloured South African. The speaker hopes that, through his experiences in London, the 'stamp / of birth, of blackness, criminality' has become 'invisible' (lines 12–13). This line may be interpreted as an endeavour on Nortje's part to obfuscate his colouredness, and especially the 'blackness' of his bloodline, by becoming 'invisible' within the city streets.

Dirk Klopper suggests that, at times, this is what exile represented to Nortje. He quotes a letter in which Nortje writes to a friend, before leaving South Africa, that he wants to be 'submerged among strangers', and Klopper comments: 'In a sense, he wanted to take on the life of strangers and become a stranger to himself. In the poetry, blackness registers this ambivalence, signifying both alienation and solidarity' (2004a: 13). These lines should not be read in isolation as suggesting that Nortje's depiction of himself as a bohemian urban poet is merely a strategy to escape any association with blackness. While his use of 'blackness' here is potentially negative, one must remember that he had not yet imbibed the vocabulary of the Black Consciousness Movement, which would allow him to include himself under an empowering rubric of inclusive black identity. This line conveys the greater freedom of identification which Nortje was afforded within Britain and within London specifically. He hopes to longer be 'stamped', as a pass or visa is stamped, with the negative construction of colouredness as 'criminality', of his origins as a shameful transgression. The freedom of London and the varied pleasures and intoxications available within the city allow Nortje to explore his identities (the 'clash of images' in 'Identity') beyond that of a coloured, exiled South African poet. This allows him, in 'Natural Sinner', to declare, boldly, in a line which is evocative both of the confessional movement and of later Black Consciousness poetry: 'I speak this from experience, speak from me' (line 14). However, as is evident in his constant shift between self-loathing and pleasure within the city and his inability in these sonnets to escape the idea of sin and confession, he struggles to erase the 'stamp' of shame.

As we have seen in these five sonnets in particular, the body is the metaphorical means by which Nortje represents his experience of London. However, there are also two key spatial metaphors which convey Nortje's relationship to London: the Underground and the labyrinth. In 'Warren Street Post Office Tower' (1970), Nortje declares, referring to a journey via the Underground: 'I like London from the bottom better' (line 19). Achille Mbembe and Sarah Nuttall, in their book on Johannesburg, draw on David Pike's *Subterranean Cities* in order to explain the metaphorics of the 'underground':

> The underground is not to be understood simply in terms of an infrastructure and various subterranean spaces (sewers and drainage systems, underground railways, utility tunnels, storage vaults and so on). The world below (the underworld) is also made up of lower classes, the trash heap of the world above, and subterranean utopias. (Nuttall and Mbembe 2008: 22)

I have already explored in Nortje's poetry his affinities, through language, with the 'lower classes' and with the figure of the 'rag-picker', akin to Baudelaire's relish of the mud. Thus, the metaphor of the Underground is potentially subversive and is combined with the trope of the labyrinth: Michael Chapman suggests that Nortje's 'mythic imagination transforms the city into a terrifying labyrinth, a motif of metaphysical exile' (1979: 70). 'Casualty' (1966), which begins in a London bar, combines these two images: 'Let me roam in the earth's filthy miracle, / the fox-holes, / the labyrinths' (lines 37–38). In his journal, Nortje writes of London: 'You can be anonymous if you want to, you can go up to Soho and upstairs to the models leaning out of tenement windows if you wish to rediscover the secrets of … the torturous labyrinth' (Oxford Journal: 50, Manuscript Collection: Arthur Nortje, UNISA). The labyrinth is therefore associated with Nortje's desire to be 'anonymous' or 'invisible', as he writes in 'Natural Sinner' (1970). Nortje delights in losing himself in the 'labyrinth' associated with its sexual pleasures, but there is a self-destructive element to these 'torturous' labyrinthine and 'underground' journeys, born out of 'an incurable malaise that makes [him] walk restlessly through the sewers of these distant cities' ('Questions and Answers', 1970: lines 30–32). Walter Benjamin, writing on the figure of the *flâneur* in Baudelaire, also uses the image of the labyrinth to convey the aimlessness of life in a capitalist society. The destination of the labyrinthine path is 'the marketplace' and represents the route of 'a humanity (a class) which does not want to know where its destiny is taking it' (Benjamin 2006: 145–146). The image of the labyrinth, through its layered associations, does the work not only of conveying an exiled South African's self-destructive drive and simultaneous immersion and estrangement within London, but also his critique of the alienation conferred by modernity.

'Sticky fingers' and 'sponsored glossolalia': reflections on global capitalism within London

Nortje's ambivalent position in relation to class in Britain and his experience of a different kind of hegemony in South Africa underpin his critique of forms of power within British society, which are especially evident in its commercial and cultural centre, London. As Bunn has noted, Britain, and specifically London, provided Nortje with a 'heady introduction to international culture beyond the carceral apartheid state' (1996: 38). As mentioned, the censorship of literature and media was at its most draconian in this period, meaning that South Africans, in the 1960s, had limited access to international media, and television was only permitted in the country in 1976, having been staved off in service of the state's Calvinist moralism. In Britain, therefore, Nortje was exposed not only to the English cultural traditions of Oxford's halls and colleges, but also to new cultural vistas in the form of British and global popular media, particularly television, which had become accessible to most Britons by the late 1960s. His journal is filled with enthusiastic reviews of films, television shows and articles in newspapers and journals.

Nortje's poetry also evinces his keen interest in current events and their mediation. In several poems, Nortje reflects on the Cold War and the fear of nuclear holocaust, as the arms race reached its height following the Cuban Missile Crisis of 1962 and the commencement of the Vietnam War in 1965. For instance, in 'Hiroshima 21 and the Lucky Dragon' (1966), he considers the aftermath of the 1945 bomb, while in 'Waiting' (1967), he considers his one-time girlfriend, Joan Cornelius, who has moved to Canada 'under the Distant Early Warning System' (line 40), the radar system in the Arctic which warned the United States of incoming Soviet bombers. In this poem, Nortje expresses how, despite the global paranoia under nuclear threats, he is more concerned about his personal isolation: the 'radiation burns of silence' and 'the solitude that mutilates', rather than 'cosmic immensity of catastrophe' (lines 41, 44, 43). Nortje's frequent use of Cold War metaphors conveys his awareness of the global zeitgeist, in which capitalism seemed both vociferous and vulnerable.

The 1960s, for most Britons, was a period of economic prosperity, 'based on full employment, rising incomes and rampant consumerism', explains Dominic Sandbrook (2006: xvi). Technological advancement and modernisation were also at their height, symbolised in London by the construction of Post Office Tower (now the BT Tower) in 1964, which serves as the setting for Nortje's 'Warren Street Post Office Tower'

(1970). In 'Mundane Monday' (1967), Nortje presents overt connections between popular media, capitalism and political hegemony in London:

> The ice-cream man is ignorant of
> telly aerials sprouting from the chimneys.
> The ice-cream van plays pop and lolly music.
> The dollhouse of his soul sprouts
> candy floss like fungus.
> He is a sugar daddy, the flower children
> laugh at his sticky fingers and they chant
> Die thy lame id
> Die thy lame id. (Lines 5–13)

The 'ice-cream' man is made to stand for consumerist desire, as his piped music calls to Londoners, inviting them to purchase and consume, just as capitalism uses advertising to create excessive desires for products. He is aligned with mass media through the verb 'sprout' referring to both the television aerials and the ice-cream man's soul; both are grotesque, compared to symbiotic fungi. The 'flower children', on the other hand, counter this sick dependency with their anti-consumerist chant, suggesting that capitalism preys upon our base desires, stimulating our 'id', and that these instincts therefore have to 'die' in a manner reminiscent of the Christian concept of dying to oneself. This is an interesting subversion of the conventional idea that the hippy, counter-capitalist movement was concerned with a return to nature and a celebration of the body's natural desires – in other words, of the id rather than the ego. In a scene that reminds one of South African police brutality, Nortje imagines the protesters playing 'cello' with a policeman's 'nightstick' (line 22), and the poem's speaker asks: 'Who do you think / invades the London Stock Exchange / but jesus and the love disciples?' (lines 24–26). Nortje once more confers Christian qualities on the hippies, by comparing them to Christ driving out the moneychangers from the temple in Jerusalem. This utopian vision of rebellion extends to a challenge of political power, with an ironic image of the 'Lord Mayor' riding through Buckingham Palace while 'the children in the park sang Penny Lane / to drown the national waltz' (lines 48–49).

Nortje's greater exposure to global media in Britain, and particularly in London, have made him aware of the proliferation of advertisements and, through these, of the pernicious lure of consumerism and capitalism, and their role in producing the modern subject. In 'Trio' (1967), he describes advertisements in an Underground station:

> Advertisements descending and descending in tune with the escalator:
> to dance astonishingly, achieve popularity, have
> excellent breath cool gait
> in a Lovable bra. (Lines 14–17)

The list of advertisements then transitions to a mention of Cold War events and their relevance to Britain; there are 'scheduled raids / by bombers based in Guam' (lines 19–20) and 'in Saigon's Evening Standard / Mr Wilson and Mr Brown find many platforms' (lines 24–35): Harold Wilson and George Brown, Prime Minister and Foreign Secretary respectively for the Labour Government of the 1960s, refused to send British troops to Vietnam. By mentioning the entrancing advertisements with their promises of 'excellent breath' and 'popularity' in the same list as these political events, Nortje draws correspondences between global forms of political power and the forces of capitalism and consumerism. Although Nortje's exilic state (both abstract and physical) has its roots in South Africa, he is aware of how London's own systems of economic, political and cultural power result in the isolation and oppression of its residents. In 'Wayward Ego' (1970), thought to be his last poem, Nortje references television advertisements to illustrate the urban condition of alienation:

> I have leaned against black railings
> to catch a glimpse through some stranger's window
> of his animate silver picture:
>
> only an old man
> sat there rapt and sad
> watching the sponsored glossolalia. (Lines 29–34)

While Nortje presents himself as the epitome of the marginal exile – looking through a 'stranger's window' for some spark of animation – it is not only foreign exiles who are isolated within London, since the old British man sits by himself, 'rapt and sad', mesmerised by the hardly intelligible patter of advertisements, characterised, as in 'Mundane Monday', as a consumerist version of religious experience.

Conclusion

In this concluding image of 'Wayward Ego', both the old man and the speaker appear as embodiments of the alienating effects of modernity and exile, and the rest of the poem also includes several of the key tropes that inform Nortje's engagement with London. The first stanza is located at a party and focuses on the heightened sensations of the speaker's body, as 'the wired nerves jump with hallelujahs / the eyes with grainy verve pierce their horizons' (lines 2–3), establishing the body as the means through which London is experienced. The next three stanzas contain a description of the speaker losing himself within sensory pleasures, 'what's done for devilment' (line 5). In this case, pleasure derives from music, 'the erotica of a saxophone wail' (line 13), once again experienced through the body, as he feels the 'beat quiver through [his] ribs' (line 12). In the fourth stanza, the mood changes, however, moving from pleasure to alienation:

> Nights on the street find us windswept, however,
> driven by the lusts of rain
> counting lampposts and lights that rattle
> under the sky that buffets whatever's movable
>
> or awash in the city tide,
> or swimming between the rage of bottles,
> floating in muck, flotsam and tossed jetsam,
> rockbottom smelling the gutter
>
> occupying the peeling bench of an autumn day
> in an urban park, urban vegetable
> not even a crackle of leaf
> or a wild flurry of spinning. (Lines 17–28)

We have once more the metaphor of the windswept leaf, representing the purposeless, rootless exile. This is combined, as in 'Chelsea Visit', with the Eliotian image of the refuse-filled and leaf-choked river. While in other poems Nortje represents the sullied underground as a potentially productive space, here the 'rockbottom' of the river is a place of inertia, symbolising the stultifying and destructive effect of exile. The alternative resting place of the leaves, a bench in an 'urban park' where they are no longer moved around by the wind but remain purposeless and dead, further links alienation with the locus of the city. As this is believed to be Nortje's last poem, it would most likely have been drafted in Oxford, yet he chooses to set its final stanzas within London's streets, underscoring the city's connotations of both pleasure and estrangement. In this poem, the last word is given to alienation through the final image of the voyeuristic exile observing the old man watching advertisements in a lonely trance.

Within the entire corpus of Nortje's poems set in London, though, I perceive a more nuanced and shifting dialectic between a sense of loss and anxiety over his coloured identity and his status as a 'nominal' exile, with productive gestures towards an active, often ironic and subversive reconfiguration of both his colouredness and his relationship towards the place of exile, Britain. London, although never Nortje's literal home while in exile, is the symbolic site through which he carries out this repositioning of his identity. This study of Nortje's poetry set in London therefore expands our understanding of Nortje's poetry beyond the tragic modes of marginality and liminality and suggests the critical vistas that emerge when we read South African literature in exile both as a response to alienation and as a meaningful engagement with the diasporic home.

Notes

1 There was an open verdict on the cause of death, and Nortje's biographers and friends are uncertain about whether this overdose was accidental or suicidal, although there is agreement, and evidence in his late poems, about Nortje's vulnerable state of mind at this point. In providing a brief summary of Nortje's life, I have drawn on Dirk Klopper's research, particularly his preface to *Anatomy of Dark* (Nortje 2000).
2 I would like to thank Dr Nadia Valman for her suggestions about the Talmudic and literary origins of this phrase.
3 The alternate spelling of 'Lut(h)uli' is in the original poem: Albert Luthuli used both spellings himself.
4 Bhabha links hybridity with coloured South African identity in *The Location of Culture* (2004), when analysing Nadine Gordimer's *My Son's Story*.
5 In Nortje's Oxford Journal, references to *Encounter* abound; see for instance p. 71, p. 88. Several South African writers, including Douglas Livingstone and Nadine Gordimer, were also published in *Encounter*.
6 Wicomb's intertextual references to Eliot might even be inspired by Nortje's allusiveness; for instance, the aforementioned title of one of the stories in *You Can't Get Lost in Cape Town*, 'Ash on My Sleeve', which derives from the final line of Nortje's 'Waiting', is in turn an allusion to Eliot's 'Little Gidding'.
7 I would like to thank Professor Cora Kaplan for alerting me to this potential reference.
8 See for instance Baudelaire's 'Sympathetic Horror' and 'Sed non Satiata'.

Detour

South African writers and London networks of black British activism

When Todd Matshikiza passes fellow black Londoners in the street, he yearns to 'throw fraternal blessing, greeting, good wishes' at them, and perceives in their faces 'them there blue lyrics', singing out that 'maybe we've got something in common'. He finds, though, that the black Londoner he greets 'wasn' looking for [his] common curry' (Matshikiza 1961a: 41). In J.M. Coetzee's *Youth* (2002), in which he looks back on the same time period in which Matshikiza was writing, his focaliser, John, observes the 'throngs of West Indians trudging back to their lodgings, muffled against the cold' and wonders what 'draws them from Jamaica and Trinidad to this heartless city where the cold seeps up from the very stones of the street' (2002: 104). Peter Abrahams may have been deeply involved in anti-colonial and anti-racist networks in London, but he also experienced fractures in his relationships with black British activists, given their diverging goals and perspectives. Failed connections between South Africans and black Britons in London during the 1950s and 1960s are symptomatic of some of the disjunctures between anti-apartheid politics and anti-racist black British resistance during that time, yet later decades, particularly the 1980s, saw greater co-operation and networking between exiled South African and black British writers and intellectuals.

The Anti-Apartheid Movement (AAM) was headquartered in London and attracted considerable support from its founding in the 1960s onwards, as the British public reacted with horror to the Sharpeville massacre which had brought into relief the violent racism of the apartheid regime. Yet, black Britons did not initially embrace this movement. In a speech delivered in 1999, Stuart

Hall noted the synchronicity of the AAM's foundation and the 'moment of large-scale Afro-Caribbean migration to Britain':

> [T]here are sometimes perplexing questions to be asked ... about the importance for the Anti-Apartheid Movement of there being an embodiment of the reminder of race in their presence actually in front of them, as Britain saw the beginnings of a society which was both multi-cultural and multi-ethnic. Undoubtedly there was an awareness among the black populations of the South African issue. And yet there was, in some ways, an inexplicable distance between these two movements. (Hall 1999)

Although black Britons in the postwar period felt empathy towards anti-racist and anti-colonial struggles abroad, historian Elizabeth Williams emphasises that in many cases domestic struggles against the 'blatant racism of British society during the 1960s, 1970s and into the 1980s' were 'all-consuming', particularly in the major cities (2015: 34). She references Stuart Hall's comments that in the face of people's 'daily struggles' against racism, 'it is not a surprise that the overwhelming political energy went into the building of resistance at a local level, rather than the building of anti-apartheid politics' (34). As Williams explains, black activists' wariness of becoming involved in AAM protests was also partly linked to their anxiety over the role of white activists in the British anti-apartheid struggle (2, 132).

From the 1980s onwards, however, black British activism against apartheid became more visible alongside resistance to domestic racism; for instance, the West Indian Standing Committee (WISC) prioritised anti-apartheid activism after the announcement of the visit of South Africa's President P.W. Botha to Britain for talks with Prime Minister Margaret Thatcher in 1984 (Williams 2015: 2). Williams suggests that the suffering of black South Africans under apartheid 'mirrored' black Britons' 'struggles against the systemic racism of Britain' and such mirroring became 'conflated into a sense of the universal struggle of black people against white oppression, which black communities saw as dating back to the beginning of the Atlantic slave trade driven largely by European avarice' (2015: 5). Black British activists perceived the racism they experienced as a lingering effect of trans-historical, global racial injustice, which both strengthened their resolve to fight domestic racism and caused them 'to empathise with people of colour elsewhere' (Williams 2015: 126). Since the late 1970s, in particular, global black consciousness politics, drawing on the Civil Rights

Movement, the Black Power movement and Pan-Africanism as much as on the South African Black Consciousness Movement, informed the 'bold anti-racism' that manifested in unrest in British cities (Williams 2015: 3). Historians of the anti-apartheid struggle have attested that the 1980s saw the international anti-apartheid struggle intensify (Thörn 2006: 120), and Williams argues that 'South African politics became uniquely part of the political landscape of Britain in a way that no other country had done since perhaps the Biafran war in the late 1960s and early 1970s' (2015: 4).

From the 1970s and into the tumultuous 1980s, South African writers in London tended to write more about South Africa than about the city in which they were exiled. During this time, black South Africans rose up against apartheid even more vociferously than in the 1960s, with increasingly well-organised protest networks and movements thwarting the National Party's attempts at achieving 'law and order'. The arts played a central role in these movements, as '[p]oets, novelists, dramatists, photographers and painters conveyed the resistance message to vast audiences' (Thompson 1995: 228). At the same time, many writers continued to live in London and many were immersed in radical networks of activism founded on common ground between their struggles against racism.

One illustration of these solidarities is renowned British poet Linton Kwesi Johnson's relationship with South African writer and critic Lewis Nkosi. When accepting an honorary doctorate from South Africa's Rhodes University in 2017, Johnson traced his 'South African connections' to his relationship with Nkosi. Johnson, who was active in anti-racist groups in London, was arrested in 1972 for writing down the details of policemen harassing three young black men in Brixton, and in his honorary doctorate acceptance speech he attributed his release to the public awareness raised by an article Nkosi had written for *The Observer* (Johnson 2017). Johnson, who was involved with radical anti-racist organisations such as the Black Panthers, the Race Today Collective and the Black Parents Movement (BPM) during the 1970s and 1980s, also acknowledged that his interest in South Africa went beyond personal relationships and was imbricated in a sense of diasporic black political solidarity, which he attributed to his Jamaican roots, quoting lyrics sung by the Jamaican reggae band the Twinkle Brothers: 'If Africa noh free / black man can't free'.

Johnson was also a regular participant in the International Book Fair of Radical Black and Third World Books, which ran from 1982 to 1995. The fair began as an initiative of New Beacon Books, Bogle L'Ouverture Publications and Race Today Publications, supported by the Black Parents Movement, the Black Youth Movement and other activist and literary groups (White et al. 2005: 17). The first three events were held in Islington, Lambeth and Acton, but from 1985 onwards it was housed in the Camden Centre near Kings Cross. The fair also included associated events in centres such as Manchester and Bradford/Leeds after 1985, but London remained the centre of this significant British literary gathering, which was 'politically a continuation in the tradition of the 1945 Pan African Congress held in Manchester which laid the basis for the post World War Two independence movements' and culturally 'a continuation of the traditions established by the Caribbean Artists Movements between 1966 and 1972' (White et al. 2005: 1). It is worth recalling Peter Abrahams's organising role in the Pan African Congress, an important milestone in the black radical British activism out of which the Fair emerged. Susheila Nasta suggests the Book Fair was one of several influential responses to the unrest of 1980s Britain amongst black British writers and activists, as the government's immigration policies tightened under Prime Minister Margaret Thatcher and tragic events such as the racially motivated fire that killed fourteen black teenagers in New Cross in 1981 led to 'a series of uprisings … which began in Brixton in 1981' (Nasta 2014: 1). Publishers and political and literary collectives reacted to the disturbingly visible effects of racism in Britain by strengthening solidarities between black Britons and African and Asian writers.

Alongside responses to these British social and political issues, the programmes of the Book Fair reveal how South Africa became an important focus, especially after the mid-1980s. Both British and South African writers played a key role in the mobilisation of support against apartheid and other global racisms. Anti-apartheid organisations such as the International Defence and Aid Fund for Southern Africa (IDAF), the Azania Liberation Support Committee and the Azania Trust exhibited at the Fair, alongside South African publishers such as Ravan Press, Skotaville Publishers and David Phillip. South African writers who participated in the fair's events included actor, director and writer Lionel Ngakane in 1982 and 1985 (Todd Matshikiza's companion at the Kensington pub where he suspected the barman was a South African policeman in disguise), as well as playwright Bheki Peterson and poet, Pan-Africanist Congress activist and founder of Skotaville Publishers, Jaki Serote, in 1986. Mongane Wally Serote participated in the fair in 1987 and poet John Hendrickse was involved in 1990. The precarious environment in which these writers, many of them radical Black Consciousness activists, operated in South Africa is driven home by a note in the 1988 programme which notes that former participant Jaki Serote was 'detained in 1987 and is still in detention' (White et al. 2005: 324) – the same note reappears in 1991.

The Fair's events and panels also frequently dealt with South African concerns. The 1986 programme speaks of the heightened global focus on South Africa in the mid-1980s. The two central forums of the fair were 'Nkrumah – 20 Years After' (White et al. 2005: 225), and 'The Struggle for Southern Africa', with the director John La Rose elucidating in his 'Call to the Bookfair' the connections between these dual themes. Just as Nkrumah's influence, 'especially after the All-African Peoples' Conference' was 'considerable and at times decisive all over the continent' and indeed globally, La Rose observes that 'the people of South Africa are challenging and amazing the world with their determination, and their willingness to die so as to end the injustice of apartheid and win their national, social and cultural liberation' (La Rose, 'Call to the Book Fair', 1986, in White et al. 2005: 229). La Rose describes the struggle against apartheid as 'an inspiring example of the numerous interventions by youth, workers, peasants, writers, artists and intellectuals around the world, who want a different and better life for the world's peoples' (in White et al. 2005: 229). The same programme reprinted Nelson Mandela's 1985 reply to Botha following his offer of conditional release, which was read at a public meeting in Soweto, in which Mandela famously asserted, 'Only free men can negotiate. Prisoners cannot enter into contracts' (in White et al. 2005: 231). This text is positioned to face an excerpt from Nkrumah's *Class Struggle in Africa*, resonating, some thirty years later, with Peter Abrahams's efforts while in London to situate the South African struggle in a larger Pan-African context of radical anti-colonialism.

When Ngũgĩ wa Thiong'o delivered his address at the opening of the sixth International Book Fair in March 1987, he similarly foregrounded the importance of the anti-apartheid struggle as a test case for global 'movements for independence from *colonialism*' and 'against *neo-colonialism*'. He asserts that 'South Africa is a unique case which sees a convergence of all of the above features: a people's movement against colonialism, neo-colonialism and for revolutionary change. And that is why South African people's struggles are really the story of our lives: a metaphor of the 20th century' (1988 programme, in White et al. 2005: 303). Unsurprisingly, the 1990 fair programme featured a free Nelson Mandela, fist raised, on the cover, along with La Rose's welcome statement, opening with the stirring lines: 'No image has been more moving, in this the last decade of the century, than the sight of Nelson Mandela, hand in hand with Winnie Mandela, taking his first public steps into the centre of freedom in South Africa' (379). The International Book Fair of Radical Black and Third World Books was one the many forums based in London which forged networks between black British writers and literary activists from Africa and Asia. South African writers were key participants, contributing to discourses of protest and solidarity circulating within 1980s London.

Another such South African forger of alliances between black British writers was Lauretta Ngcobo, whose work I discussed briefly in my introduction. Ngcobo lived in London from 1963 until 1994 and her two published novels, *Cross of Gold* (1981) and *And They Didn't Die* (1990), were groundbreaking feminist contributions to South African letters. Born in Ixopo, KwaZulu-Natal, in 1931, she was one of the few women who attended Fort Hare University, after which she taught and then took a job with a research council. Having become politically conscientised at Fort Hare, she was one of the key figures in the anti-pass women's march held in 1956. She married trade union organiser, PAC leader and treason trialist Abednego Ngcobo, who was imprisoned for two years in 1961 under the Suppression of Communism Act. Their joint political activity and the resulting surveillance by the apartheid government necessitated exile, first in Swaziland, then Zambia and finally the United Kingdom, Ngcobo and her two children arriving to join her husband in 1969. She wrote her two novels while working at a south London school and becoming involved in organisations and collectives that promoted gender and 'racial' equality.

While not a billed participant in the Book Fair, Ngcobo participated in other forums of intersecting and intersectional activism in London, contributing, for instance, to the first issue of *Wasafiri*, the British literary magazine founded in 1984 in response to 'a pressing need to open up the seemingly impermeable and parochial boundaries of British literary culture by setting up an alternative platform, a place where serious critical attention could be paid to the large number of works being published, but not recognised, by writers of African, Caribbean, South Asian and Black British backgrounds' (Nasta 2014: 1). The first issue featured an interview with Ngcobo, 'focusing on the interrelationship between literature and politics' (Nasta 2014: 2). Ngcobo was at the time the President of the Association for the Teaching of African, Caribbean, Asian and Associated Literatures (ATCAL), which was involved in *Wasafiri's* founding. This organisation shared its aims with the journal, as it sought to create a more diverse curriculum in schools and universities. At the same time, Ngcobo was deeply involved in feminist initiatives; as Barbara Boswell and Victoria Collis-Buthelezi put it, she 'created spaces where other women could write about their experiences, so that black women's writing would no longer be a 'rare' phenomenon' (2017: 3). One such literary 'space' was her edited collection of essays by black women writers in Britain, *Let It Be Told* (1987), which brought together submissions by writers such as Marsha Prescod, Valerie Bloom, Grace Nichols, South African-born Agnes Sam and Ngcobo herself. Ngcobo's introduction, Boswell and Collis-Buthelezi argue, 'outlines a trajectory of black women's writing, a move, which, at that time, was unparalleled outside of the USA' (2017: 3). In this sweeping history, Ngcobo delineates how 'Blackwomen are caught between white prejudice, class prejudice, male power and the burden of history' (1987: 3) and argues for the political cogency of a feminist, black literary collective: 'From now on we exist. Where we had no collective considered viewpoint, now we have. In books such as this, we are carving for all Blackwomen a niche in British society' (Ngcobo 1987: 34).

Such striving for visibility is required because of gatekeeping deployed by the white and male-dominated publishing industry. Ngcobo describes the British book industry, 'publishers, distributors and retailers', as 'highly regulated because it constitutes the body of knowledge and values generally called British civilization' and names British publishers 'the guard dogs of their great traditions' (1987: 16). Yet she draws attention to the 'changes in the outlook of white, male-dominated publishers', pressured by 'the feminist lobby' who saw women being promoted in publishing (17), while feminist publishing houses shifted from a narrow focus on the 'neglected needs of their marginalized fellow white sisters', compelled in response to the 'literary cloudburst of Blackwomen's writing from North America' to 'look nearer home for Black talent' (17). Virago, publisher of *Let It Be Told* and Ngcobo's novel *And They Didn't Die* (1990), is one of the 'prestigious' feminist presses she describes as becoming more responsive to black women's writing. Ngcobo's survey of the growth in publishing opportunities for black British women writers, alongside the continued challenge of getting into print, drives home her commitment to elucidating the limiting structural and institutional context in which she and other black women writers operate.

South African writer Agnes Sam, as part of her submission to the anthology, marries a similar emphasis on the guardrails set up by British publishers with a specific focus on the challenges of the South African black woman writer in exile. If publishers 'believe the Black writer to be writing for Black readers', Sam suggests, 'the question of earning a living for writing, a universal problem, is exacerbated for Black writers in exile' (Sam 1987: 72). She differentiates herself from white South African writers who are 'guaranteed an audience' in both South Africa and the United Kingdom, while 'Black South African writers who are in exile know that their works are not circulated in South Africa, and that any market basing itself on the Black reading public in England will restrict publications of their work' (72). She concludes that the 'situation of the Black South African woman writing to earn a living in England has never been touched upon by any discussion of women writers or African writers' (72), a claim which underlines the importance of Ngcobo's intervention in both her wide-ranging introduction and her editorship of such a pioneering volume.

Sam's statement extends Ngcobo's overview of the United Kingdom publishing situation with commentary on South Africa's challenges both of censorship and exile, but also of the challenges faced by black South African women writers in particular. As I discussed in my introduction, problematic masculinist idioms of urban writing have inhered in South African letters, entangled with its Romantic and modernist influences, but in the 1980s further layers of masculinist modes of protest persisted, in literary genres and in the struggle against apartheid more broadly. Lauretta Ngcobo writes in her own essay in the collection about the gender dynamics of the anti-apartheid struggles: 'I slowly came to realize that mine was a cheering role, in support of men. I had no voice; I could only concur and never contradict nor offer alternatives. ... All decision-making positions are still in the hands of men, in spite of the lessons of a rigorous political struggle' (Ngcobo 1987: 136–137). Such a statement contributes to our understanding of the limits placed on black South African women writers' self-expression.

Her critique of British publishing, on the other hand, explains why London was not always as hospitable and productive a location for South African women writers as it may have been for men. If Ngcobo was able to forge a path to publication, this was achieved through the persistent collective efforts of black feminists, and through her own active role in black feminist collectives in Britain. Exiled South African writers like Ngcobo thus shaped the direction of British publishing and anti-racist politics, even as their end goal remained forging solidarities that would help to turn the tide of apartheid in South Africa; as Ngcobo writes, 'Britain's oppression of Black people is not mine to destroy; I have battles to fight elsewhere' (1987: 138). At the same time, she provides a warning about subjugating the fight against patriarchal oppression to the struggle against racism. Cognisant of the 'seriousness' of this prediction 'in the mid-1980s' while 'watching the Black neighbourhoods burning in South Africa and our people dying in large numbers' (1987: 138), Ngcobo nevertheless concludes her essay by wondering 'if it will prove to have been easier to fight the oppression of apartheid than it will ever be to set women free in our societies' (138). Her solidarities across 'societies' are thus twofold and, at odds with some anti-apartheid activists at the time, she does not privilege the struggle against racism over the struggle for gender equality.

Although solidarities between black British activists and South African writers reverberated through the rest of the United Kingdom rather than through London alone, partly accounting for the divergent, detouring nature of this chapter, key events such as the International Book Fair of Radical Black and Third World Books and journals like *Wasafiri* which were based in London, as well as the long history of the city as a publishing hub, make it a useful lens through which to view the meaningful networks that coalesced between black British and South African writers and activists. The fractured, shifting and conditional nature of these alliances during the tense decade of the 1980s calls out for more research in order to assess the role literary-activist figures of both nationalities played in contributing to the end of apartheid and the development of a more equal society in Britain.

4

Securing the past: self-reflexive, retrospective narratives of London in J.M. Coetzee's *Youth* and Justin Cartwright's *In Every Face I Meet*

Post-apartheid South African writing has frequently been characterised as a literature of retrospection. David Attwell and Barbara Harlow noted in 2000 that 'its fields are the experiential, ethical and political ambiguities of transition: the tension between memory and amnesia' (2000: 3). Whereas the 1980s were characterised by anxiety about South Africa's future, in the early years of the new millennium, they argued, it was 'the past that sustain[ed] many of the most earnest reflections. In post-apartheid literature, the future has little future, whereas the future of the past is reasonably secure' (4). Rita Barnard complicates this temporal distinction between apartheid-era and post-apartheid literature, suggesting that it is 'not quite accurate to say that while apartheid-era literature tended to be focused on the future, post-apartheid literature has been focused on the past' (2012: 660). Instead, she argues:

> The truth is that past, present and future are not so readily disentangled when historical experience is particularly painful. ... Their forms, one might say, are palimpsestic; the narrative oscillates between contemporary events and parallel (or originary) events in the past. The temporality of post-apartheid writing ... is perhaps most characteristically traumatic: marked by recurrences, melancholia and an elegiac effect that is not readily brought to term. The present, one might say, bears the scars of the past. (Barnard 2012: 660)

Narratives about South Africa's past often exceed the country's boundaries, since so many South Africans writers, intellectuals and political figures chose to live abroad or were forced into exile during the apartheid decades and, as I have argued throughout my study, London is one of these significant alternative spaces that inform South Africa's cultural history. Moreover, as we have seen, apartheid-era literature set in London exhibits its own layered structures in that texts 'oscillate' between events in London and 'parallel' or 'originary' events in South Africa. In the works of Peter Abrahams and Todd Matshikiza, in particular, London often represents the utopian, futural orientation of these apartheid-era narratives, but writers in London also look back to the trauma experienced in the recent past in South Africa. If post-apartheid literature is characterised by retrospection that attempts to resolve the 'tension between memory and amnesia' and if it also evinces a 'traumatic', fractured sense of temporality, then it has something in common with South African literature set in London, which frequently looks backwards towards South Africa and its history, as well as back into London's past. In post-apartheid texts set in London, then, space and time are doubly layered and fractured, speaking to both the trauma of displacement and the complexities of remembering.

In this chapter, I will explore two retrospective narratives of London by South African writers, both of which employ postmodern, metafictional techniques that foreground the uncertainty of reconstructing the past. J.M. Coetzee's *Youth* (2002), the second instalment in a fictionalised autobiographical sequence, looks back on the writer's years in London in the 1960s. Justin Cartwright's novel *In Every Face I Meet* (1995) critiques and deconstructs race and class prejudice in 1990s London, in dialogue with key historical events in South Africa. Both Coetzee and Cartwright combine layered temporalities and spatial perspectives to reflect on key events in South Africa's history through narratives set in London; each writes the history of London from a South African perspective, while evoking other time periods and global spaces that are layered in London. For instance, these texts present the interlaced, overlaid nature of race discourses and racisms from London, South Africa and other spaces. Furthermore, in Coetzee's novel in particular, the postmodern form inscribes the unwriteable and unreadable nature not only of London, but also of South Africa. These two white South Africans self-reflexively and self-consciously displace their anxieties about writing, or *not* writing, about race in South Africa on to their depictions of London. Remembering and narrating the past, for these authors, is more than an 'earnest reflection' on South Africa that promotes memory over amnesia: refracted through London, remembering is a temporally and spatially kaleidoscoped project that brings into question the privilege and position of the writer.

'The poet's country': writing back to London in J.M. Coetzee's *Youth*

The epigraph to J.M. Coetzee's *Youth* is Johann Wolfgang von Goethe's motto from his *West-östlicher Divan*: 'Wer den Dichter will verstehen muß in Dichters Lande gehen' (Whoever wants to understand the poet must visit the poet's country). Without the benefit of paratextual elements – the cover of the Vintage edition features an iconic 1960s photograph of a rain-soaked Trafalgar Square – one might approach this text with the assumption that the novel will take place mainly in South Africa, the home country of the 'poet' whose memoir we are reading. However, while this fictionalised autobiography, encompassing the years 1959 to 1964, begins with Coetzee's final years as an undergraduate student at the University of Cape Town, it moves swiftly to his time in London as a computer programmer for IBM, and finally to Bracknell, where he worked on the Atlas computers for IBM's British rival, International Computers. Despite its conclusion in Bracknell, near Reading, London is the spatial heart of the book. The Goethe epigraph therefore suggests that South Africa is not the only place that the reader has to 'understand' in order to interpret his work: London is also a significant locus within the writer's story. In *Youth*, South Africa, and the writer's relationship to his home country, is explored through a narrative set in London.

Youth was published in 2002, following the publication of the controversial and celebrated *Disgrace* in 1999, and was Coetzee's second semi-autobiographical work, after his 1997 memoir, *Boyhood*. The ambiguous genre of these texts caused some confusion amongst readers. In the USA, as Derek Attridge notes, *Youth* was subtitled '*Scenes from Provincial Life II*', signalling its status as a sequel to *Boyhood*, which had borne that subtitle in some editions. In the United Kingdom, by contrast, *Youth* had no such subtitle. The absence of any titular suggestion of its loosely autobiographical status and its use of third-person, present tense narration over the conventional first-person, past tense narration of traditional memoirs led many to view the text as a 'botched novel' rather than as an innovative autobiography (Attridge 2004: 157). Attridge asserts that '*Youth* has less value as testimony than *Boyhood*', partly due to the 'startling omissions and distortions' in the narrative compared with the facts of Coetzee's life. There is, for instance, no mention of Coetzee's marriage to Philippa Jubber in 1963 (Attridge 2004: 161). Coetzee's biographer, J.C. Kannemeyer, elaborates on these omissions, pointing to a six-month interruption in Coetzee's time in England and suggesting that this alteration of chronology is in keeping with Coetzee's statement about the ambivalence between 'fictional' and 'true' biography, since both forms depend on 'selection of data and omission of data' (2012: 130). Attridge, on the other hand, suggests that Coetzee's altered personal history 'renders the notion of autobiographical "truth" particularly problematic', as the 'urge to confess' can 'distort the representation of the past' (2004: 161). While Attridge presents this 'tendency' as something to which Coetzee 'succumbs' (161), one might also regard Coetzee's rewriting of this aspect of his life story as raising questions about the ethics of writing the self.

Coetzee asserted in an interview with David Attwell in 1992 that 'all autobiography is storytelling, all writing is autobiography' (Coetzee 1992: 391) and in the same interview coined the term 'autrebiography', which is to say that autobiography is always the biography of the other, the *autre*, that one was previously; it can never be the transparently 'true' narrative of the self in the present (394). Through his distortions of the autobiographical facts of his own life, Coetzee highlights the constructed, arranged and fictionalised nature of autobiographies. No matter their claim to 'truth', all autobiographies employ the framework and tropes of 'storytelling'. Furthermore, through his use of third-person narration, Coetzee makes visible the ways in which autobiography, though it may present the writer and the self represented in the text as identical, manifests the same writer/subject relationship as novels: 'autrebiography' captures this distance between the self writing and the self depicted. Attwell suggests in *J.M. Coetzee and the Life of Writing* (2015) that '[t]he most trenchant of the purposes of Coetzee's metafiction ... is that it is the means whereby he challenges himself with sharply existential questions, such as "Is there room for me, and my history, in this book? If not, what am I doing?"' (2015: 26). *Youth* asks these existential questions in relation to place – both South Africa and London – as Coetzee interrogates his own positionality and purpose as a writer. Even though *Boyhood*, *Youth* and *Summertime* (2009), the third and most experimental of Coetzee's autobiographical 'trilogy', draw on the facts of Coetzee's history more explicitly than his other works, and thematise the life and development of the writer, traces of self-writing can in fact be found across his oeuvre, since 'all writing is autobiography'. As Attwell puts it, Coetzee's writing is 'grounded in fictionalized autobiography', so that 'the texts marked as autobiography are continuous with those marked as fiction – only the degree of fictionalization varies' (2015: 26).

In his second semi-fictionalised memoir, we might ask why Coetzee chooses to draw on the few years he spent in London, before skipping forward to the 1970s in *Summertime*, rather than recalling any of the intervening periods of his life, such as his time as a PhD student in Texas. And what is the significance of looking back to 1960s London in the early twenty-first century? The London-based narrative in *Youth* allows Coetzee to explore a crucial period in his life which informed his development as a writer and especially as a writer of South Africa. His displacement to London provided experiences that would test the idealism of a young would-be poet and would confirm the impossibility of eliding or escaping his South African origins through geographical transplantation, as Margaret Lenta argues. '[T]he reader can follow the young Coetzee on his path from rejection of this homeland, not to reconciliation, but to the wish to engage as an artist with South Africa', she suggests (2003: 166–167). Coetzee recounts in *Youth* the artistic development that led to his first novel, *Dusklands* (1974), which focuses on South Africa's past in the section 'The Narrative of Jacobus Coetzee'. In 2002, almost ten years after the end of apartheid, the narration of this development provides a reminder of the temptation faced by white writers to elide their South Africanness in London. This does not mean that Coetzee proposes that post-apartheid South African writers should only write about South Africa or should be narrowly committed to their home country. After all, in 2002, the year that *Youth* was published, Coetzee relocated to Adelaide, Australia. Rather, *Youth* is a reconstruction of his own development as a writer, in response to the loci of both South Africa and London, and a consideration of the complex relationship between the 'white writer' and South Africa.

'Nothing unique': a familiar and limited vision of London

In *Youth*, the young artist's development is traced against the backdrop of the early 1960s, the decade during which many racist apartheid statutes were enacted and resistance to those laws was met with violence, as was evident in the March 1960 Sharpeville massacre; *Youth*'s protagonist, John,[1] describes South Africa post-Sharpeville: 'nothing is as it was before' (Coetzee 2002: 37). It is no accident that three of the writers whose work I discuss in this study set their London-based narratives in the 1960s. As has been discussed in relation to both Todd Matshikiza and Arthur Nortje, during the 1960s many black and white intellectuals either left South Africa on exit visas or chose to leave the country owing to the increasingly oppressive laws and the violence that erupted in response. Likewise, Justin Cartwright left South Africa for Oxford in

1965 and then stayed on permanently in the United Kingdom. John's exit from South Africa is presented as mainly motivated by self-preservation, as he feels sickened by the toxic 'bully-boy' violence of apartheid (37) and fears army conscription, telling himself: 'I must get out before it is too late!' (39). As much as London in the 1960s afforded greater freedoms than South Africa, the city provided exiles and emigrants with a glimpse of an alternative future for South Africa, presenting utopian glimpses of a 'convivial', multiracial space (to use Paul Gilroy's vocabulary).[2] However, displaced South African writers, with their sensitivity to racial tension, were also well positioned to make visible the faultlines within this apparent utopia. Temporalities and spaces – possible futures evident in the present, and space refracted through other spaces – thus overlap in these South African writers' interpretations of 1960s London. In *Youth*, temporality is further complicated by the retrospective nature of the narrative.

Coetzee's self-reflexive project in *Youth* means that his depiction of 1960s London is partial and blinkered. The partiality of the novel's vision performs the impossibility of a complete, truthful depiction of a place, a moment in time or oneself. The self-absorbed narrative concerns John's sexual affairs, his attempts at writing, his reading and his work, with only minor digressions into social commentary, which are mostly significant in terms of their bearing on himself. For instance, he notes how '[m]odern England is turning out to be a disturbingly philistine country', one that is 'hostile' to the 'life of the mind' (49–50). This is an observation not dissimilar to Arthur Panter's equally supercilious assertion, in Jacobson's 'A Long Way from London' (1958), that London 'wasn't civilized enough' (1958: 151–152). John's observation triggers a series of questions about his own place in England: 'What then is he doing in England? Was it a huge mistake to have come here? Is it too late to move?' (49–50). Derek Attridge writes of the self-absorbed nature of *Youth*'s 'testimony':

> [W]e get some insight into the impact on white South Africans of the Sharpeville Massacre, an intense sense of London's inhospitability to foreigners in the early 1960s, and glimpses of the early stages of the computing industry and of Britain's part in the Cold War, but these are viewed through the eyes of such a limited and self-absorbed witness that readers are unlikely to learn a great deal. (Attridge 2004: 157)

Even some of these insights, such as John's recognition of the 'impact on white South Africans of the Sharpeville Massacre', are qualified by their exceptionalism amongst the self-focused narrative detail. For instance, we learn that '[w]rapped up though he is in his private worries, he cannot fail to see that the country around him is in turmoil' (Coetzee 2002: 37). Other than the Sharpeville massacre, as Kannemeyer notes, 'Coetzee does not comment on the Rivonia trial and the sentences meted out to the ANC members, nor on the night march from Brighton to London by ANC sympathisers on 13 June 1964' (2012: 117). This self-absorption is partly an indication of the narcissism of youth and is perhaps also an admission of the privilege which insulates white South Africans from these crucial events.

One of the other aspects of passing social commentary that Coetzee provides is Britain's involvement in the Cold War. At IBM, he discovers that one of the programs on which he is – at first unwittingly – working concerns data used to develop the TSR-2 bomber for the Royal Air Force. Although nothing appears to come of this new weaponry, he considers his possible complicity in Cold War politics:

> Now that it is too late, he wonders what would have happened if, while the TSR-2 cards were in his hands, he had surreptitiously doctored the data on them. ... On the one hand, he would like to do his bit to save Russia from being bombed. On the other, has he a moral right to enjoy British hospitality while sabotaging their air force? (Coetzee 2002: 83)

John also attends a rally in Trafalgar Square, not an anti-apartheid event, but a demonstration of the Campaign for Nuclear Disarmament, protesting against the British atomic weapon station at Aldermaston, although he insists he is merely an 'onlooker' (85). Later, he is confronted with Aldermaston once again, since one of International Computers' Atlas machines is situated at the nuclear research station, although John, as a foreigner, is not allowed to work on it. Once again, while John might not comment on many major political events of the 1960s, including the erection of the Berlin Wall or decolonisation of African states, he reacts to incidents and developments which have a more direct bearing on his own profession and position within London. This elision of key international events reflects John's desire to avoid politics and their constraining consequences. We see this when he reflects on the spectre of nuclear war within Britain:

> From the frying-pan into the fire! What an irony! Having escaped the Afrikaners who want to press-gang him into their army and the blacks who want to drive him into the sea, to find himself on an island that is shortly to be turned to cinders! What kind of world is this in which he lives? Where can one turn to be free of the fury of politics? (85)

The self-focused perspective of the text is thus interwoven with his desire to escape the oppressive effects of politics. In South Africa, he is caught between the apartheid regime's conscription and the uncertainty and shame of being an unwanted white resident in an African country. While of course 'the fury of politics' has much more serious consequences for black South Africans, it is nevertheless the political situation in South Africa which may encourage John to avoid being swept up in wider political events and movements altogether.

The 'limited and self-absorbed' nature of Coetzee's text is foregrounded in a metafictional passage in which John worries that he will not be able to write London:

> He does not as yet know England well enough to do England in prose. He is not even sure he can do the parts of London he is familiar with, the London of crowds trudging to work, of cold and rain, of bedsitters with curtainless windows and forty-watt bulbs. If he were to try, what would come out would be no different, he suspects, from the London of any other bachelor clerk. He may have his own vision of London, but there is nothing unique to that vision. If it has a certain intensity, that is only because it is narrow, and it is narrow because it is ignorant of everything outside itself. (63)

In this passage, John is concerned that he will not be able to represent 'England', and specifically 'London'. Paradoxically, he complains that he cannot 'do' London 'in prose', before going on to do exactly that, describing aspects of London such as crowds walking to work, the weather and typical accommodation. Just as Attridge attributes the 'limited' nature of the text to its protagonist's self-absorption, so John here claims that his perspective of London is 'narrow' because it is 'ignorant of everything outside itself'. Furthermore, John's focus on himself stands in *place* of his ability to represent London, thus drawing attention to the absences in the text. John's hesitation at representing 'England in prose' is twofold: firstly, he is concerned that he does not 'know England well enough' and, secondly, he is anxious that his 'vision' of London will not be 'unique' despite the 'intensity' of its self-obsessed perspective. His concern about knowledge of London is caught up in the newcomer's anxiety about his lack of authority to write the metropolitan space. However, his anxiety about not presenting a 'unique' vision of London suggests that John is not so much an outsider as he may imagine, since he imagines his narrative will be 'no different … from the London of any other bachelor clerk'. John's wish to create a 'unique' narrative of London suggests, furthermore, the young writer's idealistic belief that his writing must be revolutionary and novel, without forebears. We also have the sense here of London as overwritten, an idea that recurs when John begins to compare British travel accounts of South Africa to narratives of London, which will be discussed later. He is concerned that he will merely reprise tropes associated with postwar London narratives, such as the cold weather, throngs of Londoners 'trudging' through the streets to work and rundown flats, because these have become ingrained through the multitude of literary accounts, particularly texts of arrival and immigration, written about the city. This passage therefore reveals how *Youth*'s 'limited and self-absorbed witness' enables Coetzee to develop thematic concerns, as the self-reflexive narrative enacts the hesitation and ambivalence felt by the South African writer attempting to represent London. Despite John's hope that London will turn him into a writer, the city proves to be barren of inspiration, and he later turns to South Africa as setting and subject. London is therefore the catalyst for his artistic development, but not in the way in which he anticipated.

While this passage imagines John's hypothetical, as yet unwritten narratives about London, Coetzee simultaneously critiques his own text, *Youth*, by suggesting its lack of uniqueness, and pre-empts praise of its concentrated, focused 'intensity', a word that is frequently attributed to Coetzee's writing style. Jarad Zimbler notes that reviewers of Coetzee's work frequently juxtapose the 'clarity and simplicity' of his writing with similarly characteristic 'force or intensity' (2014: 2). All of John's parodied London tropes – cold weather, dilapidated accommodation and crowds going to work – are present within *Youth*. One of the first sensations he describes in London is the cold: his feet, as he sleeps on a sofa in a friend's bedsitter, are 'icy' (Coetzee 2002: 41). His accommodations are perfunctory – a room in a house with a gas cooker over which he cooks chipolata sausages – and he soon joins the 'crowds trudging to work', 'indistinguishable in his black uniform from any other London office worker' (51). Margaret Lenta has commented on the familiarity of Coetzee's London narrative and has suggested that one of the reasons that Coetzee is 'willing to blur the generic definition of his work' through the use of third-person narration in his fictionalised autobiographies, *Boyhood* and *Youth*, is to 'preserve [their] 'everyman' quality':

> Few colonials who have made their way to the metropolis in the last half-century will fail to sympathise with Coetzee's loneliness, and many will believe that they shared to an extent in his experiences in London, recorded in *Youth*. ... This everyman quality depends on the vividness with which ... London in early 1960s is rendered, as well as on the

detachment which the narrator shows towards the protagonist. (Lenta 2003: 163)

The 'everyman' quality of the book may invite self-identification on the part of some readers, but the metafictional passage about writing London suggests that even more is going on here, as *Youth* falls, in an act of self-parody, into the narrative clichés that John hoped to avoid. By providing an internal critique of the potential banality of his book, Coetzee empties the text of its authority and any claim to a Romantic vision of artistic originality. This act plays into his foregrounding of textuality and storytelling over grand metanarratives and the privileging of the author figure, throughout the book and his oeuvre as a whole.

***Youth* and experience: London as chastener**

Amongst the familiar features of narratives recounting the experiences of colonials in London, there is often an underlying trajectory of the provincial subject encountering the transformative pleasures of the metropole. In *Youth*, Coetzee reprises this trope, but in a lightly satirical manner, through his account of the provincial writer in London who is 'not built for fun' (Coetzee 2002: 77). In his idealistic paradigm of London, the young Coetzee focuses on the city's rich literary history and its potential to inspire art and poetry. At the outset of the novel's section set in London, we learn of the qualities that John attaches to London, in comparison with other cities:

> There are two, perhaps three places in the world where life can be lived at its fullest intensity: London, Paris, perhaps Vienna. Paris comes first: city of love, city of art. But to live in Paris one must have gone to the kind of upper-class school that teaches French. As for Vienna, Vienna is for Jews coming back to reclaim their birthright: positivism, twelve-tone music, psychoanalysis. That leaves London, where South Africans do not need to carry papers and where people speak English. London may be stony, labyrinthine and cold, but behind its forbidding walls men and women are at work writing books, painting paintings, composing music. One passes them every day in the street without guessing their secret, because of the famous and admirable British reserve. (41)

Although he admits that London is his second choice after Paris, he suggests that it is a place where 'life can be lived at its fullest intensity', owing to the 'secret' artistic activities of the British.

We soon learn, however, that John's experiences in London fall short of the life of art and beauty he aims for: at IBM, 'he feels his very soul to be under attack', suspecting that the company is 'killing him, turning him into a zombie' (47), and during his time off he experiences 'loneliness indistinguishable from the low, grey, wet weather of London or from the iron-hard cold of the pavements' (52). He also undertakes a series of disastrous romantic and sexual encounters. John, however, reworks these bleak moments into his vision of London as a place of testing and transformation. While Nortje was following Baudelaire's and Rimbaud's example and losing himself in the bodily pleasures of the city (or, at least, he presented this persona in his poetry), Coetzee shows his younger self as choosing to emulate 'Eliot and Stevens and Kafka', rather than following the bohemian lifestyles of 'Poe and Rimbaud' (60). In a humorously prim passage, the young man is presented as eschewing 'absinthe and tattered clothes' (60) in favour of his 'black suit':

> That era is over: his own madness, if it is to be his lot to suffer madness, will be otherwise – quiet, discreet. He will sit in a corner, tight and hunched, like the robed man in Dürer's etching, waiting patiently for his season in hell to pass. And when it has passed he will be all the stronger for having endured. (60)

John's declaration, 'That era is over', suggests that his failure to imitate the hedonism and *flânerie* of 'Poe and Rimbaud' is not only due to a personal lack, his not being 'built for fun' (77), but also because the London of postwar austerity is a disappointment and does not deliver on the belated, Baudelairean, Romantic promise of the city. Here, Coetzee echoes the experiences of other South Africans in London in the 1950s and early 1960s. For instance, the protagonist in Dan Jacobson's short story 'A Long Way from London', Arthur Panter, declares of postwar London that 'it had all been spoilt' (Jacobson 1958: 152), and Jacobson, in his novel *The Evidence of Love* (1959), describes England as 'a disappointment that endures and endures' (121). Because, as Jacobson puts it, London is a 'dream' (1959: 121), imagined by colonials who have imbibed English literature and a Romantic ideal of the city, the reality, particularly in the aftermath of the war, is strangely familiar but also a disappointment.

Furthermore, as a South African writer, John is not able to take on the role of the *flâneur* in London, as he does not occupy a position of power in relation to the city. He is not able to read – or write – the city; as he confesses, he does not 'know' London (Coetzee 2002: 63), and *flânerie* is premised on knowledge of the city. As Keith Tester explains, 'The *flâneur* is the individual sovereign of the order of things who, as the poet or as the artist, is able to transform faces and things so that for him they have only that meaning which he attributes to them' (1994: 7). John is neither able to attribute a 'unique' meaning to the objects of the city, nor does he occupy a Baudelairean, Rimbaudian relationship towards the city that entails pleasure and consumption. Arthur Nortje presents himself (or his poetic persona) as sometimes taking on the role of the pleasure-seeking, potentially voyeuristic *flâneur* because this enables him to assert his agency in the city, but John imagines his 'season in hell' to be a time of Germanic asceticism and melancholia (epitomised by Albrecht Dürer's *Saint Jerome in His Study*) as opposed to a period of Rimbaudian sensuality. Of course, as in Nortje, the late Romantic figure of the libertine or *flâneur* is not far removed from melancholia, lack or loss itself; as Tester writes, the *flâneur's* detached attitude is 'one step away from isolation and alienation', since '*flânerie* can, after Baudelaire, be understood as the activity of the sovereign spectator going about the city in order to find the things that will occupy his gaze and thus complete his otherwise indeterminate identity; satisfy his otherwise dissatisfied existence; replace the sense of bereavement with a sense of life' (Tester 1994: 7). Nortje and Coetzee thus express their sense of alienation (or that of their literary personae) in different but parallel ways: Nortje through a late Romantic, bohemian, flâneuristic relationship to the city and Coetzee through a self-abnegating, inward-looking shrinking from the city's pleasures. Both Nortje and Coetzee drew from Eliot the modernist lexis of urban alienation, and we see John's devotion to modernism later in the novel through his reading of Ezra Pound and Ford Madox Ford. Ironically, John here expresses his desire to emulate not Eliot's poetry but his bookish, bourgeois lifestyle, suggesting the conservatism of the modernist canon. If the late nineteenth-century 'era' of 'tattered clothes' and 'absinthe' is 'over', surely that of early twentieth-century writers like Kafka, Eliot and Stevens is also outdated in the swinging 1960s? John, despite updating his role models slightly, remains belated, out of touch with contemporary London.

While he eschews the lifestyles of the Romantic French poets, John maintains the Romantic trope of 'experience' leading to artistic fulfilment. Coetzee reveals the absurdity and grandiosity of the provincial artist's sense that he will become a new kind of person and poet within London. Pieter Vermeulen traces how this Romantic 'recuperation of experience', and of London, is gradually abandoned by the protagonist in *Youth*

(2007: 191). The young Coetzee comes to realise that London, rather than providing the fulfilment of his literary and sexual desires, 'is proving to be a great chastener', and the only thing he is 'learning', like a 'beaten dog', is to temper his ambitions (Coetzee 2002: 113). In a key passage towards the end of the book, he reveals the bad faith behind his original expectations of London:

> Experience. That is the word he would like to fall back on to justify himself to himself. The artist must taste all experience, from the noblest to the most degraded. Just as it is the artist's destiny to experience the most supreme creative joy, so he must be prepared to take upon himself all in life that is miserable, squalid, ignominious. It was in the name of experience that he underwent London – the dead days of IBM, the icy winter of 1962, one humiliating experience after another: stages in the poet's life, all of them, in the testing of his soul ... It is a justification that does not for a moment convince him. It is sophistry, that is all, contemptible sophistry. (164)

John reflects, retrospectively, on his misguided expectation that London – alongside Paris and Vienna – might provide a 'destiny' that South Africa could not: 'Destiny would not come to him in South Africa, he told himself; she would come (come like a bride!) only in London or Paris or perhaps Vienna, because only in the great cities of Europe does destiny reside. For nearly two years he waited and suffered in London, and destiny stayed away' (150). Thus, Vermeulen argues:

> [T]he book refuses the two most familiar models for the inclusion of experience in an artistic autobiography: it is not a straightforward *Künstlerroman*, in which the artist is 'enriched and strengthened' by his experiences in order to write the work we are reading, and in which the success of this achievement retroactively valorises these experiences; nor is it a confession that congratulates itself on its conversion into the insight into the vanity of these experiences. (Vermeulen 2007: 192)

Vermeulen suggests that the chastening effect of London in *Youth* prevents the stalemate associated with confession that Coetzee describes in his essay on Tolstoy, Rousseau and Dostoevsky, 'Confession and Double Thoughts', as a 'potentially infinite regression of self-recognition and self-abasement in which the self-satisfied candour of each level of impure motive becomes a new source of shame and each twinge of shame a new source of self-congratulation' (Coetzee 1992: 162). He not only rejects the 'contemptible sophistry' of believing that everything, whether a morally questionable sexual affair, a soul-destroying job or constant loneliness, should be recuperated as 'experience' that enriches and develops the artist, but also questions the satisfaction provided by the 'ruthless honesty' of laying bare these delusions (Coetzee 2002: 164). This thematic concern with delusion, Romanticism and confession in the book are of much broader significance than their relevance to Coetzee's depiction of London. However, London, together with the expectations and chastening reality it provides, is the catalyst for this disillusioning but radical epiphany.

Passing as a Londoner: Englishness and alienness

Another of the young protagonist's delusions that must be shattered in London is his expectation that he will be able to assimilate into Englishness, that he will pass as an Englishman and escape his burdensome South African identity. A third-person account of Coetzee's early life, foreshadowing the subject matter and narrative approach of *Boyhood* and *Youth*, is contained in an interview published in *Doubling the Point*. In this interview, Coetzee describes his departure for Britain as being 'very much in the spirit of shaking the dust of the country from his feet' (1992: 393).[3] In the same narrative, he describes how, in both Britain and the United States, he felt 'alien' and dates this feeling back to his childhood in Worcester in South Africa, during which he developed a 'sense of social marginality' as a 'child from an Afrikaans background attending English-medium classes, at a time of raging Afrikaner nationalism' (393).

Coetzee's 'alienness – not alienation' (393) therefore dates back to his early life and is not only a symptom of his displacement from his home country. Significantly, his 'alienness' is attributed to being primarily English-speaking and having an affinity with Englishness while living in the Afrikaans community of Worcester. However, in *Youth*, we see how he attempts to assuage this feeling of alienness by reinventing himself as a Londoner. Thus, at IBM, despite the numbing dullness of the corporate environment, he rejoices in his ability to converse relatively easily with an English colleague:

> A bare two months ago he was an ignorant provincial stepping ashore into the drizzle of Southampton docks. Now here he is in the heart of London town, indistinguishable in his black uniform from any other London office-worker, exchanging opinions on everyday subjects with a fullblooded Londoner, successfully negotiating all the conversational proprieties. Soon, if his progress continues and he is careful with his vowels, he will pass as a Londoner, perhaps even, in due course, as an Englishman. (Coetzee 2002: 51)

At this stage, he believes that his clothing and speech (if he is 'careful with his vowels') will disguise his South Africanness and he will 'pass' as a Londoner. Jacobson's character, Arthur Panter, similarly attempts to wear the mask of Englishness, losing 'any trace of a South African accent' and dressing 'like an Englishman', so that 'no-one could have accused him of being, in appearance, a son of the wide-open spaces' (Jacobson 1958: 153–154). The similarity between these two characters' modes of assimilation conveys once more the 'everyman' quality of Coetzee's narrative, reflecting a ubiquitous attitude towards South Africanness and Englishness amongst a certain generation of English-speaking white South Africans.

Coetzee sets out a clear trajectory of 'progress' for John in London: he hopes to graduate from South African to Londoner to Englishman. That he positions 'Englishman' as the apogee of achievement suggests the importance accorded to Englishness amongst colonial (and ex-colonial) subjects. Robert J.C. Young has suggested that Englishness has historically been a concept fashioned by 'a long-distance nationalism', by a 'far-off diasporic community' of those 'who were precisely not English, but rather of English descent: the peoples of the English diaspora moving around the world' (2008: 1). In *Boyhood* we see how, despite the young John Coetzee's Afrikaans heritage on his father's side, he harbours a deep-felt attachment to Englishness, due to his love of cricket, the English language and mythic English values such as valour and duty: 'There is England and everything England stands for, to which he believes he is loyal. But more than that is required, clearly, before one will be accepted as truly English: tests to face, some of which he knows he will not pass' (Coetzee 1997: 128). One could frame his experiences in London as fulfilling this predicted failure to 'pass' the 'tests' that Englishness provides, but the passage from *Boyhood* also suggests that Englishness was, to begin with, an ideal, invented mainly in the colonies, which is unachievable because it is mythical. He is more likely to pass as a 'Londoner' because of the multicultural and increasingly globalised nature of the city, but the category of Englishness is closed to him.

Soon, John refers to London as 'this alien city' (Coetzee 2002: 65) and comes to realise that his foreignness – his South Africanness – is ineluctable. Though he may take on the superficial trappings of London life, he will never 'pass' as a Londoner: 'As for him, he may dress like a Londoner, tramp to work like a Londoner, suffer the cold like a Londoner, but he has no ready quips. Not in a month of Sundays would Londoners take him for the real thing' (102–103). He realises, rather, that Londoners see him as 'another of those foreigners who for daft reasons of their own choose to live where they don't belong' (102), evoking concepts of 'belonging' and 'home' that governed national rhetoric around immigration in the 1960s. Becoming a 'Londoner' turns out to be just as difficult as becoming English. Despite his attachment to England and Englishness and his attempts at assimilation, he will never pass for the 'real thing'. Englishness is also revealed not to be a single identity: class-divided as 1960s Britain is, 'he will have to choose between them, choose whether to be middle-class English or working-class English' (103), yet admission to both categories is closed.

Furthermore, John develops his understanding of Englishness, and his relationship to this category, in comparison to black Londoners, whom he observes. His commentary on race in London follows a passage in which he compares himself to a refugee. While he is 'fleeing' apartheid South Africa, he doubts that a 'claim on his part to be a refugee' will be accepted by the British Home Office (104). In the following paragraph, he describes West Indian immigrants:

> He walks along Maida Vale or Kilburn High Road at six o' clock in the evening and sees, under the ghostly sodium lights, throngs of West Indians trudging back to their lodgings, muffled against the cold. What draws them from Jamaica and Trinidad to this heartless city where the cold seeps up from the very stones of the street, where the hours of daylight are spent in drudgery and the evenings huddled over a gas fire in a hired room with peeling walls and sagging furniture? Surely they are not all here to find fame as poets? (104)

Coetzee conveys the sympathy which John feels towards the West Indian immigrants who, like him, may not be refugees, but also have their own complex reasons for leaving their homelands. Like the West Indians, he shares the somatic experience of the cold felt keenly by those who hail from warmer countries: they are 'muffled against the cold', far away from 'Jamaica and Trinidad' in a 'heartless city where the cold seeps up from the very stones of the street'. John similarly finds the pavements 'iron-cold' (52) and London to be a 'huge, cold city' (57). Describing a later winter, he contrasts the 'worst winter of the century' to a South African summer spent running on Strandfontein beach (102). The word 'lodgings' is also significant, implying that these immigrants occupy temporary or makeshift accommodations rather than homes. Like the famous writers of the Windrush generation, John has come to London to 'find fame' as a 'poet', but like many immigrants he also experiences London as 'heartless' and as a place of 'drudgery'.

The above passage presents the shared ground between John and West Indians in London, suggesting that there is more in common between their experiences than between John and Englishmen. Todd Matshikiza likewise observes Caribbean immigrants walking London's streets and imagines a potential fraternity with them, based on shared experiences of immigration, but also on a sense of global blackness. John recognises that, as a white immigrant, he would not experience London in an identical fashion to these black Britons:

> The people he works with are too polite to express their opinion of foreigner visitors. Nevertheless, from certain of their silences he knows he is not wanted in their country, not positively wanted. On the subject of West Indians they are silent too, but he can read the signs. NIGGER GO HOME say slogans painted on walls. NO COLOURED say notices in the windows of lodging houses. Month by month the government tightens its immigration laws. West Indians are halted at the dockside in Liverpool, detained until they grow desperate, then shipped back to where they came from. If he is not made to feel as nakedly unwelcome as they are, it is only because of his protective coloration: his Moss Brothers suit, his pale skin. (104)

Both John and the West Indian immigrants are 'not positively wanted', which he can sense, despite and because of the 'silences' of his British colleagues. Like Jacobson, he perceives a 'paradoxical sense of exclusion and withdrawal' as a white South African in London (Jacobson 1971: 884). In order to ascertain the British attitude towards West Indians, however, he does not need to read hidden or subtle 'signs': overt expressions of racism are physically present within the city, in the form of graffiti and notices in the windows of lodging houses. He reads these 'signs', just as Matshikiza deciphers the barely coded language of racist accommodation notices in London newspapers. In the final sentence of the passage, Coetzee asserts the difference between John and the West Indian immigrants: while the British government 'tightens its immigration laws' against black colonials, it continues to allow white immigration from its former colonies. While he knows that he will never pass as a Londoner or an Englishman even though he may dress like one, he nevertheless realises that his suit and his white skin lend him a certain degree of privilege and protection against 'naked' prejudice. By comparing John to black immigrants to London, Coetzee makes visible the racism of 1960s Britain. Thus, while he may have been attempting to flee from shameful and outdated attitudes in South Africa, he finds that racism is woefully ubiquitous.

Furthermore, beyond these two more obvious comparisons – between his own experience of feeling unwelcome in London and the racism experienced by black Londoners, and the underlying comparison between racism in South Africa and racism in London – there exists a further resonance in John's sense of being not 'positively wanted'. As a descendant of white settlers in Africa, Coetzee is familiar with a feeling of being unwanted and out of place, which underlies his sympathy for the West Indian Londoners. Earlier in *Youth*, Coetzee reflects on 'the gulf fixed' between white and black South Africans because of the 'awareness of both sides' that people like himself are 'here on this earth, the earth of South Africa, on the shakiest of pretexts' (Coetzee 2002: 17). I do not mean that Coetzee intends that West Indian immigrants are in London on shaky 'pretexts': the comparison is not evenly weighted in terms of power and privilege, as Coetzee acknowledges. Rather, by comparing his own experience of prejudice as a South African in London to that of the West Indian Londoners, Coetzee reminds the reader of other experiences of 'not being positively wanted': his own recognition of being in South Africa 'on the shakiest of pretexts', and the exclusion faced by black South Africans in their home country.

The country of his heart: writing and reading South Africa in London

In *Youth*, London is revealed to be neither the crucible of experience that will refine the young Coetzee as an artist, nor the location in which he can be absorbed into Englishness and therefore shed his South Africanness. In London, the only development that occurs in terms of his writing is that, through the 'chastening' that occurs in the city, he is compelled to turn to South Africa for inspiration. The sole piece of fictional prose which we see John writing is a short story about a girl on a beach, which is set in South Africa: 'It disquiets him to see that he is still writing about South Africa. He would prefer to leave his South African self behind as he has left South Africa itself behind' (62). He 'sees no point in trying to publish it' mainly because he is concerned that its subject matter will not be translatable to English readers:

> The English will not understand it. For the beach in the story they will summon up an English ideas of a beach, a few pebbles lapped by wavelets. They will not see a dazzling space of sand at the foot of rocky cliffs pounded by breakers, with gulls and cormorants screaming overhead as they battle the wind. (62)

John's perceived audience is 'the English', which reveals how he wishes to assimilate into English society and the English literary field, even as he writes about South Africa. The gulf between London and South Africa is suggested in his realisation that he cannot communicate to English readers the sublime beauty of a South African beach. He strives towards an accurate and rich portrayal of South Africa, even as he presents the challenges of representing the landscape for English readers.

As with the passage in which he describes London while expressing his anxiety at not being able to represent the city, Coetzee here provides a vivid description of the South African beach, even as he presents John's thoughts about not being able to depict the scene. If he can imagine what English readers should picture when reading about the beach, why not simply describe the landscape using these images? John's ambivalence at representing South Africa surely has more to do with the difficulty of representing apartheid South Africa, for which the representation of the landscape is a metaphor. In *White Writing: On the Culture of Letters in South Africa* (1988), Coetzee discusses how 'white writers' who are 'no longer European, not yet African' (11) have historically struggled to 'read' and represent the African landscape. According to Coetzee, the questions that have dominated South African literature, especially poetry, have included:

> How are we to read the African landscape? Is it readable at all? Is it readable only through African eyes, writeable only in an African language? Is the very enterprise of reading the African landscape doomed, in that it prescribes the quintessentially European posture of reader vis-à-vis environment? Behind these questions, in turn, lies a historical insecurity regarding the place of the artist of European heritage in the African landscape ... – an insecurity not without cause. (1988: 62)

John is able to represent the South African landscape, but he evinces a paradoxical insecurity about his powers and imagines that the South African landscape is unreadable, particularly by a metropolitan readership. The self-reflexive, metafictional form of the text thus serves to inscribe the unreadable and unwriteable aspects of South Africa.

John's concern over the impossibility of representing the South African landscape provides an allegory of the ambivalence that white writers feel towards representing apartheid South Africa. Timothy Bewes has characterised Coetzee's work as dramatising shame, in form as well as content, as 'an event of incommensurability: a profound disorientation of the subject by the confrontation with an object it cannot comprehend, an object that renders incoherent every form available to the subject' (2011: 3). Certainly, on a content and thematic level, *Youth* is replete with references to shame, as John frequently expresses both his personal shame at his actions, particularly his sexual misadventures, but also the broader shame of being a white South African. When he imagines claiming refugee status at the British Home Office, he envisions himself testifying that he is fleeing from 'boredom', 'philistinism', 'atrophy of the moral life' and 'shame' (Coetzee 2002: 104). However, on a more formal level, and relevant to the passage above, Coetzee's shame is also a 'manifestation of the impossibility, even the obscenity, of a literary response to apartheid' (Bewes 2011: 137). By having John claim that English readers will not 'see' a representation of South Africa accurately, Coetzee presents the gap between language and subject which makes the depiction of any space – particularly one as fraught as South Africa, but also London – a problematic project. He cannot 'do' South Africa any more than he can 'do' London, not, in this case, because of a lack of knowledge, but because of the incommensurability (as Bewes puts it) between subject and writer. The difficulty John finds in 'doing' England or London 'in prose' mirrors his anxieties about representing South Africa. Just as he is self-critical of his 'narrow' vision of London, 'ignorant of everything outside itself' (Coetzee 2002: 63), so he is concerned about his authority, as a privileged 'white writer', to represent South Africa.

As John gradually turns to his home country in his writing, despite the challenges involved in doing so, his reading drifts simultaneously towards South Africa. In the Reading Room of the British Museum, he begins to read early accounts of travel in the Cape and discovers that 'it is his country, the country of his heart, that he is reading about' (147). He wonders whether he is 'proving himself unable to live without a country', which leads to a 'yearning for the South Africa of the old days' (137). In a *mise-en-abyme* moment, he reflects on his experience of reading about South Africa, in London:

> Do these Englishmen around him feel the same tug at the heartstrings when there is a mention of Rydal Mount or Baker Street in a book? He doubts it. This country, this city, are by now wrapped in centuries of words. Englishmen do not find it at all strange to be walking in the footsteps of Chaucer or Tom Jones. (137)

London is described as a fully written city, 'wrapped in centuries of words'. South Africa, on the other hand, has not, in the 1960s, been as thoroughly represented. Once more, we see Coetzee commenting upon the historical tradition of viewing Africa as an unrepresented, and unrepresentable, sublime, uninhabited space in comparison to the overwritten, overpopulated urbanscape of London. Dan Jacobson draws on this same trope in his autobiography when he calls South Africa an 'undescribed and uncertified place' (1985: 8). In *White Writing*, Coetzee refers to the historical 'fiction' of 'unpeopled' Africa, which allowed western colonialists an ideological base to conquer and people the land, and he highlights the role that the 'poetry of empty space' plays in furthering this fiction (1988: 177). We recall here Jacobson's description of Arthur Panter as a 'son of the wide-open spaces' (1958: 54). John's attitude towards South Africa, as he reads early travel accounts in the British Museum, echoes aspects of this paradigm, as he foregrounds the unwritten, even non-literary nature of South Africa. John yearns for 'the South Africa of the old days' because he is not yet able to face the challenge of representing or even forming an attachment to contemporary South Africa in all its complexity, but must hark back to a colonial past for inspiration. His first South African novel is inspired by William Burchell's *Travels in the Interior of Southern Africa* (1822). John decides he will write a novel 'as convincing' as Burchell's travel book, which will be imbued with the 'aura of truth' (Coetzee 2002: 138). This research echoes Coetzee's section 'The Narrative of Jacobus Coetzee' in *Dusklands*. It is his time in London – both the concrete availability of South African history in the British Museum and the city's chastening effects – which throws John back into a recognition of his attachment to South Africa and causes him to focus on South Africa as a literary subject, however fraught a subject it may be. Furthermore, Coetzee's recounting of John's admiration of the 'aura of truth' provided by historical travel narratives suggests the complex relationship between fiction and history.

 J.M. Coetzee's *Youth* is thus a 'Portrait of the Artist as a Young Man' *and* a portrait of 1960s London. If it is a particularly narrow, even banal, picture of the city, this is because the youthful, self-absorbed perspective of his protagonist is realised in a limited, self-reflexive narrative of London. Coetzee's metafictional text raises questions about the role of the author but also about the position of the writer in relation to the places he represents. For John, it is easier to write the Karroo of the nineteenth century than it is to depict the London or South Africa of his present, which leads to an awareness of the impossibility of eliding his own South Africanness, as well as a consideration of the difficulties of representing apartheid South Africa. London chastens both his Romantic pretensions and his hope of becoming an Englishman. This trajectory of the gradual disillusionment of the young writer illuminates the traps into which many Anglophone South African writers have historically fallen: those of Romanticism, Anglophilism and the fiction of South Africa as an empty, unreadable and unwriteable space. Thus, through his fictionalised account of his years spent in London, Coetzee traces the historical pitfalls of South African 'white writing', while providing a retrospective glimpse into 1960s London.

Marking weakness in London: Justin Cartwright's *In Every Face I Meet*

Justin Cartwright's *In Every Face I Meet* (1995) begins with a strange question: 'The boom in mozzarella, trade or consumer led?' We soon learn that this query derives from the focaliser of the novel's preface, 'freelance writer Julian Capper' (Cartwright 1995: 3), who is writing an article for a trade magazine, *The Grocer*. Given the moment and location in which the novel is set – the year 1990 in London – one can read an implied association between the title of the paper and the 'grocer's daughter', Margaret Thatcher, who had been the British Prime Minister since 1979.[4] The mercantile nature of his article also reminds one of the consumer-driven focus of Thatcher's economic approach. Capper is rushing to finish his article because he is on jury duty for two weeks, which he is anticipating eagerly:

> He knows, of course, that by the time a case reaches court it will have been repackaged (a word he uses frequently in *The Grocer*), but he believes he will be able to see behind the artificiality and the formality to the human issues. He feels that he will be exploring the real world in some way. As a writer he is always on the lookout for the real world. (Cartwright 1995: 4)

Paradoxically, Capper believes that, as a writer, he will be able to see past the ways in which the crime will be reconstructed ('repackaged') into a pre-determined narrative. He has faith in the existence of a 'real world' that can be accessed beyond discourse. However, we soon see that he is just as likely to turn the events of the case into a story upon which he imposes his own interpretations, since '[t]he defendant is not just a man on a murder charge, but a character in a drama imbued with personal significance for Julian Capper' (6) and, upon entering the courtroom, he 'thinks it is like walking on to a stage, already lit and with the scenery in place' (7). There is no 'real world' here: all is constructed, packaged like a product and as pre-ordained as a script.

When we learn that the narrative which follows this section provides multiple perspectives on the case being heard, we may read the prosecutor Mrs Badenoch's warning to the jury as an injunction to the reader: 'Let me tell you now that you may choose to believe all, or nothing, or a part of what a witness says. You may think a witness is not telling the truth in some particular, but you may still believe some of his or her evidence' (8). The last words before the narrative proper begins are 'Julian Capper is poised, his pen is ready. Mrs Badenoch turns to the jury' (8). The story we then read is therefore either a version or retelling of the case presented by the prosecution, or the account written by Julian Capper. By constructing his text within these metafictional layers, Cartwright, like Coetzee, questions the role and authority of the author, as he highlights the constructed and mediated nature of discourse around race and class in early 1990s Britain.

The novel's title evokes William Blake's poem 'London', and just as Blake's poem provided a critique of social control and inequality in London in the late eighteenth century, so Cartwright's novel comments upon the 'woe' evident 'in every face' (Blake [1789] 1992, line 3), by providing a perspective on London's underclass and by drawing attention to the way in which racism in 1990s Britain was structured around ideas of belonging and nationhood. The initial, obscure references to Thatcher in the preface expand into more overt critiques of the effects of Thatcherism within London. Through the protagonist's reminiscences about his childhood in colonial southern Africa and his obsession with Nelson Mandela, South Africa is also made present within the text, so that an implicit comparison is set up between London and South Africa.

Justin Cartwright, born in Johannesburg in 1945, left South Africa to study at Oxford University in 1965, and thereafter moved to London, where he lived until his death in 2018. Despite Cartwright's long-time residence in Britain, critics have designated Cartwright an 'outsider', a position which they have attributed to his South African origins. A review of his novel *To Heaven by Water* (2009), for instance, suggested that 'Cartwright, born in South Africa, has always had an outsider's beady eye on English life' (Feay 2009). The assumption that Cartwright is an 'outsider' to English culture is a problematic one, since the author lived and worked in England for more than forty years. Yet, as in the examples above, his alienation rather than assimilation is invoked in praise of his ability to observe English society. Like John in *Youth*, it seems that according to some critics, Cartwright can never hope to 'pass' as an Englishman, which suggests the elusive nature of Englishness. This positioning of Cartwright as 'outsider' is also, however, a perspective he consciously plays with and exploits: he has suggested that he purposely inhabits dual national roles, playing up a certain side of his identity depending on his whereabouts, saying: 'I work both sides of the street. When I'm there [South Africa], I'm fabulously South African and when I'm here [England] I probably play it down a bit' (Cartwright 2009c). Cartwright utilises his outsider/insider perspective to provide a satirical view of British society, which is particularly evident in later novels such as *The Promise of Happiness* (2004), *To Heaven by Water* and *Other People's Money* (2013). *In Every Face I Meet* was the first of Cartwright's novels to provide the type of 'state of the nation' novel for which he would become well known. Like *White Lightning* (2002) and *To Heaven by Water*, *In Every Face I Meet* also juxtaposes South Africa and London, exploring how race and 'ethnicity' are constructed in both locations.

Responding to Thatcherism: social critique and metafiction

In Every Face I Meet is narrated in the third person, mainly in the mode of free indirect discourse, and focuses on the thoughts of former rugby player and native of Swaziland, middle manager Anthony Northleach, over the course of one day that ends with his arrest for the killing of a young black British man, Jason Parchment. Cartwright also writes from the perspectives of three other characters, in third-person narratives that are focalised through one character at a time. A story focalised through prostitute Chanelle Smith alternates with Anthony's narrative from Chapter 2 of section 'Two' onwards, evoking 'the youthful Harlot' in Blake's famous poem (line 14), and Chapters 7, 13 and 15 of 'Two' provide the perspective of Anthony's wife, Geraldine. In the very short section entitled 'Three', Anthony is in hospital recovering from a gunshot wound, and framing the entire narrative, at its beginning and end, are two sections, 'One' and 'Four', set a few months later, devoted to the perceptions of Julian Capper. The narrative itself thus takes on a retrospective quality, since it begins in November 1990 with Julian Capper's prologue and then presents the rest of the narrative as a long flashback set on 5 February 1990, focalised through Anthony and Chanelle, before returning to November in the final section.

Although published only five years after the time in which it is set, those intervening years were characterised by change and upheaval in both Britain and South Africa. Of course, in South Africa, the 1990s began with the release of Nelson Mandela on 11 February, which followed the fall of the Berlin Wall in 1989. No longer able to excuse the continuation of apartheid on the grounds of the communist threat that the ANC supposedly posed, and subject to increasing international political pressure, the National Party agreed to negotiations with the ANC, which signalled the beginning of the end of their regime. In *In Every Face I Meet*, Cartwright comments upon the role of the British government in securing the release of Mandela, but also suggests their prior, tacit support of the apartheid regime: 'The papers say that Mrs Thatcher put pressure on the government to release Mandela. For more than a third of Nelson's imprisonment, she has been Prime Minister. What took her so long?' (Cartwright 1995: 43). Previously proscribed political parties, including the ANC, were unbanned on 2 February 1990, and Mandela was released the following week. Thus, *In Every Face I Meet* is set in between these key historical moments, though it was written around the official moment of national transformation: the first democratic elections in South Africa, which Cartwright dealt with more directly in *Not Yet Home*, a 1996 collection of essays and interviews about this milestone and its consequences for South Africa. Setting the novel at the transitionary stage in South Africa's history allows Cartwright to draw on the myth-making around Mandela and the future he represented. Locating the novel in London, rather than South Africa, allows him to comment upon how South Africa, and particularly Mandela, became an important touchstone for thinking about race in Britain.

In Britain, the early 1990s were also a period of political and social change, as Margaret Thatcher was forced out of her cabinet on 22 November 1990 and was replaced by John Major. Thatcher's resignation occurs between the main events of *In Every Face I Meet* and its prologue and epilogue, which are set ten months later, in late November 1990. Under Thatcher, Britain had seen major economic and social changes during the 1980s. The sale of council houses and tax cuts for high earners meant that the unemployed and low-wage-earners suffered, while the gap between rich and poor widened. Privatisation of utilities exemplified Thatcher's focus on individualism. Joseph Brooker explains how 'There's no such thing as society' became the phrase that defined Thatcherism, as '[t]he prime minister succinctly voiced the suspicion of the collective and public, that ran through much of the policy of the decade, and strongly affected British culture' (2014: 78). Thus, depending on one's perspective, Thatcher was either 'a new Churchill who had reversed decline, defeated socialism and restored Britain's place in the world' or a 'small-minded bigot, who destroyed British industry, widened inequality and unleashed a new era of greed and rampant individualism' (Jackson and Saunders 2012: 1). Cartwright's novel certainly leans towards the latter perspective in its assessment of the social effects of Thatcher's policies on British society over the previous decade.

In Every Face I Meet is not unique in providing a critical response to the consequences of Thatcher's time in government. Many British novels of the 1980s and early 1990s critiqued Thatcherism and its effects, reflecting the liberal slant of much literary fiction, but also indicating, as Brooker suggests, how the 'large-scale change and social drama' of Thatcherism led to writers 'feeding off it and channelling its energies, even as they sought to criticize many of its effects' (2014: 77). Literary responses to Thatcherism either took the form of overt political satire or included broader social commentary within their plots. An example of one of the more direct responses to the effects of Thatcherism is Jonathan Coe's state-of-the-nation novel *What a Carve Up!* (1994), which covers the period of September 1990 to January 1991, thus overlapping in part with the chronology of *In Every Face I Meet*, and likewise including the event of Thatcher's resignation. Through its focus on the Winshaw family, whose members represent powerful interest groups under Thatcher's regime with influence across spheres from banking to the media and the arts, Coe's novel explores 'Thatcherite trends' and the consequences of 'Thatcherite free-enterprise' (Head 2002: 35).

An instance of the second, less direct critique of Thatcherism is Emma Tennant's *Two Women of London* (1989), which rewrites Robert Louis Stevenson's *The Strange Case of Dr Jekyll and Mr Hyde*, with working-class Londoner Eliza Jekyll transforming into socialite Mrs Hyde with the help of the drug Ecstasy. The novella uses these two figures to draw attention to the contrasts between wealth and poverty in London that had become starker in Thatcher's Britain, so that '[t]he extremes of the contemporary city map on to the divided self of Jekyll and Hyde' (Brooker 2014: 91). Cartwright similarly provides doubles and contrasts through the multiple perspectives provided in his novel, illustrating the economic and social divide between middle-class and underclass within London. While *In Every Face I Meet* contains a framing narrative in which a juror and writer analyses the facts of the central narrative, Tennant goes even further, as the entire text is narrated through the perspective of an investigator assessing the murder supposedly committed by Mrs Hyde. Both texts thus combine a metafictional framing narrative with the reconstructive, retrospective perspectives inherent to the criminal justice system.

The combination of postmodern techniques, such as metafiction, with a critique of Thatcherism, which we see in *Two Women of London* and *In Every Face I Meet*, is a key feature of several British novels of the period. Postmodernism was the global watchword in literary fiction in the 1980s and 1990s, as:

> A range of post-structuralist and postmodern intellectuals offered apparently fundamental challenges to the very foundations of Enlightenment rationality, exhibiting preferences for the plural and the ludic, endorsing bricolage, the fragmentary and pastiche, the aesthetic possibilities of which influenced many writers who came to prominence in the decade. (Horton et al. 2014: 15)

Nick Bentley suggests that even after postmodernism reached its high point in the 1980s, and even as it was critiqued for its potentially apolitical nature, the 'blurring of the boundaries between fiction and reality' that was so significant to postmodernism 'continued to fascinate cultural theorists and novelists alike in the 1990s' (2005: 4). In Britain, postmodernist techniques were woven through literary responses to Thatcherism. For instance, Dominic Head argues that novelists like Coe and Margaret Drabble respond to 'Thatcher's infamous conviction that society does not exist' by creating 'inventive fictional forms' to 'fashion some surrogate form of social network' (2002: 35). Alternatively, the fragmented, nonlinear forms of many postmodernist novels can be seen as *reflecting* the fragmented nature of British society under Thatcher.

Cartwright's novel is not particularly fragmentary in terms of time or the linearity of it narrative, but it does reflect on its own textuality, as well as the constructed and mediated nature of discourses such as racism. His engagement with metafiction is timely, since Patricia Waugh suggests that, while metafictional tropes existed in literature even before modernism, metafictional writing of the late twentieth century was 'both a response and a contribution to an even more thoroughgoing sense that reality or history are provisional: no longer a world of eternal verities but a series of constructions, artifices, impermanent structures' (1984: 7). Frederick M. Holmes explores the ways in which Martin Amis's postmodern novel *London Fields* (1989) responds both to changes in the class structure of Britain, such as the growth of a large underclass and the instability of the middle class, and to the shallowness of postmodern society 'in which reality is culturally constructed and electronically mediated and in which people frequently behave like decentred automatons' (Holmes 2014: 161). Amis, like Cartwright, combines social critique with metafictional techniques – also including an author figure, who shares his initials with those of the author, as a key character – which reflects the mediated nature of life in 1990s Britain. In Cartwright's case, his commentary on British society, especially his critique of racism in London, is augmented by the dialogue he sets up between South Africa and London.

Racism, Mandela and messianism

Cartwright outlines the manner in which racist ideology is constructed in Britain by providing us with the perspective of a typical middle-class, middle-aged, British middle manager. Cartwright adopts an ironic attitude towards the character of Anthony, aided by the distance of his third-person narration. In the first scene in which Anthony appears, at a London Underground station, we are immediately made aware of his priorities. He is 'plumped up' with 'expectation': firstly, because 'England have beaten France 26–7 in Paris' and secondly, because 'the government in South Africa has announced that Nelson Mandela will be released soon' (Cartwright 1995: 11). Rugby, in Anthony's mind, comes first, before transformative world events, and this is worth bearing in mind as we later read about his idealistic obsession with Mandela. Anthony is also presented as an observer of Londoners, and his commentary on the Underground's commuters is immediately filtered through his awareness of race:

> Others have those London faces: low expectations, cheerful, easily amused, self-deprecating, open to hurt, strangely unworldly. Lots of black women, but less black men at this time of day. God, the bewildering variety in their faces. The blacks dress with verve. He admires it, although the young men in their hoodies and track suits, who seem to be more numerous by evening, frighten him. Anthony has reached an age when he sometimes feels unprompted stirrings of dread. These boys are dressed to combat a chill wind off Lake Michigan. They all seem to have, as the sports commentators say, upper body strength. He doesn't think of them as English, although of course they are. (12)

While Anthony is 'plumped up with expectation', he imagines that the Londoners he observes have 'low expectations'. He reads their faces and imposes his own, condescending assumptions upon them, even as he notes the 'bewildering variety in their faces', voyeuristically categorising and 'marking' his fellow commuters. Likewise, critics have suggested that Blake's 'London' can be read as evincing a scopic relationship of power towards its subjects. Pramod K. Nayar argues, for instance, that 'London' is a 'surveillance poem', in that we witness the speaker carrying out 'observation and data gathering accompanied by a social sorting of the people who might be denied the right to the city for their subversive or illegitimate activity' (2014: 328). The speaker's viewpoint is not panoptical, but is rather a perspective of '*sousveillance*', or 'surveillance at the level of the ground and the street' (330). In this passage and others within the novel, Anthony adopts a similar, voyeuristic, 'sousveillant' perspective towards his fellow Londoners.

The flattening effects of such an objectifying perspective are revealed as Anthony generalises about the commuters, especially focusing on the black passengers – 'the blacks dress with verve' – and reveals that his thinking about race plays into stereotypes of black men as criminal and dangerous, since his 'dread' is based on their clothing choices. The last line of this passage is particularly revealing of Anthony's racism, since he 'doesn't think of them as English, although of course they are'. His thoughts here are contradictory: he doesn't 'think' of the black men as English, yet he knows that 'of course they are'. The distinction here is between Anthony's underlying racism and his exclusive concept of Englishness, and his realisation that these black men are British citizens. Anthony has granted the black commuters the status of 'Londoners', but is reluctant to bestow upon them the mythic quality of 'Englishness'. As we have seen in Coetzee's hierarchy of 'Londoner' and 'Englishman', 'Londoner', while similarly a nebulous designation, is more flexible and inclusive, even more so in the 1990s than in the 1960s. Within this passage and in the novel as a whole, Cartwright reveals the contradictions present in 1990s Britain, in which black Britons were officially granted the full rights and freedoms of citizenship, but often suffered structural and personal racism in their everyday lives.

Paul Gilroy comments on the nexus between British national identity and racism in *There Ain't No Black in the Union Jack* (1987), his study of racism in 1980s Britain, writing that 'the politics of "race" in this country is fired by conceptions of national belonging and homogeneity which not only blur the distinction between "race" and nation, but rely on that very ambiguity for their effect'. Gilroy outlines the characteristics of 'new racism', a term referring to the discourse around immigrants in the 1980s, and argues that '[t]he new racism is primarily concerned with mechanisms of inclusion and exclusion' and that it 'specifies who may legitimately belong to the national community and simultaneously advances reasons for the segregation or banishment of those whose "origin, sentiment or citizenship" assigns them elsewhere' (1987: 44–45). In Cartwright's novel, Anthony evinces his interpellation into 'new racist' ideology in that he excludes the black Londoners from Englishness based on the racial and class markers of their hip-hop style clothing. That Cartwright's commentary on racism in 1990s Britain, presented through the consciousness of Anthony, was delivered in the moment in which the world was focusing on South Africa's emergence from an oppressive, racist regime is particularly relevant, since Cartwright, like Ngcobo, reveals that racism endures globally in subtle and obfuscated forms, beyond the obviously racist statutes in South Africa.

Anthony's reverence for Englishness and his racism are particularly pronounced because of his upbringing in Africa, in Swaziland, which would have still been under British rule during his childhood, as it only became fully independent in 1968. Woven through the events of 5 February 1990 are his nostalgic remembrances of growing up in rural Swaziland. Anthony frequently ruminates upon his memories of Swaziland's King Sobhuza's Ncwala (king-renewal) ceremony. These passages are brimming with exoticism, in their anthropological focus on the ritual dances, the gory slaughtering of the bull and Anthony's prurient fascination with the hidden rites 'they won't show to Europeans' (Cartwright 1995: 112). Cartwright thus illuminates the continuity between colonialism and contemporary racism within London. Just as the young Anthony is both 'thrilled and frightened' by the naked Swazi dancers, so he expresses his fear of and fascination with the black men and women on the train. The sexualisation of black subjects that underlies Anthony's racism is especially evident when, just before the novel's violent denouement, Anthony visits a strip club and observes a white and then a black dancer. He 'pays attention' to both through an objectifying gaze, but his assessment of the white dancer is more sympathetic: he wonders whether her 'work is stressful' and notes that her face is 'lean and earnest'. Anthony's impressions of the black dancer combine misogyny with racist stereotyping: 'She's a black girl who dances twice as energetically as the previous girl, as if being black demands extra physical exuberance' (160). He then compares her to Winnie Mandela: 'Her face is blank. It reminds Anthony of Winnie Mandela when she is angry, a kind of steely emptiness' (160). Whereas Anthony reads earnestness and worry in the face of the white dancer, the face of the black dancer is 'blank'; she is only legible through her incorporation into the stereotype of the physically exuberant, 'angry black woman'. Moreover, the reference to Winnie Mandela here reminds the reader of Anthony's obsession with Nelson Mandela, undermining his idealistic attachment to the ANC leader. In another moment, while reading a newspaper article about her alleged involvement with criminals, Anthony forges a direct connection between Winnie Mandela and British class politics, commenting: 'There is a seam of violence in Winnie's life. Like the under-class' (28).

The sections focalised through Anthony are particularly heavy in free indirect discourse and contain almost stream-of-consciousness passages in which his surroundings suggest observations, memories and ideas. This allows us to witness how Anthony, a typical middle-class white Londoner, and a colonial, works out his views about race and class in relation to place. A chapter set in Soho is particularly rich in spatial detail, with each shopfront described and its contents enumerated:

> The Italian grocer, its windows packed with basil and spaghetti and wheels of Parmesan, is crowded. There is so much food in there, the customers seem like an afterthought. And here's a place where they sell cut-price tickets to Milan and another sex shop where they sell underwear in red and black PVC and, if you look in, rows of dildos, some of them puckered like tripe, and here's a Chinese restaurant with the bodies of ducks hanging in the window and bowls of noodles and rice, made of plastic or something, to give you an idea of what's available inside, and over here they sell nothing but boots, which everybody in Soho wears and now he is walking past the window of a film company which advertises a film with Tom Selleck, *Three Men and a Little Lady*. And here's a tapas bar, selling Spanish and Mexican beer which everybody drinks. The richness of it all, just in these few yards. In the darkening streets – it's night but still afternoon – this is evidence of the range of human restlessness. (91)

He remarks upon the cosmopolitanism of the area as he passes the 'Italian grocer', the Chinese restaurant' and the 'tapas bar' (91). This procession of shops and restaurants representing different national cuisines is summarised in Anthony's overarching statement: 'The richness of it all, just in these few yards ... this is evidence of the range of human restlessness' (91). On one level, Anthony's joyous affirmation of the 'richness' that Soho offers could be read as a celebration of London's cosmopolitanism, as in Matshikiza's description of 1960s Soho in his *Drum* magazine column. Yet Anthony's enjoyment of Soho is based on his consumption of the goods the area has to offer. There is, for instance, a long scene at an Italian restaurant in which each dish and drink is detailed. The utility of London's multiculturalism, to Anthony and his ilk, lies in its potential to provide pleasure to middle-class consumers.

Moreover, we soon realise that Anthony, for all his professed interest in the 'range of human restlessness', is uninterested in the lives of those different from him, particularly London's underclass. While he is driving through south London, we learn that:

> Anthony knows nothing of what goes on one block from the A23. He sees the road as a façade, behind which there may be nothing at all. Occasionally, of course, he can see tower blocks where people, surprisingly, consent to live, but it is a blank, unknown landscape. (174–175)

Anthony is indifferent to what 'goes on' behind the 'façade' that is the major highway through London. Unlike the streets in Blake's 'London', and unlike the familiar streets of Soho, these poorer areas of London go uncharted within Anthony's mental cartography. The landscape, like the black dancer's face, is 'blank', and the only thing he patronisingly assumes about this space is that people 'consent' to live in council housing tower blocks; he cannot imagine that many residents may have no other option. Anthony is later forced to confront the realities of the lives of the British underclass when he is mugged by Chanelle and Jason and is then arrested for Jason's murder. Through the character of Anthony, Cartwright thus provides an example of insularity and class prejudice amongst the middle class in Thatcherite Britain.

Nowhere are the hypocrisies of the bourgeois liberal Londoner conveyed more clearly in the novel than in the sections which focus on Anthony's obsession with Nelson Mandela. In addition to Cartwright's own background, and the southern African connection provided through the references to Swaziland, it is through the Mandela passages that the nexus between London and South Africa is made particularly meaningful in the novel. Anthony has expectations of Mandela not only as a South African leader, but as a messianic figure who will reveal 'a simple but previously undiscovered truth about humanness' and who 'will stop the drift' of modern society (97). He therefore decides to fly to Cape Town with his friend Mike to witness Mandela's release, although of course the planned expedition never occurs, because of the attack by Jason and Chanelle and Anthony's arrest. The delusional, overblown nature of Anthony's idolisation of Mandela satirises the international veneration of the leader as the champion of humanistic values, which would have been at its high point at the time of this novel's publication. Anthony, for instance, believes that 'Nelson has been thinking about him, just as he has been thinking about Nelson. There is two-way traffic in these relationships' (12). Just as the opening section contrasts sport and the sublime, rugby and Mandela, so Anthony's belief in Mandela as a messianic solution is satirised in a conversation between Mike and Anthony that is based on rugby jargon:

> *Nelson is our man*, he says to Mike.
> *What position does he play?*
> *Utility player.* (69, italics original)

Anthony jokes that Mandela can take on whatever role is required of him in the 'game'. One wonders whether Cartwright edited the novel to include its rugby references following the widely mythologised Rugby World Cup of June 1995, as *In Every Face I Meet* was published in September that year. If so, then his combination here of rugby and Mandela provides a satirical gloss on the strategic and perhaps compromised nature of the alliance between the previously whites-only, Afrikaner-dominated sport and the ANC leader. Nelson Mandela famously appeared at the final game, which South Africa won, wearing the team jersey with its springbok emblem. Deborah Posel explains that '[t]he springbok had been the official emblem of the apartheid regime; as the emblem of the national rugby team, it exuded an aggressive white machismo, integral to the game of rugby but equally iconic of apartheid's nationalist chauvinism' (2014: 82), thus Mandela fulfilled his role as 'utility player' in that moment by bridging the gap between the ANC and rugby-loving white South Africans.

Anthony believes that Nelson Mandela will provide broad, humanistic knowledge to his followers: 'Nelson, he believes, will have picked up some ... basic wisdom while he was breaking stones in the lonely beauty of Robben Island' (Cartwright 1995: 67). Evoking the image of the holy man who enters a state of hermitage in order to attain enlightenment from God, Anthony concludes that Mandela's isolation from society on Robben Island will have developed his 'wisdom': 'Maybe he was freer out there ... [H]e is sure that Nelson will be bringing back from there, like Moses from the mountain, essential knowledge ... Nelson has been set free of all the humiliation and reverses that ordinary people suffer' (87). It is a sign of Anthony's privilege that he cannot imagine that, as a political prisoner, Mandela was certainly not 'freer'. Anthony's image of Mandela is based on Robben Island, from whence he imagines Mandela will be 'bringing back knowledge', but Mandela would have been in Pollsmoor prison in Cape Town from 1982 to 1988, and then in Victor Verster Prison outside Cape Town for the last two years before his release. Anthony's uncertainty about the facts of Mandela's life and imprisonment suggests his desire to accept a simplified, more easily mythologised version of Mandela's life.

Anthony's obsession with Mandela is thoroughly idealistic, and does not temper his racism; in fact, he is not interested in the meaning of Mandela's release for black South Africans. While many British anti-apartheid supporters would have been more sympathetic than Anthony to Mandela's political aims, Cartwright's depiction of Anthony's idolisation of Mandela reflects the worldwide focus on Mandela during the 1980s and the messianic framework in which Mandela was envisaged. Posel, drawing on Tom Lodge's research, points out that the Release Mandela Campaign, started in 1980, created a 'heightened international awareness' and that the campaign 'launched an avowedly reverential, redemptive version of Mandela's political and ethical significance ... as a man of extraordinary and special qualities, uniquely positioned to champion the cause of freedom in South Africa and the world at large' (2014: 73). Rob Nixon similarly traces the messianic narrative assigned to Mandela:

> During his 27 and a half years of imprisoned fame, Mandela accrued a reputation of near-Messianic dimensions. There were several reasons for this: the redoubtable convictions of the man himself; the scale and inventiveness of the international tributes enacted in his name; the peculiar progress of his relation to the media; and the sweeping power in South African history of the idiom and psychology of redemptive politics – replete with deliverance from bondage, covenants, chosen people, divine election, promised lands, apocalypse, chialism and all manner of eschatology. (1994: 176)

Anthony anticipates Mandela's release as a moment of redemption and deliverance, although he empties Mandela of his political and anti-racist significance. For instance, he imagines that 'when Nelson comes out, things will change', but rather than anticipating change in South Africa, he anticipates a host of minor victories for himself and his colleagues: that he 'will be made a director and the chairman will buy a new horse and Thelma will go to Thailand' (Cartwright 1995: 27). Through this list of petty aspirations, Cartwright sends up the way in which Anthony, who is exemplary of many other Mandela supporters, 'expects a lot of Nelson' (43).

The continuity between Anthony's Swaziland-originating racism and his idolisation of Mandela is evident in his frequent comparisons of King Sobhuza and Mandela, which seem to suggest that they are both romanticised figures of the wise 'noble savage'; Anthony believes that Mandela, as a 'Thembu prince', will have been 'thinking about the meaning' of the Ncwala ritual on Robben Island and will be 'in a position to update King Sobhuza's beliefs' (175). Anthony even thinks that Mandela will look like Sobhuza when he 'comes out' (48). Thus, Anthony's romanticisation of Mandela co-exists with his racism. Stuart Hall suggests that 'racism constructs the black subject' as 'noble savage and violent avenger. And in the doubling, fear and desire double for one another and play across the structures of otherness, complicating its politics' (1996: 445). Anthony's fear of young black men in London, which comes to a head in his encounter with Jason, is doubled, in this complicated way, with his reverence of Mandela. Anthony's ideas about Mandela thus provide a sense of how South Africa figured in the 1990s in the global imaginary and how veneration of Mandela informed British narratives of race.

Narrating the lives of London's underclass

Jason, the nineteen-year-old pimp who attempts to mug Anthony and who is shot and killed by Anthony's friend Mike, is also a Mandela supporter, although Mandela represents something very different to the young black man. Jason's expectations following Mandela's release have Pan-African and Rastafarian overtones. He tells Chanelle: 'Nelson is coming out. Our man he's coming out to lead us home ... He's coming out of captivity. He's the Lion of Judah. He is the Emperor of Africa' (Cartwright 1995: 81). For Jason, who is eking out a precarious existence as a pimp and thief, Mandela represents the hope of a possible return to Africa ('home'), venerated as Hailie Selassie reincarnate, the 'Lion of Judah'. While almost as messianic and vague as Anthony's concept of Mandela, the hope that Mandela's release represents to Jason is specifically related to his blackness and his strong identification with Africa. Anthony concedes that Mandela may also be important for black Britons; as he is passing a shop selling 'ghetto fashion' where '[b]lack boys in huge sports clothes hang out', he asserts that '[t]hey need Nelson's testament too' (97). During the mugging Anthony spots the ANC amulet around Jason's neck and 'wonders wildly if he can tell him about Cape Town' (180). What Anthony fails to realise is that the Mandela whom Jason supports is not a humanist icon who will provide a nebulous truth about existence; rather, he sees Mandela as a specifically African figure who represents redemption for all black people.

Because of the ways in which British society has failed him – he was brought up in the foster system and has little education – Jason identifies more with Mandela than with Englishness. This is evident in a symbolic moment in which Chanelle goes to the court to pay a fine, and we are provided with a description of the court's hallway:

> The floor is a mosaic, showing St George and a dragon, but so worn out by feet that St George's white horse has been almost erased and the dragon could be anything, because its fiery nostrils and its tail have been wiped out. It was Jason who told her it was St George and the dragon. At his school in Birmingham they used to have a badge like that, although only the nerds wore the school uniform, he said. Now Jason is wearing his green and gold and black necklace to show that he's a Nelson Mandela supporter. That's a badge really. (102)

The image of the patron saint of England, St George, has been almost erased, suggesting that Englishness has lost its meaning, particularly to many frequent visitors to the court, such as Chanelle and Jason. Englishness, from Chanelle and Jason's perspective, is an exclusive quality, associated with alienating middle-class values, and Jason's ANC amulet is testament to his allegiance to Nelson Mandela over any national attachment.

Cartwright's depiction of Jason and Chanelle provides an empathetic view of London's underclass, balancing out Anthony's frequently sexist, racist and class-prejudiced perspective on his fellow Londoners. Jason's interest in rap music and his use of American slang suggest the rise of hip-hop culture in 1990s Britain. While Anthony is frightened of the black men on the Underground because of their hip-hop clothing, and assumes that rapping is 'about scaring whitey' (144), Chanelle understands how Jason uses his assumption of American rap culture to acquire agency within British society:

> He's bought himself a new LA Raiders jacket and cap and new sunglasses to go with the car. He looks great, in fact he looks ready to be in a video, with one of those rap groups he likes. Big clothes with plenty of pockets. The black boys don't want to look like they have financial worries. Jason always has nice new trainers and big jackets or hoodies. When they walk down the High Road together they are telling all the little white people that they are big and loose and free. They want respect. That's what they are saying. Chanelle wonders if they can win this one, but she never tells Jason that. Jason has started calling his mates his homies, or homeboys. He likes these American words. (80–81)

Chanelle reads the symbolism of Jason's clothing choices; she knows what he and his friends 'are saying' through their outfits, which resemble those of 'rap groups' in a video. Through Cartwright's commentary on the appropriation of African American signs by black Londoners, we see how racial discourses and identity politics from other spaces are layered in London, which is also evident in the Black Atlantic resonances of Todd Matshikiza's writing. Like his allegiance to Mandela, Jason's adoption of American hip-hop regalia and language allows him to challenge his powerless position within British society, although Chanelle is sceptical of this claim to agency: she 'wonders if they can win this one' (81).

The novel's sections focalised through Chanelle provide a detailed depiction of the lives of London's underclass in the early 1990s and demonstrate how social inequality puts women in an especially precarious position. Chanelle is the 'youthful Harlot' of Blake's poem, but the 'Infant's tear' which she 'curses' ('London', line 6) is that of her own child, Bradley, who was born with health problems due to her drug use during pregnancy and who dies in a fire at the novel's conclusion. Cartwright shows how the circumstances of Chanelle's and Jason's fates are out of their control and does not present the pair as morally corrupt criminals. Chanelle's narrative frequently underscores the hopelessness of her life: 'She can't go on for much longer. Somehow she's got to get some money for Bradley and get a job ... Most of the girls end up dead before they're thirty' (76). In a scene which epitomises her class position, Chanelle peers into luxurious houses of London's middle classes, near the court where she must pay her fines for prostitution:

> There's a street near the court which looks like those streets in *Mary Poppins*. The front doors are all gleaming and there are neat trees and bushes in pots and boxes. Each house seems to be occupied by one family. She always walks up this street, even though it takes longer. Down in the basements she can see bright, tidy kitchens. The floors are tiles or wooden planks. In one kitchen she can see children sitting down at a long table. It must be a birthday party ... Chanelle is standing there, smiling, watching this as if it's on television. ... She says, this is where I am going to live with Bradley. But she doesn't believe it. She knows she's going to wind up like her mother. Or dead. (100)

Chanelle's view into the lives of others is reminiscent of the moment in Arthur Nortje's 'Wayward Ego' (1970) in which he recounts how he has 'leaned against black railings / to catch a glimpse through some stranger's window' (lines 29–30). While Nortje uses this image to illustrate the alienation he feels as a South African in London, Cartwright writes this scene to highlight Chanelle's distance from middle-class Londoners. The reader is positioned to sympathise with her, as we are given access to her thoughts, from her vicarious enjoyment of the scene to her wish that she will live in the 'bright, tidy' house with her son. She knows that this is impossible, however; 'she doesn't believe it'. Although a born-and-bred Londoner, Chanelle experiences alienation from safe, clean spaces in the city. Through her tragic character, Cartwright draws attention to the consequences of Thatcherite neoliberalism and individualism, as he shows how the underclass cannot hope to achieve the bourgeois existence that is upheld as the height of happiness. This unattainable image of class aspiration is also perpetuated by the entertainment media: Chanelle significantly views the scene 'as if it's on television'.

'Bullet points': (re)constructing the scene of the crime

The themes of race and class commentary within Cartwright's novel are most explicit within its concluding section, which returns to the court case, focalised through the juror and writer Julian Capper. Furthermore, in this final section, the retrospective nature of *In Every Face I Meet*, both in terms of the historical time in which it is set and its internal analeptic structure, is explored through metafictional references. Section Three, which precedes the court case and describes Anthony waking up in hospital after the mugging, features an epigraph by Karen Blixen: 'People work much in order to secure the future; I gave my mind much work and trouble trying to secure the past' (in Cartwright 1995: 191). Firstly, Cartwright's selection of a quotation from Karen Blixen's *Out of Africa* (1937) as an epigraph is surely not peripheral to the concerns of *In Every Face I Meet*. Blixen's account of her years as a farm-owner in Kenya is seen by many as the urtext of colonial paternalism. Ngũgĩ wa Thiong'o, for instance, critiqued Blixen's patronising depictions of black Africans in his essay, 'Literature and Society: The Politics of the Canon' (1984). Cartwright's reference to Blixen thus provides a reminder of the continuity between colonialism and racism in the metropole, which we have seen in Anthony's racist ideas, developed during his childhood in Swaziland.

Moreover, Cartwright's use of this epigraph emphasises the difficulties of retrospective narratives: it takes a great deal of 'work and trouble' to 'secure' the past. This is true of the court case in the novel, which must make sense of the shooting incident that forms an ellipsis in the text. While Jason intended for the mugging to be a straightforward robbery that would finance his new BMW, the incident ends with a violent scuffle between the three men. Anthony is shot and injured, and Jason dies of a gunshot wound. The reader, however, is not informed categorically whether it was Anthony or Mike who shot and killed Jason. The complicated reconstruction of past events which must take place in the court case is exemplary of the backward-looking nature of the novel's entire narrative, raising questions about the distortions and omissions inherent to historical narratives. Just as Coetzee employs the ambiguous genre of the fictionalised autobiography in order to suggest the difficulty of writing a 'true' history of one's own life and, by implication, of the nation, so Cartwright employs metafictional references in the trial section to question the possibility of faithfully reconstructing the past. That this set-piece about truth-telling takes place in a court foreshadows the amnesty hearings of the Truth and Reconciliation Commission, which commenced in 1996. Rather than interrogating South Africa's past, however, the trial in *In Every Face I Meet* puts English society on the stand.

The displacement of sociopolitical commentary from South Africa to London is perhaps attributable to Cartwright's resistance to writing about South Africa. He first wrote an entire work set in South Africa in 2002, *White Lightning*, and that novel is largely about the unfathomable, frustrating nature of life in South Africa. In *Youth*, Coetzee is self-reflexive about his focus on London over South Africa, in the novel itself and in John's writing. Yet, despite the metafictional nature of *In Every Face I Meet*, Cartwright does not reflect on his position as a South African writer. Julian Capper, the writer-juror protagonist of the framing chapters, may share both his profession and his initials (J.C.) with those of the novel's author, but he is not South African. Cartwright's lack of overt scrutiny of his own position as a South African writer, along with the absence of South Africans – other than an off-stage Mandela or a near-neighbour in Swazi-born Anthony – from the novel, could be viewed as a problematic blind spot, reflecting a desire to shake 'the dust of the country from his feet', in Coetzee's words (1992: 393). Using a different metaphor of relinquishment, Cartwright describes, in *Oxford Revisited* (2009), how, after moving to Oxford and being exposed to Isaiah Berlin's value pluralism, he found himself 'happily free from the heavy burden of being a white South African' (2009a: 39).

Alternatively, his aversion to direct depiction of South Africa may reflect the challenges of writing South Africa as a white writer, as it does in Coetzee's work. His focus on London can potentially be read as a retreat from South African exceptionalism towards a depiction of the racial and social faultlines in other societies, such as Britain. Although Cartwright may not reflect on his South Africanness in the text's metafictional aspects, he uses the figure of Capper to consider his role as an author more generally. Capper is not portrayed in an entirely sympathetic light. We have seen how he immediately views the trial as a fictional narrative, and from a narcissistic perspective. Capper's tendency to view events as narratives with 'personal significance' (Cartwright 1995: 6) is a self-reflexive critique on Cartwright's part concerning the position of the writer as a social critic who also transforms life and history into stories. Furthermore, Capper is proved 'wrong' by the novel's conclusion: he believes in Anthony's guilt, whereas we later learn that Mike probably killed Jason. In a particularly metafictional moment, Capper notes some of the key themes of the trial:

> [T]here is a sense – he wipes his fingers to write down some bullet points – in which the case is symbolic.
>
> The shucking of all responsibility for the weak and defenceless.
> The contempt for the unsuccessful and under-privileged.
> The promotion of business and market values above individualism.
> The attempt to preserve the status quo.
> The nostalgic belief in an earlier golden age.
> Racial innuendo. (214)

Here, Julian Capper becomes a literary critic rather than a writer, anticipating how a close reader would characterise the trial as 'symbolic' of various sociopolitical themes. His ideas are recorded as 'bullet points', punning on the gun violence of the novel's key event, and suggesting the danger of simplifying social issues within 1990s Britain into a tidy retrospective narrative. Whereas William Blake's 'London' provides a strident critique of social and political control and its consequences in eighteenth-century London, *In Every Face I Meet* is less sure of its own political and moral conclusions, even as it exposes race and class conflict in the capital. As in *Youth*, London thus provides a context for self-critique, and postmodern techniques are used to question Cartwright's position and privilege as a writer, particularly as a white South African writing about race.

The frequent metafictional references within the trial section also serve to convey the role of the media and public opinion in establishing well-worn narratives about race and class within London. The defence plays upon these clichés in order to criminalise Jason and vindicate Anthony. For instance, they hand around Jason's gun, highlighting 'Jason Parchment's criminal proclivities' (200) and distribute pictures of Jason's clothes placed on a 'dummy without a face' (202). We recall the 'blank' face of the black dancer and the 'blank' space behind the A23, when the defence presents a faceless image of Jason in which he is marked only by his 'capacious hooded jacket, voluminous trousers, dark glasses and a baseball cap with "Los Angeles Raiders" written on it', as well as his 'ANC badge' and his 'giant black Nike trainers' (202). Echoing Anthony's fear of the young black men on the train in the opening scene, the defence's display of Jason's hip-hop clothing is 'obviously designed to make him look sinister' and 'like a dangerous black pimp', despite the fact that he is 'only five foot five inches tall and barely twenty years old' (202). The defence therefore plays into racist tropes about young black men in urban areas.

The defence's characterisation of the location of the mugging is also filtered through media representations; the council estate is 'a place so notorious that it had been featured in a weekend supplement as the most dangerous place in Britain, with a mortality rate only slightly better than the slums of Kingston, Jamaica. (That's how they slip in the racial quotient.)' (200). London's underclass is rendered as foreign and as other, through the comparison of the council estate to the 'slums of Kingston'. We note once more that Capper anticipates the reader's analysis of the trial by providing his own reading of the coded language used by the prosecution. This is even more evident when he thinks that '[i]f you wanted to find a place that symbolised both the decay of the inner city and – in Julian Capper's view, more importantly – the decay of the human spirit, you would choose the Bevan North Estate' (201). The name of the estate is an ironic reference to the welfare state and its erosion under Thatcher, as it recalls Aneurin Bevan, the Minister for Health in Clement Attlee's postwar government from 1945 to 1951, who spearheaded the establishment of the National Health Service. The prosecution presents the estate as embodying the 'decay of the inner city', suggesting that criminals such as Jason are causing the corruption of London, just as the figures in Blake's 'London' are represented as cursing and tainting London's institutions of family, church and state. Further gloss of the defence's argument by Capper outlines how they believe that the case 'serves to underline the unacceptable consequences of this contempt for life in certain sections of our great capital city. The black sections' (214).

Jason's role in the corruption of the city is framed in terms of his exclusion from 'pure' Britishness:

> The defence has tried to suggest, although not in so many words, that Jason Parchment was not quite British. They can't say that, of course,

but there was an elaborate pantomime to establish that his father was believed to live in Sierra Leone and that his name on the birth certificate is Ndongo. (214)

While Jason may have changed his name to 'Parchment' in order to assimilate into British society, he has nevertheless become a 'parchment', a piece of blank paper, onto which the racism and class prejudice of British society is written. 'Michael Frame' has similarly become an empty space into which ideas of masculinity and Englishness are inserted within the narrative of the court case. The textual reference here shows the political work that metafiction does in the novel, as it suggests the constructed, fictional nature of racism, which is sustained through narratives presented in the media. Anthony did not think of the black men on the Underground as 'English', although he added a hasty 'although of course they are' (12). Similarly, although the defence 'can't say' that Jason is not British, they nevertheless present a coded narrative to this effect, which Capper deconstructs. Cartwright conveys how racism in Britain, although not as overt as the apartheid statutes which had been recently overthrown in South Africa, is sustained by discourses of belonging and nationhood. In contrast, Anthony and Mike are seen, by the defence, to epitomise English values, as Anthony 'was once selected for a trial for the England B rugby team' and is 'the son of a bank manager'. Once more, Capper spells out the defence's message:

> What the defence are saying is that if it were not for all these prostitutes and pushers and pimps, none of this would have happened to a decent man. There has been an invasion of dear old leafy England by a new, and unwelcome, culture which cares nothing and knows less about the tolerance and respect which once, not that long ago as a matter of fact, prevailed in our country. (205)

The irony here is that we know that neither Mike nor Anthony is wholly 'decent' nor 'tolerant'. Just before the mugging, Mike abuses his ex-wife, and we learn that Anthony has been unfaithful to his wife and holds sexist and racist views. The values of 'dear old leafy England' are shown to be illusory.

Finally, in the trial, we see how Anthony's idolisation of Nelson Mandela is exploited to 'free Northleach from any suggestion of racism by pretending that Mandela was his hero' (208). While the defence brings out the 'Mandela fairy story' at each turn (214) Capper feels 'compelled to point out to his fellow jurors the artifice, the rehearsal, the duplicity of this exchange. He must deconstruct it for them … He must explain to them once again the significance of trying to enlist to the cause Nelson Mandela, the single most powerful symbol of our times' (215). The undermining irony present in Anthony's musings about Mandela is thus transformed into overt critique in Capper's narrative. Whereas Jason's ANC badge is just part of his 'sinister' outfit, Anthony's desire to witness Mandela's release is presented as evidence of his tolerance. This emphasises once more how white liberal South Africans and British anti-apartheid supporters alike may have been blind to other forms of racism, even as they idolised Mandela as a humanist hero. Thus the court case is not just an attempt to 'secure' (in Blixen's words) the immediate past of Jason's murder, but also enables Cartwright, through the author stand-in, Capper, to interrogate London's past by drawing attention to harmful narratives of racism and class prejudice. However, the metafictional references that abound in the concluding section of the novel cast doubt not only on the valency of narratives around race, class and Britishness, but also on the novel's own retrospective sociopolitical commentary.

The novel's conclusion combines a detailed description of a London setting with an ambiguous commentary about truth and history. We see how Julian Capper 'passes through the metal detector out into Parliament Square, with its emblematic red buses, black taxis and Big Ben. He walks towards the Underground, past Abraham Lincoln, past General Smuts and Winston Churchill. He sees an *Evening Standard* banner: "Major to welcome Mandela"' (218). In the global imagination, London is represented by these 'emblematic' objects and places, which elide the other symbols that have currency in the city – one thinks, for instance, of the ANC emblem around Jason's neck. Capper then walks through Parliament Square, where the statue of South African General Smuts stands alongside those of Abraham Lincoln and Winston Churchill. In 1995, Cartwright would not have known that Nelson Mandela's statue would be erected in the Square in 2007, but his reference to the headline announcing newly appointed British Prime Minister John Major's forthcoming meeting with Mandela after the listing of these statues suggests that he foresaw how Mandela would be classed alongside these leaders. South Africa and London thus mingle in this concluding scene, before Capper's final realisation that Anthony was not 'able to tell the truth', because he knew, when he was arrested, that Mike had killed Jason: 'That's how it is with friends: you don't dishonour their memory' (218). Far from suggesting that Capper (or Cartwright) sympathises with Anthony in this moment, I read this final emphasis on 'truth' and 'memory' as sustaining Cartwright's focus on complicity, storytelling and historical narratives throughout the novel. A retrospective account of London, even one as contemporary as *In Every Face I Meet*, can never tell the whole story. Cartwright may be designated an objective 'outsider' by critics owing to his South African background, but, as he shows us through the compromised author figure, Capper, his narrative is liable to distortions, biases and prejudices, even as it attempts to capture the 'state of the nation'.

Conclusion

In Justin Cartwright's later novel, *White Lightning*, the protagonist, James Kronk, is a South African who has lived in London for several decades and has now returned to South Africa, where he buys a farm in the Helderberg Mountains. The novel is in many ways a response to J.M. Coetzee's *Disgrace*, as Cartwright similarly reprises and rewrites tropes of the *plaasroman* (South African farm novel). Throughout the novel, James contrasts his life in contemporary South Africa in the early 2000s with his experiences in London during the 1960s, while also recalling incidents from his childhood in South Africa. As James adjusts to rural South African life, though, he starts to lose sight of his years in London and comments that: 'You could go mad trying to reconcile the disparate landscapes of the mind' (Cartwright 2002: 148). Later he explains how his amnesia relates to space:

> The point of memory is to free yourself from the tyranny of the present. But I am enjoying a different process, freeing myself from the tyranny of the past which has constrained on me unfairly: the forgotten pea-souper is falling on London … and London's outlines are becoming unclear. I hope for this fog to spread gradually over all my past, obliterating my sins.
>
> It occurs to me that in this way, without intending it, I will have joined my countrymen, for whom amnesia is a necessary condition. (Cartwright 2002: 152)

In this passage, we see how the 'disparate landscapes' of London and South Africa come together in a consideration of the importance of memory. The dual spaces and temporalities of the text allow this passage to contain multiple meanings, just as the retrospective narratives in *Youth* and *In Every Face I Meet* are doubly Janus-faced, looking both to South Africa and London and to the present and the past. James's complaint that the 'past' has 'constrained on [him] unfairly' must surely not only indicate his pleasure in the 'forgotten pea-souper' of amnesia that is falling on his past disgraces within London. Within the context of the novel, which deals with his complex relationships with the black residents of the farm and neighbouring informal settlement, and within the South African context which forms the backdrop to the novel, this statement must surely also express the desire of white South Africans to exculpate themselves from complicity with the structural conditions of apartheid: to allow the 'fog' of 'amnesia' to '[obliterate] their sins'. While James might see amnesia as a 'necessary condition' of his 'countrymen', *White Lightning* undermines this statement through its frequent focus on remembering. Although the memories are of London, rather than South Africa, these reminiscences stress the importance of reconstructing the past to understand the present.

As in this passage from *White Lightning*, Cartwright's *In Every Face I Meet* and Coetzee's *Youth* refract the retrospective impulses of post-apartheid South African literature through narratives of London's past. This allows these authors to reveal the historical connections between London and South Africa and creates a spatially fractured, self-reflexive, partial rewriting of South Africa and London's histories, so that the dual contexts provide an opportunity for self-critique on the part of these writers. In *Youth*, Coetzee returns to London in the 1960s and presents a familiar, somewhat limited, vision of London as experienced by a white South African in the postwar period. This narrow depiction of London enacts the self-absorbed nature of the text's youthful protagonist, but also demonstrates his difficulty in writing London, which is associated with his ambivalent attitude towards writing, and coming to terms with, his home country. *Youth* furthermore presents London as a chastening city, which puts paid to its protagonist's artistic idealism and his aspiration to pass as an Englishman. The 'autrebiographical' genre of the text enables Coetzee's interrogation of his own position as a writer, while returning to the London of his youth deepens this self-analysis by augmenting its spatial dimensions, as he reimagines his younger self grappling with the challenges of representing both South Africa and London.

Justin Cartwright's *In Every Face I Meet* does not share the ambiguously autobiographical genre of *Youth*, but its metafictional framework and references nevertheless bring into question the authority of the text and allow Cartwright to trace the mediated narratives around race and class in 1990s Britain. The text's retrospective distance is shorter than that of *Youth*, but the structure of the text, around a court case, similarly invites a consideration of the instability of the past. South African-born Cartwright, a longstanding British resident, allows South Africa to intrude into his text in the form of his protagonist's obsession with Nelson Mandela, and this element is a potent illustration of the historical nexus between London and South Africa.

In these retrospective and postmodern texts, Coetzee and Cartwright destabilise and anatomise narratives about London, writing about South Africa and accounts of the past, simultaneously self-reflexively questioning their own role as writers. The fact that both Coetzee and Cartwright are writing about race may partly account for their self-questioning attitude towards their own work, as they question their own authority, as white South Africans, to write about race issues. Whether this self-reflexiveness transcends or perpetuates what Coetzee calls the 'potentially infinite regression of self-recognition and self-abasement in which the self-satisfied candour of each level of impure motive becomes a new source of shame and each twinge of shame a new source of self-congratulation' (1992: 162) is debatable. Timothy Bewes suggests that one of the chief characteristics of Coetzee's early novels was 'a sense of the impossibility of addressing the situation of apartheid "transparently" in writing, and the shame of attempting to do so'. In this 'ethically complex' situation, 'writing is possible only as betrayal of that complexity' (Bewes 2011: 152). In *Youth*, Coetzee reflects on his difficulties in writing London in order to suggest the impossibility – or at least the difficulty – of writing about South Africa directly, so that the potential narcissism of self-reflexivity is thus acknowledged, even thematised. In Cartwright's text, the metafictional references allow a certain degree of self-reflexivity, and the displacement of South African race issues onto London may suggest the uneasiness he feels writing about South Africa, but his text is less inward-looking than Coetzee's. In both texts, however, London provides the catalyst for considerations not only of Englishness and British race issues, but of the writer's own positionality in relation to South Africa and to black South Africans and Britons alike. The retrospective nature of these texts foreground both how history is contingent on the narrator and how time along with space is layered non-synchronously and in unexpected ways within London. In this way, they point beyond postmodernism and self-reflexiveness towards texts about London, such as Ishtiyaq Shukri's *The Silent Minaret*, which emphasise the unequally interlinked nature not only of South Africa and London, but of a multitude of global spaces.

Notes

1. Because *Youth*, although semi-autobiographical, is written in the third person, I will refer to the protagonist as he is known in the book: as 'John'.
2. See Gilroy (2004).
3. In his Jerusalem Prize Acceptance Speech, Coetzee used the same phrase, suggesting that, during apartheid, one's identity as a white South African could not be escaped, 'short of shaking the dust of the country off your feet' (1992: 96).
4. I would like to thank Lucy Graham for her suggestion of Cartwright's link between the title of the trade magazine and Margaret Thatcher. See, also, our co-written article, '"Bucks without Hair" and "Bullet Points": Social and Metacommentary in Justin Cartwright's *In Every Face I Meet*' (Graham and Buchanan 2014).

Epilogue

Between the cracks of the city: transnational solidarities and fractures in Ishtiyaq Shukri's *The Silent Minaret*

In Ishtiyaq Shukri's *The Silent Minaret* (2005), Kagiso, the brother of the novel's absent protagonist, Issa, is taken to visit Brick Lane, the curry-house-lined east London street at the centre of the city's Bangladeshi community:

> I was amazed. Here was a London you won't find in the postcard shops. Like the time I accompanied Issa on his illicit trip to Durban. It was though we had arrived, not in Zululand, but somewhere on the sub-continent. In Brick Lane, where Katinka took me to eat dhal, even the street signs are in another language. (Shukri 2005: 37)

In this moment, Kagiso discovers London as a multicultural city, containing and concealing diverse spaces within its streets. Later, his friend Katinka remarks of Edgware Road in north London, known for its concentration of Middle Eastern restaurants and shisha bars: 'if Brick Lane is like the Meghna flowing through its east, then this is like the Euphrates, or the Tigris, or the Nile flowing through its west' (214).

These descriptions of a London that is in fact '[m]any Londons' (214), containing communities and cultures from other locations, have something in common with the other 'South African' narratives of London discussed in this book: the recognition that London is a global rather than only an English space, a 'contact zone' (Pratt 1992: 8), in which transnational encounters occur. For instance, Peter Abrahams's *A Wreath for Udomo* highlights how London became the locus from which exiled African activists were able to plan the liberation of their home countries from English colonialism, while Dan Jacobson brings West Africa to London through the character of the Tanganyikan student in 'A Long Way from London'. Todd Matshikiza marvels at the international cuisines and entertainments in Soho, and his writing references other spaces through its jazz inflections, engaging with the transnational interplay between London, South Africa and a wider global black imaginary. Arthur Nortje's cosmopolitanism is entangled with his use of the tropes of alienated modernity, and his internationalism manifests itself through his evocation of late Romantic French poets within London. Though J.M. Coetzee's protagonist in *Youth* may be self-absorbed, even he cannot help noticing the living conditions of London's immigrant West Indian community, while Cartwright's protagonist in *In Every Face I Meet*, like Matshikiza, expresses fascination at the variety of national cultures and peoples evident on Soho's streets. As I have explored throughout this study, some of these cosmopolitanisms may draw on problematic strategies of othering, while others are more radical and productive or express the writer's own complex relationship to London. What they all have in common, however, is their emphasis on observing, identifying, invoking or superimposing multiple localities within the location of London. These cosmopolitan moments are present, of course, within narratives that are already transnational: the work of South African-born or identifying writers writing about London. We see, for instance, in the passage from Shukri quoted above, how Kagiso's observations about Brick Lane are filtered through his memories of South Africa, and specifically through a moment in time in which cultural signifiers – food, buildings, clothing – transport the traveller to a distant locality (the Indian 'sub-continent' within 'Zululand'), providing both surprise and pleasure.

Meg Samuelson, agreeing with many other critics writing in the first decade of the new millennium,[1] has suggested that a key characteristic of so-called 'post-transitional' South African writing is that the nation is no longer the key context for understanding identity. Although she suggests that the national 'remains the fundamental starting point for such wider endeavours', the 'post-transitional' moment moves beyond the supposed South African exceptionalism of the apartheid era and is 'marked by a proliferating process of scripting connections' (Samuelson 2010: 113). Samuelson uses *The Silent Minaret* as an example of an emerging South African literature, one that 'takes cognisance of the nation's embedding in the global' (113). Leon de Kock suggests similarly that, in 'new' South African literature, 'the local is of interest only as it infuses global matters of concern with a critically located inflection' (2009: 42). Rather than viewing Shukri's transnationalism as an example of something 'new', I argue that *The Silent Minaret* continues a tradition within South African writing that engages with the global, while remaining rooted within the twin locations of South Africa and London.[2] Through its critical engagement with London and other spaces, Shukri's novel exemplifies the reach of South African literature beyond both itself and the West, not only in terms of geography, but also in relation to the range of political and social concerns that this literature unpacks.

The simultaneous rootedness and extroversion of *The Silent Minaret*, like many of the other works by South Africans in London discussed in this study and South African literature more generally, can be usefully thought of in terms of Doreen Massey's concept of a 'global sense of place'. Massey argues for an 'alternative interpretation of place' constructed not out of a 'some long internalized history' but from a 'particular constellation of social relations, meeting and weaving together at a particular locus' (1994: 154). For instance, while *The Silent Minaret* is set in London and partly in South Africa, the global resonances, influences and intersections present in each setting allow the text to travel beyond itself. Rather than a demarcated area with boundaries drawn around it, 'place' is therefore read as a 'point of intersection', a 'meeting place', which includes a 'consciousness of its links with the wider world' and 'which integrates in a positive way the global and the local' (Massey 1994: 155).

'When cities crack': post-9/11 Britain and 'postimperial melancholia'

The Silent Minaret does not only celebrate the 'many Londons' and the 'London you won't find in the postcard shops' but explores the fragility of multicultural London in the aftermath of the 2001 World Trade Centre attack, and in the context of the United Kingdom's involvement in the wars in Afghanistan and Iraq and the concomitant anti-Muslim sentiment and crackdown on local 'terrorism' within the UK during the early 2000s. The novel narrativises Paul Gilroy's observed dialectic between 'conviviality' and 'melancholia' in post-9/11 Britain. Gilroy perceives British society as marked by 'postimperial melancholia', a concept he develops from Alexander and Margarete Mitscherlich's adaptation of Freud's insights around melancholia and mourning to the postwar context in West Germany (Gilroy 2004: 98). The Mitscherlichs sought to understand how, after Hitler's death, the 'German nation warded off a collective process of mourning for what they had loved and lost by means of a depressed reaction that inhibited any capacity for reconstructive practice' (107). In the postwar British context, Gilroy perceives a comparable 'inability even to face, never mind actually mourn' the loss of Empire, which, accompanied by the 'arrival of substantial numbers of postcolonial citizen-migrants' has engendered 'shock and anxiety' derived 'from a loss of any sense that the national collective was bound by a coherent and distinctive culture' (98). Although the history of Empire has become a source of shame, Gilroy argues that the work of mourning has been deferred through a process of wilful forgetting and denial. The 'war on terror' rhetoric in post-9/11 Britain is thus a continuation of this 'postimperial melancholia', repeating its 'key themes' of 'invasion, war, contamination' and 'loss of identity' (15). At the same time, Gilroy perceives in Britain an 'unheralded multiculture, which is distinguished by some notable demands for hospitality, conviviality, tolerance, justice and mutual care' (108). Although published in 2004 in response to specific incarnations of this inward-looking ideology in Britain, Gilroy's description of the melancholia that characterises British political discourse is prescient of the anti-immigration rhetoric dominating the 2016 'Leave' campaign which advanced the decision to leave the European Union.

The 'postimperial melancholia' that Gilroy perceives in Britain can be correlated with the disappointment experienced by South African writers in postwar London. When writers like Dan Jacobson describe the disparity between their expectations of London and the reality they encounter, we could read into their resulting disappointment and arguably narcissistic sadness a refusal to acknowledge the imaginary (or belated) nature of their mental picture of Britain. The dissonance experienced by liberal South African writers arriving in London reflects their coming to terms with their embeddedness in the history of colonialism. The perceived shortcomings of contemporary London are made to stand for their ambivalence about the meaningfulness of colonially inscribed ideals of Englishness and modernity, though writers like Jacobson and Coetzee are self-reflexive about this projected disappointment. While the ambivalence, shame and sadness experienced by liberal, white South Africans encountering London in the postwar period is entangled with their complicated position in relation to the struggle against apartheid, we can similarly transpose Gilroy's 'postimperial melancholia' into post-apartheid South Africa, a time and place likewise fraught with questions of remembering and coming to terms with shame and loss.

Certainly, in *The Silent Minaret*, Shukri draws out the parallels and continuities between South Africa's colonial and apartheid-era history and post-9/11 Britain to explore this contrasting dynamic between 'melancholia' and 'conviviality'. Simultaneously, he presents contemporary events in London as continuous with global forms of oppression, racism and marginalisation, particularly with regards to Muslim and Arab peoples. The fulcrum upon which these interlocking geographies and temporalities rest is the novel's protagonist, Issa Shamshuddin, the text's absent centre. Issa, a Muslim South African PhD student living in London, has gone missing. The reader never finds out Issa's whereabouts or the reasons behind his disappearance. Tina Steiner suggests that '[t]he incursions of power into the personal life of the character are portrayed as so debilitating that he sees no alternative but to join the terrorists or commit suicide' (2007: 63), whereas Jane Poyner proposes that Issa may have enacted his own disappearance, or he may have been 'disappeared' by the state in the manner of extraordinary rendition (2007: 322). In his absence, Issa's voice is only heard in fragments through his journals, his unfinished thesis and the memories of his loved ones.

The heteroglot nature of Issa's inner circle challenges the Manichean thinking behind global racisms. Issa's immediate family is made up of his mother Vasinthe, a Hindu South African Indian woman, while he has been given a Muslim name by his Muslim South African father, who left his mother just before she gave birth. His other mother, Gloria, a black South African woman, was walking through suburban Johannesburg with her two-month-old son, Kagiso, looking for work, and happened to knock on Vasinthe's door as she was about to give birth to Issa. After assisting with the birth, Gloria and Kagiso stayed with Vasinthe, and they formed an unusual South African family, despite the laws against interracial co-habitation during apartheid. Expanding this 'multiracial' circle is Katinka, Kagiso and Issa's Afrikaans friend, who rejected her racist family and eschewed their indoctrination, and Frances, Issa's elderly, Catholic, British neighbour. Each character, through their own background and their relationship with Issa, provides commentary on the South African and global resonances of the 'war on terror'.

Ishtiyaq Shukri's writing about the intersections between London, South African and Muslim spaces springs from his own background as a South African of Muslim heritage, born in Johannesburg in 1968. He has lived in London intermittently since 1997 and studied South Asian literature at the School of Oriental and African Studies. In *The Silent Minaret*, Shukri blurs the boundaries between spaces and emphasises the continuities of experience – oppressive and productive – between localities, while also suggesting the destructive nature of policed national borders and nationalisms. This border-crossing and boundary-blurring project is well illustrated by the poem that prefaces the novel, 'When Cities Crack', which begins 'When cities crack, do stories too, / their scaffolding / collapsing?', and repeats this refrain in subsequent stanzas: 'When cities crack, do memories too, / like china heirlooms / smashing' and 'When cities crack, do people too / their lives disintegrating?' (Shukri 2005: 6–7). The repeated word, 'cities', does not refer to a specific location. In the context in which it is written, one might think of New York and the World Trade Center attack, particularly because of the architectural imagery of 'their scaffolding / collapsing'. However, images of devastated cities could equally suggest the bombings of cities in Afghanistan and particularly Iraq. Thus New York and Afghanistan/Iraq, apparently polar opposites in the 'war on terror', are grouped together as cities whose experience of suffering and destruction are both shared and interconnected. This conflation of cities is also suggested by an offhand observation on the part of Kagiso, as he looks at a postcard of the Johannesburg skyline which he finds in Issa's room: 'He remembers sending the card, in the early days, soon after Issa first came to London. He likes the picture. It captures something of the city, he thinks – its drama, its ambitions. People often mistake it for New York' (42). While the 'postcard shops' of London do not accurately represent the multicultural city, this postcard 'captures something of the city', even if that 'something' is its non-specificity, its global nature. The poem 'When Cities Crack' is about more than just the commonalities between cities, but questions the kind of stories one can and should tell in the midst of destruction. Shukri concludes that he is only able to construct 'mosaic pictures hobbled together from fragments' (7).

The devastation and disintegration brought about by the 'war on terror' is reflected in the fragmented nature of the novel, which is polyvocal and is constituted by journal entries, pamphlets, news articles, sections of Issa's thesis and mobile text messages, amongst other forms. In the epigraphic poem, Shukri offers an apology and explanation for the scattered nature of the text: 'Here, I say, I've salvaged what I could, your stories … I'm sorry it's so disarranged, like ravaged cities cracking' (7). The fragmented narrative also resembles a detective story, with Kagiso, Katinka and Vasinthe acting as detective figures. The novel offers sporadic clues that never coalesce into a resolution, as Issa is not found before the conclusion. The 'mosaic' constructed from the 'cracked' fragments is a narrative which reflects the complex multiplicities contained within nations and cities, and thus this is a form which resists unified national narratives, just as the failed mystery-novel form resists closure. The poem 'When Cities Crack' not only draws connections between 'cities' through their non-specificity but also reveals the way in which cities are themselves fragile social mosaics, whose 'cracks' often reveal schisms and absences. While Shukri frequently references other cities, as in the prefatory poem, London is the central location whose fragments are pieced together and studied in the novel.

London is presented in *The Silent Minaret* as the centre of a country whose borders are being actively policed in apparent service to the 'war on terror'. However, as Pallavi Rastogi puts it, London is also a 'global city made up of numerous criss-crossing cultures' (2011: 22). Rastogi suggests that London is a 'narrative necessity' in *The Silent Minaret* and that Shukri's depiction of the 'diversity of the metropolis' references Salman Rushdie's *The Satanic Verses* (1988) and Hanif Kureishi's *The Black Album* (1993), important precursor texts dealing with the intersections between Islam and London (Rastogi 2011: 22). Rastogi's argument is that London is a 'necessity' within the text precisely because it allows Shukri to undermine the supposed one-dimensional image of 'postcard' London through his exploration of other cultures and peoples behind this obfuscating, monolithic façade. As we have seen, he does this by having the characters comment overtly on the 'many Londons' they experience; he also shows how effort and imagination is required to uncover these diverse realities within London. For instance, Katinka, inspired by her Palestinian boyfriend, Karim, is learning Arabic, and her new-found knowledge allows her to unearth London's other spaces:

> She particularly enjoys deciphering the registration plates of luxury cars from the Middle East that glide through affluent parts of the city. It thrills her that she is able to pierce the 'exotic' surface of the image and identify the real country, the very city beyond. (Shukri 2005: 99)

Through her knowledge of Arabic, Katinka is able to discover not only the 'real country, the very city' signified by the 'exotic' script, but is also provided with a glimpse of the 'very city' in which she is living, one that goes beyond exoticism. As the characters attempt to crack the code of Issa's disappearance, they also read and decipher the multiple transnational layers that London offers.

Shukri's affirmation of 'multicultural' London is patently not a validation of the state-mandated 'multiculturalism' of the early 2000s. While Tony Blair's New Labour government might have presented its policy of diversity as serving to 'advance tolerance and advocate the recognition of cultural difference' (Howarth and Andreouli 2012: 1), some have argued that Blair's focus on multiculturalism was merely tokenistic, entrenching identity politics and ghettoising ethnic groups without recognising their internal differences.[3] Shukri's critique of state-sponsored violence towards and discrimination against Muslims in Britain suggests that he views the New Labour government's avowed 'multiculturalism' as a cover for its underlying racism. His affirmation of 'the hybrid dynamic' (Shukri 2005: 66) in London and elsewhere (particularly South Africa) goes beyond identity politics or political lip-service, towards an almost utopic, fragile vision of transcultural exchange and mutual recognition.

While Shukri presents Brick Lane as a manifestation of the 'many Londons' that are present behind its 'postcard' image, this is notably an observation rooted in the early 2000s during which the novel is set. Today, Brick Lane is certainly represented in many a tourist guidebook, travel website and 'postcard shop'. The area's increased visibility on the tourist map has as much to do with its depiction in Monica Ali's bestselling novel *Brick Lane* (2003) as with the 'creative-class takeover of London's East End' that the novel was criticised as feeding into, as Sarah Brouillette argues (2014: 9). While Shukri does not foresee how Brick Lane might become both gentrified and exoticised, he warns against the potential for orientalist othering when white Londoners enter into spaces such as the shisha bars of Edgware Road. The Baghdad Café, the Arab restaurant on the Edgware Road at which Issa and Katinka meet frequently, is another symbol of London's convivial multiculturalism, representing a haven for Arab residents of the city, but also welcoming South Africans, including the Afrikaner Katinka. Although Katinka becomes a 'regular who can't get enough', before her first visit to the café, she laughs when a friend warns against going, suggesting that she 'might get rolled up in a carpet and smuggled into sexual slavery' (Shukri 2005: 219). In retrospect, she is ashamed at her complicity in the racist joke, telling Kagiso: 'Now it makes me cringe to think that I, an Afrikaner, the victim of so much stereotyping, could have done the same to others' (220). She is aware of the exoticising lens through which she initially viewed Arab peoples. Shukri's vision of transcultural exchange within London goes deeper than superficial institutional 'multiculturalism' or a consumerist cultural voyeurism, instead valorising what Gilroy calls 'the ordinary virtues and ironies – listening, looking, discretion, friendship – that can be cultivated when mundane encounters with difference become rewarding' (2004: 75).

Buckled time and blurred contexts: superimposed places and palimpsests

As in the parallel above between Afrikaners and Arabs, South Africa is made present in *The Silent Minaret* both through reminders of the interlinked histories of South Africa and London and through comparisons which enable reflections on different forms of racism in each location. The loaded effects of evoking South Africa in London are staged when Kagiso notes the graffiti in the men's toilet of the aforementioned restaurant in Brick Lane. The incident begins:

> I found myself thinking again tonight, far away and on the other side of the world, about my place of birth while I was in, of all places, the men's toilet in Brick Lane, East London.
> 'East London?' I checked, confused, when Katinka announced our destination. 'But I've only just arrived.'
> 'Not *that* East London. East London, here, where I live, in the East End, mate. (Shukri 2005: 37)

Kagiso's jet-lagged confusion, between the East End of London and the city in South Africa's Eastern Cape province called East London, highlights the interwoven histories of South Africa and Britain through British colonialism that led to a shadow 'London', with its own 'Oxford Street', being established on South Africa's south-east coast, with the Buffalo River, despite its border of tropical vegetation, standing in for the Thames. Kagiso's confusion between places also plays into the overall boundary-crossing agenda of the novel.

After the analeptic description of Brick Lane quoted at the beginning of this chapter, we return to the men's toilet, where Kagiso notices a chain of graffiti beginning: 'Bangladesh used to be East Pakistan', followed by 'Israel used to be Palestine', 'Lebanon used to be Syria', 'Ethiopia used to be Eritrea' (38) and so on. The graffiti reminds Kagiso of his birthplace, Taung, which 'used to be in the Republic of South Africa' but was incorporated into the apartheid regime-created 'homeland' of Bophuthatswana in 1977. That this list of border disputes and invocation of transnational solidarities is found within London testifies to the networks of activism and resistance central to the city's history and present. The longstanding arbitrariness and cruelty of global border-drawing, especially in the Middle East and Africa, are distilled within Kagiso's memory of his own early life within a homeland designed to contain and oppress the racial other. South Africa's apartheid history is thus compared to other historical and ongoing land disputes. Certainly, this is nothing new: apartheid has been used by many as an analogy for the Palestine/Israel conflict, ever since South African Prime Minister Hendrik Verwoerd declared in 1961 that 'Israel, like South Africa, is an apartheid state'. While Verwoerd employed this parallel to illuminate the disingenuousness of Israel's criticism of South Africa's apartheid system, the analogy was subsequently taken up as a critique of Israel's treatment of Palestinians.[4] Solidarity between Palestine and South Africa, focused on the designation of Israel as an 'apartheid' state, was foregrounded following the May 2018 Nakba Day protests in which at least fifty-eight Palestinians were killed by Israeli armed forces. South Africa responded by recalling their ambassador and comparisons between South African and 'Israeli apartheid' dominated media commentary; activist Mbalenhle Matandela called the murder of protesting Palestinians a 'Sharpeville Massacre unfolding' (2018). And in 2021, Israeli human rights organisation B'Tselem published a report which designated Israel an 'apartheid regime', similarly sparking vigorous debates in the international media.[5]

Kagiso's first instinct is similarly comparative: he thinks of linking these instances of global imperialism and oppression to the South African homeland system, by adding to the chain, 'Bophuthatswana, Venda, Transkei, Ciskei, Lebowa, Gazankulu, KwaZulu, KwaNdebele *all* used to be South Africa' (Shukri 2005: 40). However, he does not have a pen with which to write this addition, and is later glad for his omission:

> Apart from the fact that most of its readers would probably never have heard about the homelands or the immense suffering they contained, I thought it rather pointless to insert a now settled dispute alongside so many contemporary and unresolved ones. (40)

Kagiso raises questions about which histories are made visible, through his recognition of the effacement of the suffering within South Africa's homelands. Furthermore, he challenges his own tendency to think back to South Africa, by calling apartheid's land policy a 'now settled dispute' and by choosing to foreground other contemporary struggles. In the novel as a whole, Shukri moves beyond South African exceptionalism, exemplifying, as Samuelson suggests, a literature that contests 'the national as its overriding context' (2010: 113).

In Shukri's most recent novel, *I See You* (2014), the photographer protagonist Tariq explains his globally-minded approach to photojournalism, which could be read, equally, as a metafictional insight into Shukri's literary method:

You know, whenever I've held the camera up to my eye, whether that's been in Afghanistan or Libya or Palestine, I've always felt that one eye was focusing on the subject in front of me while the other considers home. So I constantly have this sort of blurring of contexts whereby I imagine superimposing the international context I'm in onto the national context I'm from. I guess that has something to do with audience and my always being aware that my photographs are essentially taken with South Africa in mind … I think that this constant looking-at-home-from-afar, this distance, has left me with a certain kind of clarity, which is more difficult to get when you're close up. (Shukri 2014: 66)

This double vision – looking back at South Africa from afar and looking at South Africa through global contexts – likewise describes the narrative perspective of Shukri's earlier novel. Furthermore, in South African writers' works set in locations such as London, the 'clarity' provided by 'looking-at-home-from-afar' not only brings the South African situation into sharp focus through the superimposition of an 'international context' onto a 'national context', but also provides a palimpsestic 'blurring' of contexts that allows commonalities or contrasts between South Africa and 'afar' to highlight characteristics of the 'international' location. As I have already suggested, a global perspective is evident in earlier South African writing about London, in which the cosmopolitanism of London enables reflection on international concerns. In apartheid-era texts by authors such as Abrahams and Matshikiza, the freedoms London affords are used as a foil to highlight the oppressive apartheid conditions to which black South Africans are subjected, but these authors move beyond instrumental comparisons of London and South Africa to comment on the discrimination present in Britain itself, while drawing in other global struggles against racism and colonialism. For instance, Matshikiza references the African American situation, while Abrahams compares South African experiences to African anti-colonialist efforts. Thus Shukri's emphasis in *The Silent Minaret* on international contexts beyond South Africa develops a transnational strand within South African literature that has been evident for many decades, especially in works written in exile, including texts set in London.

In *The Silent Minaret*, Shukri does not comment overtly on the contemporary South African situation. This project is reserved for *I See You*, in which he highlights how the power of global private security forces and the ascendancy of neoliberal interests have insidiously eroded democracy within South Africa and elsewhere. In *The Silent Minaret*, the South African past informs his characters' revelations about contemporary global politics. It is not only apartheid that is analogous to the othering and racism that is the backbone of the 'war on terror', but also the colonial past, particularly the early history of the Cape under the sway of the Dutch East India Company. Neelika Jayawardane explains how Shukri 'historicizes the dynamics of intercultural relations in South Africa in order to illustrate how the methodologies employed by previous European imperial ventures remain globally relevant and pertinent to the present' (2014: 3).

This historicisation is most evident in Issa's thesis, which explores the 'first fifty years leading up to the establishment of a permanent Dutch settlement there [at the Cape], 1652–1702' (Shukri 2005: 66). Issa's introduction to his thesis explains his focus:

> My interest is in the hybrid dynamic, the complex transcultural exchange and fusion that, though fragile and uneven, nevertheless formed an integral feature of the early settlement and ensured its development; the heterogonous[6] bartering, which, by the time of the disaster of 1948, had been almost entirely obliterated from memory. (66)

Issa's preoccupation with the 'hybrid' dynamic that existed in the early days of Dutch colonialism reflects his understanding of the value of 'transcultural exchange' that has been developed through his own multicultural family background. Issa points out the 'whitewashing' of this more nuanced history (67), as well as the eventual displacement of indigenous inhabitants that the Dutch settlement occasioned. In the interests of unpacking the complex, hybrid history of the Cape, Issa's thesis explores the origins of Islam in South Africa, especially how it was caught up in both systems of oppression and of resistance. He focuses on the figure of Abadin Tadia Tjoessoep, also known as Sheikh Yusuf of Macassar, who was brought to the Cape as a political prisoner from the Eastern Batavian Empire after resisting the rule of the Dutch East India Company (VOC) and who established the first Muslim community in South Africa: 'Throughout his imprisonment', Issa writes, 'Yusuf continued to agitate against Dutch colonial rule so that the history of Islam in South Africa is therefore synonymous with the struggle against oppression' (74).

It is Sheikh Yusuf's fate as a prisoner that forms one of the 'cracks' through which history bleeds into the present, as Issa compares this episode from his history thesis with contemporary images of prisoners at Guantánamo Bay. He sees these images on television in the Baghdad

Café on Edgware Road, in a scene recalled by Katinka as the last time she saw Issa before his disappearance. In this moment, he is reminded again of the significant opening quotation of his thesis from Erich Auerbach, that 'history includes ... the present', and of his own dissertation's central argument:

> The history of early European exploration and settlement at the Cape of Good Hope remains universally and eternally pertinent. The procedures of dispossession and domination implemented here in the fifteenth century would be repeated around the globe for the rest of the millennium, and then again at the start of this new millennium. (65)

Thus, although the connections between London, South Africa and other locations such as Afghanistan, Iraq and Palestine are based in part on the analogy of centuries-old South African history and apartheid history (a 'now settled dispute'), Shukri, through Issa's thesis, argues that '[t]o declare these events over is the recourse of perpetrators, collaborators, benefactors and perpetuators' (65). The events of the war in Afghanistan and the accompanying paranoia about 'terror', along with widespread acts of racism towards Muslims in London and elsewhere, draw Issa out from the history which previously preoccupied him more than the contemporary experiences of London, his 'adopted city' (70). Time and place seem to shift, as Issa recognises the correlations between historical and contemporary events:

> Then time buckled, history flipped and the 17th century became indistinguishable from the 21st. He found it impossible to drag himself from the present and into the past. He was no longer able to distinguish between the two ... A thesis that started off as history now reads like current affairs. (70)

As Issa watches news coverage of the wars in Afghanistan and Iraq, he perceives the transhistorical, transnational parallels between these self-interested conflicts and the actions of the VOC in the Cape and elsewhere as the company pursued its own economic interests; as Issa writes in his last e-mail to his mother, 'The past is eternally with us' (25).

In *The Silent Minaret*, different moments in time and diverse spaces are frequently superimposed over one another, reiterating Issa's Auerbachian mantra. Shukri pre-empts his later use of photography as a metaphor for ways of seeing when Kagiso stands in front of Westminster Abbey, in the spot where Nelson Mandela was photographed on his 1962 visit to London (131). Kagiso is brought to this location by Issa's inclusion of the photograph in his notebook. For Issa, and for Kagiso, Westminster Abbey is not significant because of the royal coronations and weddings it has hosted or the English kings and poets interred there, but because of its fleeting connection to South Africa's history. The photograph provides a window into this alternative history of a very British landmark. Kagiso notes that the paved area around Westminster Abbey is called 'The Sanctuary'. In a passage in his notebook, Issa imagines the everyday lives of refugees in London and refers to London several times as 'the sanctuary', for instance: 'From the top decks of buses, they scan the bustling pavements of the begrudging sanctuary, searching, desperately, for familiar scenes from home' (134). Shukri thus forges a connection between the plight of 'unwanted' and 'despised' (134) refugees supposedly provided with 'sanctuary' in London, the religious meaning of 'sanctuary' as a holy place of refuge and the moment in which Mandela was in London, a city that could have become a political 'sanctuary' for him if he had chosen to stay in Britain – recall Esmé Matshikiza imploring Mandela to stay in London – and that was of course a refuge for many South African activists. The reference to Mandela's historical visit in *The Silent Minaret* thus presents a reminder of London's important role in the anti-apartheid struggle, as well as a critique of the societal disregard for the presently oppressed who are only given 'begrudging sanctuary' within the city. Shukri therefore uses a moment from the past to speak to the present, while foregrounding the imbrication of South Africa and Britain's histories.

Just as Shukri moves beyond the South African context to include other localities, but does not abandon it and indeed finds its history 'universally and eternally pertinent' (65), so this narrative is to some extent fixed in London. The specificity of both the historical South African context and the contemporary British setting allows for persuasive illustrations of Shukri's ideas about transnational and transhistorical analogies and continuities. The most significant connection between the seventeenth-century history of the Cape and early 2000s London can be found in Issa's emphasis on the early colonial Cape's 'hybrid dynamic, the complex transcultural exchange and fusion' that was 'fragile and uneven' but also 'integral' (66). As in Issa's thesis about the Cape, London's hybrid communities (such as the Baghdad Café, where Afrikaner Katinka is welcomed as a regular) are revealed as 'fragile', since the British state responds to the World Trade Center attack by targeting British Muslims, thereby creating an atmosphere of suspicion and othering when it comes to Arab peoples within Britain.

'Cathemosdraquels' and 'Londonistan': meeting places and alienation

The 'silent' (*silenced*) minaret of the novel's title belongs to the Finsbury Park Mosque in north London, which is visible from Issa's flat. Issa notes in his journal: 'At home, minarets declare God's greatness five times a day, but here they stand silent, like blacked-out lighthouses' (66). Not only is the mosque prevented from broadcasting its daily calls to prayer, it has been silenced in a symbolic yet violent manner, since on the night of 20 January 2003 a massive police raid was carried out on the place of worship, involving battering rams and helicopters. It is this incident, which was sparked by discoveries of an alleged ricin plot in neighbouring Wood Green and by the mosque's associations with 'radical' cleric Abu Hamza, that directly precedes Issa's disappearance. Many British Muslims, such as Dr Ghayasuddin Siddiqui, the leader of the Muslim Parliament of Great Britain, criticised the raids as heavy-handed and as having the potential to 'undermine good community relations and fuel an Islamophobic backlash on the places of worship and on innocent people' (quoted in Steele et al. 2003). Following the raid, the mosque was boarded up for months before it was re-opened under a new set of trustees, and this is the state in which Kagiso finds it as he attempts to walk in Issa's footsteps through London:

> It is all boarded up, all the ground floor windows and the door covered up with corrugated iron. It strikes him that this is the only time he has seen corrugated iron in London – the metal out of which nearly all South African shanties are built, the metal of his grandmother's shack before Ma Gloria had the walls bricked. (Shukri 2005: 222)

Kagiso perceives analogies between the degradation caused by the apartheid system and the current global oppression of Muslims, drawn through the anomalous presence of corrugated iron in London. In both cases, the corrugated iron, whether used by township-dwelling South Africans as a temporary building material or to board up a place of worship in London, is a material manifestation and symbol of racism.

Frances, Issa's neighbour, also compares South Africa to London, focusing on the Finsbury Park Mosque raid, but in this case South Africa is revealed to be more inclusive than London. She recalls Issa telling her about a mosque and cathedral in Durban which stand so close to one another that they resemble one building; he and Frances imagine 'a sky that echoes simultaneously with azaan and the Angelus'. She tells Kagiso: 'It all suggested such pictures to my mind, such sounds to my ears. I can't think of such a place or imagine such mingling of sounds here. That would need to be nurtured with love and respect, not battering rams and riot gear' (82). South Africa's 'hybrid dynamic', although repressed by centuries of colonialism and decades of apartheid, can still be glimpsed in manifestations such as Durban's 'cathemosdraquel' (82). Frances sees less hope of convivial multiculturalism being sustained within London, because of the powerful anti-Islamism in Britain that manifests itself in incidents such as the Finsbury Park Mosque raid. While much South African writing about London, particularly during apartheid, compares London's relatively tolerant environment to the racism experienced by black South Africans, Shukri suggests that London in the early 2000s may in fact be less free than contemporary South Africa.

The Finsbury Park Mosque, with its alleged terrorist connections, was at the centre of the sensationalist renaming of London as 'Londonistan', because of the alleged liberty given to extremist Muslims within the city. The designation apparently derived from the French police, but was seized upon by the British media.[7] The portmanteau 'Londonistan' supposedly references the similar freedom given to extremists within Afghanistan, but also has undoubtedly racist overtones, suggesting a critical attitude towards the concentration of South Asian and Middle Eastern immigrants within London. It is the title, for instance, of a polemical book by right-wing columnist Melanie Phillips (2006), and is a term used snidely in much of the fascist British National Party's propaganda.[8] Shukri references a variant of this moniker in the scene within the Brick Lane restaurant: the waiter jokes 'Welcome to Londondstan [sic]' (2005: 38). In that moment, the term is stripped of its negative political significance and becomes a playful celebration of the fusion of cultures and nationalities within the city. It has something of the light-hearted tone of Matshikiza's 'British West Hampstead' and 'Belsize Pakistan' (1961a: 127). When combined with the underlying memory of South Africa's Bantu*stans*, evoked by Kagiso's remembering of the place of Bophuthatswana amongst global border disputes, 'Londonistan'/'Londondstan' is granted even more transnational, transhistorical layers of meaning, invoking both productive multicultural conviviality and damaging racism.

For Issa, the alienation he experiences within London and his empathy for the suffering of oppressed peoples drive him to despair: the conviviality of the Baghdad Café does not protect him from the trauma of the disturbing war scenes he witnesses there on the television, nor from the violence in the city's surrounding streets. Poyner suggests that Issa's obsessive handwashing, which is based on Islamic purification rituals, indicates that he experiences 'growing disaffection with the alien and alienating culture in which he finds himself as a disease of which he must be rid' (2007: 327). While Arthur Nortje's poetry presents his attempts to explain and counter his alienation by focusing on bodily engagement with the city, Shukri has his protagonist enforcing a barrier between his body and London's public spaces. His mother's colleague, trying to imagine what could have led Issa to either self-willed disappearance or self-destruction, tells Vasinthe 'the struggle's never over … There is a lot in Britain to alienate a young idealist. "Inglan' is a bitch"' (Shukri 2005: 226). Quoting Linton Kwesi Johnson's 1980 poem about racism and inequality in Britain, Shukri once more implies the continuities between the apartheid 'struggle' and the contemporary struggles of being a 'young idealist' (particularly one of Muslim heritage) in London.

Furthermore, Shukri traces new forms of discrimination in Britain that have developed out of a long history of racism. For instance, Issa is disturbed by a newspaper article about an incident in Lye in the West Midlands, in which British police raided a mosque to remove a family of Afghan refugees who had overstayed their right to remain in the country. To Frances, he remarks on the article's combination of images and words, such as 'battering ram', 'mosque', 'children' and 'deportation': 'What sort of society can make sentences out of such disparate words, Frances – casual, matter-of-fact sentences out of such disparate words?' (95). Frances replies: 'the same sort that only two generations ago displayed signs like: no blacks, no Irish, no dogs'. She adds: 'Things have come a long way since then', but Issa will not let this optimistic statement remain uncritiqued: 'Yes, Frances, they have – a very long way. Bigoted signs have become battering rams, detention camps and bombs. A very long way, backwards' (95). This exchange presents an unbroken thread between contemporary racism in Britain, manifested in the early 2000s in discrimination against Muslim residents, and the nationalist racism of the 1960s. Both Todd Matshikiza and J.M. Coetzee, writing in or about the 1960s, comment on the racism evident in accommodation advertisements. Shukri takes a long view of racism in Britain, suggesting that post-9/11 paranoia is simply a new form of nationalism and bigotry.

Shukri presents a concrete example of racial discrimination in the novel when Issa is questioned relentlessly at Heathrow Airport upon returning to Britain after a trip to South Africa. This incident is based on Shukri's own experiences of interrogation and surveillance as a Muslim foreigner living in London. In December 1993, Shukri was detained at

Heathrow on arrival and was asked to check in at a police station daily for the remainder of his stay, a requirement that he refused. Then, in August 2003, he was called aside for questioning after attending the Hutton Enquiry hearing in which Tony Blair presented his evidence surrounding the death of his government's weapons expert, David Kelly (Shukri 2015). In *The Silent Minaret*, after Issa is called for questioning on arrival back in London from a visit to South Africa, the other detainees ask him what his name is, and when he replies with his Arab-sounding name they confirm why he has been stopped at immigration: 'That's why. In here, we all have such names' (Shukri 2005: 181). In 2015, Shukri received widespread media attention when he faced another such encounter at Heathrow: he was detained for more than nine hours on arrival in London, was subsequently deported and had his residence stamp of nineteen years cancelled, despite the fact that his wife is a British citizen and he owns property in London. The cancelling of his indefinite leave to remain in the United Kingdom was supposedly due to his absence from the UK since 2012, although he had good cause to be away, as he was in South Africa owing to family illness, and in Yemen, where his wife headed up an Oxfam branch. In an online essay about his deportation, Shukri wonders whether immigration officials would have considered these mitigating circumstances in making their decision if his name was 'John Smith': 'But my name is not John Smith, and I have been to Yemen. That I believe sealed my fate at Heathrow and led Border Force officials to think that they could not take a chance on me, to decide that given all the options at their disposal, they would enact the harshest' (Shukri 2015). As he says through Issa's fellow detainees in *The Silent Minaret*, it is the 'names' of Muslim visitors and immigrants that elicit the 'harshest' treatment by British immigration officials. In the fragmented narrative surrounding Issa's disappearance in the novel, the Heathrow incident is certainly an important clue as to the events that may have resulted in his feelings of alienation, which may have led to his disappearance.

Missing persons, stateless people

Issa's absence, the missing centre of the novel, has two thematic purposes. Firstly, it provides a crux for the novel's overall concern with missing, erased and hidden people and histories. Issa is haunted by the city's invisibles, London's marginalised poor and especially its refugees. Kagiso finds the passage in Issa's notebook which describes the lives of poor immigrants, tortured by the trauma of their past and forced to work menial jobs in the city. It begins:

> I am sitting on Derek Lane's bench tucked away in the affluent heart of this splendid city, but, with my own accursed 'Sixth Sense', I only see the ogres – the hideous ones, the invisible ones. They roam the city, the unwanted ones, with vacant, distant stares. Absent and preoccupied, here only in unwanted, despised, brutalised, foreign body; Europe's untouchables. (Shukri 2005: 134)

Shukri's description of migrants in London is evocative of Arthur Nortje's poem 'Foreign Body' (1966), in which the poet considers his alienation from Britain: 'What substance around the foreign body / can pearl it smooth, what words can make me whole?' (lines 15–16). Issa's emphasis, in this passage, on the lexis of disappearance – 'invisible', 'vacant', 'absent' – is prescient of his own vanishing act. Issa's status as a 'missing person' is thus a symbolic performance of solidarity with those who are daily rendered invisible and forgotten within the 'affluent heart' of London. Of course, there is the other possibility, as Jane Poyner suggests, that Issa has been 'disappeared' by the British government for his suspected sympathy with Islamic extremists, in which case his absence could be read as an act of solidarity with those who are illegally arrested and extradited through 'extraordinary rendition' (Poyner 2007: 322), as well as with those who were 'disappeared' by the apartheid authorities. Kagiso, packing up Issa's bookshelves, finds the five volumes of the Truth and Reconciliation Commission's Report, and searches them 'like a telephone directory, for names, names he knows – names of the tortured, the missing and the dead' (Shukri 2005: 104). He finds the entry about the death of Steve Biko, amongst others, and considers how these atrocities were covered up through the government's web of censorship and propaganda, so that his understanding of the full extent of apartheid suffering is marked by a 'collection of blank spaces' (110). The Truth and Reconciliation Commission is also, however, presented through the words of Kagiso's colleague as a 'stage-managed whitewash' (103). Thus, Issa's disappearance contains resonances of historical absences, missing persons and obfuscations of truth in both South Africa and London.

The second thematic and symbolic significance of Issa's disappearance is found in the ways in which he evades state surveillance and monitoring by disappearing without a trace in a city whose streets are lined with CCTV cameras and whose borders are strictly policed. Jayawardane suggests that 'Issa's disappearance can, thus, be a form of resistance – a way of preventing the state from recording his movements by dissolving his physical presence from the public record' (2014: 5). As we have seen in Todd Matshikiza's writing, surveillance also formed an important part of the apartheid regime's means of control over its subjects. Black South Africans were scrutinised for potential defiance and their movements were closely monitored through the pass system. The mechanisms of apartheid policing and othering that Matshikiza describes in the 1960s are reproduced in early 2000s London in the form of state 'anti-terror' measures. Issa's resistance of the state's policing and scrutinising apparatuses feeds into his larger investment in 'constructing an identity outside of any nation state, including South Africa', as Jayawardane suggests (4).

His eschewal of the mechanisms enforcing the borders of the nation state is echoed by Katinka in a crucial moment in the text. She finds herself stuck in traffic outside Hyde Park during the Last Night of the Proms concert and is forced to listen to the flag-waving crowd singing along to the imperial anthem 'Land of Hope and Glory', which in turn reminds her of the myopic nationalism of her own Afrikaner people. Particularly, she remembers a school visit to Kimberley, where the group observes a minute of silence at the site of the first concentration camp, where Boer women and children were interned by the British. She recalls railing against the narrowness of the teacher's call to remember 'their sacrifice', as she thinks of the many black South Africans who died in these camps, but also of how the camps served as a blueprint for later, brutalising forms of incarceration: 'Our people, the Volk, weren't the *only* victims here, they were the first' (Shukri 2005: 248). Katinka's memory is a reminder, a making-visible, of the sometimes effaced, interwoven histories of British and South African racism, and is also a call to empathy with the oppressed beyond one's own 'Volk'. In this way, her memory elucidates Shukri's wider project of moving beyond narrow national contexts – either South Africa or Britain – towards solidarity with those suffering throughout the world *because* of the power of the state. This is even more overtly conveyed within the same scene, as the Union Jacks brandished by the singers remind Katinka of the moment, in 1994, when the old South African flag was taken down and the new one raised:

> Three hundred and forty-two years, she counted, finally draw to a close – wrong years, dark years, evil years, driven by the philosophy behind songs like these, all of them now, finally, behind. She felt the uniformed, straight lined, saluting little girl she once was step out of line, throw off her badges and run towards this stateless moment: no flag to wave, no anthem to echo, no eternal enemy against which to perpetually defend,

no God-chosen nation for which to die in gory glory. She looked up at the empty flagpole, the muted brass band, not wanting the stateless moment to end. (250)

Through the powerful image of the temporarily absent flag, Shukri offers a radical critique of nationalism, and presents once more the continuity between apartheid ideology and contemporary British nationalism, as evidenced by the persistence of symbols such as 'Land of Hope and Glory' and as manifested in Islamophobia. Moreover, Katinka's longing for the 'endless, limitless possibilities of the stateless moment' (250) once more reflect Shukri's desire to take his novel's concern beyond that of specifically national contexts – beyond damaging nationalisms, but also beyond exceptionalism.

In this South African novel set in London, Shukri moves beyond a comparison of national contexts, since he aims towards the transcendence of nationalisms or national identities altogether. In this way, *The Silent Minaret* differs from some of the other writing explored in this book. Todd Matshikiza, Dan Jacobson and J.M. Coetzee, in particular, consider what it means to be South African in London and what it would take to assimilate into Britishness (or Englishness). Even Nortje, despite his cosmopolitanism, expresses anxiety about fitting into British society. In 'Jesus College Bar' (1965), he wonders whether he is 'handsomer than Englishmen?' (line 7), notices the 'attention' on his 'speech and usage' (line 14) and must remind himself to '[r]elax among people' (line 20). However, the characters in Shukri's novel do not share the same insecurity or anxiety about national identity or belonging. Shukri's characters are not interpellated by nationalism but are alienated from it, and are therefore well positioned to critique nationalist ideologies. Issa's feelings of alienation in London are not due to any self-consciousness about his foreignness, but arise from his resistance to British racism. This different approach to the nation can be attributed, partly, to the novel's later moment of publication, in a post-national, global age in which the ideology of nationalism is increasingly irrelevant, even if it still draws alarming support from right-wing quarters.

The Silent Minaret is just one of several contemporary South African texts which present their South African-born characters as global citizens. For instance, in several short stories in S.J. Naudé's *The Alphabet of Birds* (2011), South Africans move between London and other destinations. London is presented as just one of many, almost interchangeable global metropolises, rather than as a place that represents either the culmination or disruption of visions of Englishness. In one of the narratives, 'Mother's Quartet', the protagonist remarks on her City banker brother's 'traceless London accent' and describes him as a 'smooth Londoner' who is 'an ideal specimen of the borderless world's financial elite' ([2011] 2015: 228–229). Here, 'Londoner', although seemingly a description of origin or attachment, implies an absence of national attachment or character. He is a different kind of stateless 'migrant', but one equally disconnected from any nation, or seemingly so, as he still has an attachment to his South African childhood, manifested in the nasturtiums from his mother's garden which he imagines growing over London night clubs and apartments during drug-fuelled hallucinations. Texts like Naudé's present a new generation of South Africans who move unselfconsciously through the world and do not approach London with the same anxieties and expectations of previous generations, although he foregrounds the alienation and despair that often accompanies these rootless characters on their travels. These characters, like Shukri's global-minded protagonist, move beyond a postimperial (or post-apartheid) melancholia, and foreground the embeddedness of South Africans within an increasingly globalised world.

Beyond London and South Africa

South African writing about London, or indeed a study of such writing, opens itself up to critique over its persistent reference to the West (or the North), represented by London, as a foil for South Africa, rather than exploring South African linkages with other southern, or non-western, locations. Over the past decade, scholarship on South African literature, and on 'transnational' or 'diasporic' literatures more broadly, has complicated the prominence of 'north-south modes of transnationalism' (Hofmeyr 2007: 3) by exploring transnational conversations and networks within the south, supplementing exilic and diasporic narratives set in the West and rethinking important but potentially overwhelming historiographies like the Black Atlantic. Shukri's writing intervenes in these spatial-temporal questions of dominance, obfuscation and memory through his novel's multilocational mapping. Shukri's interweaving of the history of Islam in the Cape, through the figure of Abadin Tadia Tjoessoep, exemplifies the excavated Indian Ocean trajectories that are central to the rethinking of South–South interconnections.

Crucially, *The Silent Minaret* concludes not in London or South Africa, but in Palestine, where Katinka has gone to live with Karim and to teach at a local school. Pallavi Rastogi argues that '[w]ith this sort of conclusion … the novel strips the West of centrality as a space, theme, and discourse, allowing a new form of transnationalism to emerge, one that links South Africa to histories and geographies – such as Palestine – to which it may not have historically been linked' (2011: 27). Katinka, in a letter to Kagiso, tells him that Qalqilya, in the shadow of 'The Wall' is 'far more horrendous than anything you've seen in the homelands' (Shukri 2005: 273). And the novel's last words consist of a text message she sends to Issa's mobile number, which underscores the connections between South African history and not London (this time), but Palestine, quoting Issa's thesis: 'Im by da wal @qalqilia. Wen jan landd @cape he plantd a hedj 2 sepr8 setlaz frm locls. Da histry of erly urpn settlmnt @da cape is unversly&eternly pertnt x' (274), text-speak shorthand for: 'I'm by the wall at Qalqilya. When Jan [Van Riebeeck] landed at the Cape, he planted a hedge to separate settlers from locals. The history of early European settlement at the Cape is universally and eternally pertinent'. Shukri thus moves his narrative beyond the well-worn but productive connections between South Africa and London. Yet London remains the grounding location of the novel. Shukri's decentring of the North can occur even in London-based narratives, as we have seen in the work of almost all the writers studied in this book. Both South–South or Indian Ocean frameworks of reading and writing, and writings of South African London that decentre or critique the former imperial hub rally around the project of 'provincializing Europe' (Chakrabarty 2000).

While Shukri stretches the text's international perspective beyond London and South Africa, both contexts, in their historical and contemporary forms, remain important touchstones of comparison and analogy in his exploration of global forms of racism and repression. He moves beyond apartheid concerns, while recognising that 'the struggle's never over' (Shukri 2005: 226). Massey argues that the specificity of a place derives from its 'accumulated history', with 'that history itself imagined as the product of layer upon layer of different sets of linkages, both local and to the wider world' (1994: 156). As I have suggested throughout this study, London's palimpsest has been written on – graffitied, like the list of conflicts in the Brick Lane bathroom, or scratched over like the deeply engraved pencil marks on Matshikiza's newspaper – by the histories of other places, including South Africa.

Although Shukri employs novel contexts and imaginative genre-mixing to forge global connections, the migratory nature of the South African novel has long been evident. While it may be that early twenty-first century South African writing reflects a wider diasporic reach, as Michael Titlestad suggests, I would argue that even 'exilic' writing, such as writing about London, has stretched itself beyond a 'dualistic home-exile conjunction' (Titlestad in de Kock 2009: 32). For South African writers, London is sometimes an escape, sometimes a foil, a map to potential futures or a window into shared histories. Writing about London engages not only with the complex linkages, contrasts and continuities between London and South Africa, but was also one of the key strands of South African literature which extended the national corpus beyond both South Africa and the West, through its engagement with the international nature of London itself.

To read South African writing about London is thus to study the development of 'South African' literature, and culture more broadly, in relation to one of the key places of exile and one of the most important international touchstones within the South African imaginary. The displacing manoeuvre carried out in this book has brought into relief some of the characteristics of a national literature that are not easily contained within its originary nation. If there are 'many Londons', as Katinka says in *The Silent Minaret*, then I have aimed to study one of these 'Londons' – the London of South African writers – while foregrounding the multiplicity and polyvocality within even this specific national perspective. For many South Africans who went into exile in London, the city represented freedom, a chance for a more open-ended identity beyond the restrictions of South Africa's apartheid-determined roles. In many cases, their dreams of reinvention were thwarted by the limits of London itself, but also by the difficulty of shrugging off their South Africanness entirely. However, if we crystallise those instances in which London represents a life beyond predetermined and limited racial or national categories, in which Matshikiza decided that 'England was going to be great fun' because he was no longer known as 'Todd 92867' (1961a: 9), then I hope to have harnessed the outward-facing, forward-looking impetus of those idealistic moments, in order to think through the nexus between London and South Africa in ways that complicate and deepen our understanding of national categories, histories and literatures.

Notes

1   See Chapman (2009) and de Kock (2009).
2   It is worth noting that Samuelson provides a disclaimer to her generalisations about 'post-transitional' literature, to the effect that 'the category of the

"post-transitional" cannot be imagined as slicing a clean break into the cultural continuum. Instead, it both bleeds into and draws its sustenance from transitional concerns and apartheid structures, while re-circuiting these concerns into new engagements' (2010: 113).
3 See, for instance, Mirza (2006).
4 See Vally (2015).
5 See 'A Regime of Jewish Supremacy from the Jordan River to the Mediterranean Sea: This is Apartheid'. *B'Tselem*, 12 January 2021. www.btselem.org/publications/fulltext/202101_this_is_apartheid. Accessed date 1 February 2021.
6 Shukri uses the botanical term 'heterogonous', rather than the more conventional, sociological 'heterogeneous' in order to continue the biological metaphor of grafting and intermixing conveyed by the 'hybrid dynamic'.
7 See Barrett (2015).
8 See, for example, 'Londonistan Strikes Again as "British" Islamist Bombs Stockholm'.

References

Archival sources

Amazwi South African Museum of Literature, letters from Noni Jabavu to Denis and Jean Keenan-Smith, 19 July 1985, 22 August 1995.

Anti-Apartheid Movement Archives, MSS AAM 1463, 'We Sing of Freedom' programme, 1963. www.aamarchives.org/file-view/category/18–1960s.html?s_f_id=4025.

BBC Genome Project, Radio Times 1923–2009, programme listings. https://genome.ch.bbc.co.uk/.

British Library Sound Archives, BBC recording reference: LP 27135, Todd Matshikiza, 'Apartheid Apart', *The Tuesday Talk*, BBC Home Service, 6 February 1962.

George Allen and Unwin papers, Archive of British Publishing and Printing, University of Reading.

Hodder & Stoughton papers, London Metropolitan Archives.

Manuscript Collection: Arthur Nortje, University of South Africa (UNISA) Archives.

Published sources

Abrahams, Peter. 1952a. 'The Plural Societies'. *The Observer*, 28 September.

Abrahams, Peter. 1952b. 'When a Black Man Comes to Town'. *The Observer*, 1 June.

Abrahams, Peter. 1952c. 'African Documentary: Degrees of Degradation'. *The Observer*, 15 June.

Abrahams, Peter. 1953. *Return to Goli*. London: Faber and Faber.

Abrahams, Peter. 1954. *Tell Freedom*. London: Faber and Faber.

Abrahams, Peter. 1956. *A Wreath for Udomo*. London: Faber and Faber.

Abrahams, Peter. 1963. 'Nkrumah, Kenyatta and the Old Order'. In *African Heritage: Intimate Views of the Black Africans from Life, Lore and Literature*, edited by Jacob Drachler. New York: Cromwell-Collier.

Abrahams, Peter. 2000. *The Coyaba Chronicles: Reflections on the Black Experience in the Twentieth Century*. Kingston: Ian Randle.

Alvarez, Al. 1962. *The New Poetry*. Harmondsworth: Penguin.

Alvarez-Pereyre, Jacques. 1984. *The Poetry of Commitment in South Africa*, translated by Clive Wake. London: Heinemann.

Ansell, Gwen. 2004. *Soweto Blues: Jazz, Popular Music and Politics in South Africa*. London: Bloomsbury.

Attridge, Derek. 2004. *J.M. Coetzee and the Ethics of Reading: Literature in the Event*. Chicago: University of Chicago Press.

Attwell, David. 2015. *J.M. Coetzee and the Life of Writing: Face to Face with Time*. Oxford: Oxford University Press.

Attwell, David and Harlow, Barbara. 2000. 'Introduction: South African Fiction after Apartheid'. *Modern Fiction Studies*. 46 (1): 1–9.

Ball, John Clement. 2004. *Imagining London: Postcolonial Fiction and the Transnational Metropolis*. Toronto: University of Toronto Press.

Ballantine, Christopher. 2012. *Marabi Nights: Jazz, 'Race' and Society*. Pietermaritzburg: University of KwaZulu-Natal Press.

Ballantine, Christopher. 2018. 'Revisiting Todd Matshikiza's King Kong'. *SAMUS: South African Music Studies*. 38: 357–360.

Barnard, Rita. 2012. 'Rewriting the Nation'. In *The Cambridge History of South African Literature*, edited by David Attwell and Derek Attridge. Cambridge: Cambridge University Press.

Barrett, David. 2015. 'Abu Hamza Trial: Finsbury Park Mosque Informant Reda Hassaine Sees His Enemy Jailed'. *The Telegraph*, 9 January. www.telegraph.co.uk/news/uknews/terrorism-in-the-uk/11333494/Abu-Hamza-trial-Finsbury-Park-mosque-informant-Reda-Hassaine-sees-his-enemy-jailed.html. Accessed 20 August 2016.

Baucom, Ian. 1999. *Out of Place: Englishness, Empire and Locations of Identity*. Princeton, NJ: Princeton University Press.

Baudelaire, Charles. [1857] 1952. 'Elevation' and 'The Swan'. In *Poems of Baudelaire: A Translation of Les Fleurs du Mal*, translated by Roy Campbell. London: The Harvill Press.

Benjamin, Walter. 2006. *The Writer of Modern Life: Essays on Charles Baudelaire*, edited by Michael W. Jennings. Cambridge, MA: Belknap Press.

Bentley, Nick. 2005. 'Introduction: Mapping the Millennium: Themes and Trends in Contemporary British Fiction'. In *British Fiction of the 1990s*. London: Routledge.

Bernstein, Hilda. 1994. *The Rift: The Exile Experiences of South Africans*. London: Jonathan Cape.

Berthoud, Jacques. 1984. 'Poetry and Exile: The Case of Arthur Nortje'. *English in Africa*. 11 (1): 1–14.

Bewes, Timothy. 2011. *The Event of Postcolonial Shame*. Princeton, NJ: Princeton University Press.

Bhabha, Homi K. 2004. *The Location of Culture*. London: Routledge.

Blair, Peter. 2012. 'The Liberal Tradition in Fiction'. In *The Cambridge History of South African Literature*, edited by David Attwell and Derek Attridge. Cambridge: Cambridge University Press.

Blake, William. [1789] 1992. 'London'. In *Songs of Innocence and of Experience*. London: Dover.

Blixen, Karen. 1937. *Out of Africa*. London: Putnam.

Bloomfield, Amanda. 2004. 'Nortje and Nature'. In *Arthur Nortje: Poet and South African. New Critical and Contextual Essays*, edited by Craig McLuckie and Ross Tyner. Pretoria: UNISA Press.

Boehmer, Elleke. 2002. *Empire, the National, and the Postcolonial, 1890–1920*. Oxford: Oxford University Press.

Boehmer, Elleke. 2008. *Nelson Mandela: A Very Short Introduction*. Oxford: Oxford University Press.

Boswell, Barbara. 2016. 'Rewriting Apartheid South Africa: Race and Space in Miriam Tlali and Lauretta Ngcobo's Novels'. *Gender, Place & Culture*. 23 (9): 1329–1342.

Boswell, Barbara and Collis-Buthelezi, Victoria J. 2017. 'And She Didn't Die: Celebrating Lauretta Ngcobo's Life and Literary Legacy (1931–2015)'. *Scrutiny 2*. 22 (1): 1–5.

Brooker, Joseph. 2014. 'Thatcherism and British Fiction'. In *The 1980s: A Decade of Contemporary British Fiction*, edited by Emily Horton, Philip Tew and Leigh Wilson. London: Bloomsbury.

Brouillette, Sarah. 2014. *Literature and the Creative Economy*. Stanford, CA: Stanford University Press.

Brutus, Dennis. 1971. 'I walk in the English quicksilver dusk'. In *Seven South African Poets: Poems of Exile*, edited by Cosmo Pieterse. London: Heinemann.

Bunn, David. 1996. '"Some Alien Native Land": Arthur Nortje, Literary History, and the Body in Exile'. *World Literature Today*. 70 (1): 33–44.

Campbell, Roy. 1949. 'The Sling' (1933). In *The Collected Poems of Roy Campbell*. London: The Bodley Head.

Cartwright, Justin. 1995. *In Every Face I Meet*. London: Sceptre.

Cartwright, Justin. 1996. *Not Yet Home: A South African Journey*. London: Fourth Estate.

Cartwright, Justin. 2002. *White Lightning*. Oxford: Isis Publishing.

Cartwright, Justin. 2009a. *Oxford Revisited*. London: Bloomsbury.

Cartwright, Justin. 2009b. *To Heaven by Water*. London: Bloomsbury.

Cartwright, Justin. 2009c. 'Justin Cartwright on Family and Future'. *Intelligence Squared*. www.intelligencesquared.com/talks/justin-cartwright-on-family-and-future. Accessed 28 March 2011.

Chakrabarty, Dipesh. 2000. *Provincializing Europe: Postcolonial Thought and Historical Difference*. Princeton, NJ: Princeton University Press.

Chapman, Michael. 1979. 'Arthur Nortje: Poet of Exile'. *English in Africa*. 6 (1): 60–71.
Chapman, Michael. 2009. 'Introduction: Conjectures on South African Literature'. *Beyond 2000: South African Literature Today. Special issue of Current Writing: Text and Reception in Southern Africa*. 21 (1–2): 1–23.
Cockin, Katherine and Morrison, Jago. 2010. *The Postwar British Literature Handbook*. London: A&C Black.
Coe, Jonathan. 1994. *What a Carve Up!* London: Viking.
Coetzee, J.M. 1988. *White Writing: On the Culture of Letters in South Africa*. New Haven, CT: Yale University Press.
Coetzee, J.M. 1992. *Doubling the Point: Essays and Interviews*, edited by David Attwell. Cambridge, MA: Harvard University Press.
Coetzee, J.M. 1997. *Boyhood: Scenes from Provincial Life*. London: Vintage.
Coetzee, J.M. 2002. *Youth*. London: Vintage.
Coombes, Annie E. 2003. *History after Apartheid: Visual Culture and Public Memory in a Democratic South Africa*. Durham, NC: Duke University Press.
Coplan, David B. 2007. *Township Tonight!: Three Centuries of South African Black City Music and Theatre*. Auckland Park: Jacana.
Cornwell, Gareth, Klopper, Dirk and MacKenzie, Craig (eds). 2010. *The Columbia Guide to South African Literature in English since 1945*. New York: Columbia University Press.
Crerar, Pippa. 2016. 'London Is Still Open for Business despite Brexit'. *Evening Standard*, 18 July. www.standard.co.uk/news/mayor/london-is-still-open-for-business-despite-brexit-mayor-launches-londonisopen-campaign-a3298211.html. Accessed 16 September 2016.
Dalamba, Lindelwa. 2013. 'Popular Music, Folk Music, African Music: King Kong in South Africa and London'. In *Situating Popular Musics: IASPM 16th International Conference Proceedings*, edited by Ed Montano and Carlo Nardi. www.iaspm.net/archive/IASPM11.pdf. Accessed 10 May 2021.
Dalamba, Lindelwa. 2018. 'Beyond the Seam: Comrades, Compromises and Collisions in Todd Matshikiza's "Jazz" Worlds'. *SAMUS: South African Music Studies*. 38: 301–334.
Davids, Nadia. 2013. '"It is us": An exploration of "Race" and Place in the Cape Town Minstrel Carnival'. *TDR: The Drama Review*. 57 (2): 86–101.
de Certeau, Michel. 1984. *The Practice of Everyday Life*, translated by Steven Rendell. Berkeley, CA: University of California Press.
de Kock, Leon. 1996. *Civilising Barbarians: Missionary Narrative and African Textual Response in Nineteenth-century South Africa*. Johannesburg: Wits University Press.
de Kock, Leon. 2009. 'Judging New "South African" Fiction in the Transnational Moment'. *Beyond 2000: South African Literature Today. Special issue of Current Writing: Text and Reception in Southern Africa*. 21 (1–2): 24–58.
Distiller, Natasha. 2005. *South Africa, Shakespeare and Post-Colonial Culture*. Lewiston, NY: Edward Mellen.

Driver, Dorothy. 1996. 'Drum Magazine (1951–1959) and the Spatial Configurations of Gender'. In *Text, Theory, Space: Land, Literature and History in South Africa and Australia*, edited by Kate Darian-Smith, Liz Gunner and Sarah Nuttall. London: Routledge.

Eliot, T. S. 1922. *The Waste Land*. New York: Horace Liveright.

Elkin, Lauren. 2016. *Flâneuse: Women Walk the City in Paris, New York, Tokyo, Venice and London*. London: Chatto & Windus.

eThekwini Living Legends. 2012. 'Living Legends 2012 Interview: Lauretta Ngcobo', *YouTube*. www.youtube.com/watch?v=oQv5wJ9APzU. Accessed 22 September 2016.

Feay, Suzi. 2009. 'To Heaven by Water by Justin Cartwright: Review'. *The Telegraph*, 28 June. www.telegraph.co.uk/culture/books/5648634/To-Heaven-by-Water-by-Justin-Cartwright-review.html. Accessed 1 July 2011.

Gagiano, Annie. 2004. 'The Sense of Exile in the Poetry of Arthur Nortje'. In *Arthur Nortje: Poet and South African. New Critical and Contextual Essays*, edited by Craig McLuckie and Ross Tyner. Pretoria: UNISA.

Ganguly, Keya. 2004. 'Temporality and Postcolonial Critique'. In *The Cambridge Companion to Postcolonial Literary Studies*, edited by Neil Lazarus. Cambridge: Cambridge University Press.

Gikandi, Simon. 1997. *Maps of Englishness: Writing Identity in the Culture of Colonialism*. New York: Columbia University Press.

Gikandi, Simon. 2006. 'Preface: Modernism in the World'. *Modernism/Modernity*. 13 (3): 419–424.

Gill, Michael (director). 1967. *Three Swings on a Pendulum*, featuring Robert Hughes, Lewis Nkosi and Olivier Todd. BBC.

Gilroy, Paul. 1987. *There Ain't No Black in the Union Jack: The Cultural Politics of Race and Nation*. London: Unwin Hyman.

Gilroy, Paul. 1995. *The Black Atlantic: Modernity and Double Consciousness*. Cambridge, MA: Harvard University Press.

Gilroy, Paul. 2004. *After Empire: Melancholia or Convivial Culture*. London: Routledge.

Gilroy, Paul. 2018. '"Imagination is Everything": Paul Gilroy Chats to The JRB about Race, Land and South Africa's Role in Overthrowing the Racial Order'. Interview by Simon van Schalkwyk, *The Johannesburg Review of Books*, 4 April. https://johannesburgreviewofbooks.com/2018/04/04/imagination-is-everything-paul-gilroy-chats-to-the-jrb-about-race-land-and-south-africas-role-in-overthrowing-the-racial-order/. Accessed 20 March 2019.

Gordimer, Nadine. 2012. *No Time Like the Present*. London: Bloomsbury.

Gqola, Pumla Dineo. 2001. 'Ufanele uqavile: Blackwomen, Feminisms and Postcoloniality in Africa'. *Agenda: Empowering Women for Gender Equity*. 16 (15): 11–22.

Graham, Lucy Valerie and Buchanan, Andrea. 2014. '"Bucks without Hair" and "Bullet Points": Social and Metacommentary in Justin Cartwright's *In Every Face I Meet*'. *Journal of Commonwealth Literature*. 49 (1): 47–62.

Graham, Shane. 2009. *South African Literature after the Truth Commission*. New York: Palgrave Macmillan.
Graham, Shane and Walters, John (eds). 2010. *Langston Hughes and the South African Drum Generation*. New York: Palgrave Macmillan.
Gunner, Liz. 2005. 'BBC Radio and the Black Artist – Lewis Nkosi's "The Trial" and "We Can't All be Martin Luther King"'. In *Still Beating the Drum, Critical Perspectives on Lewis Nkosi*, edited by Lindy Stiebel and Liz Gunner. Amsterdam: Rodopi.
Hall, Stuart. 1996. 'New Ethnicities'. In *Critical Dialogues in Cultural Studies*, edited by David Morley and Kuan-Hsing Chen. London: Routledge.
Hall, Stuart. 1999. 'The AAM and the Race-ing of Britain'. Paper presented at symposium on 'The Anti-Apartheid Movement: A 40 Year Perspective', South Africa House, London, 25–26 June. www.sahistory.org.za/archive/aam-and-race-ing-britain. Accessed 31 May 2018.
Halperin, David M. 1997. *Saint Foucault: Towards a Gay Hagiography*. Oxford: Oxford University Press.
Hannerz, Ulf. 1994. 'Sophiatown: The View from Afar'. *Journal of Southern African Studies*. 20 (2): 181–193.
Harris, Ashleigh. 2018. '"The Island Is Not a Story in Itself": Apartheid's World Literature'. *Safundi*. 19 (3): 321–337.
Hartwiger, Alexander Greer. 2016. 'The Postcolonial Flâneur: *Open City* and the Urban Palimpsest'. *Postcolonial Text*. 11 (1). www.postcolonial.org/index.php/pct/article/viewArticle/1970. Accessed 10 May 2021.
Head, Dominic. 2002. *The Cambridge Introduction to Modern British Fiction, 1950–2000*. Cambridge: Cambridge University Press.
Heyns, Michiel. 2011. *Lost Ground*. Johannesburg: Jonathan Ball.
Hofmeyr, Isabel. 2007. 'The Black Atlantic Meets the Indian Ocean: Forging New Paradigms of Transnationalism for the Global South – Literary and Cultural Perspectives'. *Social Dynamics*. 33 (2): 3–32.
Holmes, Frederick M. 2014. 'Generic Discontinuities and Variations: Crises of Authority and Innovations in Form and Technique in British Fiction of the 1980s'. In *The 1980s: A Decade of Contemporary British Fiction*, edited by Emily Horton, Philip Tew and Leigh Wilson. London: Bloomsbury.
Hopkinson, Tom. 1961. 'King Kong is Coming'. *The Observer*, 29 January.
Horton, Emily, Tew, Philip and Wilson, Leigh (eds). 2014. 'Introduction'. In *The 1980s: A Decade of Contemporary British Fiction*. London: Bloomsbury.
Houlbrook, Matt. 2005. *Queer London: Pleasures and Perils in the Sexual Metropolis, 1918–1957*. Chicago: University of Chicago Press.
Howarth, Caroline and Andreouli, Eleni. 2012. '"Has Multiculturalism Failed?" The Importance of Lay Knowledge and Everyday Practice'. Institute of Social Psychology Research Paper, The London School of Economic and Political Science Publications. www.lse.ac.uk/DPBS/About-Us/faculty/caroline_howarth/Howarth-and-Andreouli-paper-FINAL.pdf. Accessed 20 August 2016.

Hyslop, Jonathan. 2008. 'Gandhi, Mandela and the African Modern'. In *Johannesburg: The Elusive Metropolis*, edited by Achille Mbembe and Sarah Nuttall. Durham, NC: Duke University Press.
Jabavu, Noni. 1960. *Drawn in Colour*. London: John Murray.
Jabavu, Noni. 1961. 'From the Editor's Desk'. *New Strand*, December.
Jabavu, Noni. 1962a. 'From the Editor's Desk'. *New Strand*, January.
Jabavu, Noni. 1962b. 'From the Editor Abroad'. *New Strand*, February.
Jabavu, Noni. 1962c. 'From the Editor's Desk'. *New Strand*, March.
Jabavu, Noni. 1962d. 'From a Mobile Desk'. *New Strand*, April.
Jabavu, Noni. 1977. 'Smuts and I'. *Daily Dispatch*, 9 February.
Jackson, Ben and Saunders, Robert. 2012. *Making Thatcher's Britain*. Cambridge: Cambridge University Press.
Jacobs, J.U. 1989. 'The Blues: An African American Matrix for Black South African Writing'. *English in Africa*. (16) 2: 3–17.
Jacobson, Dan. 1958. 'A Long Way from London'. In *A Long Way from London*. London: Weidenfield & Nicolson.
Jacobson, Dan. 1959. *The Evidence of Love*. Harmondsworth: Penguin.
Jacobson, Dan. 1966. *The Beginners*. Harmondsworth: Penguin.
Jacobson, Dan. 1971. 'The Secret of the English'. *Times Literary Supplement*, 7 July.
Jacobson, Dan. 1985. *Time and Time Again: Autobiographies*. London: Flamingo.
James, Leslie. 2015. *George Padmore and Decolonization from Below: Pan-Africanism, the Cold War and the End of Empire*. Basingstoke: Palgrave Macmillan.
Jarrett-Kerr, Martin. 1961. 'King Kong – Making History'. *New Statesman*, 24 February.
Jayawardane, M. Neelika. 2014. 'Forget Maps: Documenting Global Apartheid and Creating Novel Cartographies in Ishtiyaq Shukri's *The Silent Minaret*'. *Research in African Literatures*. 45 (1): 1–23.
Johnson, Linton Kwesi. 2017. Acceptance speech: Rhodes University Honorary Doctorate. www.ru.ac.za/graduationgateway/honorarydoctorates/2017/lintonkwesijohnson/. Accessed 14 March 2018.
Jonker, Ingrid. 1960 trans. 1968. 'The Child Who Was Shot Dead by Soldiers at Nyanga', translated by Jack Cope and William Plomer. Reprinted 2002 in *The New Century of South African Poetry*, edited by Michael Chapman. Johannesburg: AD Donker.
Kalliney, Peter. 2013. *Commonwealth of Letters: British Literary Culture and the Emergence of Postcolonial Aesthetics*. Oxford: Oxford University Press.
Kannemeyer, J.C. 2012. *J.M. Coetzee: A Life in Writing*, translated by Michiel Heyns. Melbourne: Scribe.
Klopper, Dirk. 2004a. 'Arthur Nortje: A Life Story'. In *Arthur Nortje: Poet and South African. New Critical and Contextual Essays*, edited by Craig McLuckie and Ross Tyner. Pretoria: UNISA.
Klopper, Dirk. 2004b. 'In Pursuit of the Subject: Towards a Biography of Arthur Nortje'. *Writing in Transition in South Africa: Fiction, History, Biography*. Special issue of *Journal of Southern African Studies*. 30 (4): 869–887.

La Guma, Alex. 1962. *A Walk in the Night*. Ibadan: Mbari.
Lenta, Margaret. 2003. '*Autre*biography: J. M. Coetzee's *Boyhood* and *Youth*'. *English in Africa*. 30 (1): 157–169.
Lessing, Doris. 1975. *A Small Personal Voice: Essays, Reviews, Interviews*. London: Vintage.
'Londonistan Strikes Again as "British" Islamist Bombs Stockholm'. *BNP*. www.bnp.org.uk/news/londonistan-strikes-again-%E2%80%9Cbritish-%E2%80%9D-islamist-bombs-stockholm. Accessed 20 July 2016.
Lytton, David. 1970. 'Ingrid Jonker comes to Stratford'. In *Seismograph: Best South African Writing from Contrast*, edited by Jack Cope. Cape Town: Reijger Publishers.
McDonald, Peter D. 2009. *The Literature Police: Apartheid Censorship and Its Cultural Consequences*. Oxford: Oxford University Press.
MacInnes, Colin. 1957. *City of Spades*. London: Allison and Busby.
McLeod, John. 2004. *Postcolonial London: Rewriting the Metropolis*. London: Routledge.
Mafe, Diana Adesola. 2008. 'A Portrait of the (Tortured) Artist as a Young (Coloured) Man: Reading Arthur Nortje'. *Safundi: The Journal of South African and American Studies*. 9 (4): 427–455.
Mandela, Nelson. 1994. *Long Walk to Freedom*. London: Abacus.
Martin, Denis-Constant. 2014. *Sounding the Cape: Music, Identity and Politics in South Africa*. Somerset-West: African Minds.
Masekela, Hugh and Cheers, Michael D. 2004. *Still Grazing: The Musical Journey of Hugh Masekela*. New York: Crown Publishers.
Massey, Doreen. 1994. *Space, Place and Gender*. Cambridge: Polity Press.
Matandela, Mbalenhle. 2018. 'Nakba Day 2018 Should Mark a Turning Point in Resistance against Israeli Apartheid'. *The Daily Maverick*, 16 May. www.dailymaverick.co.za/article/2018-05-16-nakba-day-2018-should-mark-a-turning-point-in-resistance-against-israeli-apartheid/#.Wv1QvEiFPIU. Accessed 30 May 2018.
Matshikiza, Todd. 1961a. *Chocolates for My Wife*. London: Hodder & Stoughton.
Matshikiza, Todd. 1961b. 'King Kong – Making the Music'. *New Statesman*, 24 February.
Matshikiza, Todd and Matshikiza, John. 2000. *With the Lid Off: South African Insights from Home and Abroad 1959–2000*. Johannesburg: Mail and Guardian Books.
Mirza, Munira. 2006. 'Diversity is Divisive'. *The Guardian*, 21 November. www.theguardian.com/commentisfree/2006/nov/21/diversityhasbecomedivisive. Accessed 10 September 2016.
Mkhize, Khwezi. 2018. '"To See Us as We See Ourselves": John Tengo Jabavu and the Politics of the Black Periodical'. *Journal of Southern African Studies*. 44 (3): 413–430.
Modisane, Bloke. [1963] 1990. *Blame Me on History*. London: Penguin.

Munro, Brenna M. 2012. *South Africa and the Dream of Love to Come: Queer Sexuality and the Struggle for Freedom*. Minneapolis: University of Minnesota Press.

Nasta, Susheila. 2014. 'Looking Back to Look Forward'. *Wasafiri*. 29 (3): 1–3.

Naudé, S.J. [2011] 2015. *The Alphabet of Birds*. Translated by S.J. Naudé. London: Andotherstories.

Nayar, Pramod K. 2014. 'William Blake's "London" as a Surveillance Poem'. *The Explicator*. 72 (4): 328–333.

'New Strand Editor: Pick South African Woman to Revive Britain's "Most Popular" Magazine'. 1962. *Ebony*, April.

Newton, Darrell M. 2011. *Paving the Empire Road: BBC Television and Black Britons*. Manchester: Manchester University Press.

Ngcobo, Lauretta (ed.). 1987. *Let It Be Told: Black Women Writers in Britain*. London: Virago.

Ngcobo, Lauretta (ed.). 2012. *Prodigal Daughters: Stories of South African Women in Exile*. Pietermaritzburg: UKZN Press.

Ngũgĩ wa Thiong'o. 1984. 'Literature and Society: The Politics of the Canon'. In *Critical Perspectives on Ngugi*, edited by G.D. Killam. Washington, DC: Three Continents Press.

Nicol, Mike. 1991. *A Good-Looking Corpse: The World of Drum – Jazz and Gangsters, Hope and Defiance in the Townships of South Africa*. London: Secker & Warburg.

Nixon, Rob. 1994. *Homelands, Harlem and Hollywood: South African Culture and the World Beyond*. London: Routledge.

Nkosi, Lewis. [1965] 1983. *Home and Exile*. Harlow: Longman.

Nortje, Arthur. 2000. *Anatomy of Dark: Collected Poems of Arthur Nortje*, edited by Dirk Klopper. Pretoria: UNISA.

Nuttall, Sarah. 2004. 'Bodiographies: Writing the Body in Arthur Nortje'. In *Arthur Nortje: Poet and South African. New Critical and Contextual Essays*, edited by Craig McLuckie and Ross Tyner. Pretoria: UNISA.

Nuttall, Sarah and Mbembe, Achille (eds). 2008. *Johannesburg: The Elusive Metropolis*. Durham, NC: Duke University Press.

Ogungbesan, Kolawole. 1979. *The Writing of Peter Abrahams*. London: Hodder & Stoughton.

Owen, Wilfred. 1919. 'Strange Meeting'. Reprinted in *The War Poems of Wilfred Owen*, 1994, edited by Jon Stallworthy. London: Chatto and Windus.

Pechey, Graham. 2004. 'On Trek'. *Times Literary Supplement*. Issue 5274, 20 April.

Polsgrove, Carol. 2001. *Divided Minds: Intellectuals and the Civil Rights Movement*. New York: Norton.

Polsgrove, Carol. 2009. *Ending British Rule in Africa: Writers in a Common Cause*. Manchester: Manchester University Press.

Pordzik, Ralph. 1998. 'No Longer Need I Shout Freedom in the House: Arthur Nortje, the English Poetical Tradition and the Breakdown of Communication in South African English Poetry in the 1960s'. *English Studies in Africa*. 41 (2): 35–53.

Posel, Deborah. 2014. '"Madiba Magic": Politics as Enchantment'. In *The Cambridge Companion to Nelson Mandela*, edited by Rita Barnard. Cambridge: Cambridge University Press.

Poyner, Jane. 2007. 'Cosmopolitanism and Fictions of "Terror": Zoë Wicomb's *David's Story* and Ishtiyaq Shukri's *The Silent Minaret*'. *Safundi: The Journal of South African and American Studies*. 12 (3–4): 313–330.

Pratt, Mary-Louise. 1992. *Imperial Eyes: Travel Writing and Transculturation*. London: Routledge.

Ramdin, Ron. 1987. *The Making of the Black Working Class in Britain*. Aldershot: Gower.

Rastogi, Pallavi. 2011. 'International Geographies: Looking Out in Ishtiyaq Shukri's *The Silent Minaret*'. *Research in African Literatures*. 42 (3): 17–30.

Rive, Richard. 1981. *Writing Black*. Cape Town: David Philip.

Robolin, Stéphane. 2015. *Grounds of Engagement: Apartheid-Era African American and South African Writing*. Chicago: University of Illinois Press.

Said, Edward. 1994. *Culture and Imperialism*. New York: First Vintage Books.

Sam, Agnes. 1987. Essay. In *Let It Be Told: Black Women Writers in Britain*, edited by Lauretta Ngcobo. London: Virago.

Sampson, Anthony. 1956. *Drum: A Venture into the New Africa*. London: Collins.

Sampson, Anthony. 1957. 'South African Contexts'. *Times Literary Supplement*, 16 August.

Sampson, Anthony. 2000. 'Introduction'. In Todd Matshikiza and John Matshikiza, *With the Lid Off: South African Insights from Home and Abroad 1959–2000*. Johannesburg: Mail and Guardian Books.

Samuelson, Meg. 2010. 'Scripting Connections: Reflections on the "Post-Transitional"'. *English Studies in Africa*. 53 (1): 113–117.

Sandbrook, Dominic. 2006. *White Heat: A History of Britain in the Swinging Sixties*. London: Abacus.

Schalkwyk, David. 2013. *Hamlet's Dreams: The Robben Island Shakespeare*. London: Bloomsbury.

Schmidt, Elizabeth. 2013. *Foreign Intervention in Africa: From the Cold War to the War on Terror*. Cambridge: Cambridge University Press.

Schreiner, Olive. 1883. *The Story of an African Farm*. London: Chapman & Hall.

Schwartz, Delmore. 1949. *The World is a Wedding*. London: John Lehmann.

Schwartzman, Adam. 1999. 'Introduction'. In *Ten South African Poets*. Manchester: Carcanet Press.

Serote, Mongane Wally. [1972] 1999. 'City Johannesburg'. In *Ten South African Poets*, edited by Adam Schwartzman. Manchester: Carcanet Press.

Shukri, Ishtiyaq. 2005. *The Silent Minaret*. Auckland Park: Jacana.

Shukri, Ishtiyaq. 2014. *I See You*. Auckland Park: Jacana.

Shukri, Ishtiyaq. 2015. 'Losing London'. *Africa Is a Country*, September. http://africasacountry.com/2015/09/losing-london/. Accessed 17 July 2016.

Sivanandan, Tamara. 2004. 'Anticolonialism, National Liberation and Postcolonial Nation Formation'. In *The Cambridge Companion to Postcolonial Literary Studies*, edited by Neil Lazarus. Cambridge: Cambridge University Press.

Slaughter, Joseph. 2007. *Human Rights, Inc.: The World Novel, Narrative Form, and International Law*. Ashland, OH: Fordham University Press.

Smith, David James. 2010. *Young Mandela: The Revolutionary Years*. London: Weidenfeld and Nicolson.

Snaith, Anna. 2014. *Modernist Voyages: Colonial Women Writers in London, 1890–1945*. Cambridge: Cambridge University Press.

Soyinka, Wole. 2002. 'Voices from the Frontier'. *The Guardian*, 13 July. www.theguardian.com/books/2002/jul/13/poetry.wolesoyinka. Accessed 15 June 2015.

Staples, Brent. 2019. 'The Radical Blackness of Ebony Magazine'. *New York Times*, 8 November. www.nytimes.com/2019/08/11/opinion/ebony-jet-magazine.html. Accessed 20 March 2020.

Steele, John, O'Neill, Sean, Alleyne, Richard and Clough, Sue. 2003. 'Police Seize Weapons in Mosque Raid'. *The Telegraph*, 21 January. www.telegraph.co.uk/news/uknews/1419533/Police-seize-weapons-in-mosque-raid.html. Accessed 21 August 2016.

Steiner, Tina. 2007. 'Pockets of Connection against the Backdrop of Culture Talk in Ishtiyaq Shukri's Novel *The Silent Minaret*'. *Current Writing: Text and Reception in Southern Africa*. 19 (1): 53–68.

Stephens, Jan. 1943. 'The Native View'. *Times Literary Supplement*, 16 January.

Stolp, Mareli. 2018. 'Review: King Kong, Legend of a Boxer, dir. Jonathan Munby'. *SAMUS: South African Music Studies*. 38: 361–366.

Tennant, Emma. 1989. *Two Women of London*. London: Faber and Faber.

Tester, Keith. 1994. *The Flâneur*. London: Routledge.

Thomas, Martin. 2002. 'The British Government and the End of French Algeria 1958–62'. *Journal of Strategic Studies*. 25 (2): 172–198.

Thompson, Leonard. 1995. *A History of South Africa*. New Haven, CT: Yale University Press.

Thörn, Håkan. 2006. *Anti-Apartheid and the Emergence of a Global Civil Society*. Basingstoke: Palgrave Macmillan.

Titlestad, Michael. 2004. *Making the Changes: Jazz in South African Literature and Reportage*. Pretoria: UNISA.

Tlali, Miriam. 1975. *Muriel at Metropolitan*. Johannesburg: Ravan.

Turner, Mark W. 2003. *Backward Glances: Cruising the Queer Streets of New York and London*. London: Reaktion Books.

Vally, Salim. 2015. 'Solidarity with Palestine: Confronting the "Whataboutery" Argument and the Bantustan Denouement'. In *Apartheid Israel: The Politics of an Analogy*, edited by John Soske and Sean Jacobs. Chicago: Haymarket Books.

van der Vlies, Andrew. 2007. *South African Textual Cultures: White, Black and Read All Over*. Manchester: Manchester University Press.

van der Vlies, Andrew. 2011. 'Zoë Wicomb's Queer Cosmopolitanisms'. *Safundi: the Journal of South African and American Studies*. 12 (3–4): 425–444.
Vermeulen, Pieter. 2007. 'Wordsworth's Disgrace: The Insistence of South Africa in J.M. Coetzee's *Boyhood* and *Youth*'. *Journal of Literary Studies*. 23 (2): 179–199.
Vladislavić, Ivan. 2010. *Double Negative*. Cape Town: Umuzi.
Wade, Michael. 1972. *Peter Abrahams*. London: Evan Bros.
Walkowitz, Judith R. 2012. *Nights Out: Life in Cosmopolitan London*. New Haven, CT: Yale University Press.
Wanner, Zukiswa. 2014. *London–Cape Town–Joburg*. Cape Town: Kwela.
Waugh, Patricia. 1984. *Metafiction: The Theory and Practice of Self-Conscious Fiction*. London: Methuen.
White, Sarah, Harris, Roxy and Beezmohun, Sharmilla (eds). 2005. *The International Book Fair of Radical Black and Third World Books: A Meeting of the Continents: History, Memories, Organisations and Programmes 1982–1995*. London: New Beacon Books.
Wicomb, Zoë. 1987. *You Can't Get Lost in Cape Town*. Reprinted 2000. New York: The Feminist Press.
Wicomb, Zoë. 1998. 'Shame and Identity: The Case of the Coloured in South Africa'. In *Writing: South Africa*, edited by Derek Attridge. Cambridge: Cambridge University Press.
Williams, Elizabeth M. 2015. *The Politics of Race in Britain and South Africa: Black British Solidarity and the Anti-Apartheid Struggle*. London: IB Tauris.
Wilson, Elizabeth. 1995. 'The Invisible Flâneur'. In *Postmodern Cities and Spaces*, edited by Sophie Watson and Katherine Gibson. Oxford: Blackwell.
Woeber, Catherine. 1995. 'Error in the Religious Equation: Images of St Peter's School in South African Autobiography'. *English Academy Review: Southern African Journal of English Studies*. 12 (1): 58–69.
Woeber, Catherine. 1997. 'A Long Occupation of the Mind: Peter Abrahams's Perspective on His Education'. *English in Africa*. 24 (2): 87–104.
Woolf, Janet. 1985. 'The Invisible Flâneuse: Women and the Literature of Modernity'. *Theory, Culture & Society*. 2: 37–46.
Woolf, Virginia. 1925. *Mrs Dalloway*. London: Hogarth.
Xaba, Makhosazana. 2009. 'Noni Jabavu: A Peripatetic Writer Ahead of Her Times'. *Tydskrif vir Letterkunde*. 46 (1): 217–219.
Xaba, Makhosazana. 2019. 'On Noni Jabavu and the Return Home'. *Johannesburg Review of Books*, 5 August. https://johannesburgreviewofbooks.com/2019/08/05/on-noni-jabavu-and-the-return-home-makhosazana-xaba-celebrates-one-of-south-africas-foundational-literary-centenarians. Accessed 21 February 2020.
Young, Robert J.C. 2008. *The Idea of English Ethnicity*. Oxford: Blackwell.
Zimbler, Jarad. 2014. *J.M. Coetzee and the Politics of Style*. Cambridge: Cambridge University Press.

Index

Note: Literary works can be found under authors' names.

Abrahams, Peter 26–28, 29–59, 68, 77–78, 80–81, 83, 103, 183, 235, 245
   Coyaba Chronicles, The 27, 28, 32, 34, 36, 38, 45–46, 48, 51
   Dark Testament 30–32, 35
   Path of Thunder, The 28, 62
   Return to Goli 35–52
   Song of the City 28, 34–35
   Tell Freedom 29, 30, 42–45
   Wreath for Udomo, A 45, 52–58, 68, 235
Anti-Apartheid Movement 123, 125, 179–180
Attridge, Derek 190–191, 193
Attwell, David 188, 191

Ball, John Clement 16
Barnard, Rita 188
Baudelaire, Charles 11, 20, 154, 156, 157, 159–161, 164, 171, 173, 198, 199
belatedness 2–3, 19–20, 68, 77, 154, 198, 199, 238
Bewes, Timothy 206–207, 233
Bhabha, Homi K. 152, 153
Blake, William 210, 211, 215–216, 219, 224, 227, 228

British Communist Party 27, 37–38, 39, 40, 41, 47, 83
Brutus, Dennis 18, 141, 142, 144, 145, 150
Bunn, David 148, 154, 155, 157, 161–162, 174

Campbell, Roy 146, 159
capitalism 155, 174–176
Cartwright, Justin 209–233, 236
   In Every Face I Meet 189, 209–233, 236
   White Lightning 211, 226, 231–232
Coetzee, J.M. 77, 83, 88, 156, 179, 189–209, 226, 232–233, 236, 238, 251, 255
   White Writing 156, 206, 208
   Youth 77, 88, 179, 189–209, 226, 232–233, 236
Cold War 25, 38, 53–54, 124, 135, 174, 176, 193, 194
coloured identity 31, 94, 120–121, 148, 152, 153–154, 156, 163–165, 166, 169, 171, 172, 178
Confessionalism 155, 169, 172

INDEX

contrapuntalism 8, 97, 113–114, 119, 120, 131, 136, 137, 149, 150
cosmopolitanism 98, 103, 105, 130, 131, 149, 160, 169, 171, 218, 236, 245, 255

Dalamba, Lindelwa 99, 106
Davids, Nadia 94
De Certeau, Michel 12, 126, 131
Denniston, Robin 101, 102, 111–112
disappointment 14, 18–19, 22, 63–68, 77, 89–90, 91, 134, 159, 198, 238
Distiller, Natasha 40, 42, 44–45
Driver, Dorothy 10
Drum magazine 10, 96, 97–98, 99, 101, 102–106, 108–110, 111, 113

Eliot, T.S. 2, 19, 20, 140, 144, 154, 155, 157–158, 160, 169, 177, 198, 199
Englishness 6–7, 15, 60, 65–67, 83, 108, 201–203, 210, 216–217, 223, 229, 255–256
exile 2, 13, 18, 58, 61, 125, 128, 140–141, 142–148, 149, 151–154, 158, 160, 161, 165, 172, 173, 176–178, 186, 258

flâneur 10–11, 22, 130, 156, 160–161, 163, 167, 169, 173, 198–199

gender 8–12, 85–86, 91, 184–187
Gikandi, Simon 2–3, 7
Gilroy, Paul 98, 105, 216, 237–238, 242
Gordimer, Nadine 11, 14–16
Gunner, Liz 97–98, 105

Hall, Stuart 179–180, 222
Harlem Renaissance writers 26, 28, 31, 34, 43–45, 103–104

International Book Fair of Radical Black and Third World Books, The 181–184
Islamophobia 249–252, 255

Jabavu, Noni 10, 11–12, 80–91
Jacobson, Dan 14, 19, 25, 28–29, 59–78, 90, 193, 198, 202, 204, 208, 235, 238
Beginners, The 29, 66
Evidence of Love, The 29, 62, 66, 198
'Long Way from London, A' 61, 62–77, 193, 198, 202, 208
Time and Time Again 29, 60, 62, 65, 72–73
jazz 93, 95, 99–106, 117, 125, 126–127, 131, 133–134, 149
Johnson, Linton Kwesi 181, 251
Jonker, Ingrid 19–20, 90, 146

Kalliney, Peter 2, 13, 157
King Kong 93, 97–111, 123, 131
Klopper, Dirk 143, 148, 152, 172

La Guma, Alex 144, 159
liberal humanism 26, 29, 37, 39, 40–46, 59–61, 71, 75, 76, 77
liberalism 40, 42, 48, 50, 57, 58, 61, 69, 70–71, 75–76, 81–82, 86, 134
Lytton, David 19–20, 89–90

Mandela, Nelson 4–7, 117, 123, 135, 150, 183, 184, 211–212, 215–223, 229–230, 247–248
Massey, Doreen 237, 257
Matshikiza, Todd 17, 59, 83, 93–137, 179, 189, 236, 245, 254, 255, 258
Chocolates for My Wife 17, 99, 101–102, 106, 109–119, 120, 121, 124, 126, 127–131, 132–134, 136–137

McDonald, Peter 144
McLeod, John 7, 16, 19, 65, 68
metafiction 191, 195, 197, 206, 208, 210, 213–215, 225–227, 229, 230, 232, 233
mission schools, South Africa 5, 6, 41, 45, 61, 71, 106
modernisms 2–3, 12–13, 31, 113, 141, 157–158, 199
multiculturalism 218, 241–242, 250
Munro, Brenna 164–165, 166

Naudé, S.J. 255–256
neo-Toryism 69, 70, 71, 74–75
Ngcobo, Lauretta 8–9, 11–12, 184–187
  Let It Be Told 8–9, 185–187
Nixon, Rob 10, 103, 104, 106, 108–109, 221
Nkosi, Lewis 20–22, 103, 105, 112–113, 181
Nortje, Arthur 1–3, 10, 17, 77, 83, 140–178, 199, 255
Nuttall, Sarah 143, 157, 170, 173

Padmore, George 27, 38, 50–52, 56, 57
palimpsests 16–17, 132, 188, 245, 257
Pan-Africanism 26–27, 37–38, 51–52, 54, 55, 62, 77, 181, 182, 183, 222
Plath, Sylvia 155
Polsgrove, Carol 39, 52, 53, 58
postmodernism 214

queer subjectivities 164–168

Rimbaud, Arthur 165, 198, 199
Robben Island 17–18, 149, 150–151, 220, 222
Romanticism 41, 46, 48, 154, 156–157, 166, 172, 186, 197, 198–199, 201, 208

Said, Edward 114
Sam, Agnes 186–187
Schreiner, Olive 12–13
Serote, Mongane Wally 3, 155, 183
Shukri, Ishtiyaq 12, 233, 235–258
  I See You 244–245
  Silent Minaret, The 235–258
Snaith, Anna 12
Soho 19–20, 130–131, 171, 173, 218–219, 236
South Africa House 17, 115–117, 135, 149
surveillance 17, 116–117, 119, 121, 124, 128, 131, 184, 216, 251, 253–254

Tambo, Oliver 7, 43, 123
Tester, Keith 161, 199
Thatcherism 182, 209, 210, 212–214, 225, 228
Third Programme, BBC 35, 46, 50, 80, 84, 111
Three Swings on a Pendulum 20–22
Titlestad, Michael 99, 105–106, 110, 113–114, 117, 126, 127, 258
Trafalgar Square 17, 27, 115, 123, 126, 127, 148, 149, 151, 162, 190, 194
Turner, Mark W. 167

Van der Vlies, Andrew 157
Vladislavić, Ivan 18

Wasafiri 184–185
Wicomb, Zoë 153–154, 157, 164
Williams, Elizabeth 180–181
Windrush generation 14, 25, 90, 203

Xaba, Makhosazana 80, 81, 84

Young, Robert J.C. 7, 202